TEACHING IN THE PRESCHOOL

TEACHING IN THE PRESCHOOL

JERE E. BROPHY
The University of Texas at Austin

THOMAS L. GOOD
The University of Missouri-Columbia

SHARI E. NEDLER
University of Colorado at Denver

Harper & Row, Publishers
New York   Evanston   San Francisco   London

Sponsoring Editor: Michael E. Brown
Project Editor: Robert Ginsberg
Designer: Emily Harste
Production Supervisor: Will C. Jomarrón

Cover illustration by Jack Unruh

Teaching in the Preschool

Library of Congress Cataloging in Publication Data

Brophy, Jere E
    Teaching in the preschool.

    Bibliography: p.
    Includes index.
        1.   Education, Preschool.   I.   Good, Thomas, L.,
1943–   joint author.   II.   Nedler, Shari E., joint
author.   III.   Title
LB1140.2.B76   372.21   74-14463
    ISBN 0-06-042393-5

This book is fondly dedicated to
Cheri and Joe Brophy,
Heather and Jeff Good,
and Michael, Karen, and Don Nedler,
our primary instructors in child development
and early childhood education

CONTENTS

PREFACE

Although day-care centers and nursery schools have existed for years, they became commonplace only in the 1960s with the advent of Project Head Start. Prior to that time, they were organized primarily as programs to provide play experiences to foster social and emotional development, and were patronized primarily by middle- and upper-class families. However, with the establishment of Head Start centers and other preschools planned primarily for poor children, this emphasis on play and social-emotional development was often supplemented (in some extreme cases even supplanted) by an emphasis on stimulating the young child's intellectual development and preparing him for school.

This revolution began with great enthusiasm and positive expectations. Given that much of the child's intellectual development occurs in the years before school, and given that poor children enter school already well behind their middle- and upper-class peers, it seemed reasonable to expect that, if poor children were provided with a planned educational setting and experiences similar to those that middle- and upper-class children enjoy in their homes and family life, early education could eliminate the cumulative disadvantage shown by poor children (the older they get, the farther they fall behind their middle- and upper-class peers in measured intelligence and school achievement). Early results were encouraging: Children enrolled in early education programs made noteworthy gains on IQ tests and other measures, suggesting that their relative disadvantage had been eliminated or greatly reduced. However, with a few notable exceptions, follow-up studies discouragingly revealed that the gains children made in experimental programs gradually dissipated after they left the programs, so that a year or two later they no longer enjoyed any advantage over similar poor children who had not had preschool experiences. These data were interpreted by many (most notably Jensen, 1969) to mean that early education experiments had failed and that the elimination or reduction of the cumulative disadvantage of the poor could not be accomplished through early education.

Like many others who have been involved in this endeavor, we disagree with Jensen and those who would dismiss the educationally oriented preschool as having failed. Instead, we agree with those who insist that a more accurate summation of the available data reveals *not* that early education has failed, but that for the most part *it has not yet been tried.* Although no single "optimal" preschool model has emerged, and none may ever emerge which is optimal for all children, common key factors have been identified in those preschool programs that have succeeded in obtaining significant gains in student academic performance and in maintaining these gains over several years' time (Karnes, Zehrbach, and Teska, 1972a; Weikart, 1969). These key factors include the systematic teaching of planned objectives, a low child-to-teacher ratio, and active and enthusiastic involvement of the parents. One or more (usually all) of these factors were absent in the programs that failed to have a significant and lasting impact on children. Thus, despite the many failures and frustrations, the existence of several successful programs demonstrates that well-designed and staffed preschool programs with planned objectives can achieve a sustained beneficial effect on children, even though most early education programs have yielded disappointing results to date.

The major purpose of this book is to prepare teachers to capably operate *successful* preschool programs. In our attempt to accomplish this, we have tried to provide a wealth of specific and detailed information that is likely to be of practical use to such teachers. We have drawn upon the theoretical and empirical literature on child development, socialization, early education, and teacher education, distilling from it the information, guidelines, and suggestions that we think are most useful for preschool teachers. Where research data were unavailable, we have drawn upon our own experience in an early education program and on the suggestions of teachers and supervisors who have worked in such programs. Our primary guiding principles in preparing the book have been clarity of communication and purpose; thus, we have eliminated as much jargon as possible and have tried to write clearly and unambiguously. Also, we have limited our coverage of child development, socialization, teacher education, and related topics to those areas that have *direct* bearing on the needs of the preschool teacher. Reading lists are provided for those who wish to pursue these topics in greater detail.

Fortunately, day-care and early education programs are not going to disappear; in fact, present signs suggest that they will become a permanent part of our society and will serve children from every segment of the population. We say fortunately because, as previously stated, we believe that existing data show that such programs can be successful if certain key elements are present. Thus, we believe that preschool programs are important for child-care purposes alone. However, an additional, more powerful set of forces emanating from a series of social changes in our society has virtually assured that day-care and early education programs will be demanded and supported in the future. We refer, of course, to the many changes that have occurred in connection with the women's liberation movement, particularly the tendency of women to become seriously career oriented rather than thinking of work as only an interim activity until they have a baby. This change in commitment to a career, among other factors, has led increasing numbers of women to have fewer babies than they had in the past, and to desire to return to their jobs sooner. Whereas previously even career-oriented women usually did not return to work until their youngest child entered elementary school, it is becoming increasingly common for women to return to work as soon as their child is toilet trained, or, in some cases, when he is about six months old. Thus, there is every reason to expect a sustained and even increased demand for high quality day-care and early education services.

The present volume is intended for caregivers and future caregivers in all kinds of preschool settings and programs, although it should be especially useful for those who will teach in early education programs involving some kind of planned curriculum. Several chapters deal with curriculum and instruction in the preschool, and the book as a whole assumes that some part of the daily program will be spent in planned activities based on pre-selected objectives. Thus, caregivers working in such settings should find the book most useful. However, the principles for curriculum and instruction usually apply as well to the unplanned, spontaneous instruction which teachers give during "teachable moments" that occur every day in all pre-schools, so that the curriculum and instruction chapters should be quite useful and applicable to teachers who are not working from a planned curriculum as well.

To help draw attention to this distinction, we have systematically (and arbitrarily) differentiated our use of the term *preschool* from the terms *early education* and *early education programs* throughout the book. The term *preschool* is used to refer to *any* type of preschool or child-care program, ranging from programs designed particularly for disadvantaged children, which have a very heavy academic emphasis, to programs designed for more advantaged children, which have an almost exclusively social-emotional emphasis. In contrast, the terms *early education* and *early education programs* are given a more specific meaning. These are used when we wish to restrict the discussion to programs which have an *academic emphasis* (structured curriculum with planned lessons sequenced to proceed towards specified objectives), especially programs planned for disadvantaged children.

The terms *advantaged* and *disadvantaged* also appear regularly throughout the book. They are not intended as absolute labels denoting qualitatively different groups of children or families; they merely denote a family's *relative* standing in the society at large on a complex of interrelated variables. Thus, in general, advantaged families have more and better education, larger incomes, more material possessions, more desirable homes and neighborhoods, and more self-determination and societal power than disadvantaged families. Education is probably the most important single variable here, but all are mutually interrelated. These two terms were selected from a larger number of terms with similar meanings, partly because we feel that they are especially appropriate because they do not carry some of the unfortunate connotations that other terms carry, and partly because we wished to use the same terminology throughout the book whenever it became relevant to draw distinctions between advantaged and disadvantaged people.

We recognize that our use of such terms involves oversimplification because of their relativity and because all generalizations made about "the advantaged" or "the disadvantaged" will not hold for each individual who fits either of these labels. However, inequalities among families and individuals in our society are quite obvious, and they often have important implications for child development and for how a preschool program can best meet a given child's needs. Thus, we use the terms whenever they appear relevant, but readers should bear in mind that these are *relative* terms which apply to *groups* but which may or may not apply to a given individual.

The main theme of the book will be the role of the teacher in *optimizing* the cognitive, social, emotional, and general personal development of each individual child. Thus, developmental stages in physical, mental, and personal development will be discussed, but this sort of information will be presented in the context of *how the teacher can use it* to make decisions about the kinds of experiences and treatment that each child needs. Thus, our primary stress is on the teacher as a decision maker, using information from child development generally and from observations of individual children in particular, in order to optimize the general development of each child.

Cognitive-linguistic development and social-emotional-personal development will be treated as correlated and interrelated outcomes of the same basic set of facilitative behaviors on the part of the teacher. This approach is based partly on our own experience and partly on data from several sources showing that adult behavior which fosters optimal cognitive-linguistic development usually also fosters social-emotional-personal development, and vice versa. Sometimes these two general areas of child development are presented as separate from each other, and occasionally they are even presented in a way that makes them seem somewhat contradictory, as if adult behavior that fostered one kind of development would somehow retard development in the other areas. We believe that attempts to separate these areas (except for the purpose of discussing specifics) are artificial and mis-leading, and that, with the exception of certain unfortunate extremes, teacher behavior that fosters optimal development in one area will probably also foster optimal development in other areas. This fundamental assumption per-meates the book because it is basic to our approach to early child care.

Although we have tried to present a large volume of detailed information and suggestions, it would be a serious mistake for the reader to attempt rigidly and blindly to apply the suggestions in cookbook fashion. We have nothing against cookbook approaches in theory; in fact, if we believed it were possible, we would attempt to write a "cookbook" for teachers and other adults working in early child-care settings. However, the job of pro-viding an optimal environment for each child is far too complex and demand-ing for a cookbook approach to achieve much success. Only a relatively small number of do's and don't's apply regularly to all or most situations. There are a large number of principles and methods that will succeed with regularity if they are applied at the right time and in the right way, but it is up to the teacher to recognize the situations which call for their applica-tion and to follow through with appropriate behavior. This is much more complex and challenging than the cookbook application of a few simple procedures.

It is for this reason that we stress the role of *the teacher as a decision maker*. Successful teaching requires the teacher not only to master a large number of strategies for use with young children, but also to develop powers of observation and diagnostic skills that will optimize the teacher's behav-ior—selecting and using strategies best suited to the needs of an individual child at a given time. This is obviously a very sophisticated and demanding level of teaching. Although this optimal level of teaching will not come quickly or easily, we believe that it can be taught and learned in systematic fashion, provided that the teacher has or acquires the necessary dedication, observational and diagnostic skills, commitment to professionalism and self-improvement, willingness to receive and use feedback, and a basic enjoy-ment of young children and a desire to work with them.

The book has been written primarily for future teachers, both professional and paraprofessional, who are preparing for careers working with young chil-dren. It should also be useful for in-service teachers in these same settings, for preservice and in-service teachers at the kindergarten and early ele-mentary grade levels, for educators and supervisors of preservice or in-service teachers in the above mentioned groups, and for parents. Although our own experience with preschool settings has been concentrated most heavily in schools and other settings which have used the early childhood programs of the Southwest Educational Development Laboratory, the book has been written for the general audience of teachers and future teachers involved in early child care. Thus, unless otherwise noted, the principles and methods we suggest are presented because we believe that they are important and applicable to good preschool programs in *all* settings, not just those which are similar to the program with which we are most closely identified.

We have tried to strike a balance between global and minimally useful generalities on the one hand, and overly specific and rigid assertions on the other. Frequently the applicability of a given principle or method will depend upon the kinds of children enrolled in a program and the goals of the program's designers. Where this is the case, we have tried to be as specific as possible in drawing the relevant distinctions among available options and their respective advantages and disadvantages in different situations, rather than to stress only one of the available options when it might be inappropriate or even harmful in certain situations. Also, we have tried to be prescriptive, providing as much information as possible about what teachers *should* do rather than about what they should *not* do. Where complex teacher behavior is required, we have tried to analyze its component parts and to present each step in the proper sequence in order to simplify communication and to provide a procedural model that can be followed in appropriate situations.

Although the book could be used at almost any point in teacher preparation (including in-service education), it probably will be used most ideally and effectively in preservice courses or in-service training experiences which include classroom observation and practice teaching with provision of feedback. Teachers and other adults, just like children, find material presented in lectures and textbooks to be most useful when they get opportunities to observe its application and to experiment with it in realistic situations. Also, research on the nature of the concerns and interests of student teachers (Fuller, 1969) has shown that firsthand experience in working with children and in carrying out such concrete tasks as setting up a classroom, planning schedules, and mastering basic classroom management techniques are of more immediate and pressing concern to inexperienced student teachers than more abstract matters such as questioning strategies and the planning of individualized instructional sequences (for more on this, see Katz, 1970). Thus, we strongly recommend that instructors follow this scheme in working with student teachers, both to maximize their motivation and interest and to minimize their anxieties: Where it is possible to correlate classroom discussion of the book with the experiences of student teachers, instructors will probably be most successful if they attempt to gear their treatment of topics to the immediate needs and interests of student teachers rather than to proceed through the chapters in a set order. This might mean, for example, beginning with the chapters on setting up the classroom, classroom management, and getting off to a good start, and saving the chapters on child development, assessment, and diagnosis and reteaching for later in the year.

ACKNOWLEDGMENTS

This book represents a distillation of the theoretical and empirical research literature that has influenced our thinking as professionals involved in early childhood education and the practical knowledge we have accumulated from observing, teaching, and exchanging views with preschool teachers. The theorists and researchers who have influenced us most are primarily those listed in the references and, especially, in the readings suggested at the end of each chapter.

The students and preschool teachers who have influenced us are far too numerous to attempt to mention individually. However, we have maintained a continuing and productive dialogue with one large and identifiable group of preschool teachers and administrators working at various locations using either the Bilingual Early Childhood Program or the Bilingual Kindergarten Program developed by the Southwest Educational Development Laboratory (SEDL) in Austin, Texas. Dr. Nedler has been the director of these two programs, and Dr. Brophy and Dr. Good have been associated with them as staff development coordinators and consultants. Many of the practical ideas suggested for preventing or solving common preschool teaching and administration problems were developed after observation of and/or discussions with these people.

Dr. Good wishes to acknowledge the administrative support provided to him at the University of Missouri-Columbia by the Center for Research in Social Behavior (Bruce J. Biddle, director). Also, we wish to thank the teachers, parents, and children of the University of Texas Child Development Center (Johanna Hulls, director) and of the Rabbit Hill Children's Center (Robert Williamson, director), both of Austin, Texas, for their cooperation in helping us to obtain the photographs in the book. Photographs were taken by B. J. Brown of Austin, Texas, and by Andrew Tau at the University of Missouri

Child Development Laboratory (Dr. Virginia Fisher, director). We also want to acknowledge and express our appreciation for this help.

Typing, editing, and aspects of manuscript preparation were provided by Mike Baum, Arlene Brophy, Dr. Carolyn Evertson, Sue Gunn, Fran Head, Janet Honea, Sherry Kilgore, Judy Melvin, Dr. Shirley O'Bryant, Mike Tebeleff, and Jean Waltman. Critical reviews and suggestions were contributed by Marcy Frick, Suzi Good, Gail Hinkel, Dr. Nancy Moore, Dr. Shirley O'Bryant, Dr. Sherry Willis, and Dianne Wilson. Dr. O'Bryant was especially helpful.

Finally, we wish to acknowledge the instructional debt we owe to the seven individuals to whom this volume is fondly dedicated—our children.

Jere E. Brophy
Thomas L. Good
Shari E. Nedler

TEACHING IN THE PRESCHOOL

INTRODUCTION: SOME BASIC CONSIDERATIONS

Jane Global sat at her desk and looked around the classroom. The day had been long, discouraging, and frustrating. She remembered how exciting her teacher preparation program had been, and how much she had anticipated her first teaching job. Somehow, nothing was working out as she had imagined, and she was beginning to dread each day. As she thought back over what had happened that day she remembered the steady rain, which was just beginning to slacken. The bus that picked up the children had arrived twenty minutes past schedule. The weather had been so bad that all playground activities had been canceled. Within two hours it seemed as though every child in the room was either whining, throwing equipment, or moving around aimlessly. The schedule that Jane had worked out in her head late the night before was simply inappropriate for a rainy day.

While waiting for the bus to arrive that morning, Jane had decided to reschedule the day for free-play activities, and she had placed as much equipment as possible out on the shelves. There was no time to discuss the change of plans with her teacher aide, who rode the bus with the children and arrived with them. Jane remembered that Mary and Bobby, her two most disruptive pupils, had spent most of the day fighting with other children or throwing temper tantrums. Her teacher aide had been no help whatsoever. Throughout the day she had ignored the mess that was accumulating on the floors and on the tables, and she seemed totally confused regarding her duties and responsibilities. Jane was beginning to feel that if her aide couldn't show more initiative and more concern about her job, she would simply have to ask for a replacement.

To make matters worse, one of the little girls had suddenly vomited in the middle of the classroom and the janitor, who was busy in another part of the building, could not come in to clean up the mess. All Jane had on hand were some paper napkins that were totally inadequate for the job. She

1

sponged the child's clothes off as best she could, but the odor pervaded the classroom for the rest of the day. In the midst of all this confusion, Mrs. Rogers, Bobby's mother, arrived for a classroom visit. Jane had invited her to sit in the corner of the room and observe the children, but she noticed that after fifteen minutes Mrs. Rogers quietly stood up and left the classroom. Having parents drop by unexpectedly was really a nuisance, but Jane knew that parent participation was a policy of the school and there was really nothing she could do about it.

Now, as a fitting end to the day, Jane was waiting for Mrs. Brown to arrive. Mrs. Brown had been scheduled for a parent conference that afternoon and it was obvious that she didn't care enough to take the time to come by. Jane was really beginning to wonder if teaching was what she wanted to do. The working hours had sounded great and teaching was always something you could fall back on, but she was beginning to wonder if she really wanted to spend all of that time with young children.

When Mary Withit woke up that morning and heard the rain pounding the roof she hurried to get to school early. She knew that the bad weather would probably delay the bus and that the children would arrive late. She would need all of that extra time to prepare for the day. When Mary arrived at the school, she immediately went to her desk and got a copy of the rainy-day schedule that she and her teacher aide had prepared earlier in the school year. She knew that her aide, who rode the bus with the children, would check the bulletin board when she arrived at school in order to review any last minute changes. The bad weather would give them a chance to try some new musical group games with the children, Mary thought. She and her aide had listened to records a few weeks before, and had selected two or three activities that they felt the children would particularly enjoy.

Mary's eye quickly scanned the equipment and materials in the various learning centers, and she decided to make a few changes. She found some books on rain and weather and placed them in the book area. Some outdoor dress-up clothes and an umbrella had been stored in the closet; she put these in the housekeeping and role-playing areas. She checked her art supplies and added two baskets of collage materials to the shelves where they would be readily accessible to the children. Finger painting also would be a good rainy-day activity, and the children were ready to try mixing two colors. She prepared paints for the whole group.

Mary reviewed the checklist that she and her teacher aide had been keeping on each child's progress. She would divide the children into small groups, and she and her aide would each demonstrate some new uses of equipment that had not been placed in the classroom previously. Finally, she pulled out her copy of *The Three Bears*. By now the children were thoroughly familiar with the story, so that today would be a good time to try some role playing and dramatization. The children arrived twenty minutes late, and, as they were putting their coats away, Mary's aide quickly checked the posted schedule. She asked Mary a few questions about the equipment she was to demonstrate, and then helped the children assemble for a large circle meeting.

Mary told the children that since it was raining, they would change their usual routine and do some new and exciting things. She briefly outlined some of the activities that had been planned, and then she asked the children if there were any other special stories, games, or activities they would like to include during the day. After the circle meeting, the children moved into independent and small-group activities. The day moved along nicely. The children, the teacher, and the teacher aide cooperated in cleanup. The children had been taught that they were responsible for replacing equipment on the shelves after they had finished using it. Mary handled some minor spills while her aide made certain that the collage materials that had fallen on the floor were picked up and replaced in the baskets.

One unexpected disaster happened when a little girl vomited suddenly in the middle of the classroom. The janitor was busy in another part of the building, but Mary had an emergency bucket and mop in the bathroom. She quickly cleaned up the floor and then helped the little girl change into some other clothes which her mother had sent to school earlier in the year.

About 10:30, Mrs. Rogers, Bobby's mother, came into the classroom for a scheduled visit. Mary was delighted to see her, and since they had already discussed at a parent's conference some of the things that Mrs. Rogers could do in the classroom, Mary simply handed her three cards which described some of the things she could do with small groups of children. Mrs. Rogers quickly scanned the posted schedule and moved quietly to the book area. Within five minutes a small group of children had gathered, and Mrs. Rogers was reading one of the class's favorite stories.

When the children left at the end of the day, Mary reviewed the events that had occurred. Her aide would be coming back after the children had been delivered safely home, and they would have about thirty minutes to plan for the next day. Mary felt good about how smoothly the day had gone. She was delighted at the amount of satisfaction she derived from her job as a teacher. Even when she was in college she enjoyed working with young children, and the hours of volunteer work that she had done had really paid off in terms of helping her to feel comfortable and confident in her classroom. Her teacher aide was a tremendous help and seemed to anticipate where she would most be needed. Having parents come in as volunteers was enjoyable and a lot of help.

Mary had visited each one of the parents before school started, and they had already had three parents meetings at school in the evening. Mary had prepared a number of suggested activities for the mothers and fathers and these were easily accessible on small file cards. Having an extra adult in the classroom was always helpful for both the teacher and her aide. Mary remembered that Mrs. Brown had been scheduled for a parent conference after school. She knew that Mrs. Brown, who did not have an automobile, would not be able to make it in the bad weather, so Mary decided to stop by on her way home and reschedule the visit. Mary looked forward to the rest of the school year. Working with these children was exciting and challenging, giving Mary the opportunity to apply all that she had learned as well as forcing her to constantly acquire new skills.

Jane Global and Mary Withit share the same title. They are both early childhood teachers. One does not have to be an expert in the field to realize that the children under Jane's care are going to be spending their time in an environment that is less than optimal for their development. Mary's pupils, on the other hand, are fortunate to find themselves in a truly supportive environment. The difference lies not in the physical facility, the equipment available, the number of adults in the classroom, or the educational background of the teachers and teacher aides, but rather in the attitudes, awareness, and commitment that Mary Withit brings to her profession. Mary Withit chose early childhood teaching because she knew that she enjoyed working with children. She expected the hours to be long, she expected the job to be demanding, and she knew that she would have to capitalize on the assistance that other adults could offer. Her preparation and education is an ongoing experience for which she assumes full responsibility. It did not end when she finished her formal academic work in college. She believes that her job is important and that programs for young children cannot be entrusted to adults who are not fully aware of the complexity or demands of the teaching profession. Jane does not deliberately fail to do her job, but because of her misconceptions and ignorance concerning the role of a teacher, she functions ineffectively in the classroom.

We believe that the classroom teacher is the key to the success of any preschool program. She must be prepared, however, to continually work toward improving her skills and expanding her knowledge. All of you must ask yourselves if *you,* as future teachers, are willing to invest the time, the energy, and the deep personal commitment necessary to fill this role properly. As prospective teachers, it is important for you to understand what early education programs can and cannot do. For example, despite the hopes and optimism associated with Project Head Start, it has become clear that early childhood education cannot provide a cure for broader social problems.

The following sections review briefly some of the needs that early childhood education can legitimately address. Different kinds of early education centers are described, as well as various teaching functions and staffing patterns. As prospective teachers you should be aware of the range of professional opportunities that exist within these different settings and how they affect the roles a classroom teacher assumes.

IMPORTANCE OF EARLY EDUCATION

For centuries early education has been a concern of educators. Pestalozzi, Froebel, Montessori, the McMillans, and Susan Isaacs are only a few of the historical figures who have worked actively to expand our knowledge of the importance of the child's early experiences. Although the major efforts of these educators were directed toward slum children in various European countries, the impetus in the United States prior to the 1960s was toward middle-class children. Zigler (1972), in reviewing some of the research studies conducted in the 1930s and 1940s regarding the effectiveness of preschool education for middle-class children, concluded that there were no cognitive differences (as measured by achievement tests) between middle-class children who attended nursery school and those who did not attend school. Although some gains were reflected in the area of social skills for those who attended nursery school, by the third or fourth grade these differences had disappeared. The evidence indicates that traditional early education programs do not necessarily accelerate the cognitive development of middle-class children from good homes, possibly because these programs have emphasized the same kinds of skills these children are already acquiring. Additional research is needed before any further conclusions can be drawn regarding the effects of nursery school attendance on the middle-class child's intellectual, social, or emotional development.

Project Head Start, which was created as part of the war on poverty in the 1960s, represented a national commitment to provide comprehensive services for disadvantaged preschool children. Although definitive data regarding the effects of early intervention were not available at the time of its inception, the Head Start program appeared to represent a promising strategy for insuring quality educational opportunity for all members of society. Children from economically impoverished families were failing in school at an alarming rate, and available evidence suggested that early intervention could make a critical difference.

The work of Bloom (1964), Hunt (1961), and Hess and Shipman (1965), among others, seemed to confirm the importance of environmental factors in facilitating the development of the young child. Yet, although many experimental programs have been developed, to date research findings regarding the effectiveness of early intervention are still inconclusive. Generally, intellectual gains have dissipated gradually after the children left the program, except in those programs where parents were actively involved in working with their children at home, and where the preschool program was followed up by further intervention after the children reached elementary school. One must interpret the research findings related to Head Start with caution, however, due to the serious problems that still exist regarding adequate measurement instrumentation, particularly in the areas of social and emotional development. Nevertheless, despite the optimistic hopes of the 1960s, it is clear that early education has not, as yet, fulfilled its role as the hoped-for panacea that would cure the educational and social ills of our nation.

In spite of the lack of conclusive research evidence, there is a great need for early education programs. An overriding consideration is the shortage of day-care centers and other preschool facilities that can provide services for certain groups of children who otherwise would be left unattended. More and more women have moved back into the work force, both for economic reasons and to pursue independent career interests. The increase in divorce rates in this country has created a large number of one-parent families that are in dire need of adequate child-care services available at reasonable cost. According to the findings of a recent survey (Keyserling, 1972), many groups of children urgently need day-care services. Among these are 6 million children under the age of 6 whose mothers work. About one-third of these children come from families with annual incomes either below or close to the poverty line. Less than 10 percent of these children attend licensed day-care centers. Most of them are either cared for in their own homes or in the homes of relatives or neighbors. If the mothers did not work, many of these families would be forced to go on welfare.

Other groups desperately in need of quality child care include children of mothers who are attending school or trying to upgrade their vocational skills, young children with handicapping conditions who need specialized services, and children of mothers who are ill or are themselves handicapped. These families usually can afford *reasonable* costs, but quality day care is usually either unavailable or beyond their means.

Approximately 2.5 million children under the age of 6 come from poverty-level families where the mother does *not* work. In addition to being economically disadvantaged, many of these children do not get enough of the environmental stimulation necessary for optimal cognitive development.

There is little question that adequate child-care services and facilities are not available for all of the children who are in need of them. Unless these services are provided, many of these children will not realize their full intellectual, social, and emotional potential. If child-care services are to be provided for the children of this nation, then high standards must be maintained in the quality of the programs offered, the competencies of the teaching staffs, and the physical facilities provided.

MEETING BASIC NEEDS

We know that the development of the young child is a continuous process that is influenced by all of the events the child experiences. Early education can be a tool for responding to certain basic needs critical to the young child's fullest development.

The first of these needs is related to the child's health. The effects of inadequate nutrition have been clearly documented. Most early education programs offer ancillary food services to the child during the time he attends school. This is a primary need that must be met before the child can be expected to learn. Other health needs include medical and dental checks, vision and hearing checks, and related preventative measures.

The second need involves the identification of physically handicapping conditions that could affect the normal development of the child. Early education programs can provide a setting and an opportunity for early screening of young children that can enable us to prevent rather than try to remedy serious disabilities.

The third need relates to how language develops in the young child. Research findings (Lenneberg, 1969) appear to support arguments for the existence of a biological base in language development, with characteristics innate to the human organism routinely operating to insure development of a complete language structure. However, certain conditions seem necessary for optimizing the way a child is able to *use* the language system (structure) available to him. These conditions include the availability of adult models, the kind of feedback the child receives from the model, and the availability of meaningful opportunities to explore the *functional* use of language.

The fourth need that early education programs can fulfill particularly well is the child's need to have many opportunities to interact directly with his environment. The child's intelligence can be influenced by the quality of the environment and experiences available to him. Of particular importance during the early years are many varied encounters with concrete materials, which provide the child with an opportunity to operate on his own environment. This natural exchange between the child and the inanimate and social environment surrounding him forms the base for the more abstract thinking that occurs at later ages. Effective early education programs can respond to this need by constructing an optimally supportive environment.

A fifth need to which early education can legitimately address itself is the social and emotional development of the young child. There are many social, emotional, and motivational factors that directly influence the child's general level of competency. If a child feels good about himself, if he believes he is capable of achieving, if he gets along well with his peers, and if he has reasonable expectations of success reinforced by his daily encounters at school, then we can expect his cognitive potential to be realized.

Cognitive and affective development cannot be separated in an early education program. Any developmental factors that can be shaped by the environment are most certainly related to both the child's social and emotional growth. The impact of early education in shaping the child's affective development can be considered its most important functional goal.

We have briefly discussed some needs that early education can realistically meet. Preschool teachers cannot separate their caretaking responsibilities from the continuous process of setting goals for the child that are appropriate to his developmental needs. Children from poor homes in particular, because of the limited resources available to them, usually do not get the quantity and quality of stimulation needed for optimal cognitive, social, emotional, and physical development. Often the middle-class child has special needs that must be met. Early education programs can help fill these gaps by creating an environment that will enable the child to benefit from both present and future educational opportunities.

VARIATIONS IN CENTERS AND STAFFING PATTERNS

Early education programs can function in a variety of settings. Teachers should be aware of their differences, as well as the advantages and disadvantages of choosing one setting over another. Since each of these settings utilizes particular kinds of staffing patterns, teachers should be aware of the resources that might be available in any one of them. The type of setting and the staffing pattern will definitely affect the functions and responsibilities of a teacher.

There are a large number of private, profit-making preschool programs. These are usually owned by one individual and generally they cater to a middle-class clientele. Typically they offer a half-day program with heavy emphasis on the child's social and emotional development.

Many churches sponsor private preschool programs. The clientele tends to be middle class, although often some children from low socioeconomic groups are also enrolled. Again, most of these programs tend to offer half-day sessions with heavy stress on social and emotional development.

A number of private, nonprofit agencies also sponsor preschool programs. These include settlement houses, neighborhood agencies, and family-service agencies that cater mainly to children from low socioeconomic situations.

In addition, there are a number of different kinds of day-care centers that have been established to serve the children of mothers who work outside of the home. These may be private, profit-making organizations; private, non-profit-making centers supported through special federal funding; and, in rare cases, public, nonprofit-making centers supported through state funding.

These day-care centers are of three basic types. One type offers *custodial* care only. Major concerns are with guarding the safety of the child, providing him with food appropriate for his age, and offering him the physical care necessary while his mother works. *Cooperative* day-care centers offer, in addition to custodial care, ancillary health, educational, and social services. Typically, arrangements for these ancillary services are made through cooperation with other agencies. *Omnibus* day-care centers offer, in addition to the services described above, a variety of health, educational, and social services that are provided through the efforts of their own staffs.

Head Start programs, another type of early education setting, offer both half-day and full-day services. These programs are federally funded, and can be administered by a variety of agencies including public schools, community agencies, or model-cities programs. The majority of the children served are drawn from low socioeconomic backgrounds.

A number of preschool programs have been established under the auspices of universities, colleges, and public schools. These centers are usually demonstration schools that serve primarily as observation and participation facilities for high school and college students.

Teachers should be aware of the many variations that can exist in any of these settings. Children can be in attendance anywhere from three to eleven hours daily. The program can be housed in a separate building, in an elementary school, in a neighborhood agency, or in an industrial center. The socioeconomic backgrounds of the children served can include those from low-income homes, middle- to high-income homes, or a mixture of each. The licensing requirements, particularly for day-care programs, are largely a state and local prerogative. Because of this, there will be great variations in the number of children served, the adult–child ratio, and the kinds of ancillary services that are provided as part of the programs. Finally, the academic and experiential requirements for any staff position will vary according to the particular setting and the guidelines under which the center operates. One should expect to find a greater degree of variation in early education programs than in the typical public school setting.

Jobs and Staffing Patterns

There are many variations in staffing patterns that are unique to particular centers. An ideal staffing pattern would include:

1. Child Development Program Director. This person would administer and coordinate the total program. Prerequisites for the position would include an M.S. in child development, at least three years of teaching experience, and some administrative experience.
2. Director of the Educational Program. Prerequisites would include an M.S. in child development and/or teacher preparation, at least two years of teaching experience, and at least one year of teacher education experience.
3. Director of Social Work. Prerequisites would include at least a B.A. in social work and three years of field experience.
4. Director of the Nutrition Program. Prerequisites would include a B.A. in home economics and at least two years of field experience.
5. Director of Parent Activities. Prerequisites would include a B.A. in education and/or child development and/or social work as well as at least two years of relevant field experience.
6. Supervising Teacher. Prerequisites would include a B.A. in early child-

hood education or child development and some relevant work experience.

7. Teacher Aide. Prerequisites would include a high school diploma as well as informal experience working with young children.

Most early education programs are unable to provide the ideal kinds of staff resources described above. Teachers should be aware of the staff resources available to them, as well as of how the different positions relate to each other.

Teacher Functions

The role of the classroom teacher is exceedingly complex. Teachers should be prepared to fulfill many different functions. The teacher's major role is to create an environment where children can develop a love of learning. Most time will be spent interacting with the children, but in order to be effective in this role, the teacher must be aware of other, equally important responsibilities. The first of these relates to her duties as a program planner. The teacher is responsible for selecting the daily program objectives that must be converted to learning activities for the children. In order to plan effectively, the teacher should not only be aware of the entry-level skills that the children bring to school, but also the individual progress made by each child as the year progresses. This diagnostic function is critical if the teacher is to be able to individualize the curriculum and effectively meet the needs of each child. The teacher should have a systematic way of recording this progress, and must use these records to make decisions regarding the selection of program objectives.

Classroom management is another important function. In addition to diagnosing and selecting program objectives, the teacher is responsible for developing appropriate daily and weekly schedules, for grouping the children for various classroom activities, for anticipating special needs related to the purchase of materials, and for handling the unexpected events that create the "teachable moment" to which every teacher must sensitively respond.

The supervising teacher is responsible for planning for the other adults assigned to the classroom. This includes the teacher aide, parents, students, and other volunteers. There is a direct relationship between the effectiveness of these adults and the quality of the experience they receive from the supervising teacher. The teacher should be prepared to spend the necessary time for both planning and actual training.

Another responsibility relates to the teacher's liaison function with parents. The most successful early education programs have been those that have actively involved parents. At minimum, the teacher must be prepared to make home visits, to organize group meetings at school, and to arrange for parents to observe in the classroom.

Finally, teachers have a responsibility to cooperate, communicate, and interrelate their efforts with those of other staff members at their particular center. Even when working in a self-contained classroom, this kind of cooperation is essential. The operation of the total program will be enhanced if each of the staff members is willing to exchange ideas, to assist others in acquiring new skills, and to systematically review the goals of the total program and assess how effectively these goals are being achieved.

These are the skills that distinguish competent teachers from inefficient ones. As professionals, they must be willing to commit the time and effort necessary for individualizing a program in order to meet the needs of each child. This involves planning, scheduling, training, working with parents, and communicating with other staff members.

Kinds of Curricula and Programs

There are a number of commercially or experimentally developed preschool curriculum materials currently being used in early education centers. These programs typically consist of a series of written descriptions of learning activities appropriate for use with the young child, supportive media and learning equipment necessary for implementation, and, in some cases, diagnostic instruments to assist the teacher in assessing the progress of each child. In many centers, however, the teachers are expected to develop their own program within the guidelines of the philosophical orientation of the particular center. Although much has been written about the differences between program models and philosophical orientations, there are only a limited number of factors that characterize the different approaches used. Each teacher must make a personal decision with regard to each of these factors. If teachers at a particular center do not believe that the strategies implicit in the program model or philosophical orientation being followed are appropriate for young children, they will not be able to function effectively in that preschool setting.

One of the major areas of difference is in the theoretical orientation that underlies the ongoing preschool program. Theorists such as Montessori stressed the creation of a planned environment in which the child chooses materials and paces his own learning. Montessori developed a large number of graded, didactic materials that form the base for the instructional program and are the primary teaching tools used in the classroom. Those preschool programs influenced by Piaget, in contrast, believe it inappropriate to prearrange behavioral objectives for the child. The teacher's role is to follow up on the child's interests at a level of interaction that is consistent with his developmental functioning. A program influenced by Skinner or Gagné would assume that there is a predetermined sequence of objectives that can be systematically presented to the child. Here, the teacher's role is to present these activities sequentially and to systematically reinforce the desired response. Some models are based on an eclectic theoretical base, since at the present time the empirical support for any theoretical position is not comprehensive enough to fully account for how a child learns.

Another major area of difference is whether the program is process oriented or content oriented. Programs that are process oriented stress the development of sensory-perceptual and cognitive abilities such as skills related to discrimination, memory, temporal sequencing, and abilities that underlie classification skills. Content-oriented programs tend to stress the academic-skill areas that are emphasized in the early elementary grades. These include the development of skills and knowledge related to content areas such as language arts, science, mathematics, and reading.

The objectives of various programs differ greatly in terms of how explicitly they are stated. Some program models have developed behavioral objectives that very clearly state the desired criterion behavior. Other program models include objectives that are rather open ended, and which can be adapted and/or modified by the individual classroom teacher.

Another source of variation, related to the kinds of objectives included in a particular program model, is the matter of whether or not the objectives are presented in a teacher-imposed sequence or in terms of child selection. Some program models have developed objectives that the teacher is expected to implement sequentially. Other program models have developed objectives for the children, the sequence of presentation being determined by the child and his interests, rather than by the teacher.

The degree of structure inherent in the model will also differ greatly. Some program models rely on the presentation of many structured learning experiences that have been developed for the children. Other models stress unstructured learning experiences that are usually initiated by the child and capitalized upon by the teacher. Structure can also vary with regard to the degree of autonomy allowed a teacher. In some models, the strategies for planning and implementation are very clearly described. In others, the teacher has a wide degree of freedom in planning as well as implementation.

Another area of difference is in the use of various presentation modes. Some program models stress only a didactic approach to instruction. Others vary the presentation modes to include not only direct instruction, but also games, dialogue, and discovery.

While all of the program models agree that motivational factors play a critical role in any preschool program, the strategies of reinforcement can differ greatly. There is general agreement that intrinsic motivation is the terminal goal, but the techniques for helping the child achieve this goal are vastly different. Some program models stress the use of extrinsic rewards. These will take the form of tokens that can be exchanged for small toys, activities the children particularly enjoy, or candy which is given for reinforcement purposes. Other models stress the use of contingent social reinforcers such as words of praise, a pat on the head, or a hug. Still other models believe that the environment should be structured to respond to the child, providing intrinsic reinforcement as the child interacts with the materials available in the classroom.

The amount of parent participation and the objectives of this participation also differ in various programs. In some models, parental participation is minimal, and teachers are not expected or encouraged to involve the parents in the child's educational experiences. In other models, parents not only participate in decision making related to staffing, school policy, and the actual curriculum taught, but they also assist the teacher in the classroom in a teaching capacity.

In summary, the factors you must consider when reviewing a particular program model include the theoretical orientation of the model, type of content, explicitness of objectives, degree of autonomy allowed the teacher and child, structure of the learning experiences, presentation modes, strategies of reinforcement, and nature of parental participation. Each of these factors will directly affect the way you function in the classroom and will determine your role as a teacher.

CONCLUSIONS

In this chapter we have briefly reviewed some basic considerations and issues in early education today. We have seen that research findings do not, at this time, clearly support early intervention as the magical solution for optimizing the intellectual, social, emotional, and physical development of the young child. We have examined other reasons for providing services to young children who would otherwise be left unattended. We have seen that early education can respond to many of the child's basic needs, such as health, physical development, stimulation of language development, appropriate interactive opportunities with the environment, and social and emotional development.

Different kinds of centers, jobs, and teacher functions were briefly described. Great variations are possible in each of these areas, and teachers must be aware of the particular conditions that prevail in any center in which they hope to be employed. Other major differences exist with regard to the kind of curriculum being implemented in any particular center. Some of the factors that vary include the theoretical orientation, the kinds of objectives being implemented, the teaching strategies employed, and the degree of structure inherent in the model.

We have also suggested that finding a satisfying role in early education depends upon a match between your needs and the demands of the field and the specific job. There are a number of questions that a person considering a teaching career should ask himself. These questions involve basic decisions concerning future professional commitments.

- Have I had enough experience with young children to know that I really want to work with them?

- Do I want to work with particular kinds of children who would be served only in certain settings?
- Am I willing to commit the time and effort involved, which go beyond the scheduled working hours, in order to be an effective teacher?
- Do I know what theoretical and philosophical program orientation I am most comfortable with in terms of future teaching commitments?
- Are the goals of the program where I am considering employment realistic and consistent with what I believe to be important for young children?
- If a particular program model is being implemented at a center where I am considering employment, am I comfortable with the approach being used?
- Does the center where I am considering employment have clearly defined staff roles?
- How much responsibility will I have for training and supervision of other staff?
- Do career opportunities and a chance for growth exist at the center where I am considering employment?

These questions must be answered sooner or later by anyone who is seriously considering teaching as a professional career.

QUESTIONS

1. What characteristics do teachers of young children need to possess?

2. What attitudes about teaching in general, and about children in particular, are associated with effective teaching?

3. Describe in your own words the organizational skills that differentiate Jane's and Mary's teaching styles. Does Mary's superior organization come at the expense of classroom spontaneity?

4. Describe in your own words the major factors that characterize the different preschool programs that may be implemented.

5. Part of Jane Global's problem was that she was teaching in nursery school for the wrong reasons and had inappropriate attitudes and expectations. What are *your* reasons for wanting to be a preschool teacher? Have you observed or taught enough yet to know whether your expectations are realistic? If not, arrange to do so as soon as possible.

6. What kind of preschool program would you like to teach in (public or private; half day or whole day; high or low socioeconomic-status [SES] children; etc.)? Why? Have you had enough firsthand experience to be able to answer these questions with confidence?

7. If you were setting goal priorities for a preschool program, what goals would you stress heavily and what ones would you minimize or ignore? What does this tell you about your own values and preferences regarding the type of preschool in which you want to work?

8. Discuss your goal priorities with those of classmates, especially ones who disagree with you. Are differences due merely to oversights, or do you have important philosophical differences in some areas? If so, can these be resolved?

9. Survey different types of child-care services in your community. Describe the type of children that you think would benefit most from each (children of working mothers, low income, middle income, etc.).

10. Observe in three different kinds of child-care facilities (e.g., all day, nursery, Montessori, kindergarten). Describe in your own terms how they differ. Some of the factors you might use to distinguish programs include: child-adult ratio, SES of children, teacher training, organization of staff, funding, use of aides and volunteers, and types of services offered.

11. During observations in preschool programs, make note of provisions for protecting the health and safety of the children. Attempt to find specific instances of effective or ineffective planning.

12. From what you know about 3, 4, and 5 year olds (from reading and direct experience), what actions do you consider "typical" for them that are also dangerous? Can preschool be programmed to be relatively risk free? Should preschool programs be free of risks? Are some risks part of healthy development? How does a preschool teacher distinguish between normally and excessively dangerous situations?

READINGS

Anderson, R. and Shane, H., eds. *As the twig is bent.* Boston: Houghton Mifflin, 1971.

Caldwell, B. "The rationale for early intervention." *Exceptional Children, 36* (1970). 717–726.

Cazden, C. "The neglected situation: a source of social class differences in language use." *Journal of Social Issues, 26* (1970), 35–60.

Cicirelli, B. et al. *The Impact of Head Start: an evaluation of the effects of Head Start on children's cognitive and affective development.* Washington, D.C.: Office of Economic Opportunity, 1969.

Froebel, F. (W. N. Hailman, tr.) *The education of man.* New York: Appleton, 1887.

Keyserling, M. *Windows on day care.* New York: National Council of Jewish Women, 1972.

Montessori, M. *Dr. Montessori's own handbook.* Cambridge, Mass.: Bentley, 1964.

Piaget, J. *The origins of intelligence in children.* New York: International Universities, 1952.

Swift, J. "Effects of early group experience: the nursery school and day nursery." In M. Hoffman and L. Hoffman, eds. *Review of Child Development Research,* Vol. 1, 249–288. New York: Russell Sage, 1964.

LEARNING

This chapter deals with conditions that facilitate learning in young children. Information (based on available data) describing the effects of "deprived" and "enriched" environments on child learning is also discussed in a review of early education programs. We will attempt to single out those findings that appear to have important implications for early education programs. The research reviewed will be selective and representative rather than systematic and exhaustive. Our goal here is to communicate in broad terms the implications suggested by research for preschool programs.

Information drawn from a variety of sources reveals some useful facts and principles that provide direction for practical application. However, there are few universal truths that apply to *all* children in *all* situations. Our hope is that the information to follow will "unfreeze" commitments to educational beliefs that are not grounded in fact. Knowing that some things do not work or sometimes are untrue (e.g., praise is always effective, children from lower-class homes all have difficulty in learning) may help keep attention focused on trying to help children by adjusting the curriculum or teacher behavior. Too often educational dogma and commitment to an inflexible curriculum cause teachers to persist in behaviors that are not in the children's best interests.

In describing factors that affect child learning, we shall minimize theoretical considerations and instead concentrate on research evidence and its educational implications for practice (for additional exposure to theory, consult the readings listed at the end of the chapter). First, we believe that presently available evidence does not compel commitment to any particular theoretical position. That is, data do not exist to show that any one program is best for all children. Beyond this, we recognize that early education programs that *borrow* concepts, principles, and empirical insights, as they relate to the specific needs of their children, are apt to be most successful. For example, a child who needs adult guidance should be provided such guidance even if he is enrolled in a program that minimizes adult structuring. The research findings reviewed below show that all programs of educational intervention have both strengths and weaknesses, so that their *relative desirability* is dependent upon the needs of the children enrolled.

Finally, the chapter following this one will review information describing the *affective* growth of young children. This separation is a convenience that allows special emphasis to be placed upon both cognitive and affective learning. Obviously it is somewhat artificial, because the process of acquiring information about the self (sex roles, self-concept, etc.) is in some ways similar to how a child learns about the external world. To avoid repetition, most of the research investigating mother–infant interaction will be discussed in the next chapter, although it clearly is relevant to the present discussion as well.

BRAIN DEVELOPMENT
The effects of environmental stimulation on brain maturation or organization are uncertain. Except for severe trauma or prolonged exposure to debilitating environments, brain maturation seems unaffected by the environment. Premature babies, for instance, generally are not brain damaged nor do they suffer long-term effects from their birth. Similarly, children who are subjected to a brief period of acute starvation usually recover fully, although chronic undernourishment leads to smaller adults (Tanner, 1970).

Nutrition is important to the physical development of the brain. Thomas (1972), after reviewing several studies attempting to relate nutrition and childhood learning, suggests that malnutrition in the first few months is associated with both mental and physical retardation. The effects of malnutrition after the first year are relatively easier to offset than such early malnutrition. Early nutrition may be especially crucial because brain growth is so rapid during the first year of life. Physical growth also shows the importance of early deprivation. Eichenwald and Fry (1969) suggest that a child who is half-starved during the first six months may be permanently stunted, but if the starvation occurs after age 2, it is less likely to produce lasting physical effects.

Although the results of nutrition studies are indirect (many factors are uncontrolled—children who suffer nutritionally usually also experience a general environmental impoverishment), they are generally consistent. They suggest that the body and brain can withstand a great deal of adversity. Within limits, poor nutritional beginnings can be offset by adequate nourishment later. Also, adequate nutrition is conducive to healthy physical development of the brain even beyond year 1. Whether the effects of inadequate nutrition depress the physical growth of the brain or affect learning by depressing the child's attention and motivation (low blood-sugar level, etc.), or both, is not clear, but malnutrition definitely is associated with depressed learning. If a child is to be alert and responsive to his environment, adequate nutrition is mandatory. Clearly, then, preschools dealing with very young children, especially children from low-income families, should have programs to assess and if necessary supplement the children's nutritional requirements. Provision for nutritional requirements is likely to become even more important given the recent increase in food prices and the difficulty of purchasing inexpensive protein.

What else do we know about the development of the brain? We know that the growth of the brain, especially primary tissue, occurs very rapidly. After birth, motor maturity appears to come first, followed by sensory, visual, and auditory maturity (Tanner, 1964). Diggory (1972) suggests that most brain growth after birth involves the development of associative tissue rather than tissue growth in primary sensorimotor areas. That is, most brain growth after birth occurs in building the pathways that connect and coordinate communication between primary areas—motor, sensory, auditory, and visual. It has been estimated that the brain has achieved 90 percent of its growth by age 6.

Bayley (1970) reports that mental test scores show variable rates of growth among children in the first three or four years of life, which then become fairly stable. The implications here for programs of educational intervention seem clear: The brain does not unfold and grow at an even, predetermined rate. Although we cannot explain the role environment plays, it seems clear that environmental experiences do facilitate or depress the degree to which innate cognitive potential is reached.

Bayley's results draw some support from a longitudinal study of infants. Kagan et al. (1971) made an intensive study of a variety of measures, testing children at 4, 8, 13, and 27 months. He noted that stability coefficients did not rise above 0.5 (and most were considerably below this level), and concluded that cognitive development is quite variable in the early years, so that an individual's growth pattern can change over a short period. He suggests, though, that this low stability may be due to the inadequacy of the measuring instruments rather than to real changes in the child. Nonetheless, the data appear to suggest that planned, systematic intervention could lead to notable positive changes in child behavior.

Change may be difficult for some children to achieve, however. The most stable children in Kagan's sample were those in the top and bottom 15 percent on each measure. Thus, inherent ability and the consistency of the environment may reduce the probability of change in some children. Follow up of such children may make it possible to articulate more clearly the effects of intervention or subsequent "normal" environmental experiences on their strategies for processing and responding to environmental stimuli.

In summary, the brain matures very quickly in comparison to other parts of the body. Indeed, much of the primary tissue is present at birth, and brain development beyond the first year is mostly the building of connecting pathways between the primary location-centers in the brain. Furthermore, it appears that before about age 4, it is difficult to predict the subsequent mental development of children. Children who do poorly at age 2 may (even without direct intervention) become top scorers at age 3. Eventually, though, the habits, attack skills, and cognitive structures that a child develops begin to stabilize, so that information about a child's mental performance from one year will show a moderate correlation with the next year's score. These correlations become progressively higher as the child becomes older.

It thus seems reasonable to expect that preschool programs that begin at early ages (3 or younger) will produce greater gains than those that begin working with children at later ages. There are some data to support this view, but the nature of the support varies with the nature of the program and follow-up efforts, the age at which the child entered the program, and other factors.

Finally, we might suggest that, within rather wide environmental circumstances, the primary tissue area of the brain achieves maturity rather quickly. To the extent that experiences facilitate or depress cognitive development, they should affect the way in which the associative highways are built. Subsequently we shall present a brief explanation of this from the viewpoint of cognitive psychology. However, before doing so, it is desirable to discuss some of the evidence about environmental circumstances that can affect brain development.

EFFECTS OF DEPRIVATION

We start our search with an examination of the results of a study of animal behavior. In such studies it is possible for researchers to directly manipulate and strictly control the environment, so that the *only* difference between groups in these situations will be the experimental treatment. Thus, any changes in learning rate, brain size, or whatever can be directly attributed to the experimental treatment. Such control is neither possible nor desirable in human research in this area.

Krech (1968) completed a series of experiments exploring the effects of early stimulation on the brain development of rats. Rats from the same litter (to neutralize heritability as a factor of performance) were assigned either to an enriched environment or to a basically sterile, unstimulating one. The enriched environment afforded a number of luxuries not normally available to rats in general or young rats in particular. These experimental rats lived in well-equipped cages (creative playthings, ladders, running wheels), and as they grew older they were stimulated by new learning tasks and rewarded with sugar. Meanwhile, their brothers and sisters who were assigned to the opposite condition lived in barren cages and were rarely stimulated. Subsequent testing showed that the enriched rats outperformed their deprived counterparts. Furthermore, at the end of three months the rats were killed, and their brains were analyzed microscopically. The enriched "smarter" rats were found to have much more developed cortexes than the deprived rats (the cortex is the "gray matter" of the brain that mediates higher mental processes).

Thompson and Grusec (1970) have pointed out that, in general, early experience studies have failed to examine the effects of the treatment on older animals or humans. Thus, one could argue that it was the enrichment per se that made the difference, and that the fact that it was done with a young human or animal is not a critical factor. For example, since rats generally do not receive enrichment, is it not possible that adult rats subjected to the same treatments would also show the same effects? In any case, Krech's program of research clearly shows that an intensive (atypical) environment influenced performance and mental growth.

Spitz (1945) conducted the first large-scale study of institutionalized human infants who were less than 1 year old. He compared the "naturalistic" development of two groups of infants which were placed in two different environments. Some of the infants studied were reared in a foundling home for children whose mothers could not support them. The other infants, children of delinquent girls who were in a penal institution, were raised in a nursery at the institution.

The nursery had toys for the children to manipulate; they could see beyond their cribs; and they had care from (and interaction with) their own mothers or full-time mother substitutes. The unfortunate children in the foundling home were often deprived of perceptual stimulation (sheets consistently hung over the foot and side rails of their beds), and they only interacted with adults during meals. Observers reported that at ten to twelve months of age, these children lay on their backs (the soft mattresses made it impossible for them to roll over) and played with their hands and feet (their only toys) for long periods of time.

Spitz found that the developmental quotient scores of the foundling-home infants showed a dramatic reduction between the first four months of life and age eight to twelve months. He conducted a follow-up study two years later and concluded that the unstimulating conditions under which these infants lived had had irreversible negative effects on their development. Although this study has been criticized extensively, subsequent work by others has shown similar effects on infants reared in extremely barren early environments.

Skeels et al. (1938), however, report data suggesting that even extreme deprivation effects can be countered to some extent by intervention—remediation efforts initiated when children are 1 year old. He first studied two 1-year-old emaciated and inactive baby girls who were considered feeble-minded and unadoptable, and thus had been transferred from an orphanage to a state school for the mentally retarded. These infants were placed in a ward with mentally retarded women (whose mental age measured only approximately ten years), who showered them with affection and attention. Six months later, the girls were approaching normalcy.

To further test the possible benefits of an enriched environment, Skeels placed several more children in a home for the mentally retarded. The apparent results of the more stimulating environment were dramatic. During their stay in the home, the experimental group showed a mean gain of 27.5 IQ points, whereas a control group in an unstimulating orphanage showed losses of about 26 IQ points. Two-and-one-half years later, the experimental group had gained an additional 4 points and the controls had gained almost 6. Thus, the experimental group showed a gain of 32 points while the control group registered a loss of 20 points. Roughly twenty years later, Skeels (1966) conducted a follow-up study and found that the achieved success of the experimental infants was representative of the population of the United States as a whole—hence, normal. Most of these experimental infants had been adopted and reared in homes. As a group, these children completed an average of 12 grades of school, matured into normal adults, married, and were self-sufficient.

The statistics for the control group were grim in comparison. Most of these infants subsequently were transferred to schools for the mentally retarded, and none were ever adopted. Very few married or became self-supporting. Those few who held jobs performed only menial tasks, and in 1959 their median yearly income was $1,200.

The Spitz and Skeels results suggest that *extreme deprivation* may have dramatic effects upon the mental progress of very young children. Perhaps the effect of environment is greatest when the brain is developing physically. However, it seems clear that acute deprivation in the first year of life will retard subsequent mental development if not followed by quick intervention efforts. Furthermore, the Skeels study clearly shows that affective variables such as minimal contact with a loving adult in a continuing relationship are crucial to development.

SOCIOECONOMIC (SES) DIFFERENCES IN LEARNING

The examples discussed above are atypical, extreme examples of deprivation. What differences do variations in environment make in the lives of children who are raised by their own parents? There is great variance in the care and interaction that a given child might receive, because parents differ widely in their interests in their children and in the amount and quality of time that they can and do spend with them.

It is known that children coming from lower SES backgrounds as a group perform less well on intellectual and achievement tests than children from higher SES backgrounds (see Rohwer, 1970, for example). However, many individuals who come from lower-class homes score very highly, and numerous individuals from high SES backgrounds do poorly, both on performance tests and in school.

At present the causal aspects underlying these SES differences are unknown. Whether the tendency for lower performance in low SES children stems from aptitude (inherited from parents), lack of environmental stimulation (which depresses cognitive development), discrimination (e.g., assignment of less-successful teachers to lower-class schools, little contact with achievement-oriented students), nutrition, or some other variable is unclear and probably impossible to answer in any final way. The key question for early education is: Can intervention programs make a meaningful difference in the life of a child who has fallen behind other children?

Hess (1970) points out that, at times, there is too much stress on *group* differences, so that aspects of lower-class background are presented as gross and pervasive characteristics of an entire group. Thus, we must be wary of the dangers of overgeneralizing group differences and of applying them inappropriately to individuals. A review of some of the variables that often show SES differences may provide a list of the ways in which environment influences child growth (to the extent that it does). Hess, for example, after emphasizing the pervasive influence of values (he views the attitudes that low-SES parents develop as more likely to be the consequences of environmental factors rather than the causes), lists the following as likely mediators of environmental deprivation:

Physical conditions
Space
Comfort
Home and community resources
Display of order and routine versus disorder and unpredictability in child's
    physical and verbal exchanges with adults

Hess suggests that the *type* of parental control and the cognitive appeals on which it is based are more important than the *amount* of parent control. As we will see in the affective learning chapter, the children of parents who do not use physical power as a discipline technique, who are generally consistent in their demands, and who explain the consequences of the child's misbehavior for himself and others are more likely to learn that the world can be predicted, and are more likely to explore it actively.

Again, however, it is important to stress that the cause of the relationship is always in doubt when we talk about correlational research. When we do not manipulate or control the relevant conditions (and the home conditions for young children have rarely been manipulated as part of an experimental program), we cannot say that consistency or other factors *cause* child behavior. We simply know (in a correlational situation) that the two things co-occur. Some third variable (less dense environment, etc.) may be the key. However, correlational studies gain strength when data are replicated across several different SES levels and show that parents who behave in certain ways tend to have certain types of children. In these situations no direct proof exists, although the confluence of information suggests that the common parent behaviors are especially likely to be causal. We will not stop after each study to note the limitations of correlational research; we use this general note to stress that whenever results are summarized from natural rather than experimental conditions, we know only that variables co-occur.

Wolff (1972) suggests that the disadvantaged child often: (1) has no stable representation of the real world (we will discuss how a child learns to represent the world in the following section); and (2) has no intrinsic motivation to structure and differentiate the world. Similarly, Murphy (1972) suggests that children from disadvantaged homes do not play with words or materials as middle-class children do, and they do not project sequences of action and then play them out. This failure to "play" with the environment at an early age may be correlated with later behavior. For example, Fantz (1966) found that lower-class children aged 6 or 7 spend less time looking at visual patterns in experimental situations than middle-class children.

Schroder, Driver, and Streufert (1967) have hypothesized that an environment that is either too simple or too complex may inhibit cognitive development, especially conceptual development. The child who has too many aspects to attend to and not enough guidance from adults may find it difficult to integrate discrete stimuli into a coherent pattern. Similarly, a barren environment may not provide enough material to integrate.

Others argue that lower-class parents usually do not help their children to use language efficiently for thinking and problem solving. A common finding is that the frequency and usage of language differs markedly in high- and low-SES homes. Bernstein (1958, 1961) has argued that lower-class adults use language primarily for social reasons and tend not to use it much for logical reasoning and problem solving. Language, then, is used less in lower-class homes, and when it is, it is more likely to be used in restraining or controlling the child than in helping him to explore his world.

The homes of some disadvantaged children may be *simultaneously* over- and understimulating. For example, in a crowded environment replete with seemingly random noise and movement, the child may have too many stimuli to attend to. It has been claimed that lower-class youngsters have less opportunity to acquire auditory discriminations (Hunt, 1961; Bloom, Davis, & Hess, 1965; Deutsch et al., 1967). Their homes have high noise levels, but they do not receive the repetition, explanation, and general patterning of sounds that are needed to develop their capacity to make fine auditory discriminations. Children's inability to attend to important stimuli fully and to place such stimuli into a meaningful context may be a contributing factor to school failure. To the extent that this hypothesis is true, these children's ability to listen to teacher directions and to read would be hampered.

Finally, we might note that mothers in low-SES homes consistently are found to view their role differently and to behave differently than middle-class mothers. For example, Klatskin, Jackson, and Wilkin (1956) report that lower-class mothers are inconsistent on the dimension of rigidity/permissiveness. Among the qualities that Smilansky (1968) found to differentiate advantaged from disadvantaged homes were: friends to play with, toys, time with adults, and direct teaching in a playful fashion. Furthermore, advantaged mothers saw themselves as teachers; disadvantaged mothers did not. Such differences in parental perceptions and home stimulation experiences were seen even more clearly in research by Hess, Shipman, Brophy, and Bear (1969).

We have discussed some research suggesting that early experience is important, and we have seen that many children from disadvantaged homes live in environments that differ from those experienced by more advantaged children. Now let's return to a question raised earlier to see if such differences in experiences might influence cognitive development.

COGNITIVE DEVELOPMENT: A POINT OF VIEW

How do we explain the growth of associative pathways that make it possible for the brain to retain, differentiate, and use discrete items of stored information in problem-solving situations? Piaget, perhaps the most influential cognitive psychologist, has argued that early mental growth depends upon the child's opportunities for sensorimotor interaction. Thought is viewed as the interiorization of sensorimotor interaction. That is, the child learns to interiorize information about objects by feeling, sucking, chewing, dropping—generally exploring the external world. This view of cognitive growth through direct sensorimotor input is consistent with the general development of the brain, in that motor and sensory maturity precede visual and auditory maturity. Thus, the child is not equipped to learn by merely watching or looking—he needs direct experience to differentiate his world. Therefore, it would appear that the child who does not have the opportunity to manipulate objects will proceed less quickly than the child whose natural curiosity and drive for competency is facilitated by the environment (recall the inactive, immobile infants in the Spitz study).

The child changes and learns as he develops each day; he learns to do new things he couldn't do before. Early stimulation programs try to speed up and enrich this development by exposing the child to novel and interesting experiences not available in his home environment. Such programs are based on the works of Piaget and others suggesting that much learning occurs spontaneously as the child encounters new stimulation.

There is no direct proof for this claim, but there is ample indirect evidence for it. For example, Fantz (1966) found that 2-week-old infants preferred patterned stimuli over homogenous color, and at four months preferred the human face to nonsense figures. Recall the unfortunate infants in the Spitz study who had sheets covering the side rails of their beds. Their chances to see and respond to the environment were minimal. As a result, their ability to differentiate (and subsequently to prefer) patterned stimuli was not developed fully.

Young children *can* learn without manipulating, touching, or "experiencing" objects. Bandura (1963, 1968) has demonstrated that children can learn by listening and looking. In this instance, 3-year-old children who were afraid of dogs learned to approach them after watching a child play with a dog on film. And, as we will show later, a child's direct experience of seeing may depress his learning in some instances. We point out these exceptions to the notion that the child should be an active learner because there are numerous things that children can learn without active involvement. This becomes more true as the child becomes older. *However, the young child, especially the young child from a disadvantaged background, will learn most readily through concrete manipulation.* Thus, a desirable feature of preschool programs for disadvantaged children is that they be replete with objects and experiences requiring learner manipulation and coordination.

In review, then, cognitive psychologists suggest that infants have a basic drive to explore the world and to become more competent. Furthermore, this active curiosity is conceived to be innate but capable of flourishing or being inhibited depending upon the environment. Bruner (1966) especially underlines the regulatory role that the environment plays, and suggests that a biologically mature human does not develop complete symbolic representative systems unless adults or educational experiences have helped him as a child to structure his world in complex, highly differential ways (Anglin, 1973). Thus, thinking and problem-solving abilities will not develop "automatically" through maturation; their development must be stimulated.

Early infant growth is controlled primarily by sensorimotor input, so that Piaget has labeled this growth period as the *sensorimotor stage.* The child learns about his world through his actions: What he knows is what he *does.* Careful observations of young children show that when they accomplish a new behavior (e.g., rolling over, touching a toe, saying the "m" sound), they practice the behavior repeatedly. New knowledge (skills, if you prefer) for the infant is acquired through his exploratory behavior. The new knowledge touches off a period of practice, practice, and more practice, leading to eventual mastery, which touches off a new cycle of exploration, practice, and more practice.

The child internalizes motor action through this *mastery cycle,* gradually differentiating shapes, functions, and so on, and in time creating primitive mental structures for representing the world. The practice-mastery cycle helps to assure that the child will acquire corrective feedback from the environment, which will enable him to refine his distinctions.

LEARNING IN 2- TO 5-YEAR-OLD CHILDREN

Diggory (1972) suggests that if a child is to organize his world there must be a basic consistency to it. Environments that do not teach the child that things go in certain places or that activities can be pursued in certain places but not others probably confuse the child. Such children are not encouraged to learn that they can understand and organize the world, nor do they learn to discriminate their world as sharply (a place for painting, a time for talking). Thus, it would seem especially important for the 2- to 5-year-old youngster to be exposed to a preschool program that allows him to see the structure that exists in the environment and learn that materials and activities can be organized. The traditional nursery-school notion of dividing the room into discrete areas (housekeeping, art, block play, etc.) is believed to help the child to break down the environment into perceptual "chunks" that are manageable.

As we will note from time to time, no single preschool program or philosophy has a lock on good ideas. We suspect that the provision of clearly delineated room areas (an idea stressed by traditional nursery schools) is good for all children of this age range. Cluttered walls and areas that overlap (and perhaps overstimulate the child) probably make it more difficult for him to focus his attention. We disagree, however, with the idea of nursery schools supplying *only* free play for disadvantaged children. This is probably effective for middle-class youngsters who have learned how to examine objects and use equipment (more on this later), but disadvantaged youngsters need more direct assistance in learning to use new objects and equipment. A completely new range of possibilities forces too much on the child; a good balance between successful repetition and application of old skills and this imposition of new demands is more desirable.

For example, the child who has learned to put objects other than food into his mouth is constantly forced to discriminate foods from other objects by his mother's directions; Gradually he learns that only food goes in the mouth. Similarly, after learning to pick up a utensil, he may then learn to bang it indiscriminately. Progressively, however, he learns to bang his pegboard but not his mother or the table. Existing structures (skills, concepts, discriminations) help the child to assimilate incoming information when possible (e.g., a crayon, like a pencil, can be used to make marks). This process is called *assimilation*. It is predominant in the general exploratory behavior of the child and the playful exercising of abilities that he possesses. That is, the child practices what he already knows how to do, or he assimilates a new object by relating it to something with which he already is familiar.

Accommodation, on the other hand, forces the child to adjust his behavior to new demands by developing new structures. He doesn't already know what to do, so he must learn new behavior through imitation or experimentation.

Both assimilation and accommodation are important. The child who merely practices existing skills (assimilation) will make only minimal progress, and at times will engage in dangerous behavior (eating paint chips, etc.). The more active the child is, the more likely he is to find situations that provide demands that are discrepant from his existing structure. These demands force him to make finer and finer differentiations, ultimately creating broader and more diverse ways of representing the world (accommodation).

The words assimilation and accommodation are not important in and of themselves. We use them here simply because they are popular in the literature. The important point is to provide a dynamic environment that simultaneously: (1) allows the child to practice existing skills in a satisfying way, (2) occasionally prompts him to adjust and grow, and (3) provides optimal stimulation for growth. Too few demands are likely to leave the child at his present level, and too many demands (accommodation requests) are likely to lead to frustration and withdrawal.

Eventually, the child advances from sensorimotor ways of representing the world to ways that include primitive symbolic modes. Children who imitate their parents or play house show that they have developed images of things that they have observed. And, if given ample opportunity and encouragement to practice, they will become progressively more adept at perceiving and representing their world through imagining and role playing. Children's play is a very important part of their development. Through play they are beginning to develop a way of representing and predicting day-to-day events.

These fledgling attempts to represent the world symbolically, which begin about age 2, are part of a new stage called *preoperational* by Piaget. This stage involves the progressive refinement and coordination of the child's knowledge of the world. During the preoperational stage, children have difficulty in coordinating more than one perceptual feature at a time. A commonly stated example is the fact that most 4-year-old children know which is their right hand, but it will be a few years before they realize that their right hand will be on the opposite side if they turn around. Again, the term we use is not important. We use preoperational here because it is a commonly understood term. Its major implication is that while the child usually perceives isolated items of information accurately, he cannot fully coordinate all incoming stimuli.

Bruner (1966) has noted that during the preoperational stage the child can represent his world in three basic ways: in his actions (enactively), in images (iconically), or in words (verbally/symbolically). When the child has fully integrated the three representational modes and can attend to several perceptual features simultaneously, he has developed to an *operational* level of thinking.

Since the focus of this book is on the young learner (ages 2 through 5), let's take a look at the special learning problems of the 2- to 5-year-old youngster. As we have noted, children in the preoperational stage have a difficult time coordinating more than one perceptual feature at a time. Thus, preschool programs for very young children must be designed to help children learn such coordination. In particular, preoperational children need special help in organizing their perceptual skills. The surface qualities of objects can be very confusing to children who at this age are dominated by what they perceive in the immediate environment. Indeed, without help, younger children will not benefit from iconic instructional materials (pictures, shapes), even though older ones will. Often they need concrete objects in order to achieve true understanding.

In one study, Corsini, Pick, and Flavell (1968) improved the ability of young children to remember a block pattern. Kindergarten children did not spontaneously use paper visual models as memory aids. However, it proved to be very easy to train them to do this. Apparently, young children do not necessarily lack the *ability* to use iconic cues in attempting to remember a task, but often they are *unaware* that they *should* be using them. A related problem is the coordination of the language system with the imagery system. The child may not automatically label verbally the discrete aspects of the stimuli he sees, even though he may be aware of them and discriminate them accurately. Adults apparently can help here by regularly labeling colors, sizes, shapes, names, and other attributes of objects ("John, give me the *thin brown pencil*").

The usefulness of verbal explanation was demonstrated in a study by Ryan, Hegion, and Flavell (1969). In this experiment, preschool children were taught to use pictures as cues for remembering the spatial locations of toys. For instance, they learned to use a picture as a guide for placing zoo animals appropriately in a cage. For the younger children (3 years old), *verbal explanation* was more helpful than *nonverbal modeling*. The task was too complex for the children to learn through their own observations, but they could learn it when their attention was directed to the relevant stimuli and they were given verbal labels and explanations.

These two studies suggest that children can be trained to coordinate their perceptual capacity in order to attend more closely to incoming information and *learn* ways to use this input. Because they have previously explored the world mostly through sensorimotor activities, they apparently do not automatically use their perceptual abilities as soon as those abilities mature physically. Just as experience is necessary in the sensorimotor period, experience, especially guided experience, is necessary if the preoperational child is to use his developing perceptual capacities to maximum advantage.

Rohwer (1969) helped children to learn lists of paired words by providing the child with a sentence (a way of representing the relationships). Rohwer used three types of sentences depicting the following types of relationships:

conjunctive   the cat and the table
prepositional   the cat is under the table
verb: action   the cat bites the table

He found that stating an action relationship produced the best learning, not only in children of preschool age but also in older children and adults.

He repeated the study using pictures depicting the relationships as well as the three sentence types. He found that action sentences, regardless of what kind of picture accompanied them, still best facilitated the young child's learning of the paired words. Younger children (kindergarten and first graders) were helped more by hearing the action sentence, whereas older children learned more readily by seeing the action picture. We suspect that younger children would have been helped more by manipulating objects or a combination of manipulation and action sentences than they were with just action sentences. Again, young children learn mostly through physical manipulation.

Apparently a child develops competence for decoding and using complex sentences before showing an ability to copy even simple geometric forms. However, it is also important to note that the child can utter complex sentences before he can comply with all the logical actions suggested in those sentences. Thus teachers of young children need to realize that pictures may be misleading to children unless the teacher helps them to see by providing verbal mediators, allowing them to act out picture sequences, and so forth, and that children may utter sentences without understanding what they say. Growth is always uneven, but in dealing with the preoperational child it is especially important to realize that perceptual cues are often ambiguous. Perhaps the best way teachers can help children is to assist them in developing language as a tool for sorting and using perceptual information constructively. Preschool programs can help children build links between perception and language in numerous ways, but especially helpful are tasks that help children coordinate information coming from several input channels simultaneously (e.g., the teacher asks the child to say, "I am going to stand up, pick up the yellow square, and then walk over and place it over Johnny's head," and then act it out; the teacher allows children to pour water into dissimilar beakers and then pour the water back into the original containers).

Below are some ideas (adapted from Diggory, 1972) that seem to be useful suggestions for preschool programs that deal with preoperational children.

1. Provide the child with opportunities to differentiate and integrate his own experiences in all areas, but provide adult assistance in helping him to

recognize important cues (i.e., balance structured teaching with free play and discovery).

2. Continue to build on previous sensorimotor experience (e.g., provide opportunity, materials, appropriate guidance) by expecting the child to become more sophisticated in his use of materials (making patterned strings of beads, painting with more detail, constructing intricate block designs, etc.).

3. Conceptual development is still facilitated by action at this age; encourage this growth by action games and sequences: counting by stomping and clapping, singing in rhyme, and manipulation of all sorts will facilitate mental and physical development.

4. Recall that a child is easily distracted and misled by what he sees, so that he needs many experiences that will assist him in coordinating imagery and verbal labeling and in distinguishing the stable, invariant properties of objects from nonessential aspects such as color and shape.

5. The coordination of action, picture, and word should be encouraged. Children can be asked to talk to you about pictures and actions, to find pictures of their words, and to act out those words. Games or activities that require the simultaneous use and integration of visual, auditory, and motor modes are especially helpful.

6. Encourage use of the early forms of symbolization, and provide time for children to engage in imitative actions such as dress up, play with puppets, and so on.

7. Expand verbal competency in general (more on this later).

**LANGUAGE
DEVELOPMENT**

The child's ability to respond to and benefit from language is a key to his conceptual attainment. Indeed, language is one basic ability that separates man from other animals. We know that young children use language in a qualitatively different way than adults. For example, Fraser, Bellugi, and Brown (1963) report that 3-and-1-half-year-old children could repeat sentences by rote before they could point to pictures that represented the key elements of these sentences. McNeill (1966) has reported that children under the age of 7 give different kinds of word associations than adults do. Children provide more relational classifications (a tree is to climb, etc.). This again shows the *action focus* of the preoperational child's knowledge—mostly, he knows what he sees and does.

Several experiments suggest that children can be taught to *use* language to accomplish tasks they could not do otherwise. It has been found that children under 6 do not spontaneously use their verbal skills in problem-solving situations the way older children do. For example, Flavell, Beach, and Chinsky (1966) found that kindergarteners used verbal rehearsal (silent repeating of relevant words and phrases) much less frequently than third graders in a picture-recall task.

In some instances, young children fail to produce appropriate verbal mediators. For example, a child may actively respond to a picture and mentally attach a name or label to it. Such mental representation greatly facilitates his retrieval of information about that image. Another child may note the picture visually but fail to make any active verbal response to it. This is called *production deficiency,* which occurs when children physiologically and neurologically mature enough to produce a response or a language association fail to do so because they have not become aware of this ability.

This observation has led Flavell and others to the production deficiency hypothesis, which suggests that general language practice might help children use language to solve problems in new situations. That children can use verbal mediators to good advantage has been demonstrated in several experiments. One of the more interesting studies initially identified first graders who spontaneously used verbal rehearsal in a picture-recall task and others who did not (Keeney, Cannizzo, & Flavell, 1967). As might be expected, those children who *actively* rehearsed verbal mediators for the pictures (producers) scored higher on recall tasks than children who did not rehearse (nonproducers). However, after training, the nonproducers scored as high as the producers. Subsequently, the children were given the opportunity to stop rehearsing if they cared to do so. None of the producers stopped, but all of the experimentally trained nonproducers did. Thus, training can facilitate short-term performance, but the opportunities and factors that have led children to become producers or nonproducers (perhaps motivational intensity or attention) have produced verbal mediation habits which are *not* altered by brief techniques. (This is one example of a recurring problem: the tendency for experimental gains to dissipate once the treatment ends.)

The implications of such basic research findings are not entirely clear, but they do suggest that verbal habits and the processing of information *can* be influenced. Thus, even though we cannot specify what the particular *form* of the language program should be, it does seem clear that verbal training or language development and activities should be a part of every preschool program. Vygotsky (1962) articulated a major theory underlining the importance of verbal mediation skills. He believed it important for children to learn how to talk about problems in social settings and to develop language skills, and that this social speech of children aged 2 to 4, which helps them label and explore their world, gradually becomes inner, covert speech that facilitates thinking. At first children talk only to others for social reasons, but they gradually learn to use language to talk to themselves for thinking and problem solving.

Interestingly, Kohlberg, Yeager, and Hjertholm (1968) have found that children who talk to themselves also talk more to other children. Furthermore, they report that bright children's egocentric speech (talking aloud to oneself) peaks at age 4, whereas average children do not peak until about age 7. Apparently, the exercise of egocentric speech is the child's way of teaching himself to use verbal mediators for thinking and problem solving. Much like counting on one's fingers, egocentric speech is a tool for solving problems that the child has not yet learned to solve through silent thought.

Obviously, then, the young child's egocentric speech should not be negatively sanctioned or viewed as immature by the teacher or parent. It is a clear sign that the child is attending to his environment and actively trying to describe and understand it. A relevant question then, is: How should the parent or teacher react to the child's spontaneous verbalizations? Research has shown that to ignore such speech is self-defeating in the long run, because lack of parent monitoring and responsiveness are negatively correlated with the child's intellectual performance (Brophy, 1970; Schaefer, 1969).

Cazden (1965) studied this question directly by exposing 2½-year-old working-class children to two specific treatments forty minutes a day for three months. One treatment emphasized providing the child with a correct grammatical model by expanding the child's spontaneous utterances. If the child said "Doggie bite," or "Kite high," the adult expansions might be "Yes, he's biting," or "Yes, the kite is high." As McNeill (1970) has noted, expansion is modeling in reverse. Rather than the adult initiating the statement and having the child repeat it, the child receives the correct language model after initiating the interaction himself.

The other condition of Cazden's study was an enrichment condition. In this situation, the adult commented upon what the child said. If the child said "Doggie bite," or "Kite high," the enrichment response might be "Yes, he's very bad," or "It's very windy." Thus, this condition didn't simply expand the child's statement; it related it to other information.

Language tests administered before and after the experiment showed that while expansion students made modest gains in comparison to controls, enrichment students' gains were much larger. Language practice benefited all students, but the information provided in the enrichment treatment was of particular value.

The theoretical aspects of this study have been discussed at length (see, for example, McNeill, 1970), and it has been contended that under certain conditions expansion may be the best way to react to the spontaneous language of children, although data to support this view have not yet been presented. In contrast, the value of enrichment responses seems well-established.

To us, the desirable effects of the enrichment approach stem from its naturalness and its conversational aspects. A child's reaction to expansion may be a frustrated "I thought I said that." In contrast, enrichment may be psychologically more fulfilling because the message shows the child that he has been heard and advances the conversation to a new dimension. In time, such responses may implicitly teach the child to *respond* to others' speech rather than merely to engage in imitation or parallel conversation. Indirect support for this point of view can be drawn from a study showing that language drills correlated *negatively* with pupil-gain scores on six *abstract* language measures, whereas the teacher's communicative skill correlated positively (Soar, 1970).

The Cazden study suggests the desirability of responding to the child's spontaneous language. Also, the verbal-mediation literature reviewed above establishes the importance of helping the child to use language in learning tasks. Children who have the opportunity to interact with responsive adults will make language gains. However, when children have not been encouraged to actively use spontaneous speech or to interact with responsive adults, they may need special language training. We have seen in verbal-mediation experiments that short-run treatments will not correct such basic deficiencies; more intensive treatments are needed.

Blank and Solomon (1968, 1969) have developed a tutorial approach to teach children to use language to think, reflect, and make inferences rather than just to describe immediate experience. They stress the functional use of language rather than grammatical correctness or isolated vocabulary learning. Children are taught to attend selectively, to imagine future events ("If the key falls off the table where will it be?"), to engage in sustained sequential thinking (follow a series of directions), to develop awareness of the uses of language (give the adult directions to follow), and to develop the ability to categorize (recognize similarities and differences in sorting things).

In this section we have highlighted language because it is a key aspect of the preoperational child's development. After the sensorimotor period, the child develops imagery and verbal capacities for representing the world. Children who are helped to coordinate these emerging modes for dealing with the world, and especially those children who have ample opportunity to talk with adults, are likely to develop as energetic, alert learners. Also, children with limited early language experiences are especially likely to benefit from special programs that systematically teach language skills.

PRESCHOOL PROGRAMS: DO THEY WORK?

Having introduced the topic of systematic programs for young children, it is important to discuss whether experience in such programs is categorically good or if some programs are more useful in some aspects or for some learners than other programs. Here our goal is to briefly summarize what is known about preschools, rather than to intensively examine the curriculum or effects of particular programs. Interested readers are referred to Beller (1973) for an excellent review of the effects of specific programs.

The number of IQ points that a program "saves" or "develops" is not important per se. Thus, it is not possible to say categorically that any program failing to develop 15 IQ points is unsuccessful. Within some IQ ranges, an increase of only a few IQ points may represent a significant gain that helps children to live a comparatively richer and fuller life. Jencks et al. (1972) made a similar point with regard to achievement scores, noting that for low-SES-status children the ability to read at the eighth- versus twelfth-grade level is of no major importance (in terms of earning power), but the difference in helping children to read at the eighth-grade level versus not reading at all is of critical importance.

Success is clearly a relative term, and whether or not this label is applied to a preschool program depends upon the expectations that one holds. If one expects all children to become lawyers and doctors, the long-run effects of our initial wave of preschool programs are apt to be viewed with disappointment. However, if one's goal is to help potentially illiterate and unemployable adults to become employable and able to live autonomous lives, then some of our present preschool programs should be viewed as quite successful. Preschool programs as we know them today are probably not enough to bring *all* disadvantaged children up to middle-class performance levels within a single generation, although it is reasonable to expect that enrollment will benefit *most* children and will help many to reach middle-class standards.

Beilin (1972), for example, has noted that if 20 to 25 percent of each generation of disadvantaged children could equal the intellectual performance levels of successful middle-class students, we would have a true social revolution. Helping the children of former preschool enrollees (who develop into mature, responsible adults with stable employment and who provide stable homes for their own children) will clearly be an easier task than helping the children of unemployed parents to develop educational skills.

The goal of any preschool program is to help the child to use *advantageously* the mental ability he possesses and to enhance his existing cognitive potential to the maximum degree. The preceding discussion was not meant to establish low goals, but simply to point out that the ill effects of prolonged poverty probably cannot be eliminated in a single decade, and to urge readers and funding sources not to give up on preschools prematurely.

Preschool programs reasonably can be expected to make a major *relative* difference in the lives of most of their graduates. It is possible to help children develop their normal skills (by not letting normal potential recede to 80 IQ points through lack of stimulation, etc.), so that they enter grade school with a chance for successful mastery, allowing them to at least complete high school and to develop marketable skills necessary for a successful life.

The difference between IQ scores of 80 and 100 is an important one in our society, not because IQ scores are significant in and of themselves, but because we regularly find that persons who score in the 80s do not normally complete high school, do not obtain good jobs, and so on. What is important is not IQ but rather the life conditions that accompany it. Thus, in our view, the success of a preschool program must be viewed from the perspective of how it helps children to maintain and use effectively the mental ability they possess. Programs that help children to register positive but modest IQ gains may still be very successful if the children involved learn to use existing talents more effectively in making achievement gains. Indeed, the best way to look at preschool programs is not through IQ scores, but through the specific and demonstrable skills that children have mastered in the program. Again, we remind readers that success is a highly relative term, and that different researchers use different criteria.

Some programs have been designed to tutor *infants,* so that they can be stimulated before the cumulative effects of a disadvantaged environment occur. In general, such studies show that moderately trained adults can make a difference in infants' performance on standardized tests (Schaefer, 1969; Painter, 1969; Palmer, 1968, 1969, 1970). It will be interesting to see the effects of this early training on performance in subsequent years when these children progress through elementary school.

As we noted above, some research suggests that such gains may be a "saved from loss" effect, in that the long-term difference between experimental and control children is due more to a decline in the performance of controls than to gains for experimental children (Schaefer, 1969). Nonetheless, early childhood education remains important when viewed from the perspective of employability and quality of life.

Apparently, early education curricula need not be extensive, and tutors need not go through an extensive training program to enable children to register initial gains. Palmer, for example, reports that the specific techniques of two different experimental programs made little difference: The chance for the infant to interact with experienced adults was more important.

Early education programs have also been designed to train parents to interact with their own children. Initial results from the Florida Project (Gordon, 1971a, 1971b) were modest, but subsequent longitudinal follow-up testing showed some progress. The results from two other programs have been even more promising: The Verbal Interaction Mother/Child Home Program (Levenstein, 1970, 1971; Levenstein & Levenstein, 1971; Levenstein & Sunley, 1968), and the DARCEE Infant Program (Forrester et al., 1971). Interestingly, the results from the Verbal Interaction Mother–Child Home Program are similar to the Palmer results, in that the specifics of the mother–child program did not appear to be especially important. Apparently, providing the mother with awareness and some key interaction skills is enough. The critical variable here may be the opportunity for the child to receive stimulation from an adult on a regular basis. Within limits, optimizing child growth may be that simple: Just provide time and interest from a concerned adult.

There are few data on *group* programs for children under 3, in other words day-care centers. The available research suggests that infants are not impaired by day-care services, despite their spending prolonged periods of time away from their mothers, and they may be helped (Caldwell & Richmond, 1964; Honig & Brill, 1970; Robinson & Robinson, 1971). Furthermore, there is evidence to show that a child's attachment to his mother (or mother's to child) is not damaged by day-care enrollment (Caldwell, Wright, Honig, & Tannenbaum, 1970). Such results have to be interpreted with caution, however. These studies involved day-care programs that maintained an adult–child ratio of one to four and where each child received some personalized interaction and attention each day. Unfortunately, we know that these are not the conditions under which all day-care centers function, and there are abundant stories (all too often grounded in fact) about private home-care environments where children spend much of their days in playpens or in front of TV sets. Prescott and Jones (1967) have found conditions to vary so widely from center to center that the term "day care" has no program implications per se. Therefore, it is best to assume that day-care centers are facilitative environments for young chidren *only* if they view their educative function seriously and maintain a reasonable adult–child ratio.

DO PROGRAMS HAVE IMPORTANT EFFECTS?

We have discussed research results showing the desirable effects of adult interaction on institutionalized infants, and have reviewed data suggesting that adult–child interaction in tutorial situations and language programs has notable effects on the child's intellectual functioning. We have also examined some data on children in group settings and have found that well-managed day-care centers at least have positive short-range effects on children. We will now discuss the literature dealing with the effects of preschool programs on both short-range and long-range intellectual performance.

It is exceedingly difficult to generalize about preschool programs. Programs differ markedly in their goals, teacher–child ratios, competence and training of staff, and the tests used to certify their effectiveness. In addition, one program may last for a year, whereas another program may run for several years. Also, children's ages and characteristics such as IQ vary widely from program to program.

Some studies of programs have shown no benefits for the experimental children, although none have revealed negative effects. Others show mixed results, and still others produce consistently positive results, with experimental students outperforming controls. To further complicate matters, some studies demonstrate that carefully designed and implemented programs have no immediate or short-range benefits, but produce long-range benefits for the experimental students that do not occur for the control students. Other studies show precisely the opposite pattern. Obviously, the nature of research on organized programs of preschool education is very complicated. We refer the reader again to Beller (1973) for more details. In the discussion we will summarize the highlights of available research and provide our reactions to it.

It is not really surprising that studies have produced conflicting results. Children differ in their needs, and if preschool programs offer a set standard curriculum (which most of the early preschool programs did), it seems clear that a given program will work better for some children than for others. Thus, research is not likely to categorically certify the superiority of any particular program for *all* young children. The success of a program depends upon what child experiences precede and follow it and on what measures are used to evaluate it.

As would be expected, preschool programs tend to show better results when the "test of success" is compatible with the immediate short-range goals of the program. Programs that emphasize verbal drills are apt to do well on short-range tests of language performance, while programs that emphasize play or structured independence are more likely to register gains on symbolic expression and discrimination learning, respectively. Several investigators have attempted to compare the relative effectiveness of different preschool programs, but these studies consistently show that no single program is generally superior across a variety of measures (Beller, Zimmie, & Aiken, 1971; Bissell, 1971; Karnes, 1969; Miller & Dyer, 1970a, 1970b, 1970c, 1971; Weikart, 1971).

Beller (1969, 1972) has shown that child characteristics are important in determining the effects of preschool programs. He found that the timing of educational intervention had no important effects on children who were high on autonomous achievement striving in the first grade. Children without preschool experience who were high on this measure quickly caught up with students who had had early preschool experience. However, children low in autonomous achievement striving benefited from early preschool programs. The subsequent achievement of such children was depressed if they had not been in early education programs. Due to the decline of the extended family and the greater frequency of situations in which both parents work, the percentage of middle-class children who are high on autonomous achievement may decrease unless the preschool program fulfills this function.

Thus, enrollment in a preschool program is more important for some children than for others, even though their IQ scores may be identical. Again, such differences help to explain why there is no one superior program equally suited to all students. But this does not mean that there are no differences among programs. Some programs consistently show superiority over others on *some* dependent measures. Ultimately, the desirability of a program depends on the degree to which it provides for the needs of the children involved.

Apparently there are many roads to academic success. We noted earlier that no single preschool program has a lock on good ideas. In the following chapters, when we present practical ideas for running preschool programs, we will draw ideas from a variety of perspectives. However, before leaving our review of research on preschool programs, we must note that some things do appear to make a difference. The failure to find a single superior program does not mean that "anything goes."

Two of the comparative studies cited above deserve further comment, because they illustrate points that have general application. Weikart (1971) compared three different programs and concluded that these programs had similar effects. Furthermore, he suggested that children can profit from any curriculum that offers a wide set of planned experiences. He concluded that the major role of the curriculum is to mobilize teacher behavior toward the realization of *specified goals*. The suggestion is not that preschool programs make no difference, but that among preschool programs founded on clearly specified curricula (with accompanying training materials), there will be no major differences across a variety of dependent measures. However, programs that do not articulate curricula or offer training guides for teachers will not match the gains of planned, structured programs. The specific curriculum may not make a difference, but the presence or absence of a coherent, planned set of learning activities to help the child integrate his experiences appears to be very important.

Beller (1973) implicitly qualifies Weikart's suggestions by positing that a major ingredient of successful preschool programs is the presence of an intensive relationship between teacher and child which provides the child with a stable set of experiences. Thus, a curriculum that sanctions (or creates) an environment in which the child can interact often with an adult, either singly or in very small groups, appears to be headed in the right direction. Unfortunately, many preschool programs lack this intense, personalized adult–child interaction.

As noted previously, Miller and her associates have conducted research comparing several types of preschool programs (1970a, 1970b, 1970c, 1971). After the children had completed one of four programs, they entered either an academically oriented "Follow-Through" kindergarten or a regular kindergarten. Rather consistently, children benefited more from the Follow-Through kindergarten than from the regular kindergarten. Apparently, sustained emphasis on developing specific skills is much more effective than isolated or one-shot intervention efforts. Although the academic stress in the Follow-Through programs is not the only factor that may be causally related to child growth (the child–teacher ratio was six to one as compared to thirty to one in regular kindergarten), other studies also suggest the importance of continuing comprehensive programmatic efforts.

For example, Hyman and Kliman (1967) present data to suggest that Project Head Start gains were more likely to hold up if the children attended a middle-class school rather than a lower-class school. A middle-class public-school environment allowed children to sustain their advantage over non-Head Starters.

Home involvement also appears to be of major importance. Bittner, Rockwell, and Matthews (1968) report that children of parents whose participation in programs was extensive were more likely to retain their gains than other students. Similarly, Holmes and Holmes (1969) found that children whose parents volunteered them for the programs did better than children whose parents had to be persuaded to enroll them. Most of the data are correlational, but they suggest that programs which include sustained follow-through activities, active parental involvement, an academic focus, and a relatively high teacher–child ratio are most likely to be associated with long-lasting increments in children's intellectual functioning.

Preschool programs do affect the learning of children, and such effects are generally positive. The precise nature of these effects is determined by such factors as the kinds of children enrolled, program goals and duration, staff training, and so forth. Earlier we cited Weikart's claim that the presence of *any* defined curriculum is in itself beneficial because it helps teachers to organize and mobilize their efforts. However, it is also important to note that curricula sometimes call for vastly different types of teacher behavior.

Some curricula provide teachers with specific guidelines for teaching a sequence of lessons, while others merely present general goals and leave the selection of content and materials to the individual teacher. Bissell (1971) has provided data from a large longitudinal project showing that teachers in traditional nursery schools and in Montessori programs show more variance in implementing their curricula than do preschool teachers in academically oriented programs. The academically oriented preschool programs rather consistently presented teachers with a highly structured, skill-oriented set of lessons with specific objectives and training. Such training and supervision packages produce teacher behavior that is consistently in line with program goals, whereas teacher behavior in less structured programs is more varied.

TEACHER BEHAVIOR

As we noted in the preface, there are no "magical" teacher behaviors that are guaranteed to be successful. The usefulness of a particular behavior depends upon the specific curriculum goal and the individual learner, among other variables. However, there are certain points or principles that do have generally predictable effects; these points will be emphasized as they become relevant in subsequent chapters.

Here we want to offset the common but misguided belief that children learn best with minimal direct adult involvement. This is simply not true for disadvantaged children. When programs do not emphasize learning, such gains are not forthcoming. Unfortunately, there is some reason to believe that teaching academic skills is not seen as an important activity in all preschool endeavors. Prescott, Jones, and Kritchevsky (1967) noted that, in the ten day-care classrooms which they observed, lessons directed toward intellectual growth accounted for less than 10 percent of available time.

Part of the reason that little specific information is available on effective teaching behavior in preschool programs is that there have been few observational studies of early education teaching. Gordon and Jester (1973), in a comprehensive review, could find only about 20 observational studies. However, the existing information consistently suggests that responsive (flexible) but direct and active teacher styles produce the best results with disadvantaged children. For example, Swift (1964), in attempting to dimensionalize discrete program aspects that contribute to a program's effectiveness, noted that a prerequisite for success was the need for the teacher to be actively engaged in teaching children intellectual and social skills.

Here we are clearly suggesting the desirability of the teacher's involvement in *directing and guiding a child's learning*. At the risk of redundancy, we want to emphasize that an adult can help the child to see the world more efficiently. Although it is possible that the teacher can overstructure a child's learning environment, the problem typically lies in the opposite direction.

CHILDREN'S LEARNING: MORE DATA

There are two important recent reviews of children's learning and cognitive development that can be profitably discussed now. These reviews consider research areas that we have not systematically explored previously in this chapter, and they provide implications for preschool programs.

Stevenson (1970) summarized a vast amount of literature (experimental-laboratory studies of learning) and concluded that no learning theory accounts for all the data. Interestingly, the most salient features of child learning that he noted were vast individual differences in arriving at correct answers. These individual differences could not be attributed to any one factor. Intelligence was significant, but still it was only a moderately important factor. This suggests that brighter children *tend* to learn more quickly or more thoroughly than less able children, although many low-aptitude children equal or exceed the performance of brighter ones. Thus, other factors are at least as important as intelligence in predicting student learning (e.g., personality variables such as perseverance).

Rather consistently, Stevenson's study demonstrates that environmental variables often have different effects on children at different developmental levels. This corresponds with our review of preschool programs and our conclusion that the effectiveness of a learning situation depends upon the match between program goals and the child's developmental status. Stevenson also points out that middle-class children's (the subjects in most of the experiments included in his review) motivation to learn was high, apparently because of their interest in pleasing themselves or the experimenters rather than from a hope for external reward. This is indirect evidence, but it provides some basis for believing that children do want to explore new situations and to learn from new experiences unless this curiosity has been dampened by an aversive environment.

Finally, it is interesting to note that, from Stevenson's perspective, the two most frequently encountered sources of difficulty for children who did poorly in laboratory learning experiments were: (1) failure to attend to stimuli, and (2) inability to determine the critical features by which stimuli differ. As we have noted repeatedly, it appears that a child's ability to perceive and coordinate information from stimulus objects can be facilitated by verbal-mediation training as well as the simple opportunity to converse with adults. Given that the two problems discussed above are general handicaps to learning, it is necessary to build strategies for removing these weaknesses into preschool programs, especially into programs for disadvantaged children who do not often have interaction with adults that involves close attention to specific objects and discrimination training in comparing and contrasting different objects.

Rohwer (1970) makes a major attempt to relate data and concepts found in developmental psychology to education. In the course of his review, he identifies four prerequisite competencies that the young child must possess if he is to make adequate mental advancement. Like Stevenson, Rohwer suggests that *attention* is a very important factor. He suggests that visits to schools with low achievement records often reveal classes with high, chaotic noise levels and teachers who spend vast amounts of time simply trying to gain student attention. Brophy and Evertson (1973) have made the same observation. Again, it would seem that preschool programs for the disadvantaged need to achieve at least a minimal level of structure so that children can learn to focus attention for sustained periods of time.

The other three prerequisites that Rohwer cites are: *behavior tempo, perception,* and *language.* Behavior tempo is broken down into three skills: (a) ability to react to the verbal instructions of others, (b) ability to give verbal instructions to oneself, and (c) ability to delay making an overt response in order to scan and process information. Obviously, it is desirable that children who do not possess these skills get the opportunity to learn them. The Blank-Solomon program, for example, places emphasis upon helping the child to learn that he possesses and can use language for solving problems.

The other two prerequisites mentioned by Rohwer have emerged in other discussions in this chapter. Perception, for example, is the ability to *differentiate* aspects of the environment. And we have noted that both too much (e.g., noise) or too little stimulation may retard development. In addition, we have stressed that a major function of preschool programs is to help the child coordinate his perceptual input with his motor and language development. Language, the third factor mentioned by Rohwar, is a critical skill vitally necessary for advanced conceptual development and *must be viewed as the crux of preschool cognitive development.*

Stevenson's and Rohwer's reviews drew upon different research evidence, but they reached some quite similar conclusions. Both agree that there are dramatic differences in individual learning rates, and Rohwer in particular uses such findings to argue the case for individualized instruction. Educators for some time have been arguing this need, but Rohwer stresses the fact that only recently have we been able to see how vastly the learning rates of children differ.

The need for individualized curricula also flows directly from our previous observation that no single program has proven its universal effectiveness. Thus, another implication for preschool programming is the need for individualization and flexibility within a program structure. Obviously, no preschool program operating with a restricted budget can run a completely individualized program. However, it does seem reasonable to expect a program to allow for ample instruction time in small-group learning situations, and to provide clear procedures for allowing students who learn specified skills to advance. At the same time, it should give children who do not master the material new opportunities to learn it. Clearly, a learning system that combines the economy of large-group activities (where appropriate) with small-group and individual instruction is complex, and it needs *specific* instruments for monitoring the progress of all children at any given time. Later we will discuss such a learning situation and fully explain the feedback system that allows teachers to make instructional decisions.

CONCLUSIONS ABOUT EARLY LEARNING

In the course of this chapter, we have examined information from a variety of sources and have drawn a number of conclusions:

1. Acute early environmental deprivation is likely to retard physical and mental development, and such effects are difficult to overcome.
2. Less dramatic effects that are limited to short periods of time generally have no permanent impact on development.

3. However, if disadvantaged environments are extended over several years, they depress the mental progress of young children.

4. Intensive tutoring programs appear to have highly desirable effects upon young children.

5. Group preschool programs are complex and difficult to interpret due to the variety of programs that exist and the different criteria that have been used for evaluative purposes. However, the short-range effects of these programs appear to be consistently positive.

6. The long-range effectiveness of group programs varies with such factors as level of curriculum specificity, teacher preparation, length of program, extent of parental involvement, presence or absence of follow-through activities, and child–adult ratio.

IMPLICATIONS FOR PRESCHOOL PROGRAMS

Within these general conclusions, we have noted numerous implications for preschool programs. We view such implications as some of the relevant criteria that one might use in answering the question: How do I pick a preschool program? Let's state these implications (many of which were mentioned earlier in the chapter):

1. No one theoretical approach can be justified on the basis of empirical data as the single best approach. The desirability of a particular program depends upon the match between the program and the needs of the children in that specific target center.

2. Given that children within a target area will show varying needs, it would appear desirable to adapt or modify a program so that individual needs can be dealt with *programmatically.*

Since much of our discussion has stressed programs for disadvantaged learners, the following implications are intended for that diffuse but somewhat narrower segment of the total preschool population:

3. Children need a planned environment to help them learn that events can be predicted and to help them differentiate the world (as well as the common-sense advantage for the teacher of separating noisy and quiet play areas).

4. Within this physical structure, children need a chance to explore manageable "chunks" of the environment, as well as to experience intensive relationships with adults who help them to label and differentiate aspects of the environment.

5. Besides a chance to explore per se, children need to develop skills that will enable them to learn and to play independently. This is best accomplished by a well-planned curriculum that specifies particular learning activities to enhance growth in distinct areas (visual, motor, etc.). A mea-

surement system providing specific data on each child's progress should be included.

6. Teachers appear to teach a curriculum better when:
    a. the teacher–child ratio allows the teacher time for frequent and responsive interaction with individual children,
    b. their teaching philosophy is compatible with program goals,
    c. they are given a detailed plan for organizing and teaching planned activities, and
    d. they are allowed to deviate from the curriculum when it makes sense to do so.

7. Language appears to be a critical factor in children's growth, and it should receive *special and complementary* emphasis in all curriculum areas. The teacher's reaction to the child's spontaneous language is especially important. Such responsiveness helps to establish the fact that a child can become a dominant force in his own learning (through his language).

8. Just as we suggest that the curriculum needs to be internally consistent (e.g., language vocabulary in motor lessons should not be in advance of other areas) and, hence, comprehensive, we suggest that effective preschool programs need *active parental involvement* and built in follow-through activities. Nutritional and medical help are also important in carrying out truly comprehensive programs.

The implications of the studies and ideas reviewed in this chapter will be presented in detail later in the book. By now the reader has seen that research on environments and programs for young children is complex and does not lead to simple prescriptions. No one type of program will serve the needs of all children. The goal is to provide the child with the type of environment that he needs rather than to adhere to a "pure" program type. We hope that the complexity of the discussion in this chapter will expand the reader's awareness of problems without being overwhelming. To provide tentative direction (e.g., how to diagnose and find time to deal with the learning problems of young children), we have outlined a variety of ideas and ways to approach problems. These ideas appear later in the book. Most important, the literature reviewed here indicates that children's abilities *can* be influenced notably by enrollment in preschool programs. However, preschool enrollment per se is not an answer. We know that some programs and some teachers make more of a difference than others. (For a full discussion of research suggesting that some teachers have more impact on children than others, see Good, Biddle, & Brophy, 1975). Only more research will reveal those important program aspects and teacher characteristics that are critical in promoting the developmental needs of certain types of children.

QUESTIONS

1. In understanding young children's learning, why is it more appropriate to center upon the type of parental control rather than the socioeconomic status of the parent?

2. Explain in your own words how a home environment might be inappropriately overstimulating and understimulating at the same time.

3. Explain in your own words the importance of concrete play and manipulation in developing the cognitive capacity of the young child.

4. Describe three learning activities to use with young children that would require simultaneous use and integration of visual, auditory, and motor modes.

5. If a young child of age $3\frac{1}{2}$ uses a great deal of egocentric speech, should parents or teachers be alarmed? Why?

6. In what ways are egocentric speech and the use of verbal mediators similar?

7. Write out 15 sentences that a 3- or 4-year-old child might spontaneously verbalize. For each sentence, indicate two or three ways in which an adult might appropriately respond.

8. Why is it inappropriate to evaluate preschool programs through IQ scores? Can a preschool program be successful if it does not raise the IQ points of children attending the program?

9. Explain in your own words the reasons for the relative lack of success in early preschool programs.

10. Since the young child learns mostly by doing, will he learn as much playing by himself as he will if there is an adult present to ask questions and make comments? If not, why not? What is the function of adult verbalization with children who learn mostly by doing?

11. Hunt (1961) has stressed the need to provide just the right match in presenting new material to children. This means that the new material is related to what the child has already learned and assimilated, but that it also challenges him to accommodate (learn new concepts or skills). What sort of balance between old knowledge (assimilation) and new learning demands (accommodation) would provide the best match for a teacher in a particular situation?

READINGS

Beller, E. "Research on organized programs of early education." In R. Travers, ed. *Second handbook of research on teaching.* Chicago: Rand McNally, 1973.

Blank, M. *Teaching learning in the preschool: a dialogue approach.* Columbus, Ohio: Merrill, 1973.

Bloom, B. *Stability and change in human characteristics.* New York: Wiley, 1964.

Bruner, J. *Toward a theory of instruction.* Cambridge, Mass.: Harvard University Press, 1966.

Dale, P. *Language development.* Hinsdale, Ill.: Dryden, 1972.

Diggory, S. *Cognitive processes in education.* New York: Harper & Row, 1972.

Ginsberg, H. and Opper, S. *Piaget's theory of intellectual development.* Englewood Cliffs, N.J.: Prentice-Hall, 1969.

Good, T., Biddle, B., and Brophy, J. *Teachers make a difference.* New York: Holt, Rinehart & Winston, 1975.

Hess, R., Brophy, J., Shipman, V., and Bear, R. *The cognitive environments of urban preschool children.* New York: Pergamon, 1976.

Hunt, J. *Intelligence and experience.* New York: Ronald, 1961.

Jensen, A. "How much can we boost IQ and scholastic achievement?" *Harvard Educational Review, 39* (1969), 1–123.

Kagan, J. et al. *Change and continuity in infancy.* New York: Wiley, 1971.

Rowland, G. and McGuire, J. *The mind of man.* Englewood Cliffs, N.J.: Prentice-Hall, 1971.

3
AFFECTIVE DEVELOPMENT

In this chapter we will highlight several aspects of affective development. Studies will be presented to illustrate some of the forces that determine how children develop attitudes toward themselves and others. It is not our goal to present an exhaustive review. However, the research we review is representative of salient aspects of affective development.

In the preceding chapter we acknowledged the difficulty of separating affective and cognitive growth, and noted that separate chapters were designed to allow for a fuller and more focused discussion of these two major developmental areas. Bear this in mind as you read the present chapter.

In discussing *affective* growth, we will be talking about how a child develops self-insight, how he develops his social capacities, how he becomes aware of his body and personality, and how he learns to deal with his own emotions and to react to others and their needs. In particular, we want to pinpoint those antecedent conditions that are associated with the development of persons who have high positive regard for their own worth and who are also interested in and respectful of the legitimate needs of others and the rules of social behavior. Thus, this chapter will stress how a child learns to *differentiate* his feelings, evaluations, and attitudes about himself and others.

AFFECTIVE GROWTH CAN BE INFLUENCED

The process a child uses to differentiate aspects of his affective world does not differ from the one he uses to discriminate in his cognitive world. Parent verbalizations, information from others, and his own exploration and discoveries enable the child to become aware of his relative size, his cooperativeness, his ability, and so forth. Gradually he learns how to handle aggression, frustration, and other feelings that arise in social conflict situations. The child learns how to react to situations (behaviorally and emotionally) on the basis of what he observes and how he is treated when he makes

47

a response. Infants who are consistently prevented from crawling on the good couch, from banging, from tearing, and from general exploration probably learn eventually to look to others to initiate and/or direct their behavior.

Burton White and his colleagues at Harvard are studying the development of "competence" in young children (White, 1972). The first research step of this group was to define competence, since they could find no literature that described the behavioral characteristics of well-developed 6-year-old children. A definition of competence was achieved by: (1) selecting a broad range of 400 3-, 4-, and 5-year-old children; (2) collecting observational data to target 50 children for extended study; and (3) intensely observing the children and discussing them with their teachers to identify those characteristics that distinguish highly competent children from less-competent children (half of the children in the intensive sample were chosen because of their high overall competence and half because of their low competence, but lows were judged to be free of any gross pathology). Those social and nonsocial characteristics that distinguished the two groups are noted below. However, it is useful to note that in some cases differences between high- and low-competence children were minimal (e.g., in motor and sensory capacities).

Social Abilities

1. To get and maintain the attention of adults in socially acceptable ways.
2. To use adults as resources.
3. To express both affection and hostility to adults.
4. To lead and to follow peers.
5. To express both affection and hostility to peers.
6. To compete with peers.
7. To show pride in one's accomplishments.
8. To involve oneself in adult role-play behavior or to otherwise express a desire to grow up.

Nonsocial Abilities

1. Linguistic competence, in other words, grammatical capacity, vocabulary, articulation, and extensive use of expressed language.
2. Intellectual competence—the ability to:
   a. sense dissonance or note discrepancies.
   b. anticipate consequences.
   c. deal with abstractions such as numbers, letters, rules.
   d. take the perspective of another.
   e. make interesting associations.
3. Executive abilities—the ability to:
   a. plan and carry out multistepped activities.
   b. use resources effectively.
4. Attentional ability—the ability to maintain attention to a proximal task and at the same time to monitor peripheral events (called *dual-focus ability*).

After two years of project work, the investigators reached the conclusion that most of the qualities that distinguish low- and high-competence 6-year-olds *were* observable by age 3. To know which children would be competent 6-year-olds, one only needed to look at their behavior as younger children (the competent 6-year-old was the competent 5-year-old, etc.). Hence project data suggest that children's social competence develops and stabilizes early in life. This is but one study; however, the importance of affective experiences during ages 2 and 3 are highlighted. A third phase of this research program (what antecedent parent behaviors are associated with socially competent youngsters?) will be discussed later in this chapter.

To speak of learning (e.g., how to deal with frustration) is not to deny the presence of genetic influences on such personality variables as reflectivity or passivity. Certain propensities are present at birth, notably arousal level or temperament. However, all personality factors can be influenced favorably by a positive environment. For example, Kagan, Pearson, and Welch (1966) have demonstrated that reflectivity (thinking before acting rather than acting impulsively) can be *learned through exposure* to experienced, reflective teachers; Meichenbaum and Goodman (1971) have shown that it can be *taught directly.* In yet another study, Bandura and Mischel (1965) have shown that a child's tolerance for delay of reinforcement can be increased through modeling procedures.

Similarly, a variety of research has shown that restless, aggressive, and reticent-introverted behavior can be altered radically. The point we wish to make is a simple one: Virtually all "personality" components that a preschool teacher discovers in a young child can be changed. However, there is some research to suggest that by middle childhood a child's self-concept stabilizes, so that change, while still possible, is more difficult to achieve.

Behaviors and school patterns (e.g., repeated failures) that continue over time eventually lead children to form stable self-assessments ("I'm no good," "People like me," "I can't learn," etc.) that are difficult to change. Indeed, children who develop strongly rooted views of themselves may continue to be unhappy even if they subsequently learn to perform adequately. Such children *feel* inadequate no matter how much they achieve or how highly they are regarded by others.

Children who learn that they are successful are motivated to persevere in normal, ambiguous, or difficult school situations such that success becomes a style. So, too, for happiness and other stances toward life. Typically, the happy child has learned to change unpleasant conditions, whereas the unhappy child has learned to accept unpleasant conditions. No doubt personality variables (especially coping skills) will become more important and basic aptitude relatively less important in learning situations that allow children to progress at their own individual rates. Clearly those who want to learn and feel that they learn will prosper in such a situation.

The parent and the preschool teacher can play an extremely valuable role by helping young children not only to develop coping skills, but also to develop realistic expectations, to accept limitations, to evaluate performance realistically, to respect individual differences among peers, and to engage in cooperative play and activities. In summary, preschool teachers *can* help children to learn to accept themselves and others, thereby helping to provide the foundations for happy, satisfying lives.

We shall return to the teacher's role, but first we shall discuss how a child builds a theory about himself (his self-concept) and the special role that parents play in helping the child to learn who he is and how he feels about himself.

AFFECTIVE GROWTH PARALLELS COGNITIVE GROWTH

We stressed earlier that either too much or too little stimulation can hinder cognitive development. This is true for affective growth as well. There must be a good match between what the child encounters and what he can handle emotionally. Children at age $2\frac{1}{2}$ who can play cooperatively for 15 minutes are doing well. However, a child of this age cannot be expected to play only with his own toys for long if he is in the company of other children and their toys. Allowing a 3-year-old to play next door is probably appropriate and stimulating for him, but sending him four blocks up the street to the grocery store is asking for a disaster.

These examples may seem a bit extreme, but adults often harbor incorrect notions about the emotional capacities of young children. In particular, they sometimes act as if they expect children to behave as adults. The point is that either too much or too little of almost anything (support, freedom, etc.) can be harmful. Erikson (1963) has argued this point effectively, showing that outside pressure which does not mesh with the child's inner control is likely to create an angry or anxious child.

In essence, a child's self-awareness develops in the same way as his knowledge about objects in the external world. The child learns about himself through intensive dialogue with concerned adults, by having a chance to experience events (testing his limits), and through his play alone and with other children. *Thus, learning about oneself depends upon concrete experiences and feedback from others.*

Epstein (1973) has pointed out that the more extensive a child's self-theory (the more aware of his feelings the child is and the more concepts he has for coping with different situations), the more open he is to new experiences. *Assurance* and *control* help the child to become progressively more differentiated (to have more awareness of feelings, more coping skills). The child who interacts with concerned adults normally becomes increasingly aware of himself and more willing to accept new situations and demands. Children who characteristically avoid new experience often function with a limited self-view.

Epstein points out three reasons why an individual may form a limited, restricted self-view: (1) lack of the cognitive capacity to differentiate and generalize; (2) stress and anxiety, which may make him afraid to explore; and (3) lack of experience. He suggests that persons who have inadequate self-views because of limited experience are not as resistant to change as those who are fearful of new experiences. This is of course good, articulate common sense. Children (or adults) who are not alert or capable of discriminating their world will not see how they can act in the world. Similarly, children who are fearful may know what to do but be inhibited from asserting many of their interests. Cognitive or affective malfunctions will hinder growth in both areas.

COGNITIVE ASPECTS OF MORAL DEVELOPMENT

The interdependence of cognitive and affective factors can be seen clearly in the area of moral development. Kohlberg (1964) has noted that the child's ideas about right and wrong are dependent not only on his experiences and socialization, but also on his level of cognitive development. During the sensorimotor period (roughly, the first two years of life), the child has no true concepts of right and wrong, just as he has no true concepts of anything else. At this stage the child is essentially an amoral, hedonistic creature whose behavior is conditioned by its consequences. Activities that are encouraged or rewarded by parents or other persons in the environment are continued, while those that are discouraged or punished tend to disappear. Kohlberg calls the child at this stage *premoral,* because, even though the child's behavior is somewhat predictable from knowledge about what has been rewarded and punished, he does not act out of any general sense of right and wrong.

Morality in the sense of general notions of right and wrong begins in the preoperational stage. As the child develops strong attachments to his parents and other significant persons in his environment, he becomes motivated to do things that will please them and avoids doing things that will hurt or anger them. At first these moral ideas tend to be isolated do's and don't's, but as the child moves into the stage of concrete operational thinking, he or she begins to combine and integrate separate moral ideas into a generalized concept of the "good boy" or "good girl." The child is now a truly moral being, in the sense that his actions are affected by general ideas about right and wrong. However, these general ideas came from the outside—the child picked them up from his parents and significant others and adopted them for himself, usually without much thought. One implication of this is that the child's moral ideas will not always be well integrated with one another, so that some of them may be contradictory, and at times he may do things that are innocent from his perspective but which are considered immoral from the perspective of an adult.

A common example of this lack of integration, and one that tends to infuriate parents and teachers working with young children, is lying. Most adults strongly resent lying, and are apt to react negatively and punitively when they encounter it in children. However, a lie told by a 3-, 4-, or 5-year-old is not the same as a lie told by an adult. Usually children of this age have not developed the cognitive structures required to integrate and systematize their thinking in any particular area, including morality. As a result, they are capable of telling quite obvious lies (for example, claiming that they did not do something that you have just watched them do, even though they know you have seen them), without understanding the implications of their claims from the viewpoint of the adult. The child will not see the interaction as particularly important, and will not realize its implications, so that he will be amazed as well as afraid when he sees the adult become frustrated and enraged (if the adult reacts in this way). The child will eventually learn to change his behavior as his cognitive structures develop and as adults patiently and repeatedly point out any contradictions with reality in what he says and reiterate their expectation that he will tell them the truth. However, this will take considerable time and many repetitions, and adults who work with children of this age must be patient, because it is simply unrealistic to expect the child to learn adult morality as a result of just one or two experiences.

Although the emergence of a stable "good boy" or "good girl" morality during middle childhood may make it seem otherwise, the child does not develop a truly systematic and internally integrated morality until adolescence and the onset of formal operational thinking. Most children simply repeat what they have been told about right and wrong without seriously thinking about it or questioning it until this time, so that morality is still essentially a reflection of what they have gotten from others.

However, once children begin to question and think about moral ideas, they begin to form their own values and opinions and to gradually develop a system of moral ideas about right and wrong. At this point, the child is doing much more abstract and personal thinking than before, and he now approaches morality from the viewpoint of his own considered judgments rather than by blindly applying rules that he has learned from others. In sum, although the specifics of a child's behavior in general and his morality in particular can only be explained by examining his formative experiences (this will be discussed later in the chapter), the child's morality cannot be fully understood without taking into account his cognitive development.

The interplay between these two major factors is better understood in the area of moral development because of the investigations of Kohlberg and others, but the same kind of interplay is involved in all of the other affective areas discussed in this chapter as well. The level of cognitive development is not a direct cause of particular affective traits or behavior, but it will affect the processes through which affective traits or behaviors are expressed and will set some limits on the degree to which a child can develop within a given time span.

The interplay between level of cognitive development and children's morality also has implications for parent and teacher behavior. Behavior that might be appropriate in responding to problems caused by a 2-year-old might be disastrous in dealing with a much older child, while extended discussions and explanations that are important for developing insight and responsibility in older children would be wasted on a child in the sensorimotor stage or the early preoperational stage. Thus, in making decisions about how to handle a problem posed by a particular child, it is necessary to take into account not only his behavior and the behavior of anyone else who might be involved, but also his level of cognitive development.

PERSONALITY DEVELOPMENT: PSYCHOANALYTIC VIEWS

Psychoanalytic theorists like Erikson and Freud view personality development as a problem of adjusting to a series of personal crises. If the child successfully resolves such conflicts, his development proceeds in a healthy, natural way. However, if conflicts are not successfully resolved, the child's personality may remain fixated at an immature level (for example, continual overreacting to authority).

Different theorists have their own labels for the crisis periods through which children must work. However, the various names assigned to these periods are not important; far more crucial are adult recognition of the child's problems and provision of help in dealing with them. Some psychologists take the position that the specific dilemma is not as important as the fact that each stage represents a child–adult conflict over the child's increasing competencies: How the adult reacts to the child's emerging competencies will determine the extent to which the child is desirous of and capable of living an autonomous life.

A discussion of some of the specific stages provides glimpses of the general problems that children must confront in their affective development. The child's personality growth from birth to 2 years (often called the oral period) is marked by his initial inability to differentiate himself and his food from other aspects of his environment. He behaves as though any object exists to be placed in his mouth. Progressively, he begins to differentiate between himself, food, and mother. A universal characteristic of this period is his dependence upon others to satisfy his needs. Erikson (1959) argues that the *dependable* satisfaction of these needs is necessary if the child is to believe and trust in his world rather than develop an attitude of mistrust and anxiety. The infant who is satisfied is able to venture out and explore the world and experience success on simple events (which in turn touches off more exploratory behavior). The infant who mistrusts the world begins to retreat and to become passive, fearing the consequences of exploring the unfamiliar.

Murphy (1972) stresses the importance of the mother in developing the infant's trust and subsequent exploratory behavior by noting that the more feedback the child gets, the greater his drive to explore and discover new skills. Eventually, then, the child comes to have a "let's play" attitude and the belief (trust) that his behavior will evoke play with his mother. Without this belief (built upon concrete experiences), the child is less likely to engage in exploratory behavior.

The adult model and his responsiveness to the child, then, play a major role in *motivating* the child to explore the world. Spitz (1972), for example, notes that no teaching machine would induce a child to imitate his father's walk or voice. In short, a common assumption of psychoanalytic theory is that children who do not have a chance to interact with responsive adults have reduced opportunities for concept formation because they are not stimulated to explore their environment without fear.

Children during the ages of 2 to 4 pass through a stage (commonly called the anal stage) in which the toileting process may become a crisis. Again, however, it should be noted that toilet training is but one issue that involves child–parent conflict. In general, the child must reconcile conflicts between pleasing or displeasing himself and pleasing or displeasing his parents. Other issues that involve the child's increased competence (eating certain foods, riding a tricycle to a neighbor's house, etc.) also present conflicts, *and they lead to real experience through which the child learns more about himself.* Can he *initiate* behavior without undue risk? Does he know why he can and cannot do certain things? Can he talk to his parents, or is it better to avoid them? Through such conflicts the child learns a great deal about how his parents view him, and this *information* communicated by parents shapes the child's view of himself. Later we will provide specific examples showing that the *forms* of parental control used consistently in conflict situations also have notable effects upon the child's subsequent development.

During ages 4 to 6, children pass through a stage (commonly called the oedipal period) in which their attachment to the opposite-sexed parent is strong and they may begin to fear the same-sexed parent. According to psychoanalytic theory, the child begins to identify with the aggressor (same-sexed parent) in order to curry favor and avoid punishment. So, the child adopts his or her habits, mannerisms, and so forth. Regardless of whether one accepts the validity of the oedipal hypothesis, there is general agreement that in this period the child is concerned with "Who am I?" questions, and that sex-role identity is a special concern. Again, parent reactions to the child's behavior can either facilitate or retard the child's progress.

Some psychologists interpret behavior in this period as another competence problem. They reject the psychoanalytic explanation based on unconscious fears and motives and substitute a social learning interpretation, noting that the child's real problem is coping with the realization that he is weaker, slower, and generally less competent than his parents. Parents who help their child realize that in time he will be as competent as adults, and who also encourage him to develop realistic goals and comparisons, will do much to help the child look forward to new growth and experiences. In contrast, children who are led to believe that their relative weakness is permanent are apt to become more passive. Bowlby (1951) notes that the child's motivation to take over controlling and planning functions is dependent upon a positive and responsive relationship with those who are trying to teach him.

Maccoby and Masters (1970), in a major review of childhood attachment and dependency, find some support for the psychoanalytic assertion that a child's perceptual capacity is regulated by infantile attachments. In the psychoanalytic view, the child's perceptual world initially is diffuse; gradually he differentiates himself from the external world through pleasure and pain experiences.

In summary, if one accepts cognitive development theory, the implication is that socialization (including self-awareness) proceeds like any other environmental input, and that knowledge of feelings, and so forth, must be mediated through the cognitive capacities of the child. During *infancy* and *early childhood,* cognitive and affective development proceed hand in hand.

We have presented a way of examining children's personality development that makes frequent mention of psychoanalytic writings. In part we do this because this theoretical viewpoint has been most concerned with the effects of early childhood experience upon subsequent development. However, this viewpoint (for the issues we are presently discussing) can be integrated with the cognitive-learning viewpoint presented in the previous chapter. Both approaches underline the importance of concrete experiences and the role of parents in influencing child growth; both suggest that the child learns about the world and about himself by *doing* and by observing the treatment he receives from others.

To trust others, the child must have his basic needs met in a reasonably consistent, satisfying way. To develop curiosity about the world, and to enjoy initiating new acts, the child must be allowed to explore. Concrete experience is the cornerstone of affective and cognitive development for young children.

SELF-ESTEEM

We have presented arguments suggesting that close affective involvement with a responsive adult is important for a child's development. Now let's review data supporting this proposition. Schaefer (1969) has investigated relationships between maternal affective behavior during tutoring activities and cognitive and affective measures of children. The mothers' negative affect was associated with negative affect in the children, and it related negatively to the children's intellectual performance. For example, Schaefer found that negative parent attitudes (hostile involvement, detachment, irritability, punishment, withdrawal) assessed when infants were 16, 30, and 36 months old correlated −0.38, −0.34, and −0.40, respectively, with Stanford-Binet IQ scores at 36 months of age.

There are data to suggest that child attachment may facilitate attentive play. Mothers' attentiveness to their 5- and 6-month-old infants was positively correlated with the infants' attention to and manipulation of test objects (Rubenstein, 1967). However, Schaffer and Emerson (1964) found that sheer *availability* of the mother was not a significant factor in the intensity of an infant's attachment. The important variables were (1) maternal responsiveness (quickly attending to a crying infant), and (2) amount of interaction (*kind* of interaction was not that important within the range of dimensions explored). Furthermore, it was noted that, when a child formed an attachment to an adult other than his mother, it was someone who stimulated him. Somewhat similar conclusions were reached by Ainsworth and Salter (1963) in their study of Ganda infants. They noted that the more caretaking and interaction time a mother spent with her child, the more firmly attached he was to her. It would seem that the *amount of time* mothers spend interacting with infants is a stronger bonding factor than expressed affection, at least at this age.

There is evidence to suggest that affective parent behaviors may influence the cognitive attentiveness of even very young infants. Korner (1964) noted incidentally (while conducting another study) that when crying infants were picked up and placed on a shoulder they become visually alert and actively scanned the environment. Korner and Grobstein (1966) designed a study to examine the effects of these "soothing" behaviors on 45- to 79-hour-old infants. It was found that when infants were picked up and held on the shoulder, they usually became visually alert. There was considerable variation among the infants, but the study does illustrate the close relationship between affective (responsiveness of adult, tactile stimulation) and cognitive behavior (intense visual exploration).

Medinnus and Curtis (1963) studied 56 mothers of children from a cooperative nursery school program for children 3 to 5 years old (parents occasionally had teaching responsibilities in the program). These researchers found a positive correlation between maternal self-acceptance and child self-acceptance. Parents who are satisfied with themselves are no doubt in the best position to help young children to develop positive views of themselves. Excessive concern with one's own problems makes it very difficult to deal with someone else's needs. This is so in part because self-preoccupation limits our ability to "see" the needs of someone else.

A broader attempt to identify the antecedents of self-esteem was undertaken by Coopersmith (1967). He developed a measure of self-concept that yielded quite stable scores for fifth-grade children, suggesting that the individual arrives at a general appraisal of his worth sometime preceding middle childhood. The instrument was used to investigate the antecedents, consequences, and correlates of self-esteem in a series of interrelated studies. First, subjects were selected who differed in measured self-esteem. These fifth graders were then subjected to a clinical evaluation (tests and interviews) and were observed in a series of laboratory experiments designed to measure desirable self-esteem characteristics (initiative, for example). In general, the clinical evaluations and behavioral observations supported the view that high and low scorers on the self-esteem test perform differently. Behavioral differences emerged in these three distinct areas: (1) anticipation (lows expect to fail and to be rejected), (2) reaction (lows are afraid to be different or to have unpopular ideas), and (3) self-preoccupation (lows show excessive self-concern).

In addition to the clinical and behavioral measures of the child, Coopersmith attempted to identify the *antecedents* of self-esteem by interviews with the child and his mother. Obviously, self-reports have to be regarded with some skepticism, especially considering the fact that the mothers were attempting to recall their behavior of several years in the past. Nevertheless, the results are persuasive. Mothers of children with high self-esteem consistently reported: (1) nearly total acceptance of child, (2) clearly defined and enforced limits, and (3) respect and latitude for individual action within the defined limits. These reports also were marked by the *absence* of: (1) rejection, (2) ambiguity, (3) disrespect, and (4) harsh emotional punishment.

Interestingly, Coopersmith had begun his study with the expectation that high self-esteem in children would be associated with home environments that provided little structure and much freedom. His reaction to his finding that children benefit from restricted freedom took two major forms: (1) the child needs some stability if he is to engage in self-evaluation and to explore freely and compare past and present performance; and (2) restricted freedom may help the child to learn that his environment can be manipulated. Again, we are confronted with the fact that the person–environment *match* is an important factor in self-growth. Too much or too little responsibility probably retards growth, while a more moderate, optimal amount apparently fosters it.

Even adults are able to tackle only manageable "chunks" in reacting to the world. For example, Epstein (1967), in a study on parachuting anxiety, has suggested that the quickest and best way to master anxiety is to allow awareness of new threatening aspects to emerge only after old ones are overcome. We can assimilate only so much information or stress before the debilitating effects of excessive anxiety set in. Parents and preschool programs can help children to develop affectively and cognitively by seeing to it that they are not given either too much or too little information, structure, and so on.

Children continually exposed to adults who make random, unpredictable demands upon them and who punish them inconsistently and in highly emotional ways will learn to distrust and dislike adults and develop the idea that their self-worth is insignificant. Anticipation of rejection from others will eventually teach the child to lower his self-esteem to protect himself. Once formed, such depressed self-evaluations and perceptions are difficult to change. The child's anticipating judgments about his probable performance ("I can," "I can't") come to control his behavior and become self-perpetuating (the child doesn't try because he "knows" he will fail).

Other implications in Coopersmith's data also deserve comment. *Acceptance* is a key in that it allows the child freedom to find his own emotional match. If he has to worry constantly about parents' or teacher's love, a child obviously will risk or initiate very little. Also, the importance of *consistency* is suggested by the Coopersmith study. The restricted-freedom factor means *nothing* unless it is also accompanied by adult respect for legitimate child behavior that exists within the rule-governed limits (later we will see that *how* these rules are communicated is also important). This component provides the match by allowing the child autonomy and responsibility in areas he can handle, while gradually adding new themes within the existing limits (e.g., making a nondestructive and nondisruptive mess if he is willing to clean it up). Clearly, the child does not grow optimally unless he has the opportunity for *real* but *manageable responsibility.*

PARENTAL CONTROL AND MORAL DEVELOPMENT

Earlier we described the work of Kohlberg and others on the development of *moral judgment.* Another major area of research has explored the antecedents of parent behavior upon the subsequent *moral behavior* of the child. Hoffman (1970) provides an extensive discussion of discipline methods of parents and the moral development of the child, and readers interested in a comprehensive treatment are referred to that source. Hoffman notes that it is possible for a person to internalize three ways of controlling his behavior:

1. Conditioned fear or anxiety ("I might get caught, and no cookies for a week").
2. Positive identification with an absent reference group or person ("Cardinal players always hustle, tell the truth, do the best they can," etc.).
3. Viewing moral standards as obligations to oneself ("I believe . . .").

These alternatives roughly correspond to the three major stages of moral development described by Kohlberg (1964). Hoffman also points out that there are three major child-rearing approaches:

1. *Power-assertive discipline* (parents use physical punishment, threats, deprivation of privileges).
2. *Love withdrawal* (parents express their anger in a direct but nonphysical manner: They ignore the child, refuse to speak or listen to him, isolate him).
3. *Induction* (parents explain why they want the child to change his behavior: They point out consequences to himself or others, appeal to child's pride).

Both power-assertive and love-withdrawal techniques are highly punitive. Indeed, as Hoffman points out, love withdrawal may have more powerful emotional effects than power-assertive techniques. Power assertion by the parent at least is over quickly, but love withdrawal is more prolonged for the child, and often he cannot *predict* when it will end. Children need to learn that they can predict environmental events, and any love-withdrawal technique (isolation, for example) should be used (*if* it is used) only with clear information telling the child when the punishment will be over. Induction techniques appear to be optimal, especially within an atmosphere of affection. Being loved provides the necessary emotional security (trust) for considering the opinions and needs of others.

After reviewing a considerable volume of literature, Hoffman notes that the most reliable finding in parent–child research is the *negative* relation between power-assertion techniques and all indicants of moral development. Frequent use of parental power assertion is associated with weak moral development in middle-class children. Induction and affection are associated with advanced moral development, but these relationships are not as strong or consistent as the negative ones for power assertion. Love withdrawal had *no* strong or consistent relationships with moral-development measures.

In lower-class families, *no* consistent relationships were noted between children's moral development and the nature of parent discipline. Among several possible explanations offered by Hoffman is the suggestion that power assertion is the predominant form of discipline in lower-class homes, and that it washes away the effects of induction (a perceived threat is perhaps always present, even when induction is used). However, the inconsistency of the environment and the reduced interaction time between parent and child, which also typically appear in lower-class homes, may also reduce the effectiveness of induction techniques in these homes. Countless other variables could be at work (i.e., behavior patterns that differ in middle- and lower-class homes), and the simple truth is we cannot explain the lack of relationship in lower-class homes.

In addition to naturalistic studies, Hoffman reviewed a variety of laboratory studies investigating the effects of power assertion. Interestingly, he observed that independent of the timing or intensity of punishment, children showed greater resistance to temptation when they had previously experienced *posi-*

tive interactions with the punisher (more so than did children who had received only impersonal contacts).

Hoffman tentatively concludes that affection does play an indirect role in helping children to internalize moral actions by orienting the child to the parent in a positive way, thus reducing the parent's need to resort to power assertion or love withdrawal. We would add that, in the absence of respect and affection for the adult, it will be difficult to use *induction* techniques. Lorenz (1972), for example, has stressed that young people are able to accept tradition only from people they respect and love.

Baumrind has also been concerned with the effects of parental control techniques on child behavior. She noted that self-controlled and alert children typically have parents who are controlling and demanding but also warm, consistent in a rational way, and receptive to statements or requests from the children (Baumrind, 1967). She labeled this form of controlling but loving responsiveness as *authoritative* parent behavior. Parents of children who tended to be discontented and distrustful were controlling but emotionally unresponsive and less warm than other parents. This parent style she labeled *authoritarian*. Children who were least controlled and nonexplorative typically had parents who were relatively warm but noncontrolling and nondemanding (note that freedom without parental direction did *not* lead to maximal curiosity and exploratory behavior in children).

Subsequent investigation largely supported the original findings but qualified them somewhat by noting that parent behaviors are better viewed as *clusters*. No single parent behavior relates in a direct one-to-one way with child behaviors independent of child sex, etc. (Baumrind, 1971). Nonetheless, *authoritative* parent behavior is most frequently associated with children who develop the capacity for assuming responsibility and engaging in independent action.

Baumrind (1971), on the basis of her own studies and other research data, presents several propositions that appear to describe the relationship between parents' personal practices and the development of social responsibility in their young children. Some of her generalizations are paraphrased below:

1. The *modeling* of socially responsible behavior has a positive influence upon the development of social responsibility, especially if the model has a close relationship with the child.
2. *Nonrejecting* parents are more potent models and reinforcing agents than rejecting parents, and to the extent that nonrejecting parents value and reward socially responsible behavior they are more likely to obtain it.
3. Parents who *explain* their requests are more effective than parents who do not encourage verbal exchange about rules and demands.

Baumrind also presents propositions describing parental practices and the development of independence in young children:

1. Early environmental stimulation and complexity of interaction foster independent functioning.
2. Both passive-acceptant and overprotective parental practices slow the development of independence, compared with active encouragement optimally matched to the child's developing capabilities.
3. Parent support for the child's self-expression and independent functioning is helpful unless parents are unwilling to make demands upon the child.
4. Firm control can be associated with subsequent child independence as long as the child has some opportunity to experiment and can *make decisions* within the established rules.
5. Reliance upon reinforcement (reward and punishment) to control child behavior without the frequent use of appeals to reason (induction) often leads to dependent, compliant, or passively resistant behavior.
6. Moderate use of power-oriented techniques for discipline control, when used by self-confident parents who frequently use induction tactics, does not necessarily interfere with the development of independence in young children.

Thus, the results from three separate lines of inquiry—Coopersmith, Hoffman, and Baumrind—yield a consistent set of findings. The focal points of agreement reside in the view that young children will internalize values, preferences, norms of behavior, and so forth, and generally will conform to parental expectations when parents:

1. Take time to explain the demands they make on children.
2. Help children realize the possible consequences of their actions by providing explanations and using other induction techniques.
3. Set identifiable and realistic standards of behavior for children.
4. Consistently enforce these limits but allow the child to experiment within them.
5. Are generally warm toward children and responsive to the questions, protests, and so forth, that they raise.

ANTECEDENT PARENT BEHAVIOR: A BEHAVIORAL EXAMINATION

Earlier in the chapter the work of White and his colleagues was mentioned. This project is relevant to the present discussion because these researchers presently are attempting to relate *parent behavior* to the growth of competence in children (rather than interviewing parents or asking them to fill out questionnaires). These investigators developed the viewpoint that competence could be predicted very early but that marked divergence in child functioning did not begin until sometime during the second year of life. Hence, the decision was made to study parent behavior with 2- to 3-year-old children. Below we will only report the *tentative* highlights of their research, which is still in progress. An extended discussion of sample selection, instrumentation, and general methodology can be found elsewhere (White, 1972). Differences between mothers of high- and low-competence children include:

1. Mothers of low-competence children appear to be more restrictive than mothers of high-competence children (use more playpens and gates to restrict gross movements of children).
2. High-competence children receive more live language than low-competence children, who get the bulk of their language from television sets.
3. Homes of high-competence children are filled with manipulable, visually detailed objects, and the child is consistently encouraged to explore.
4. Mothers of high-competence children are more likely to react to the child's present interest rather than "mother's" interest. However, high-competence mothers do not always respond to child requests, nor do they frequently engage in extended (e.g., five minutes) direct teaching. Rather, White notes that the bulk of maternal teaching is opportunistic, and occurs mostly in reaction to some child initiative.
5. Successful parent-teachers have a generally favorable attitude toward life. For example, none of the successful mothers are seriously depressed or excessively unhappy about life. Furthermore, successful mothers seem to enjoy their children much more than mothers of low-competence children.
6. Finally, *successful mothers come from all socioeconomic strata.* Their two most important resources are *energy* and *patience.* Furthermore, mothers of high-competence children spend less than 10 percent of their time interacting with their infants. The obvious conclusion that follows from these observations is that the *quality* of parent–child interaction is considerably more important than the *frequency* of such interaction.

In general this research fits in nicely with the general theory and the review of desirable parent behaviors discussed above. However, the study points up an important difference between parent interactions with infants and young children. (For a discussion of parent–infant interactions see studies reviewed earlier in the chapter: Ainsworth, 1963; Rubenstein, 1967; Schaffer & Emerson, 1964.) Apparently, the *frequency* of contact is more important for *infants,* but the *quality* of that interaction becomes more important *later.*

Also important here is the evidence that competent mothers and competent children come from all SES levels. More evidence will be presented on this point in Chapter 13; however, it is very important to note that there is wide variance (high, middle, and low scores) in parent and child behaviors across SES levels, so that many lower-class children are similar to the stereotypic view of the middle-class child, and many middle-class children conform to the stereotype of lower-class children.

SEX ROLE DEVELOPMENT   Mischel (1970) has noted that sex-role stereotypes and standards serve as guides in the self-evaluative process, but that there is wide variance within any domain of sex-typed behavior (aggressive females and passive males are not difficult to find). It is clear that an individual's conception of his sex role will influence his behavior and self-evaluation. Typically, a male who prefers quiet indoor play to rough outdoor play at age 6 receives systematic negative feedback likely either to change his behavior or to damage his self-evaluation.

Sex roles are helpful to the extent that they help a child to differentiate himself *accurately* and to prepare for his adult role. However, the value of *rigid* sex-role definitions has been questioned recently. For example, Block (1973) argues that the highest plateau in the development of sexual identity is not masculinity or femininity in the traditional use of these terms, but is instead a sense of self that is secure enough to permit the individual to manifest human qualities sometimes labeled unwomanly or unmanly. The person should have some *flexibility,* and not be restricted within rigid limits.

Although rigid sex typing in primitive societies was a functional necessity, there is little justification for rigid sex typing in modern, industrialized nations. In fact, rigid sex-role definitions probably unduly limit the experiences of young boys and girls so that many satisfying experiences and potential occupational roles are denied to both sexes. Maccoby (1966) concluded, after a comprehensive review of the literature, that optimal cognitive functioning depends on a balance between the feminine-passive and masculine-active orientation. In other words, the tempering of rigid sex typing may facilitate cognitive functioning. Indeed, changing cultural patterns (for example, the increasing number of mothers who enter, or re-enter, the work force while their children are still very young) will cause both males and females to adopt a wider range of potential roles. Flexibility is gradually replacing rigidity here.

A point argued above is relevant to the present discussion: Young children need firm attachment to a loving, responsive adult if they are to actively explore their perceptual world. This is not to say that the female exclusively should assume the mother role for the infant, but *someone* (be it the father or some other caretaker) must play the part. We have seen that time spent in *actively responding* to the child appears to be the chief responsibility of the mother figure. Fathers can no doubt play this role, although as a group they have had little training for it (little girls change diapers—little boys push trucks).

To reiterate, at present the reasons underlying our traditionally rigid sex-role prescriptions are fast disappearing. At one time, survival depended upon a clear division of labor. Physical strength was necessary for many male roles, and it made sense to prepare young boys for the hunter's role (encouraging aggressive, self-initiated behavior). Such role specificity for males

Even very young children typically show sex-typed interests in their play choices. The boy above has chosen to saw wood, while the girls below are preparing dough.

Children enjoy pretend play involving adult roles. You can encourage this by providing props, such as the clothing, doll, soap, and sink shown here.

made it desirable to train young girls to run the home in the absence of male aid (hence passivity, dependability, etc., were encouraged in young girls).

Now it is possible for persons of both sexes to choose from a wide range of roles, depending upon their interests and competencies. Thus, it appears desirable for young children of both sexes to have the opportunity to play with all available toys and to sample a full range of experiences rather than to be restricted only to those activities "proper" for boys and girls respectively. What is proper is no longer the traditional list; the proper activities for a given child are those that match his interests and skills. Boys will enjoy making cookies and preparing food in preschool programs, and girls will enjoy climbing as high as the available equipment allows.

However, we don't mean to suggest that anything goes. Certain societal obligations and pressures are real, and failure to meet them endangers present and future society and causes personal problems for the children involved. Consider the example mentioned above. Young children need a close, continuing relationship with a responsive adult. Whether a father, a mother, or another caretaker performs this function probably makes no critical difference. What does matter is that the role be capably performed by someone. (However, as noted in the preceding chapter, day-care centers may or may not provide such responsive environments.) Failure to provide for this experience is an unfortunate abandonment of adult responsibility, and it may have undesirable effects on children.

Similarly, to suggest that children should sample a variety of roles is not to imply that no demands or restrictions should be placed upon them. Irresponsibility, dishonesty, and physical abuse of others, for example, cannot and should not be tolerated. We simply suggest that all children should have the chance to become autonomous, reliable, self-starting adults, and that useful experiences should not be denied to a child because of his sex. As we have noted elsewhere, verbal facility and school achievement should be included among our expectations for boys as well as girls, and independence and assertiveness should be goals for girls as well as boys. (So, too, for other individual difference variables: Children should be treated on the basis of present cognitive and affective status rather than race, SES, physical attractiveness, etc.) In general, the student role needs to become more individualized, more action oriented, and more interesting and enjoyable for young learners (Brophy & Good, 1973).

AFFECTIVE AND COGNITIVE GROWTH AFTER THE FIRST FEW YEARS

We have argued that cognitive and affective growth are virtually indistinguishable during the first few years. Subsequently their relationship becomes less clear as cognitive and affective behaviors become less interdependent (Johnson, 1967; Neidt & Hedlund, 1969). For example, certain students make consistent learning progress despite an intense dislike for teacher, school assignments, or school.

However, in general it appears that favorable affective states and good mental growth patterns co-occur. Kahn and Weiss (1973), in a major review of affective growth in public school, suggest that the relationship between attitudes and achievement is functional and reciprocal, such that academic success helps to create school satisfaction, which thus increases the possibility of future successes.

After children have been in school for a few years, attitudes toward teachers and schools (although important per se) may no longer be closely related to student-achievement scores. Students in middle childhood who have obtained a reasonable level of autonomy and who see the need for school achievement may be motivated to learn despite dull, uninspiring teaching and irrelevant assignments. However, most children, and especially younger children, will respond most favorably to adults that they like and respect.

TEACHER AFFECTIVE STATES ARE IMPORTANT

In this chapter we have presented data suggesting that parents' self-esteem is often mirrored in the behavior of their children. Insecure, anxious adults are likely to raise insecure, anxious children. Similarly, the affective states of teachers influence their students' behavior and attitudes. For example, Aiken (1970) has noted that the most important factor affecting student attitudes toward mathematics is the teacher's attitude. Teachers who find mathematics enjoyable communicate this attitude to their students.

The influence of teacher attitudes on student behavior is perhaps most dramatically represented in a longitudinal case study by Rist (1970). Rist followed a group of youngsters from kindergarten through second grade. Distressingly, he noted that the kindergarten teacher placed the children with the greatest needs at the back of the room, making it difficult for them to have teacher contact. The pattern initiated in the kindergarten classroom continued each year. These students were grouped by themselves or with other slow learners, so that they seldom had contact with other students and with the teacher. Furthermore, these students often became the targets of hostility or derision from other students. Such findings explain why children who start school with neutral or positive attitudes often develop negative attitudes.

Brophy and Good (1974) have demonstrated that certain teacher attitudes (indifference, rejection, concern, attachment) are related to differential teacher behavior toward children. Strong feelings that teachers hold toward children are likely to be communicated in teaching behavior, especially if teachers are unaware of or deny those attitudes. Similarly, teachers' expectations for child performance have been shown to be related to differential teacher behavior. In some cases, teachers treat low-achievement children in inappropriate ways (seldom call on the child, don't wait long enough for the child to respond, frequently criticize, infrequently praise, etc.) which guarantee that these students will make minimal progress (Brophy & Good, 1974).

Subsequently we will discuss how teachers can help one another to become aware of blind spots that lead them to treat children in self-defeating ways. Generally, when teachers' affective states interfere with their teaching, it is because they are *unaware* of their attitudes or the behaviors they produce. Once aware of their actions, teachers usually can modify their behavior readily.

Good and Brophy (1973) discuss at length the influence of teachers' expectations and attitudes on their behavior and, ultimately, on child behavior, and discuss in depth ways in which teachers can minimize such effects. Briefly, teachers who enjoy teaching, who like children, *who view their primary responsibility as helping children to learn,* who avoid stereotyping children on the basis of test scores, and who provide for the differences in children's learning rates are on the road to successful teaching.

In summary, teacher attitudes and general affective feelings will usually be expressed in teaching behavior, even if the teacher is unaware of them. Teachers who are confident and generally secure in their teaching role are much more likely to have a favorable impact on children than teachers who lack confidence or are insecure. Again, it is important to stress the point made in the previous chapter: Programs must select teachers who are compatible with the goals of the program and/or provide extensive and explicit training help to create the conditions necessary for active and appropriate teacher involvement. This is because such procedures help to enhance the affective states of the teachers, and ultimately the affective states of the learners.

INDIVIDUAL DIFFERENCES: A SPECIAL AREA FOR AWARENESS TRAINING

We have stressed the importance of teachers' appropriate reactions to individual differences in learning rates. Sensitivity to *individual differences* of *all* types is especially important if the teacher is to promote maximum social–emotional growth of students. Some children will learn material more quickly than others, and some will perform (run, hit a ball, draw, etc.) better than others. These are facts that teachers must accept and help children to accept. The important goal to be taught is not to "beat others"; it is to learn as quickly as one can or to perform up to one's capability and to help others attain their top capacity.

Teachers who encourage children to appreciate and accept individual differences (appearance, race, preferences, performance) as things that are natural and to be expected are doing much to help children develop reasonable expectations and interest in others who appear to be superficially different from themselves. Probably no single factor is as detrimental to the formation of a positive learning self-concept as invidious comparisons across children. To expect children to make equal progress is grossly unreasonable. Progress for children needs to be measured in terms of their individual gains over time rather than how they compare with other students. Comparing children with one another guarantees that most children will suffer by being compared with the few students who learn most quickly.

The teacher's attitude is critically important in determining how children react to individual differences among themselves. Teachers who openly communicate the fact that some children will learn more quickly on certain tasks and who also convey respect for and tolerance of individual differences will do much to help children respect or at least accept a wide variety of differences. Perhaps the most crucial teacher attitude is the belief that affective variables are important and that the teacher can and should actively work toward the realization of individual goals. What specific goals are worth working toward? Many lists exist, but one especially useful (brief but communicative) set of goals was presented by Dinkmeyer (1971). A modified version of these goals follows. (The DUSO program has been developed by Dinkmeyer to help teachers to reach these goals.)

1. Developing an adequate self-image and feeling of competence.
2. Learning giving–receiving patterns of affection.
3. Moving from self-control to effective peer relations.
4. Learning self-control.
5. Learning to become involved and to respond to challenges.
6. Learning to be competent, to think of oneself as capable of mastery.
7. Learning to be emotionally flexible and resourceful.
8. Learning to make value judgments and choices and to accept the consequences of one's choices.

ACADEMIC SUCCESS

In helping young children from educationally disadvantaged homes to build desirable affective attitudes (especially a positive school-related self-concept), academic success is vitally necessary. Children need to learn that they are responsible for their learning and that they *can learn.* Too often teachers want to teach disadvantaged children for the wrong reasons. Smothering sympathy and concern for these children lead some teachers to want to make them "happy" by allowing them to do whatever they want to do in whatever way they choose. However, in terms of a general self-concept or state of happiness, there is no reason to believe that disadvantaged children suffer in comparison with children from affluent home environments (Trowbridge, 1972).

What is missing is the feeling that the child can control events. Many children from disadvantaged homes have learned that they are subject to the capricious whims of adults and have learned strategies for coping (silence in the presence of an adult, physical retaliation to peer aggression, etc.) that do not pay off in the school situation. Such children have a problem consisting of at least three dimensions when they begin school:

1. They feel that they cannot control events in their lives.
2. They have developed successful coping strategies at home that do *not* work in school.
3. *They have not developed cognitive abilities related to academic skills (use of language, etc.)* to the degree that children from more advantaged homes have.

Under these circumstances, the attempt to make children happy in preschool programs seems to be pointless and self-defeating *in itself.* To begin with, many of these children are happy in their immediate environment; frustration does not set in until they enter first grade. Also, we have seen that unrestricted freedom is *not* associated with affective growth. Furthermore, since these children will need specific cognitive skills to make progress (and stay happy) in school later, it would seem that the conditions necessary for affective growth are best fulfilled by following a curriculum that provides a balance of well-planned, teacher-directed activities as well as opportunities for independent exploration. To do less is to short-change the children.

Weikart (1967) provides data that reasonably can be interpreted to suggest that school success *enhances* the development of a positive self-concept as a learner. In 1962 he began a preschool program and has followed the progress of his students in elementary schools. In general, his program was not very effective in raising the aptitute of students, but nevertheless, the academic achievement of these children in elementary school has been notably better than that of controls. Apparently, Weikart's children learned to use their abilities more effectively. Initially, elementary school teachers' ratings of these children (on such variables as social behavior, adjustment, etc.) were no different than the ratings of control children. However, in subsequent years, after the children had accomplished a measure of school success, teacher ratings rose significantly.

It would seem, then, that for young children affective indicators of general motivation such as enjoying learning are by-products of academic mastery and success, assuming of course that the teacher is a concerned adult who respects children, is willing to react to their needs, and is consistent in interacting with them.

More evidence to suggest that the popular dichotomy of affective *or* cognitive gains is a false one is provided by Karnes (1973). She compared the social development of children who in the previous year had participated in either a traditional nursery school program or a highly structured, academically oriented program. Follow-up questionnaires (filled out by kindergarten teachers who had no information about children's earlier program participation) revealed no differences between the two groups of children on six of the eight items.

However, on two of the items (confidence in approaching new tasks and child's self-concept), teachers rated the children who had attended the structured program significantly higher than children who had attended the nursery school program. This is especially interesting because explicit goals of the traditional nursery school included the enhancement of children's social and emotional growth. Successful participation in a *well-planned,* academically oriented preschool program may benefit the child's affective growth as well as his cognitive growth. Children who interact with affectively responsive adults no doubt will reap cognitive gains as well.

IMPLICATIONS

In concluding the chapter, we want to highlight some of its most salient points by linking them to suggestions or guidelines for preschool programs listed below.

1. Affective growth (differentiating one's feelings and attitudes) proceeds, during the early years, in the same way as cognitive development. Children need ample opportunity to become aware of individual differences and to learn to *accept* such differences. Such acceptance comes about partly by watching the teacher consistently model acceptance with other children, but also through direct concrete experiences (role playing) in understanding how others react in particular situations. Teachers can help children to differentiate complex feelings by helping them to develop their own induction techniques ("Frank, how would you feel if Johnny hit you?").

2. Affective growth, just as cognitive growth, requires matching the child's present affective skills with new demands. Too many or too few demands (freedom, structure, etc.) retard development. Given the complexity of such matching, it is best to build into the curriculum materials and activities that help facilitate affective growth. For example, programs designed to achieve cognitive goals can be geared to reach affective ones as well. A unit on body awareness might ask the child to place his hand over or under an object or to sit under or jump over objects. Desirable programs also will build affective dimensions into the unit, such as exercises to differentiate one's body, explore feelings, and engage in cooperative play.

3. Adult feedback is crucial for affective growth. Especially important is the need for acceptance, warmth, consistency, control, and the ability to react

responsively to children when they approach. The child's "worth" is clearly modeled by the teacher when the child seeks him out. The child who is put off eventually learns that he doesn't matter. In day-care centers, it seems especially important to be sure that children receive *regular* involvement with responsive adults.

4. Most problem behavior can be corrected in a preschool program (fear of adults, inability to cope with frustration, etc.). However, one problem that seems to be somewhat general among disadvantaged children is the feeling (often correct) that they are dependent upon others. Programs that follow consistent schedules and activities early in the year will help those children to adapt more quickly to the preschool program. But beyond this step, it seems that children need help in developing self-evaluation and productive-coping skills in the face of frustration. Teachers who regularly model problem-solving behavior ("Now if I lost my pencil I would . . ."; "If my friend were mad at me . . .") will help children learn how to break emotional crises into manageable chunks and to discover that problems are potentially solvable within the limits of their own resources.

5. Present societal conditions make the teacher of rigid sex roles self-defeating. Preschool programs can profitably help children achieve more flexible role definitions (humans are responsive social beings) and help them become open to a wider range of experiences.

6. We have suggested that teacher attitudes often lead to self-defeating behavior in the classroom which the teacher usually remains unaware of; thus, it seems important that preschool staffs develop a way of monitoring their classroom behaviors for unintentional effects (more on this in a later chapter).

7. Finally, we have stressed that affective development proceeds best in a real setting where children are given *real* responsibility and are expected to master objectives. Meaningful affective growth seems impossible to achieve independently of a situation in which the child is *mastering* new skills. We suggest that planned preschool academic programs which provide for such mastery experiences, in addition to fostering social–emotional development, will develop affective and cognitive achievement faster and better than programs limited to only one of these areas.

In this chapter we have presented in broad, general terms an outline of affective growth—how it develops and how it relates to cognitive development. In the chapters that deal with the "now" aspects of running a program, we will illustrate specific plans for promoting affective growth in detail. Our concern with affective growth will not be treated as a separate topic, however. By and large, affective, humanistic concerns will receive tandem treatment with the cognitive aspects of running a preschool program. Before we begin such practical discussions, it will be useful to identify ways of selecting and designing appropriate curricula for young children. After an important look at goals and objectives, we will be in a position to discuss how to reach these goals.

QUESTIONS

1. Explain how a child's trust in his parents and in the predictability of their behavior leads to greater exploratory behavior on the part of the child.

2. In what ways might parents who fail to accept themselves have detrimental effects upon their children's ability to develop self-acceptance? Be specific in your responses.

3. List five ways in which the nursery school teacher might arrange for a 3-year-old child to have real but manageable responsibilities.

4. What responsibilities might be given to a 4-year-old child that should not be given to a 3-year-old child?

5. If parents or teachers use isolation as a discipline technique, how might they structure the situation so that it does not have psychologically debilitating effects on the child? (That is, so the child is sure that he is still loved.)

6. Define induction techniques in your own words. Write three paragraphs describing three different situations in which a young child has misbehaved. For each of the situations write induction techniques that a parent could appropriately use.

7. Distinguish between authoritative and authoritarian parent behavior.

8. List ten different things that a preschool teacher could realistically do to help children develop appropriate sexual definitions.

9. In what ways could you help to reduce overly rigid sex typing?

10. Describe three specific ways in which teachers could help children to develop greater tolerance and respect for individual differences.

11. Illustrate these general comments by designing one detailed lesson activity that would help children to gain greater insight and respect for differences in human behavior.

12. Discuss your answers to questions 8 and 9 with classmates, noting any apparent contradictions in assumptions about "good" sex-role development or ways to achieve it. Are these value differences, or can they be resolved through discussion and/or investigation?

13. How can a young child tell an obvious lie and yet not be lying in the same sense that an adult would be if he did the same thing?

14. Some authors suggest that adults protect a child's self-concept by avoid-

ing telling him that he is wrong and by trying to prevent him from becoming aware of his shortcomings. Is this good advice? Why or why not?

15. Sometimes parents will punish a child for behavior that is not yet under his control (toilet accidents, crying or whining, poor speech), and will ask you to do the same. What should be done in such situations?

16. Suppose one of the children becomes very interested in using "dirty words" and begins to teach them to the others? What should you do about the child? What should you tell a parent who demands that the child be suspended unless he stops this behavior immediately?

17. Some children will not be able to do things, like button coats or put on boots or mittens, and will need help from you. What should you do if other children begin to tease them about this?

18. In what way are academic success and a child's self-concept related? Must one necessarily precede the other? Explain your answer.

READINGS

Baumrind, D. "Current patterns of parental authority." *Developmental Psychology Monographs, 4* (1971), Part 2.

Blank, M. *Teaching learning in the preschool: a dialogue approach.* Columbus, Ohio: Merrill, 1973.

Coopersmith, S. *The antecedents of self-esteem.* San Francisco: Freeman, 1967.

Dinkmeyer, D. "Top priority: understanding self and others." *Elementary School Journal, 72* (1971), 62–71.

Goslin, D., ed. *Handbook of socialization theory and research.* Chicago: Rand McNally, 1969.

Johnson, D. "The affective side of schooling experience." *Elementary School Journal, 73* (1973), 306–313.

Kahn, S. and Weiss, J. "The teaching of affective responses." In R. Travers, ed., *Second handbook of research on teaching.* Chicago: Rand McNally, 1973.

Karnes, M. "The evaluation and implications of research with young handicapped and low-income children." In J. Stanley, ed. *Compensatory education for children ages two to eight.* Baltimore: Johns Hopkins Press, 1973.

La Benne, W. and Greene, B. *Educational implications of self-concept theory.* Palisades, Calif.: Goodyear, 1969.

Maccoby, E. *The development of sex differences.* Stanford Calif: Stanford University Press, 1966.

McCandless, B. and Evans, E. *Children and youth: psychosocial development.* Hinsdale, Ill.: Dryden, 1973.

Mussen, P., ed. *Carmichael's manual of child psychology.* 3rd ed. Vol. 2. New York: Wiley, 1970.

White, B. "Fundamental early environmental influences on the development of competence." In M. Meyer, ed. *Third symposium on learning: cognitive learning.* Bellingham, Wash.: Western Washington State College, 1972.

4
WHAT ARE APPROPRIATE CURRICULA FOR YOUNG CHILDREN?

One of the primary roles of the school is to transmit basic knowledge to the child and to assist him in mastering this knowledge so that he will be able to draw upon it in thinking, making decisions, and solving problems. In order to carry out this function, schools typically develop or adapt curricula. Early education programs can select curricula from a large number of different models. These vary from traditional approaches that stress the social and emotional development of the young child to the more academically oriented models that stress skills such as reading, mathematics, and writing. All of these models seek to transmit the basic knowledge and skills they feel are most important for the young child to master.

Prior to the establishment of Project Head Start, most early education programs were designed to serve children from middle-class backgrounds. The curriculum focus of these programs was on the child's social, emotional, physical, and sensorimotor development. The underlying instructional strategy for this program model was the use of organized and free-play activities that were intended to provide opportunities for the child to know himself, understand his relationship to others, and become familiar with some of the rules of society. This curriculum model, with its major emphasis on socialization and emotional development, was generally thought to be appropriate for all children.

In contrast, a major concern of Project Head Start was to provide an educational environment that would meet the needs of *poor* children. These children came from homes that generally were quite different from those of the more advantaged middle-class child. A large percentage of these disadvantaged children failed and eventually dropped out of school. The Head Start movement stimulated educators to examine the factors that appeared to influence these failure rates, and to analyze these factors in terms of their implications for curriculum development.

Bloom (1964), Bruner (1966), and Hunt (1961) agreed that the first five years of life were important in determining the development of basic competencies. Each of these educators appeared to support the notion that the environment of the young child could have a tremendous influence on the acquisition of competence and coping skills. Other researchers (Weikart et al., 1970; Karnes, 1969) were focusing on the differences in achievement between children of the poor and their more advantaged counterparts. By age 5, the average IQ of poor children was at least 5 to 15 points below that of middle-class children, and on other measures of competencies, particuarly those related to verbal abilities, poor children were lagging even further behind.

Bruner (1972), in discussing the functioning of children from different socioeconomic backgrounds, described three interconnected influences associated with poverty. The first of these pertains to opportunities the child might have to master and use goal-seeking and problem-solving behaviors. This can lead to differences in the degree to which the child feels a sense of power regarding the effects of his own actions, and can influence the child's behavior in school in terms of goal setting, expectations of success or failure, and willingness to delay gratification. Another factor influenced by poverty is the child's linguistic development. As children are exposed to many different experiences and are provided with opportunities for practice, they learn to use language in many different ways. The third factor appears to be related to the interactive patterns surrounding the child. His attitudes toward others and himself are shaped by his relationships with peers, teachers, and parents. As these expectations are communicated, the child's concept of himself begins to form and mold.

GENERAL MODELS

Those involved in curriculum development during the 1960s were aware, in varying degrees, of the factors identified and discussed by Bruner and others. Four different kinds of curriculum models emerged from the work of that period, and the assumptions underlying these models were based in varying degrees on the concepts of: (1) the culturally disadvantaged, (2) the culturally different, (3) the intellectually disadvantaged, or (4) the economically/environmentally disadvantaged model. Although overlap exists between these theoretical positions, each model can be related to certain unique assumptions specifying the locus of the problem.

The Culturally Disadvantaged Child

The earliest position one finds identified in the literature is that of the culturally disadvantaged child. These children were generally described as poor, and living outside of the mainstream of American society. They were members of minority groups living within a subculture that had rules and values considerably different from that of the middle-class community. The child spoke a language that was either a dialectical form of standard English, or a foreign language such as Spanish, Chinese, or Navajo. Curriculum models built on the premise that the child was culturally disadvantaged stressed the creation of an environment that would offer all the advantages experienced by the middle-class child. This model was reflected in the programs used during the early days of Head Start. The classes were modeled on the schedules and activities offered within the traditional early childhood programs. The basic assumption was that, if one provided the poor, culturally disadvantaged child with the same advantages offered to the middle-class child, one would be able to assist the poor child by substituting the majority culture for the inadequate minority culture. Bissell (1970) categorizes these programs as permissive environment models.

**The Culturally
Different Child**

The concept of the culturally different child influenced the development of another curriculum model generally described as cognitively oriented. The assumption underlying this model was that the child, because of cultural differences, faced a conflict between the goals and values of the home and those of the school and society at large. One of the major goals of this model was to assist the child in acquiring mastery of those behaviors and skills necessary for success in school. The goals of this model did not include substituting one culture for another; rather, they acknowledged the differences that exist in the attainment of school-related and home-related goals and values so that home–school conflicts would be reduced.

**The Intellectually
Disadvantaged Child**

Another major preschool curriculum model (structured information) was based on the assumption that poor children came to school intellectually disadvantaged. The 4-year-old child from a poor family was already far behind his middle-class counterpart, as a result of less adequate intellectual stimulation. The curriculum, therefore, emphasized the acquisition of academic skills that would enable the disadvantaged child to begin to catch up with his more advantaged peers. The designers of this model did not believe that any time should be spent on what they called "filler activities," such as music, art, or dramatic play. While the child was in school, his time was scheduled so that he was involved with an adult who directed his learning experiences according to clearly specified goals and objectives.

**The Economically/
Environmentally
Disadvantaged Child**

The fourth curriculum model (structured environment) was based on the assumption that the child's inadequacies were due to a home environment that could be characterized as economically disadvantaged. Because of this, the family support system (economic, emotional, and intellectual) was generally limited in its capacity to support the total development of the child. Models built on this premise attempted to construct what were generally described as responsive environments. These environments were designed to respond to the needs of the child through both the materials placed in the classroom and the adults who interacted with the child. The hope was that schools could fill the gap created by poverty and prevent the concomitant emotional and intellectual problems that emerge as a result of this condition.

AREAS OF AGREEMENT Despite the fact that the assumptions for each of the curriculum models described above were different, the general goals of the models were quite similar. The arguments regarding the cause of children's inadequate functioning continue, although large areas of agreement have been reached relating to general curriculum goals that are appropriate for young children, both poor and advantaged.

All of the models stress the importance of the child's self-concept. There is total agreement regarding the necessity for the child to develop positive feelings about himself, his abilities, and his general self-worth. There is, however, great variation among the different models in the strategies employed for achieving subgoals related to a positive self-concept, such as intrinsic motivation and feelings of competence.

All of the models (with the possible exception of the structured-information programs) emphasize the importance of the child's interactions with others. The skills of interpersonal relationships are emphasized both for peer-group relationships and adult–child relationships. Development of these skills is stressed through informal play activities, teacher-directed activities, and other strategies that rely on environmental feedback.

All of the curriculum models stress the importance of developing the child's intellectual abilities. Most often, these abilities are described as those necessary for thinking and effective problem solving. The instructional strategies for achieving this goal range from active, child-initiated experimentation (such as play) to adult planning and guidance, with many variations in between.

Generally, there is also agreement that information-processing skills, such as sensory-perceptual and language abilities, support and are necessary prerequisites to the development of intellectual abilities. Each of the curriculum models includes activities and instructional strategies that are related to achieving this particular goal. Typically these strategies are reflected in experiences that focus on assisting the child to compare and contrast objects, to use language to describe events, and to learn to discriminate and abstract attributes of the world around him.

Thus, although the differences between the various curriculum models have been widely publicized, it is important to note that general agreement does exist regarding the overriding goals of early education. In many cases the actual learning activities tend to be quite similar regardless of the curriculum model being implemented. The differences in the models emerge most clearly and can be most easily contrasted and compared by examining the kinds of objectives, instructional strategies, and degree of structure implicit within the program.

COMPARISON OF SOME MAJOR CURRICULUM MODELS

Bissell (1970) provides some useful operational definitions of objectives, strategies, and structure. For the purposes of the discussions in the following section, we shall define *objectives* as the ends towards which the program is directed, *strategies* as the plans of action through which classroom activities are conducted, and *structure* as a measure of the amount of external organization and sequencing of the children's experiences. Figure 4.1 provides an overview of the major contrasts between the four curriculum models.

The Permissive-Environment Model

The permissive-environment model basically represents an adaptation of the adjustment-centered preschools designed originally for middle-class children. Examples of this kind of program would include the Bank Street Program, the Weikart Traditional or Unit Program, and the programs developed by many Project Head Start centers. The objectives of this model are often described as oriented toward the development of "the whole child." Program objectives focus specifically on intellectual and language development, sensorimotor development, social and emotional growth, and the attainment of a sense of well-being. The instructional strategy is based on allowing the needs of the children to determine the specific activities of the program. The teacher's role requires responding to the children's needs by capitalizing on informal opportunities that are relevant for learning. The curriculum model can be characterized as having a low to moderate degree of structure. This means that no lists of sequenced behavioral objectives have been developed for the teacher. It is the teacher's responsibility to individualize the program by capitalizing on informal opportunities so as to meet the unique needs of each child. The success of this model is dependent upon the skill of a master teacher who is not only aware of the developmental functioning of each child, but can also relate the child's present level of functioning to successive and developmentally appropriate levels of mastery.

The Structured-Cognitive Model

The structured-cognitive curriculum models are more concerned with the development of aptitudes and attitudes directly related to the learning process, rather than with the development of "the whole child." Examples of this type of program model would include the Hodges, McCandless, and Spicker diagnostically based curriculum, the early childhood program of the Institute for Developmental Studies, and the DARCEE Program. The major objectives of the model focus on the development of learning processes, with heavy emphasis on language growth. Other objectives include the devel-

FIGURE 4.1
Contrasting features of four curriculum models.

	Permissive Environment	Structured Cognitive	Structured Information	Structured Environment
Objectives	Emphasis on whole child	Emphasis on aptitudes and attitudes related to learning processes	Emphasis on specific information and skills, content oriented	Process oriented
Strategies	Teacher responds to child's needs	Teacher directed, both prescribed and guided interactions	Teacher directed, prescribed interactions	Teacher as mediator, self-instructing materials
Structure	Low to moderate	Moderate to high	High	Moderate

opment of perceptual, attentional, conceptual, and language skills; the development of motivation conducive to learning; and the development of a positive self-concept. The instructional strategies require the teacher to direct activities in which the children participate. This participation at times is prescribed, but often it occurs in a flexible manner. The teacher plans activities on a daily basis and guides the learning of the children. The degree of structure inherent in this model ranges from moderate to high. The process objectives are sequenced in a hierarchical order. Behavioral objectives have been developed and are usually paired with specific criterion-level performance tasks related to each of the more general content objectives. Although many of the activities are presented within a structured-game format, the teacher guides the learning at prescribed times established in the daily schedule.

In contrast to the permissive-environment curriculum model, the structured-cognitive programs select and organize learning experiences within a structured setting. Rather than just capitalizing on informal opportunities for learning, this approach uses a structured-game format as its major teaching strategy. Karnes (1973) states that the game format was adapted because it provided:

1. A positive approach to learning.
2. An opportunity for the teacher to establish a high degree of structure.
3. Flexible programming of process, content, and attitudinal variables.
4. A hierarchical ordering of concepts.
5. Opportunities to utilize paraprofessionals and parental assistance.
6. Immediate feedback for parents and teacher.
7. High motivation.
8. Repetition that is not mere rote.
9. Opportunities to enhance self-image.
10. Opportunities for individualized instruction in a small-group setting.

This model generally provides the teacher with very specific guidelines for implementing the curriculum model in any particular classroom.

The Structured-Information Model

The structured-information model is basically content oriented and concerned with identifying those academic areas likely to cause the greatest amount of difficulty for young children. The objectives of the program, therefore, are aimed toward teaching specific information and skills. The knowledge emphasized within these objectives includes concepts and rules involved in language usage, arithmetic, and reading. The designers of this model believe that the child will develop a positive self-concept as he has successful achievement experiences related to the mastery of academic readiness skills. The instructional strategy calls for the teacher to direct all of the learning activities, with the children participating in prescribed ways. The approach is didactic and is dependent on the teacher's guidance of each learning experience. This model is the most highly structured of all the curriculum models to be described in this section. The objectives are specified in a hierarchical order with criterion measures for determining mastery. These objectives are all of the content type, and a separate learning period is set aside for instruction in each content area. The Bereiter-Engelmann (1966) academic preschool is the most widely known of the curriculum models that fall into this category. Since the program designers believe that the poor child must master specific knowledge if he is ever to catch up with his more advantaged middle-class counterpart, other kinds of activities such as music, art, and dramatic play are not included or emphasized in the program. In summary, this model rejects the traditional concept of the play-oriented nursery school as an appropriate preschool model for poor children. No effort is made to reproduce a middle-class environment for young poor children; instead, the goal is to assist the children in mastering those academic skills considered necessary for future success in school.

The Structured-Environment Model

The fourth curriculum model, referred to as structured-environment programs, responds to the environmental deficits that the children bring to school. Typical of these programs would be a Montessori program or the New Nursery School developed by Nimnicht, Meier, and McAfee. The basic objectives are process oriented, and are concerned with developing sensori-motor, perceptual, and classificatory skills, and increasing the child's attention span. In addition, the Nimnicht model stresses the development of language skills.

Generally, the teaching strategies are dependent upon the use of self-instructing classroom materials that provide corrective feedback to the child. The teacher demonstrates the proper use of materials and observes the children regularly in order to monitor the degree of learning that is occurring.

She acts as a mediator between the children and the materials only when such mediation is absolutely necessary—for instance, if the child is using the materials inappropriately. The structure within this model can be described as moderate. There are no preplanned instructional objectives, but rather, the environment is planned in such a way that the materials are designed to instruct and hold the child's interest. The child is free to choose the materials he wants to work with and to pace his own rate of learning and mastery. The teacher functions as a facilitator of learning. In order to be effective in this role, the teacher in the structured-environment model must be a master, sophisticated in her knowledge of how young children learn. In addition to merely possessing such knowledge, the teacher must also demonstrate the ability to generalize it appropriately by individualizing the curriculum model to meet the needs of each child.

Nimnicht (1972) describes the activities of his model as autotelic, that is, the activities are self-rewarding and do not depend upon rewards or punishments that are unrelated to the activity. He believes that the essential satisfaction for the child should come from the activity and not from something external to the actual experience. This means that the program must be individualized to provide many ways for children to learn a specific skill. The teacher chooses the materials to include in the learning environment. Then, the environment is planned in terms of the objectives to be accomplished. Individual, small-group, and large-group activities are included in the curriculum, but the child is free to explore all of the available choices. Within broad limits, he can spend as much time on any activity as he likes; no one will ask him to stop one activity to begin another. The child, in a responsive classroom, is encouraged to make discoveries about his physical and social world. The learning environment is designed to provide opportunities for the child to discover things for himself and to learn to solve problems.

A major goal of this model is learning how to learn rather than learning specific content. The structured-environment curriculum model stresses the creation of an environment that responds to the child through the materials placed in the classroom. Language development is emphasized in varying degrees, depending upon the particular program being implemented. The traditional Montessori programs do not focus on the development of language skills; however, some American adaptations of the Montessori method do stress language development and verbal interaction between teacher and child (Kohlberg, 1968).

RESEARCH FINDINGS

Bissell (1970) examined the effectiveness of these different models when implemented with disadvantaged children. The findings indicated that the structured-cognitive and structured-information programs were consistently more effective than the permissive-environment and structured-environment

programs in producing cognitive gains among experimental
presents three conclusions based upon her interpretation o

1. Preschool programs that include the general objectives of fo,
   tive growth, that emphasize the development of language ski
   include teacher-directed strategies, which provide a high degre   .,uc-
   ture for the children's learning experiences, are more effective in producing cognitive gains than programs that lack these characteristics.
2. The most effective programs in terms of producing cognitive gains appear
   to be those that are high on the dimension of quality control: those models
   that have well-trained staff, a high degree of supervision, and a low student–teacher ratio.
3. *Nondirective programs tend to be most effective with less disadvantaged*
   lower-class children, while directive programs appear to be equally effective with all lower-class children or more effective with the more disadvantaged lower-class children.

In this section we have examined some of the similarities and differences
between major preschool curriculum models. Research findings such as Bissell's appear to support some instructional strategies as being more effective
than others for young, economically disadvantaged children. Some of the
more critical factors that have been identified include the socioeconomic
status of the child, the kinds of objectives included in the program, the
amount of emphasis given to language development, the degree of structure
provided for the teacher, the competencies of the teaching staff, and the
student–teacher ratio. In the following section, we shall examine the implications of these findings as they relate to the creation of a supportive environment and appropriate curricula for young children.

**SOME UNIVERSALS:
ENVIRONMENTAL
CONDITIONS NECESSARY
FOR LEARNING**

Caldwell (1968, 1973) suggests that we can identify certain factors as
necessary conditions for supporting the development of the young child.
Each of these factors has direct implications for curriculum decisions that
can be applied to meet some of the universal needs of children. They
include:

1. Concern for the child's health and safety.
2. A high frequency of adult contact.
3. A positive emotional climate that fosters the development of trust.
4. An optimal level of need gratification.
5. Adults who respond appropriately to the young child's behavior.
6. A minimally restrictive environment that encourages the child's
   exploration.
7. An environment that assists the child in confirming and predicting events.

8. An environment that provides a variety of meaningful cultural experiences.
9. An environment rich in play materials that supports the development of sensorimotor processes.
10. An environment that provides an appropriate match for the child's level of development.
11. An environment directed by adults who plan and develop objectives for the child.

Earlier (in Chapter 2) we advanced some general implications for programs that stemmed from research on child learning. Many of these factors are consistent with those cited by Caldwell. The following section explores the implications of these factors for the development of a preschool program. In Chapter 5 we will discuss how these general program factors provide the base for selecting curriculum goals that can then be converted into objectives and learning experiences for young children.

CURRICULUM IMPLICATIONS

1. The program should reflect concern for the child's health and safety.

Discussions in earlier chapters have addressed the issue of meeting the child's basic physical needs. The evidence regarding the effects of poor nutrition and inadequate health care clearly supports the necessity for any preschool program to meet these primary needs. Although the hours of operation of any preschool program will vary, ranging from half-day to full-day care, the services offered must include adequate food service, physical facilities that consider the child's health and safety, and provisions for handling unexpected emergencies or accidents.

2. The program should provide for a high frequency of adult contact.

Research findings (Bissell, 1970; Weikart, 1969; Karnes, 1970) regarding effective curriculum models are consistent in reporting the effectiveness of a high adult–child ratio that insures a relatively high frequency of contacts. These contacts are of particular importance for the preschool child who learns through both incidental and intentional interactions. Language development can be enhanced as the child is given opportunities to interact with responsive adults who function as models.

It is not always possible to employ a large number of adults in a preschool classroom with a relatively small number of children because of problems such as staff turnover or lack of funds. There are, however, other options that can be exercised in order to insure a relatively high adult–child ratio and to provide for frequent adult contacts. Some of these options include extensive use of parent volunteers, high school students enrolled in child-development courses, or community volunteers—including elderly persons. In scheduling the daily program, the teacher can optimize the frequency of contacts by dividing the class into small groups that cycle through alternate activity periods. This planning strategy provides some assurance that the teacher will equalize contacts with all the children in the classroom on a daily basis. By training the volunteers who work with them, teachers can insure that additional contacts between the children and other adults in the classroom will be capitalized upon in as optimal a fashion as possible.

3. The environment should reflect a positive emotional climate that supports the development of a sense of trust.

Everyone who works with young children will accept this statement as a truism; however, very few teachers are aware of its full implications. Most curriculum models incorporate goals and objectives that focus on the development of a positive *self*-concept. Teachers are well aware that the child needs to be provided with experiences and opportunities in which he can function as a competent, respected person. Teachers generally provide adequate reinforcement for the children entrusted to their care, but rarely do they focus on the development of relationships between the different children in the classroom. Typically, children engage in social interaction informally throughout the day, and unless difficulties arise, the teacher rarely interferes with these developing relationships. If a child is to learn to trust others as well as himself, much more attention must be given to the development of an awareness of feelings related to the "other." While most curriculum models acknowledge the importance of adult interaction in assisting the child to develop a self-concept, no curriculum model addresses directly the question of developing an awareness of others. This is a legitimate area for program concern, and one that the teacher must be prepared to address and plan for in daily programming for the children. Too often, teachers stand back and avoid intervening when children are involved in free-play activities. While it would not be appropriate for the teacher to be a constant participant in these situations, it is appropriate for her to be an attentive observer, ready to intervene and capitalize upon a teachable moment for stressing the development of those interpersonal skills that underlie a sense of trust. For example, suppose two children on the playground were to argue over taking turns on a tricycle. Even though they can probably resolve this argument themselves, a teacher can profitably intervene and help the children verbalize their feelings about sharing and taking turns. Empathy and understanding of the feelings of others is vital to the development of a sense of trust. In addition to spontaneous situations, the teacher's curriculum planning should address the issue of assisting the children in learning how to verbalize their feelings regarding others with whom they interact.

4. The program should provide an optimal level of need gratification.

This goal does not necessarily mean that all of the child's physical, emotional, and intellectual needs must be immediately met. There are times when teachers are justified in planning activities or making demands upon the child that can result in degrees of frustration. Learning to deal with frustration within a supportive setting can assist the child to develop and mature. The teacher must become a master in creating a moderate amount of disequilibrium that will force the child to reach toward the next level of skill mastery. In daily planning, the teacher should consider including learning experiences that will increase the child's attention span, reinforce his attitudes and behavior related to persistence (sticking to a task), and develop his "can do" attitude. Creating an optimal level of need gratification requires a teacher who systematically records the progress of each child and plans appropriately for both group and individual needs.

5. The program should include adults who respond appropriately and consistently to the young child's behavior.

This statement underscores the critical importance of the adult in the classroom. Previous discussion focused on the need for a low student–teacher ratio, the necessity for small-group instruction, and the importance of a qualified teaching staff. Regardless of the curriculum model being implemented, the success of any program is totally dependent on the skills that the teacher and other adults bring to the classroom. Planning and communication between members of the staff must occur on a regular, ongoing basis. It is impossible to act consistently if the adults in the classroom have not agreed on the overall program goals and have not discussed the specific daily objectives. Agreement must be reached as to what constitutes valued and appropriate behaviors, as well as the techniques that will be used to reinforce such behaviors when they occur. It is not uncommon to find in the same classroom a teacher who values and rewards verbal responses and exploratory kinds of behavior and a teacher aide or volunteer who values limited verbal responses and acquiescent, nonexploratory types of behavior. The differential reward systems utilized by these two adults can only confuse the children regarding the kinds of behaviors valued at school. Curriculum planning must include clear statements concerning the kinds of behaviors and behavioral goals considered to be important for each child in the classroom. In addition, agreement must be reached as to the strategies of reinforcement that will be used for both group and individual kinds of responses. In order to assure consistency in the quality of adult support offered to the children, the teacher should periodically observe the teacher aide or other volunteers working in the classroom and provide them with feedback regarding their appropriate or inappropriate behavior. Teachers should also make every effort to have either a supervisor or a fellow staff member observe their own behavior for a period of time as they interact with the children.

6. The classroom environment should be minimally restrictive and encourage the young child to explore freely.

The child needs a variety of direct experiences if he is to learn to differentiate his world. It is important that preschool provide him with opportunities to do more than simply watch or look. The teacher can plan the classroom environment to meet this condition. There is no reason why the environment cannot be completely responsive to the child's exploratory behavior. Very often, rules are established for preschool classrooms that are unnecessarily restrictive. Teachers very often impose these rules because (1) they are unfamiliar with how young children learn and develop, (2) the school principal appears to value quiet kinds of child behavior, or (3) the teacher values quiet behavior. A minimally restricted environment, conducive to freedom of movement, can easily be created. Young children have very little difficulty following reasonable rules of behavior. These rules, however, must be carefully explained to the children before they can be accepted. Teachers, early in the school year, should plan to spend time establishing agreed-upon rules of behavior with the children and then to systematically assist them in learning how to enforce and abide by these rules. Within limits, the children can patrol their own environment and control their own and others' behavior. If the teacher and other adults in the classroom are consistent in enforcing the limits that have been set on any particular kinds of behaviors, the children will soon function naturally within the constraints of rules. In an environment that is relatively free of restrictive regulations, the curriculum can offer planned activities as well as spontaneous experiences that encourage the development of curiosity, exploratory behavior, and creativity.

7. The environment should assist the child in confirming and predicting events.

Children from poor homes tend to live in environments that are minimally predictive. Daily schedules are liable to be erratic, meals are served sporadically, and bedtime varies from day to day. The curriculum planned by the classroom teacher can be designed to help the child integrate his experiences in a predictable, systematic manner. Predictability in environmental events assists the child in developing stability and confidence in his own abilities. As he begins to get consistent feedback from the school environment, the child can be helped to learn how to set realistic goals for his own behavior. Skills such as predicting, coping, and self-evaluation can be mastered as the child confirms and revises his expectations of both objects and events. Again, the extent to which these events occur depends in large measure on the teacher's skill in planning, observing, diagnosing, and replanning.

8. The program should provide a variety of meaningful cultural experiences.

This provision is likely to be overlooked in those preschool programs catering to children of the poor, particularly those who come from a minority culture or ethnic group. Most early childhood teachers tend to bring a set of middle-class values and a middle-class experiential base to the classroom. The majority of teachers who work with poor children usually have not had extensive contact with members of that particular group. Unwittingly, and often out of ignorance, this lack of understanding is reflected in the curriculum that such teachers design and develop. Teachers can model their version of standard English when speaking to the children. However, the language that the child brings from home should not be rejected. By correcting what the child says and how the child says it, even patiently, teachers reject the language the child brings to the classroom situation and in doing so, they reject the child in large measure. There are a number of strategies that teachers can use to respond to the needs of children from different cultures. They can make every effort to become familiar with the children by visiting their homes and talking with their parents. They can use neighborhood people as resource teachers for the class, both regularly and on special occasions such as holidays. They can encourage parents to work in the classroom and to assist them in becoming sensitive to the nuances and behaviors of children which differ from those of a middle-class group. When funds for a teacher aide are available, this person can be selected from the same neighborhood as that of the children enrolled in the school. The teacher's attitude in valuing other cultural traditions is probably crucial in any honest effort to expand and extend the culture of the classroom. This curriculum effort goes far beyond transmitting mainstream, middle-class cultural values; instead, it requires that the teacher actively accept and learn about the values and traditions of minority groups. Curriculum planning incorporates the major ideas and values that can be presented as familiar concepts to the children, and at a later point in time can be contrasted with other values from the mainstream culture with which the child will eventually come into contact.

9. The classroom environment should be rich in play materials and support the development of sensorimotor processes.

This statement should not be interpreted as a plea for the purchase of expensive toys and equipment. Too often, teachers and parents purchase toys that can be used in only limited ways. The kinds of toys or learning equipment available in a classroom, however, are of critical importance. The child learns through play activities about the world and finds an outlet for complex and often conflicting emotions. These experiences are necessary if the child is to learn to express his feelings and master reality. Teachers must not only consider the kinds of materials that they will place in the classroom, but also how they will be used by the children. Teachers who select materials must know the level at which each child is functioning. They must observe the group in free-play activities, and rotate materials as often as is necessary. Merely rotating materials, however, does not insure that children will use them and work with them. If teachers truly believe that manipulative equipment and play experiences are a necessary condition for learning, they can optimize the occurrence of these events through careful planning. First, they can demonstrate the use of equipment in a clearly focused, dramatic presentation. They can highlight and point out the intricacies of a toy or game as they demonstrate some uses and options inherent in it. In addition to actual demonstrations, the teacher can use effective pacing and spacing strategies for maintaining interest in working with toys in the classroom. Careful attention to the amount of time devoted to both free-play activities and directed-teaching activities can offer an optimal level of pacing and spacing of learning experiences. Varying the kinds of activities offered will tend to insure interest in the scheduled events.

10. The program should provide an appropriate match for the child's level of development.

This statement is consistent with the principle of the match as described by Hunt (1964). Curriculum planning includes the programming of experiences that are presented by the teacher, as well as the creation of an environment that is responsive to spontaneous experiences appropriately matched to the child's current level of functioning. Educators agree on the importance of achieving the "match"; however, this is an extremely difficult concept to operationalize in terms of an actual curriculum. Few teachers are trained in the techniques necessary for successfully individualizing the curriculum and matching the content to the children in the class. In the following chapter we shall discuss some techniques appropriate for accomplishing this difficult task. The match, when successfully achieved, leads to the attainment of the most crucial goal for the preschool child: learning to learn. This includes motivating the child to find pleasure in learning as well as developing his ability to attend to others and to engage in purposeful action. The child must eventually learn to delay immediate gratifications and to work for more distant rewards and goals. Throughout this process, he continues to look toward adults as sources of information and feedback. If the preschool curriculum does not serve this goal, then it becomes totally dysfunctional in terms of meeting the child's long-term motivational needs. The concept of the match is a strategy that, when implemented appropriately, will motivate the child to become a lifelong learner.

11. The program should be directed by adults who plan and develop objectives for the child.

If teachers are to plan their curricula, they must be prepared to specify the objectives they consider important for children. This is an area that most early childhood educators still prefer to avoid. There is great confusion about what we, as adults, feel is important for young children to learn. When one examines the curriculum models described in the previous section, it becomes obvious that widely divergent teaching strategies eventually are translated into equally divergent types of specific objectives. We can safely state that children can learn more from contact with adults than from contact with each other. Learning can be vastly enriched by meaningful contact with adults. Teachers must consider this in planning their curricula and specifying their objectives. While definitive, universal objectives have not yet been agreed upon, there is a great deal that we do know about how young children develop and learn. We know, for instance, that mastery of adaptive skills is critically important. We have a fair idea as to the range of probable responses available to different developmental ages. We are aware of the rapid development of language skills during the preschool years, and know that adult interaction can enhance the child's language capabilities. Common sense tells us that certain skills can be acquired most efficiently and effectively through didactic presentations, while other kinds of skills require discovery and active exploration on the part of the child.

Finally, although teachers can be comfortable with the principles stated above in terms of setting objectives for young children, they can also be reassured by the knowledge we have regarding the plasticity of the young child. Certainly, preschool programs can do much to enhance the child's development; even when this environment is less than optimal, the child will tend to survive our inappropriate efforts and he will flourish and learn as we come closer to creating an environment that is truly supportive.

SUMMARY

We have reviewed some of the major experimental curriculum models that were developed during the 1960s. Each of the models was compared in terms of its program objectives, classroom strategies, and the degree of structure inherent in the children's learning experiences. A number of environmental conditions that appear to be universally important were discussed as they related to program and curricula decisions. The following chapter will describe some techniques for converting these universals into program goals, curriculum objectives, and learning experiences for the young child.

QUESTIONS

1. When planning a program under any of the models described, give specific examples of what you, as a member of the teaching staff, would do (or plan) to provide for children's health and safety needs. (Street, playground safety; nutrition; handy first-aid kit; bus or car safety.)

2. Situation: A parent comes for a visit. Plan three activities he or she can participate in or help with. How would you organize a chart, card file, or notebook to use as a resource for adult volunteers?

3. Taking the example of the tricycle dispute described in the chapter, how would you as the teacher intervene effectively? Give specific examples of actions and verbalizations.

4. Rules: Make a list of necessary rules and how they would be established, explained, and maintained (toileting, snacking, resting procedures, taking turns, keeping noise level down). Would these rules change as the year progressed? Explain your answer.

5. Choose a piece of equipment, game, or toy, and demonstrate to the class or a small group as you would to a group of children (use with children if possible). Mention to the class when it would be presented in daily schedule, time of year, unit of work, concept(s) being developed, whole-group or small-group context.

6. During (or as a result of) your observations, try to classify the school's program according to the scheme in Figure 4.1.

7. If observations are not possible, view video tapes of programs in action and attempt to identify the curriculum model.

8. You are working in a program that utilizes parent volunteers and high school students enrolled in child-development classes. How can these relatively untrained people be used successfully? In what activities would they be involved? How would (or could) you plan with them? (Don't forget the communication of objectives.)

9. Observe and record three situations in which the adult is helping children to develop a sense of trust through his actions or guidance. If you have observed teacher behaviors that make children feel insecure, describe them and explain.

10. Make a list of emotionally loaded words sometimes used to describe children and their behavior—selfish, stubborn, lazy, and so forth. How does the use of such words influence objective observation? How could you describe the same types of behavior using words or phrases without these emotional connotations?

11. Some claim that the children or families we have called disadvantaged are merely different, that the characteristics and behavior of advantaged people are not objectively superior to those of disadvantaged people.

These writers feel that preschools and teachers should adjust to the characteristics of the children they serve, rather than foist middle-class values on them. Others see this position as unrealistic romanticism. Where do *you* stand on this issue? Find out through discussions and debates with classmates. Is this a real issue, a false issue, or some of both? Make sure you are clear here, because your answer has great implications for the types of settings in which you should work and the program goals and fellow teachers you will be comfortable or uncomfortable with.

12. Analyze your program-goal preferences. Are they based on a particular theory (or theories) of child development? Experience? Expert opinion? Observation? Reaction against unhappy experiences you had as a child? Unquestioned assumptions? Think and make notes about program goals until you know both *what* you prefer and *why* you prefer it.

READINGS

Beller, E. "The evaluation of effects of early educational intervention on intellectual and social development of lower-class disadvantaged children." In E. Grotberg, ed. *Critical issues related to disadvantaged children.* Princeton, N.J.: Educational Testing Service, 1969.

Bernstein, B. "Social class and linguistic development: a theory of social learning." In A. Halsey, J. Floud, and C. Anderson, eds. *Education, economy, and society.* New York: Free Press, 1961.

Bissell, J. "The cognitive effects of preschool programs for disadvantaged children." In J. Frost, ed. *Revisiting early childhood education.* New York: Holt, Rinehart & Winston, 1973.

Blank, M. and Solomon, F. "How shall the disadvantaged child be taught?" *Child Development, 49* (1969), 47–61.

Butler, A., ed. *Current research in early childhood education.* Washington, D.C.: NEA, American Association of Elementary-Kindergarten-Nursery Educators, 1970.

Evans, E. *Contemporary influences in early childhood education.* New York: Holt, Rinehart & Winston, 1971.

Gray, S. and Klaus, R. "The early training project: a seventh-year report." *Child Development, 41* (1970), 909–924.

Grotberg, E., ed. *Critical issues in research related to disadvantaged children.* Princeton, N.J.: Educational Testing Service, 1969.

Parker, R., ed. *The preschool in action.* Boston: Allyn & Bacon, 1970.

5
FROM CURRICULUM GOALS TO LEARNING EXPERIENCES

Early education programs, fortunately or unfortunately, have not yet agreed upon a universally accepted body of knowledge or skills that are considered most important to be transmitted to young children. This situation is in stark contrast to elementary programs, where agreement regarding academic content has been reached. Teachers, parents, and the general community know that in the elementary years students will study and master the skills of reading, writing, mathematics, social studies, art, music, and physical education. Objectives and goals have been specified for each grade level, and, while the particular curriculum or organizational structure will vary among school districts, the terminal goals for content areas are fairly consistent from one curriculum model to another.

One does not find this kind of consistent agreement in the content emphasized in the program models for early education discussed in the previous chapter. For instance, a permissive-environment model such as Bank Street stresses cognitive and socialization skills. These skills are developed through a process approach to areas of language arts, mathematics, and science. The Karnes structured-cognitive model emphasizes the acquisition of academic and social skills. Content areas include reading readiness, mathematics, science, and social studies. The responsive-environment model emphasizes learning how to learn rather than specific content, and classroom activities focus on the development of intellectual abilities and a positive self-concept. Finally, the structured-information model accents skills in academic areas, with particular concentration on the verbal interaction that occurs between teachers and children. The content areas include language, reading, and arithmetic, with art and music used to reinforce the language program.

Perhaps the major area of difference between early education and the elementary-level programs lies in the teacher's role. Generally, elementary school teachers are expected to be directly involved in the teaching-learning process. They plan the daily schedule and are expected to play a key role in interacting with, supervising, and directly instructing the children. Clear-cut agreement regarding the teacher's role has not been reached in early childhood education. The position taken by the authors is that the teacher should be responsible for planning; diagnosing, instructing, and evaluating the child's progress. The teacher, as a decision maker, becomes responsible for designing a program that uses various presentation modes such as direct instruction, guided-discovery learning, free-play activities, and tutorial sessions in order to appropriately meet the needs of each child. Teaching becomes, therefore, an extremely complex task requiring the application of both knowledge and skill in developing a suitable program.

This chapter will examine strategies for program development that teachers can use as they move from the more general goals of early education to the design of specific learning experiences for their children.

GOALS OF EARLY EDUCATION

When the goals of the various curriculum models are examined, it becomes evident that there are large areas of overlapping concern in different early education programs. The variations extend along continua of cognitive, affective, and psychomotor goals. Probably all of the models, regardless of their philosophical orientation, could agree that the following statements represent reasonable and important goals for young children because they reflect skills that are prerequisites for all subsequent learning.

Goals of early education should include:

- Assisting the child in mastering expressive and receptive language skills that are necessary for the development of problem-solving and thinking abilities.
- Assisting the child in the development of sensory-perceptual skills.
- Assisting the child in developing gross and fine motor skills.
- Assisting the child in acquiring interpersonal skills necessary for interacting effectively with peers and adults.
- Assisting the child in acquiring intrapersonal skills necessary for achieving personal autonomy.

Although there would be very little argument regarding the substance of these statements, various models would emphasize specific goals in differing degrees.

One of the teacher's major responsibilities in developing or adapting a curriculum is to relate program goals to specific learning experiences. We are going to assume that there is a foundation of core skills that is necessary for *all* children to master if they are to experience success in school. The nature of these skills will depend on the age of the child, his present level of functioning, and his socioeconomic background. For example, one would not expect a 3-year-old to be capable of attending to a learning experience such as a story for as long a period of time as a 5-year-old, since the attention span of a child is a direct function of his chronological age as well as the cumulative experiential background he brings to the classroom. One would expect a child who comes from a poor home to have already fully grasped the concept of sharing. This child, in all likelihood, has shared possessions in his home all of his life. A child from an advantaged background, on the other hand, would probably have to be taught that toys and learning materials must be shared, that each child has to wait his turn, and that, indeed, his turn will come. We cannot generalize that all advantaged children have one set of characteristics and all poor children have another set, but teachers should be aware of differences that children bring to school which are a function of their chronological age, cultural background, developmental age, and socioeconomic status.

Traditionally, early education programs have featured arts and crafts, music, games, language-arts experiences, free play, and little or no direct teaching. Program goals have focused primarily on the child's social and emotional development rather than his intellectual development. Some research findings indicate that when the academic performance of children who have attended early education programs is compared with children who have not, there are no differences in the level of achievement. We have seen, however, emerging evidence (Bissell, 1970) which indicates that planning, teaching to objectives, and regular interaction between the teacher and the child can have positive effects on the child's level of functioning. Moving from the assumption that the teacher must play a major role in planning if the child is to learn, the following questions become critical: What kinds of skills do young children need to master? Why are these skills or abilities important? How does the teacher translate these goals into specific classroom learning experiences?

WHAT DO CHILDREN NEED TO LEARN?

If the child is to learn on his own or to benefit from direct teaching, he must master some basic skills. Teachers must be prepared, therefore, to convert the general goals of early education into instructional objectives. The following section illustrates how each of the broad goal statements can be related to content areas and specified instructional objectives. The objectives for the children will vary according to their chronological age and development level. The following list of objectives is not intended to be comprehensive, but merely to give examples of appropriate objectives for various age levels.

Language Arts

Goal: To assist the child in mastering expressive and receptive language skills that are necessary for the development of problem-solving and thinking skills.

Three-year-olds should be able to learn to:

• recognize, name, and describe simple objects and pictures.
• describe simple experiences and events.
• recognize simple functions of objects.
• select instances of a concept.
• identify self by name.
• pantomime simple stories.
• name three objects in a picture.
• develop understanding and use of vocabulary related to classroom routines (snack time, restroom, etc.).
• develop vocabulary for social communication and interaction (through co-operative games, discussing experiences, singing games, field trips).

Four-year-olds should be able to learn to:

• follow simple instructions.
• ask and answer questions.
• describe and compare experiences and events.
• describe functions of objects.
• acquire basic knowledge of self and culture.
• respond to questions about similarities and differences of objects.
• develop vocabulary for expressing observations.
• develop vocabulary for thinking and problem solving.

Five-year-olds should be able to learn to:

• follow and give complex instructions.
• ask and answer various questions.
• identify and describe sequences of objects or events.
• demonstrate an understanding of models.
• understand and describe concepts related to their knowledge of self, culture, and the natural world.
• describe similarities and differences in objects and pictures.
• use information learned in various experiences to solve problems.
• develop the vocabulary for self-expression (through talking about personal experiences and feelings, telling stories, dramatic play).
• increase his vocabulary for describing complex observations.

Sensory-Perceptual Skills

Goal: To assist the child in developing sensory-perceptual skills.
Developmentally appropriate skills for 3-, 4-, and 5-year-olds include both

visual discrimination abilities as well as auditory perceptual skills. Tactile discrimination abilities can also be included under this general heading.

To develop visual discrimination abilities, 3-year-olds should be able to learn to:

- match, sort, and name basic colors and shapes.
- sequence objects by size.
- identify positions of objects.
- classify objects by general categories.
- duplicate three-dimensional designs with objects (beads, pegboards, inch cubes).
- reproduce a sequence of at least three items from memory.
- recognize similarities and differences in a variety of objects.

To develop auditory perception abilities, 3-year-olds should be able to learn to:

- attend to and respond to the presence and/or absence of sound (music, environmental sound).
- locate the direction of sound.
- recognize gross differences in sound characteristics (loud or soft, fast or slow).
- reproduce a simple sequence of instrumental sounds.
- discriminate and match environmental sounds with pictures.
- listen to and state the basic content of a simple story.
- follow a series of two directions with the appropriate motor actions.
- identify a specified word in a sentence context.

To develop visual discrimination abilities, 4-year-olds should be able to learn to:

- match, sort, and name a variety of colors, shapes, and sizes.
- sequence objects and pictures by size.
- classify items by one attribute (color, size, shape).
- recognize and name a variety of pictured locations.
- classify pictures by categories.
- duplicate two- and three-dimensional designs with objects.
- identify missing parts of pictures and shapes.
- reproduce and name a sequence of at least three items from memory.
- recognize similarities and differences in a variety of pictures.

To develop auditory perception abilities, 4-year-olds should be able to learn to:

- respond to the presence or absence and/or location of sounds and other sound characteristics.

- name gross differences in sound characteristics (loud or soft, fast or slow).
- name a variety of environmental sounds and match these sounds with their associated pictures.
- use imitative and creative expression in the recall of poems and role play of stories.
- retell the events of a story in sequence.
- follow a series of three directions with motor actions.
- identify a specified word in a story context.
- identify pairs of words that rhyme.

To develop visual discrimination abilities, 5-year-olds should be able to learn to:

- describe and discriminate properties of objects (color, size, shape, length).
- identify properties of color, size, shape, length.
- classify objects by properties.
- identify missing parts of objects, shapes, letters, and numerals.
- duplicate two-dimensional designs with objects (parquetry blocks).
- match, sort, and name letters and numerals.
- reproduce a series of letters or numerals from memory.
- reproduce and name a sequence of four items from memory.
- identify and describe similarities and differences.
- sequence objects, pictures, and symbols from left to right.

To develop auditory perception abilities, 5-year-olds should be able to learn to:

- identify likenesses and differences in sound characteristics (loud or soft, fast or slow, high or low).
- state whether two sounds are the same or different.
- role play stories, with expression involving the appropriate sequence of actions and dialogue.
- name pairs of rhyming words.
- identify minimal word pairs, stating whether or not they are the same.
- follow a series of four directions with the appropriate motor actions.
- match the initial sounds to pictures or letters.

Motor Skills

Goal: To assist the child in developing both gross and fine motor skills.

Children, through play activities at home, usually develop the basic motor skills that are necessary for eye–hand coordination. Most children, however, need to practice these skills, and preschool programs offer many opportunities in the form of games, music activities, and playground time for this sort of practice.

Three-year-olds should be able to learn to:

- imitate simple body movements and positions.
- walk forward and backward and change direction on the floor and walking board.
- move spontaneously to music.
- follow a simple walking pattern.
- roll, catch, and bounce a ball.
- perform a given action quickly or slowly.
- perform a given action from verbal instructions (one or two actions in each sequence).
- move through a simple obstacle course.
- use clothing frames appropriately (buttons, snaps, zippers).
- spoon and pour beans.
- cut simple patterns (fringe, straight line) with a scissors.
- manipulate equipment (line up chairs, stack objects).
- manipulate clay.

Four-year-olds should be able to learn to:

- move body parts as directed.
- perform balance tasks on walking board (forward, backward, sideways).
- perform hopping and jumping tasks.
- move expressively to music.
- follow a walking pattern.
- throw and catch a ball, beanbag, or balloon.
- throw a beanbag towards a target.
- reproduce a rhythm pattern (fast or slow).
- remember and perform two or three actions in order.
- manipulate equipment (be able to place objects appropriately).
- spoon and pour uncooked rice.
- cut more complex patterns with scissors.
- perform chalkboard movements (up–down, top–bottom).
- discriminate through touching various textures, shapes, and sizes.
- perform simple paper-folding tasks.

Five-year-olds should be able to learn to:

- perform walking, marching, skipping, galloping, hopping, and bending tasks.
- perform broad-jumping tasks.
- play action games (relay races, hopscotch, marbles).
- reproduce a complex rhythm pattern.
- point to a specified position while blindfolded (on, over, under, or below).
- throw a beanbag to a specified target.

- describe action of self and others.
- copy simple letters, patterns, and shapes.
- cut, place, and paste as required.
- trace around and inside stencils.
- sew on burlap or cloth.
- make horizontal lines, vertical lines, and slanted lines with boundaries.

Interpersonal Skills

Goal: To assist the child in acquiring interpersonal skills necessary for interacting effectively with peers and adults.

Objectives related to the acquisition of interpersonal skills extend from ages 3 to 5 along a developmental continuum. A child of this age range should be able to learn to:

- cooperate with others in the classroom by following rules, by helping to establish rules, and by learning to modify rules when necessary.
- share and take turns.
- give help to other children when asked to do so.
- engage in discussions and activities that involve adults and other children in the classroom.
- play cooperatively.
- help on simple tasks such as cleanup, serving snacks, and so forth.
- verbalize feelings related to events that arise in the classroom.

Intrapersonal Skills

Goal: To assist the child in acquiring intrapersonal skills necessary for achieving personal autonomy.

Many intrapersonal objectives deal with affective abilities as well as skills that underlie attitudes and aptitudes related to school learning. Again, these objectives extend developmentally throughout the preschool years and, as such, are a concern of the preschool teacher working with various age levels. In general, the preschool child should be able to learn to:

- care for his own physical needs such as dressing, toileting, and eating.
- attend to tasks for increasingly longer periods of time.
- assume independent responsibility for completing tasks.
- indicate his willingness to attempt successively more difficult tasks.
- work for delayed rewards.
- respond to social reinforcement (smiles, supportive words) rather than concrete rewards.
- critically evaluate his own work.
- set realistic goals for himself.
- work independently.

WHY ARE THESE SKILLS OR ABILITIES IMPORTANT FOR THE YOUNG CHILD TO MASTER?

Language Arts

Learning how to think and solve problems is prerequisite to confidence and success in a scientific society that requires individuals to cope with a vast body of knowledge. The child's ability to think, reason, and solve problems is dependent upon his conceptual development during his early years. Early education programs should, therefore, provide an environment that is responsive to the child's activities, that provides him with opportunities to observe and understand relationships, and that supports his use of language to express thought. The teacher, in planning activities based on the kinds of objectives discussed in the previous section, should guide the child from understanding and producing simple language forms toward more elaborate patterns. Gradually, the child should learn to describe objects, narrate events, generalize, explain, and predict a variety of ideas. The competencies necessary for manipulating language in situations requiring various levels of cognitive skills can best be developed through actual experiences. Other activities, such as finger plays, nursery rhymes, and reading books and poetry, can also be used in a variety of ways to stimulate the child's language development. The teacher must learn to capitalize upon both planned and unplanned moments to assist the children in mastering the kinds of skills that underlie the effective use of language.

Sensory-Perceptual Skills

Developmental maturation in visual and auditory processes is a prerequisite for success in school. Through visual discrimination activities, the child develops the ability to observe, describe, and understand what he sees. These skills prepare the child for reading-readiness activities. In order for the child to recognize, understand, and integrate what he sees, he must perceive that objects in his environment have invariant or constant properties, and he must be able to perceive these objects in relation to their positions in space, in relation to himself, and in relation to other objects. In addition to learning skills related to constancy and spatial relations, the young child must learn what to focus on at certain times and how to change his focus. The ability to focus and maintain attention is essential for learning to read. Activities such as finding a picture or letter embedded within a design or hidden beneath distracting lines, or outlining overlapping figures, require the child to focus on the central object or picture. The child also must learn to categorize and group different things according to some common properties. Through his visual sensory-perceptual skills, he should learn to group items, first according to a single property and then according to two or more properties simultaneously. As these perceptual skills are mastered, he also begins to use language to explain why he has grouped certain items together.

Mastery of auditory-perceptual skills is necessary for the child's understanding and use of the information he hears. Language development and reading-readiness skills are improved as he learns to use his auditory abilities. The exact degree of auditory efficiency necessary for learning to read normally is unknown. However, Gates (1947) observed that the more familiar the child is with the sound characteristics of words, and the more skillful he is in identifying and blending the sound units of words, the better equipped he is to use phonetic techniques.

Myklebust (1954) reports that, although reading is primarily a system of visual symbols, many auditory skills are essential for its acquisition. These skills include the ability to distinguish similarities and differences in sounds, to perceive a sound within a word, to synthesize sounds into words, and to divide them into syllables. If a child cannot perform these auditory functions, he will have difficulty learning to read. Preliminary findings by Rosner (1972) provide evidence that competency in auditory skills is more related to success in beginning reading than are visual skills (which appear to be related to success in mathematics).

Training the child's listening abilities involves, therefore, teaching him to discriminate sounds, to select relevant sounds and disregard others, to associate sounds with their sources, to perceive rhythm patterns, to remember and repeat sound patterns, and to use language sounds to solve problems.

Motor Skills

There is a close relationship between the development of motor skills, a sense of body image, and later success in higher-level learning tasks. The relationship between motor-skill training and sensory stimulation was considered in the early work of Itard (1932) and Seguin (1907). Piaget (1952) describes early sensorimotor learning activities as fundamental building blocks for later, more complex perceptual and cognitive development. Others have also considered the relationship of motor abilities to visual abilities (Frostig & Horne, 1964), to speech problems (Belgau, 1967), to reading readiness (Lazroe, 1969), and to reading achievement (DeHirsch et al., 1966).

Gross motor skills deal with the total musculature of the body or large portions of it. Development of these skills is necessary if the child is to handle his body well. These skills begin to develop as soon as the child has gained basic control of his posture and balance; however, as he develops, he must continually adjust and reorganize his posturing and balance patterns. Handling the body appropriately in various situations requires generalization of motor movements and intentional control of the body. Many of the objectives listed in the preceding section are designed to assist the child in acquiring these specific kinds of skills.

As the child develops proficiency in gross motor skills, he gradually refines his movement patterns to require the use of more specific muscles. This process requires time and careful learning. Muscular control of the eyes, hands, and fingers, as well as coordination of eye and hand movement, is necessary in daily tasks such as dressing and in classroom activities involving object manipulation. Coordination of the eyes and hands (plus understanding of oral instructions) is also required for later success in learning to read and write. The teacher, in planning the program, must provide time for the child to practice the fine motor skills necessary for later learning. Another crucial consideration is the child's need to practice using language to describe his own movement.

Inter- and Intrapersonal Skills

The child's interaction with those around him, as well as his feelings about himself, are necessary ingredients for the development of a positive self-concept. As he masters and extends the competencies related to the specific abilities listed above, he begins to develop the feelings of competency necessary for coping successfully with school-related tasks. These skills are developed through all of the content areas typically included in an early childhood curriculum. Creative activities, however, such as art, music, dance, and rhythm, provide the teacher with additional opportunities to observe the progress of the children as they acquire inter- and intrapersonal skills.

Art activities provide opportunities not only for sensorimotor experiences and for extending and reinforcing concepts, but also for freedom of expression. The emphasis in art activities should be on the child's enjoyment and participation rather than on a perfected product. Children should feel free to use art materials in their own ways, because this freedom of expression will enable them to project their inner selves into their art work. For young children, the ability to handle feelings and impressions through words is still somewhat limited, and access to nonverbal forms of expression provides another way for them to communicate. Thus, art has developmental value for many children.

Children also can express their feelings through music by listening, by moving vigorously, by beating a drum, and by singing. Music can be introduced in many ways and can be used every day. The incorporation of music in children's activities will affect their moods and attitudes. Appropriate times for music are rest time, story time, art time, and, of course, a special time set apart just for listening. The goal should be to help the child express himself and his feelings through music.

HOW DOES THE TEACHER TRANSLATE GOALS INTO PARTICULAR LEARNING EXPERIENCES?

In the previous sections we have discussed some goals that appear to be important for young children, and some of the reasons for their importance. One of the major tasks for a teacher is to translate these goals into daily learning experiences for children. The following section will outline and discuss the steps necessary for achieving a broad educational goal through a series of specific learning experiences. The process involves:

1. determining where the child is.
2. selecting the objective.

3. planning the activity.
4. presenting the activity.
5. evaluating attainment of the objective.
6. recycling or progressing to the next level.

Determining Where the Child Is

Ideally, teachers should be able to gather basic information about the children in their class prior to the beginning of school. Information can often be collected through home visits by asking parents specific kinds of questions related to their child's present developmental level. Unfortunately, it is not always possible for teachers either to know which children will be assigned to their class, or to have the opportunity to make home visits prior to the formal opening of school.

Teachers should check folders of children who have already attended school in order to see what kind of information is available. Basic information such as the child's age, medical history, and any unusual problems is usually recorded on typical registration forms and other school records.

Let us assume that no information regarding the children is available to the teacher. How does the teacher begin to assess the entry-level skills of 20 to 25 children and then use this information to respond to individual needs? The amount of information that can be collected is unlimited, but the key to effective information gathering is to know in advance how the information will be used. The teacher must decide what kind of information is most important to gather on each child, and then must decide how to use this information in making program decisions.

Let us assume that Mrs. T and her teacher aide are expecting 22 newly enrolled 3-year-olds in their class. Mrs. T and her aide are making basic decisions regarding program goals in preparing for the first weeks of school. During the early weeks they will be primarily concerned with:

• assisting the children in their initial adjustment to school.
• learning as much as they can about each child's abilities.
• planning a daily program that will allow each child to feel comfortable about his ability to participate, while at the same time giving the teaching staff information about the child's level of functioning.
• working toward establishing a routine that includes one-to-one interaction, small-group activities, large-group activities, and a daily schedule that is stable but at the same time allows for reasonable flexibility.
• making certain that each child becomes comfortable with the adults in the classroom.

Mrs. T and her aide discuss the kinds of information they will need to collect in order to determine each child's level of functioning. First, they review some intrapersonal skills that they hope most of the children have already acquired. These include being able to attend to their own toileting needs, feeding themselves, attending to a task for a short period of time, engaging in classroom conversations, waiting their turn, responding positively to social reinforcements, asking questions, and demonstrating some curiosity and exploratory behavior. Mrs. T and her aide list each one of these behaviors and agree that during the first two to three weeks of school they will each systematically observe different children in the classroom as they are engaged in various kinds of activities. Each will keep records on whether or not the children demonstrate these particular kinds of behavior. They also agree to use volunteers assigned to their classroom to observe different children.

Next, Mrs. T and her aide discuss some interpersonal skills that they consider important for 3-year-olds. These include working cooperatively with other children on certain tasks, asking adults for help, following rules that have been explained, sharing materials and equipment, helping other children when necessary, and engaging in conversations with adults and children. They agree that observations will be conducted in much the same way as agreed upon for intrapersonal skills. These observations will extend for two to three weeks, and each adult in the classroom will systematically observe different children at various times of the day.

They briefly review some gross and fine motor skills that they feel are important for 3-year-olds to master. Mrs. T and her aide decide that they will observe the children when they are on the playground and record information pertaining to gross body movements such as walking, running, jumping, and balancing. They schedule some simple games during the first few weeks of school that will involve imitating simple body movements, moving spontaneously to music, and following simple instructions. They also agree that during art activities they will watch the children's dexterity with scissors, crayons, and free pasting. Small-group sessions or independent work times can be used to observe the children's manipulative skills. The teachers then list some of the basic sensory-perceptual skills they consider important. They decide that during planned interaction sessions with the children they will systematically observe whether or not the children can match, sort, and name basic colors and shapes. They also plan some small-group activities such as duplicating three-dimensional cube-inch block designs and working with puzzles. Mrs. T asks her aide to observe the children when they are in the housekeeping and block-playing areas and to ask questions about the position of the furniture and blocks. Musical games are planned that will require the children to attend and respond to the presence and absence of sound, as well as other games that will require the children to recognize gross differences in sound characteristics.

Some simple language activities are planned that will enable Mrs. T and her aide to assess the children's level of language functioning. Stories are selected to be read to small groups. After each reading, the teachers will

FIGURE 5.1
Observation Form

Skills	Name										
Intrapersonal											
Toileting											
Feeds himself											
Attends to tasks											
Engages in classroom conversation											
Waits his turn											
Responds to social reinforcement											
Asks questions											
Displays curiosity and exploratory behavior											
Interpersonal											
Follows rules											
Works cooperatively with other children											
Shares											
Asks adults for help											
Helps other children											
Motor											
Gross body-movement control											
Imitates body movements											

ask simple questions requiring the children to name and describe objects and pictures related to the story. During circle time they will encourage the children to describe simple experiences and events that have occurred at school or at home. They want to determine if each child can identify himself by name, and can label at least four parts of his own body. Finally, they decide to record any spontaneous events that might indicate whether or not a child has mastered a particular language skill.

Figure 5.1 shows how their checklist looks after the skills have been entered and the chart prepared for classroom use. Mrs. T and her aide will spend at least two to three weeks working with and observing the children, assessing the strengths and weaknesses of each child. Notice that space

Figure 5.1 (*Continued*)

Skills	Name												
Moves spontaneously to music													
Follows instructions with motor response													
Cuts with scissors													
Stacks objects													
Sensory-Perceptual													
Matches, names, sorts basic colors and shapes													
Duplicates 3D designs													
Identifies positions of objects													
Attends and responds to presence and absence of sound													
Recognizes gross differences in sound characteristics													
Language													
Recognizes, names and describes simple pictures													
Describes simple experiences and events													
Identifies self by name													

Comments_____

has been left at the bottom of the checklist for additional observations that might occur spontaneously. Once the teachers feel that they have recorded a sufficient amount of information, they are ready for the next step. This involves analyzing the information, and on the basis of this analysis, selecting the objectives for their daily program.

Selecting Objectives

According to Mager (1962), an objective is an *intent* communicated by a statement describing a proposed change in a learner—a statement of what the learner is to be like when he has successfully completed a learning experience. The teacher, after analyzing what the children can and cannot do, sets goals in areas that need further work. She then analyzes the general goals in terms of specifying objectives that can be converted into learning experiences. For example, suppose that most of the children in the class were not able to match, name, and sort basic colors and shapes. The teacher would then have to decide which colors and shapes were important for the children to be able to match, name, and sort. Let us assume that, for 3-year-olds, the decision was that they should be able to match eight basic colors, name four basic colors, and sort four basic colors. The objectives for shapes might consist of matching five basic shapes, naming three basic shapes, and sorting three basic shapes. These terminal objectives would then be broken down into a number of smaller tasks that, as they were mastered, would assist the child in eventually attaining the final objectives.

Once the objectives have been specified, additional decisions regarding the actual learning experiences must be made, including the kinds of stimuli that will be used in the learning activity, the response level expected of the child, and the criterion behavior that will indicate that the child has indeed mastered the particular objective. In selecting the stimuli, the teacher should remember that there are different levels of materials that can be used with young children. The stimuli can be either concrete (actual objects), representational (picture), or symbolic (written word). In the case of an objective related to learning colors, the actual materials used in the learning experience could range from cube-inch blocks of various colors, to colored pictures, to the word "blue" printed on a sheet of paper. The teacher must be aware of the developmental differences that influence how young children learn. In order to actually assimilate and accommodate new information, the child should move sequentially from concrete stimuli first to the representational and then to the symbolic levels. The materials used in learning activities for 3-year-olds should, for the most part, consist of concrete objects such as cube-inch blocks, while 4- and 5-year-olds could work at the representational level.

Just as stimuli can vary in complexity, the levels of response required of the child can also range from simple to complex. For example, the teacher might expect the child to give a motor response such as identifying (child points to, selects, matches, puts together, puts a mark on), imitating (child performs a motor task as modeled), or demonstrating (child makes a motor response in which he shows knowledge of function, representation, comprehension of directions). The teacher can also require a verbal response that can range from imitating (child performs verbal task as modeled), naming (child gives correct label), describing (child describes properties, categories, relationships, events, similarities, differences, or functions), or evaluating (child makes a judgment). To return to the example of an activity related to color, the responses can range from the child's matching or putting to-

The same materials can be used differently with children who differ in age and/or familiarity with the materials. The boy, who is new to the beads, is simply stringing them randomly. The girl, who already knows how to do this, is following the pattern shown on the card. Both tasks involve bead stringing, but the latter is more complex.

109

gether a number of colors that are the same, to naming the colors, to describing the color as one property of an object.

Finally, for each objective and subtask that leads to the terminal objective, the teacher must specify the criterion behavior or acceptable level of performance. Early in the sequence, the teacher and her aide might be quite satisfied if the child works with two or three basic colors. Very gradually, as the child demonstrates mastery, he will add other colors to the sequence of tasks, so that it will require a higher-level response.

Planning the Activity

Before actually planning an activity, teachers should review all of the information they have acquired about the children in their classrooms. Questions to ask include: What kinds of activities would really interest particular children? Are there differences in learning styles that need to be considered in planning any learning experience? Is there a novel approach that can be used to elicit interest? How can an activity be made more exciting for the children? How can the complexity of the task be increased without overwhelming the children? Observation of children does not end after the first two to three weeks of school, but should be an ongoing activity for the teacher and aide that constantly provides new information regarding the level of functioning of all the children. Only by using this information is the teacher able to plan appropriate learning experiences for the class.

The first decision involves the content vehicle to employ for presenting any particular objective. Different labels may be used to describe the kinds of activities teachers feel are important for children. One may use subject-matter labels such as science, mathematics, language arts, art, and music, or one may describe these activities by using terms such as sensory-perceptual activity, motor activity, cognitive development, and creative expression. The teacher should remember that the content label is merely a vehicle for assisting the child in mastering a particular skill or objective, a tool to use selectively in order to motivate the child and hold his interest. Choices, therefore, include music, art, dramatic play, finger plays, science, field trips, stories, or games of various kinds. For example, any one of these content areas could be selected for presenting concepts related to color. In planning the whole sequence of objectives related to mastery of the terminal goal, the teacher might select each one of these content areas at one time or another for communicating various subobjectives. This would be appropriate in terms of pacing strategies and novelty, as well as capitalizing on various learning styles of the children.

Once the decision regarding the content vehicle for the particular learning experience is made, the teacher must then consider the kind of material to use for the actual activity. Are the materials to be concrete objects, pictures, or some other symbolic representations? What about a combination of these various kinds of materials? Will the materials be available in the classroom? Does the teacher need to collect these materials or bring them from home? Will the materials be meaningful to the children? Is there special preparation involved? How many sets of materials will be needed for all the children in the classroom? The teacher's major concern at this point is to select the particular materials to use, to make sure that they will work with the children, and then to do any advance preparation necessary. The teacher should be concerned not only about the immediate activity to be presented to the children, but also about all of the follow-up kinds of activities that lead to the terminal goal. While the detailed preparation will not occur until a later time, the need to collect various kinds of materials must be anticipated.

The next concern regards the grouping of the children. The teacher must decide how many children will participate in the particular activity: The total class? Smaller groups? One to one? Will the groupings be preplanned, or will the teacher informally select children and interact with them on a tutorial basis? Will the teacher initiate the activity, or wait for a child to indicate a "teachable moment?" The teacher and her aide must agree on the grouping strategy that will be used in presenting the activity to the children. Unless there is clear communication during this planning phase, the efforts of the two adults in the classroom will not be mutually supportive. Plans for grouping children should result in actual written lists of their names and/or listings of any other kinds of grouping decisions that are finally reached.

The next consideration is the physical setting for the learning experience. Depending upon the kinds of decisions that have been made concerning grouping, materials, and content vehicle, the teacher must now decide where the learning activity will actually be presented. Some of the choices available are the floor, a small table, a large table, a circle of chairs, a corner of the classroom, or a learning center. The physical setting must be supportive of the kinds of interactions that the teacher anticipates will occur. For instance, if the children are to label colors that they see in objects scattered about the classroom, they probably should sit in a small circle in the middle of the classroom where they would have clear visual access to the objects placed around the room. If, on the other hand, the children are to sort a number of small objects by color, it would then be appropriate to have the children sit at a table where the objects could be placed in containers and sorted with a minimal amount of confusion. The teacher and aide might role play the activity in various parts of the classroom before they make their final determination of the most appropriate physical setting. As they talk through the activity and manipulate the materials, they can easily identify potential problems and avoid them with careful planning.

Once the physical setting for the learning experience has been selected, the teacher needs to consider the total environment of the classroom. The environment can be either supportive or nonsupportive of particular kinds of learning experiences. For example, if the decision has been made to work with small groups of children in a corner of the classroom on color concepts, the teacher ought to be certain that the learning area is not next to the block area where loud, active play might be occurring. The noise would distract the children working with the teacher, and would impede attainment of the objective. Another consideration would be wall displays in the classroom. If the objectives for the class relate to color concepts, then the wall displays ought to be supportive of these kinds of objectives. The materials placed in the classroom are also part of the total classroom environment. These should be selected to reinforce the particular concepts being stressed by the teacher. Choice of materials extends to the kinds of books in the book area. If the teacher and aide have planned sufficiently well in advance, then time would have been allowed to visit the public library and check out additional books that reinforce particular concepts. It is here, in planning the classroom environment, that the teacher's creativity can totally support the program goals and objectives. There are always options for going far beyond the behavioral objective, which are limited only by the teacher's imagination. The objective is a starting point, and the teacher, by anticipating and planning carefully, can create a learning environment totally supportive of the selected goals.

The next decision the teacher must make relates to the presentation mode. Will the learning experience be teacher directed or child selected? If it is child selected, the teacher must be certain that appropriate materials are placed in the classroom where they are easily accessible to the children. In making this decision, the teacher should consider what would be the most efficient and economical use of time. There is no doubt that many kinds of skills can be mastered most effectively when children are ready to master them on their own. For example, learning to button a sweater will take a tremendous amount of practice for the normal 3-year-olds. It would be rather inefficient for the teacher to schedule a daily buttoning lesson. Opportunities for each child to button his own clothes will occur naturally, and the teacher should be aware that each is increasing his skills as time progresses. Teachers should be ready to step in and assist when necessary, but should allow the child as much time for practice as he needs. There are other kinds of skills, however, that can be mastered more effectively with programmed instruction planned by the teacher. The teacher must decide what the most effective presentation mode will be for mastering these kinds of skills and abilities. Some of the choices available include discovery learning, didactic presentations, inquiry modes, class projects, or drills directed by the teacher. Teachers can also select self-corrective activities that the children may work on individually with minimal supervision. The teacher's major responsibility is to prepare the environment through careful planning and then to provide opportunities for as much practice as necessary to achieve a particular goal.

The teacher's next concern regards the kinds of motivational strategies to be used to hold the children's interest. It is most important that the teacher and aide consistently reinforce each other by using the same general approach to motivating the children in their care. It would be most inappropriate for one teacher to use social reinforcement while the other teacher uses token or concrete reinforcements. The teacher and aide must decide what motivational strategies they will use to interest the children in the activity initially, to hold their interest throughout the activity, and to reinforce appropriate behavior at the end of the learning experience. The techniques from which they can select include novelty, surprise, mystery, pacing and spacing strategies, media, social reinforcement, feedback to the children, and contingency-management techniques. The motivational strategies will and should vary among different groups and activities. Again, the selection of strategies will depend on how much the teachers know about each child's level of functioning in the classroom. This means that observation of the children will be an ongoing activity throughout the school year.

Figure 5.2 summarizes the different kinds of decisions a teacher must make whenever an activity is planned. Let us suppose that Mrs. Young, who teaches 4-year-olds, has selected the following instructional objective as a terminal goal for the children.

The children will be able to reproduce and name a variety of pictured locations.

We shall assume that Mrs. Young's planning is taking place early in the school year and she is just beginning to schedule activities that will assist

FIGURE 5.2
Planning an Activity

Decisions	*Options*
Content vehicle	Science, math, language arts, music, art, geography
Stimuli	Concrete objects, representational (pictures), symbolic
Level of response	Motor (identify, imitate, demonstrate), Verbal (imitate, name, describe, evaluate)
Physical setting	Floor, table, large circle, learning center, outdoors
Total environment	Wall displays, learning materials, learning centers
Presentation mode	Child selected, teacher directed (discovery, didactic, inquiry, demonstration, self-corrective materials)
Motivational strategies	Social or concrete reinforcement, novelty, surprise, pacing, mystery

the children in eventually mastering the terminal goal. She decides to plan an activity in the content area of language arts. Because most of the children are attending school for the first time, Mrs. Young decides to use concrete materials and to call for motor responses. She decides that she will work with small groups in the housekeeping area where she will arrange manipulative objects such as pots, pans, dolls, and toy animals that can be placed in various locations within the learning center. She plans to demonstrate to the children how to place objects according to specified positions by telling a story that requires dramatizing and role playing the actual placement of objects. As a motivating strategy, she plans to use surprise to hold their interest by hiding raisins inside of objects where the children will be sure to find them as they follow her directions.

An experienced teacher makes these planning decisions quickly and automatically. Teachers new in the classroom will find that practice accelerates the process and that decision making will become easier as the school year progresses.

Presenting the Activity

The actual techniques appropriate for use in presenting activities to young children are described in Chapter 9. The main considerations include getting and holding the attention of the children, insuring everyone's participation, balancing group and individual responses, individualizing instruction for different children, judging when and how to terminate a lesson, and making time to work more intensively with the children who need it most.

Evaluation and Assessment

After the activity has been presented, the teacher must make a judgment as to whether or not the children have actually achieved the objective. The criterion behavior or acceptable response should have been clearly specified in the original objective. The teacher and the aide should have prepared a checklist to enable them to monitor the progress of each child. In addition to assessing whether or not the children had achieved the objective, the teacher and aide should also have observed the kinds of errors or problems encountered by the children as they worked on the particular objective. Teachers cannot make decisions regarding reteaching or special work without being fully cognizant of the kinds of errors the child has made. The error pattern will determine whether or not additional practice, reinforcing activities, independent activities, or assigned tasks should be scheduled. There are several options available when teachers are assessing the progress made by the child.

Let us assume that the teacher has presented a particular activity to a small group of children. Out of a group of six children, four achieved the objective within a reasonable period of time, while two continued to have problems. The teacher decides to dismiss the children who have achieved the objective and to work further with the children who are having problems. Through questioning and observation, the teacher attempts to identify the kinds of errors being made. In the case of the color lesson, for example, perhaps the children can match basic colors, but are not able to state the color label. Once the error has been identified, the teacher can make some basic decisions regarding how to reteach the children who have not achieved the objective. The teacher first reviews the progress made by the entire class and identifies all the children who have not achieved the objective and then makes some decisions regarding how to regroup these children: which will continue to work in small groups, which will work on a one-to-one tutorial basis, which will practice individually. The teacher's next decision concerns the kinds of activities to plan for achieving the objective. Again, choices include an independent activity tied to particular materials in the classroom, an assigned task that can be explained to the children and then carried out independently, or a reinforcing activity that can be presented by the teacher to individual children. The teacher's main consideration is to make certain that the child is provided with appropriate opportunities for practicing and mastering the particular objective. Again, checklists are prepared so that the children's progress may be carefully monitored.

For those children who have achieved the objective, the teacher and aide prepare to recycle through the series of steps necessary for converting goals into particular learning experiences. They move to the next level of objectives and systematically select specific objectives, plan the learning activity, present the activity, evaluate, and assess. The actual curriculum and program should emerge from the needs and abilities of the children. The teacher and the aide, through careful planning, individualize the program and build upon the strengths that the children bring to school. By having a clear idea of terminal objectives for the children, teachers should be able to analyze the tasks necessary for achieving the terminal goals and plan appropriate activities. Observation and assessment are ongoing tasks that provide teachers with the information necessary for making appropriate decisions. Analysis of the information is the key to effective learning if the teacher truly is to function as a facilitator of the teaching-learning process.

SUMMARY

In this chapter we have examined some of the principles necessary for translating curriculum goals into learning experiences. We have seen that general agreement does not exist regarding a body of knowledge or skills that should be taught in preschools. There is general agreement, however, about the kinds of broad learning goals considered important for young children. Three major questions have been addressed:

- What do children need to learn?
- Why are these abilities or skills important?

• How does a teacher translate these goals into particular learning experiences?

Some examples were presented that illustrated how a broad goal could be converted into particular learning experiences. The process described in the chapter should generalize to all of the skills and abilities listed under the various skill areas. Will it work for you? Why not select a program goal and try to translate it into a learning experience for young children?

QUESTIONS

1. How can the teacher capitalize on show and tell time to develop more elaborate language patterns (describe, narrate events, generalize, predict ideas)? Provide specific examples and be able to demonstrate effective techniques in role-play situations with classmates.

2. Choose a book, finger play, or poem, and develop a series of language activities or lessons using it effectively.

3. Describe two unplanned situations and illustrate how they could be used to increase the child's effective use of language.

4. Plan a series of classification activities. Would they be used with individuals, small groups, entire groups?

5. Find and/or develop games, activities, lessons, and evaluation techniques for helping children make sound discriminations.

6. Develop an information sheet to be filled out by the parent. What important information would you collect? Why?

7. Observe a teacher presenting a lesson. What techniques are employed? Are they successful?

8. Plan lessons or activities to help those who do not reach the objective after initial presentation of the lesson. Be specific. If possible, make a plan for children who have not mastered content in an actual program. Use test results as the basis for your planning and then teach the lesson. Did it succeed? Why or why not?

9. What resources in the immediate community could be developed into areas of interest?

10. Select rhythm and music activities that encourage the children to verbalize their body movements. Are there other places in the schedule where this verbalization can be encouraged?

11. Some teachers and writers oppose structured curricula because they believe that adult-directed activity will interfere with the child's "natural" curiosity. Is this true? Is curiosity a "natural" trait that automatically blossoms unless stifled, or is it learned? If learned, how is it learned?

Discuss this with your classmates, trying to separate *facts* from *unproven assumptions.*

12. Some writers and teachers oppose planned curricula because they believe that such instruction is unnatural and unbalanced, that it prevents the teacher from "teaching the whole child." Is this wholly or partly correct? What does "teaching the whole child" mean? What criteria would you use to determine whether a program was unbalanced (overstressing objectives in some areas at the expense of important objectives in other areas)?

13. We often use SES and other group indicators because they are useful in pointing out differences among children that may have implications for differential curriculum/methods planning. However, SES and similar concepts refer to *groups;* they are much less useful in planning for *individuals.* What characteristics *are* useful for planning an individualized curriculum for *each* child?

14. Lists of important curriculum goals for 3-, 4-, and 5-year-old children were given in the chapter. What are some notable age-related differences in these lists? What are the reasons for these differences? Have any important goals been omitted from the lists?

15. Suppose you "don't have time" for record keeping such as that illustrated in the chapter. What should you do? Discuss your answer(s) with classmates. Is there agreement?

READINGS

Almy, M. "Spontaneous play: an avenue for intellectual development." *Young Children, 22* (1967), 246–277.

Burns, P. and Lowe, A. *The language arts in childhood education.* Chicago: Rand McNally, 1966.

Cazden, C. "Children's questions: their forms, functions and roles in education." *Young Children, 25* (1970), 202–220.

Clure, B. *Why didn't I think of that? A teacher's resource book for early childhood education.* Glendale, Calif.: Bowmar, 1971.

Karnes, M. *Helping young children develop language skills: a book of activities.* Washington, D.C.: Council for Exceptional Children, 1968.

Lowenfeld, V. *Creative and mental growth.* New York: Macmillan, 1964.

———. *Young child and his art.* New York: Macmillan, 1954.

Read, K. *The nursery school.* Philadelphia: Saunders, 1966.

Smith, R. and Leonhard, C. *Discovering music together: early childhood.* Chicago: Follett, 1968.

Todd, V. and Heffernan, H. *The years before school: guiding preschool children.* Toronto: Macmillan, 1970.

6
THE PHYSICAL ENVIRONMENT OF THE PRESCHOOL

THE PRESCHOOL AS A WHOLE

Although a wise teacher who respects the children is by far the most important single variable in determining the quality of a child's preschool experience, several other factors play a vital role. One of these is the quality of the preschool environment, especially the room or rooms in which the teacher and children spend most of their day. A carefully planned and equipped preschool provides the child with safe and pleasant surroundings. It also maximizes his opportunities to work and play independently through the use of design principles that minimize hazards and obstacles and enable the child to meet his own needs as much as possible. The same design principles that make for an optimal preschool from the viewpoint of the child also make for an optimal environment for the teacher, since they help minimize accidents, delays, interruptions, and other inconveniences.

In this chapter we will try to illustrate the ideal preschool environment. Even though few readers will ever be in a position to design and implement their own plans for a preschool, all will have the opportunity to modify the environments in which they will work to some degree. Most teachers find that a clear specification of the ideal situation is very useful in assessing the strengths and weaknesses of their own preschool and in developing ideas and priorities for needed changes. Thus, while it is true that most teachers will have to accept and to work within certain constraints which are beyond their control, it is also true that steps can be taken to improve any preschool environment. Often important improvements can be made at little or no expense. Bear this in mind as you read the chapter. If you work in a preschool that has physical features which cause you problems, remember that you do not have to accept them passively. Ask yourself how things could be improved, and follow through on any ideas you develop about making such improvements.

Ideally, the preschool should be self-contained, situated with its own buildings on its own grounds, separate from elementary schools or other institutions. Most observers also agree that it should be *small*, containing no more than three or four classes. This arrangement will minimize traffic and safety hazards, and will maximize flexibility by eliminating many of the problems of scheduling, equipment sharing, and other administrative constraints that become necessary when a preschool is very large or when it is attached to an elementary school.

Ideally, all the school buildings should be ranch style, eliminating the stair climbing that can be a problem for young children. The front entrance should include a sheltered pickup and delivery area, located in the middle of a one-way, drive-through access road set back from the main street (see Figure 6.1). This arrangement will allow children to get in and out of cars or buses at an area safely removed from street traffic, and the covered entranceway will eliminate the need for umbrellas or special clothing on rainy days.

The outside play area should be behind the school building, away from the street. The entire play area, but especially any parts that border on streets, should be surrounded by a wire-mesh fence five or six feet high. Such a fence will not impair visibility, but it will keep the children and outside play equipment (except for a few stray balls) inside the play yard.

Wire endings at the top and bottom of the fence should be blunted or rounded, so that children who stick their arms or legs under the fence or who try to climb it will not cut themselves. Gates should be fitted with locking mechanisms that are either high up or complex to operate, so that children too young to use the gate without supervision will be unable to open it. One gate should be situated as close as possible to the pickup area, and a walkway should extend from this gate to the pickup area. This arrangement will facilitate pickup when the children are playing outside (as they often are) just before pickup time.

Where the preschool is part of a larger school and all of the above conditions are not possible, try to approximate them. Preschool classrooms should be located on the *first floor,* and should be clustered together *near the entrance* used by the preschoolers. If possible, pickup and delivery of preschoolers, especially if they are below kindergarten age, should be scheduled separately from the mass entrances and exits of older children. Young children can easily get lost in the confusion of a large crowd, and they are sometimes injured because they are not alert or agile enough to stay out of the way of older children who may not be watching where they are going as they move through the halls. One way to accomplish this separation is to use different arrival and departure times, such as having the preschoolers come to school fifteen minutes after the other children and leave fifteen minutes earlier. However, this is often impractical because many parents will be coming to pick up both preschoolers and older siblings. The result

FIGURE 6.1
Covered school entrance recessed from the street; fenced-in outside play area with gate and sidewalk leading to pickup area.

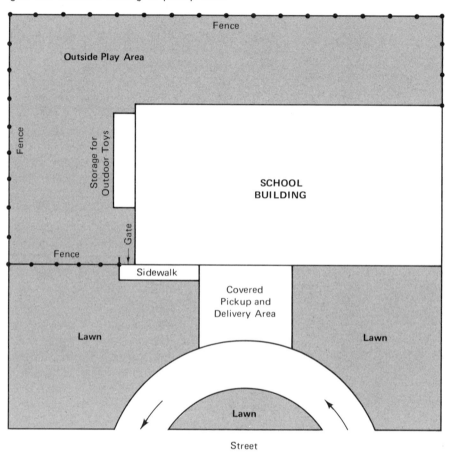

will be an irritating delay for such parents and an increase in the backup of traffic. An alternative solution is to arrange for preschoolers to enter and leave through their own exclusive gate or doorway, which should be apart from the entrance used by the older students.

SCHOOL VEHICLES
Buses, cars, or other vehicles used by the school to transport children will have to conform to state or local regulations and inspections, and staff who drive them will be required to have chauffeurs' licenses, not just ordinary drivers' licenses. Even if the school does not transport children on a daily basis, it is likely that transportation arrangements will have to be made for

field trips and special events. Thus, it is vital that you be familiar with legal requirements applying to your school, and that you take steps to insure that you are in compliance with them.

All children, whether transported by the school or by their parents, should be firmly belted into their seats. This should be standard policy for school-operated vehicles, and it should be frequently stressed to parents who drive their children to school as well. School-operated vehicles should carry a fire extinguisher in good working order, a complete emergency medical kit, and an up-to-date list of the relevant names and emergency phone numbers for each child enrolled in the school. The vehicle itself must be inspected periodically according to state or local regulations, and drivers should be encouraged to check out any suspicions about the condition of their vehicles. Anticipatory and preventive maintenance will minimize the chance of accidents. The school should carry liability insurance covering injury and medical costs for anyone riding school vehicles. Such insurance usually has provisions declaring it null and void if the safety precautions discussed above are not kept in effect continually.

School personnel should have lists of car pools and of persons authorized to pick up each child, and policies about what to do when an unauthorized person calls for the child will be needed. Bus drivers or parents will need a policy concerning what to do if no one is home when the child is being delivered from school.

SLEEPING ARRANGEMENTS

Most whole-day programs, and some half-day programs involving very young children, include a scheduled rest or nap time. Usually it is most convenient to provide each child with a mat or cot to use at these times. The mats or cots should be stored in the classroom in cupboards that make them easily accessible. In the interest of preventive hygiene, each child should have his own mat or cot labeled with his name or some other identification device. To facilitate removal and replacement, mats or cots should be kept in precisely the same place so that the child can remove and return his own cot without difficulty. Where cots are unavailable and the children sleep on mats, rugs, mattresses, or other padding that rests directly on the floor, the padding should be color coded or otherwise designed so that the difference between the bottom side and the top side is easily recognizable. This will insure that dirt from the floor clings only to the underside of the padding and not to the side that the child rests on.

Very young children may require cribs or baby beds with side bars to prevent them from falling out. Ideally, sleeping facilities for children who need a prolonged nap, rather than a brief nap or a sleepless rest, should be permanently set up in dark, quiet rooms either located away from noisy areas or soundproofed. If space is at a premium, collapsible wooden or plastic cribs that can be quickly unfolded and assembled should be available. Prior to nap time, they should be set up in the designated sleeping room, which should be as quiet as possible. A staff member should be on duty in this room at all times during the nap period, ready to tend to the needs of any distressed child. It is important that this be done quickly, both for the child's own good and to avoid the contagion problem that may occur if other children wake up or begin to imitate the distressed child.

Nap schedules should be as flexible and individualized as possible. Children who want or need a long nap should be allowed to sleep undisturbed, and those who do not need a nap or need only a short nap should be allowed to leave the sleeping room and return to active play as soon as they are fully awake and unlikely to go back to sleep. The individual nap needs of young children are extremely varied, although most children show an individualized pattern. Daily records kept over a period of two or three weeks will establish the nap time that each child needs when he enters the school. These should be rechecked from time to time, however, since the habits and needs of most children will change as the year progresses.

MEALS

Virtually all preschools serve meals and/or snacks to the children. Obviously, facilities and meal-preparation procedures should meet the highest safety, health, and nutritional standards, using the state and local guidelines as minimal criteria. In addition, certain less obvious aspects of food serving are also important. First, food service should be arranged so that the children can do as much as possible independently. Furniture should be scaled to the size of the children (booster chairs, low tables for toddlers, etc.). Ideally, the child should be able to lean over his plate when he eats, and the distance he must cover in moving food from the plate to his mouth should be minimal. Glasses or cups should have handles and/or be slender, so that the child can easily get his hand around them. Plates and drinking vessels should be light and unbreakable. Any food slicing necessary should be done before the food is served, since preschoolers usually cannot handle knives well enough to cut their food successfully. If the children have to carry any food from a serving counter to their seats, the food should be given to them on trays. Younger children should have bibs or napkins that tie on or slip over the neck, preferably with pockets at the bottom to catch spilled food. All of these considerations minimize the teacher's problems and maximize the child's independence by making it possible for him to eat by himself as much as possible and to minimize his spills and accidents.

In scheduling the frequency and size of meals, bear in mind that compared with adults, young children need to eat smaller meals but to eat more frequently. Thus, they should not be expected to eat large amounts at scheduled meal times (although many will), and snacks should be served between meals (juice or milk with cookies, fruit, cheese, dry cereal, or crackers). As with their sleeping habits, young children's eating habits vary tremendously, although most children will show an identifiable pattern. This should be taken into account. Heavy eaters should be served more than light eaters, and each child's individual preferences generally should be followed. Except in the case of prolonged and repeated behavior that endangers the child's health, it is pointless to coax or cajole a child into eating something he does not want to eat or to withhold additional food from a child who is still hungry.

Also, some children are allergic to certain foods. Parents should be questioned about this when the children are enrolled, and any information about food allergies should be used in planning and serving meals. If a child is allergic to a common food that cannot simply be excluded from the school menu, staff should be sure that the child does not eat or drink it and that some appropriate substitute is provided.

EMERGENCIES

The preschool should have a dispensary or emergency room for use when a child is sick or injured. Ideally, this should be a small, specifically equipped room, although any room with a bed or cot and easily accessible emergency equipment is acceptable, even if it is normally used as an office or a storeroom. In any case, the room should be physically separated from the playrooms and other rooms used by the children, so that a sick or injured child can be treated without distractions and without disturbing the other children. In addition to a bed or cot, which should be permanently set up and ready for immediate use, the room should contain a fully stocked first-aid kit; information on first aid and emergency treatment of poisons, burns, and injuries posted on the wall; and up-to-date listing of the relevant emergency phone numbers for each child in the school. A specific staff person, trained in first aid, should be designated to take responsibility for action and decision making in emergencies. If this person is one of the teachers, the emergency plan should also specify who is to assume responsibility for that teacher's class, so that the teacher can be freed immediately to handle the emergency. If the child obviously needs medical attention, or even if there is serious question (possible broken bone, possible concussion, possible poisoning), steps should be taken to insure that the child gets medical treatment as quickly as possible. First, the child's doctor should be called and informed of the situation; his advice should be followed from that point. If the doctor directs that the child be brought to his office or to an emergency-care facility, the parents should be called immediately. This is because in many states doctors will not treat a child unless the parent is present and gives consent, even if the parent has previously filled out a medical

consent form. Thus, if the child is sick or injured seriously enough to require treatment, you must get not only him, but also one of his parents to a doctor.

If you must get the child to a doctor as quickly as possible, do not wait for the parent to come to you. Instead, call the parent, quickly explain the situation, and instruct him to meet you at the doctor's office or emergency facility. Then take the child there yourself as quickly as possible. If the parent needs transportation and the child's home is nearby or on the way to the medical facility, you can save time by stopping at the home to pick up the parent. These time-saving measures can be crucial in some cases.

Regardless of the specific sequence of action taken in a given case, a cardinal rule to remember whenever medical advice is needed is to call the doctor before calling the parent. The doctor will need to talk to you, not the parent, since you usually will be in a better position to tell him the facts of the situation. Also, the doctor must decide where the child should be examined and treated. By calling him first, you can get this information immediately and have it available when you call the parent. Calling the parent first in these situations would only waste time and would probably result in several unnecessary phone calls and discussions.

In less serious situations, where the child simply appears to be sick but not in immediate need of medical attention, it is better to call the parent and let the parent decide what to do. In this case, the child should be allowed to lie quietly on the bed or cot and wait for the parent to pick him up. Until the parent arrives, the child should be supervised constantly by a staff member to insure that his condition remains stable and that he does not become upset.

Be sure that you know your school's policies about first aid. Only doctors are authorized to administer prescription drugs, but a great many drugs can be purchased and used without prescription. Some schools allow their staff members to dispense such nonprescription drugs as cough lozenges, aspirin, and nasal sprays according to their own judgments; others require specific permission from the head of the school; and still others forbid this practice altogether.

OUTSIDE PLAY AREA

Many teachers and parents see outside play as analogous to recess in the elementary school—a break in activities without any important educational or developmental purpose. However, outside play should be seen as an important aspect of the preschool program, since such play is vital not only to the physical development but also to the social and intellectual development of preschool children. Thus, the outside play area should be thoughtfully designed and equipped, and its use should be planned as systematically as in-class learning activities are planned.

Every preschool should have an outside play area, and ideally it should be self-contained and reserved for the exclusive use of the preschool children. If the same play area must be shared by preschoolers and older children, outside play schedules should be staggered so that the preschoolers have exclusive use of the play area during the time they are using it. The ideal play area will vary with the age of the children and the degree of adult supervision of outside play. The size of the play area will naturally depend upon the available space. However, in planning from scratch, or in deciding how many children to accept in your preschool, recommended guidelines are 35 square feet of indoor space and 75 square feet of outdoor space per child.

One important feature, already mentioned, is that the play area should be completely fenced in. Another is that it should contain grass, sand, and other soft surfaces, as well as a hard surface. Ideally, the hard surface should be smooth cement rather than rough concrete or asphalt. Slippery and dangerous surfaces such as gravel should be avoided. Unless there is some reason to the contrary, running games such as tag and Red Rover should be played on the grass rather than on the hard surface, to minimize injuries. The hard surface should be used for wheeled toys, jumping rope, and certain ball games and circle games.

The grassy area should contain trees suitable for climbing and picnic tables that can double as climbing toys or imaginary forts, ships, and so on. Depending upon the situation, part of the soft surface might be set off as a garden, a digging patch with dirt and shovels, or an animal enclosure. Trees that are tall enough and have sturdy limbs can provide the support needed for swings made from auto or truck tires attached to a limb with a sturdy rope. Most children enjoy these improvised swings more than commercial ones, and as a rule they are safer, although even here care should be taken to see that the tire is only a foot or two from the ground and that the rope is short enough to prevent a child from accidentally crashing into the tree trunk. Also, swings should be away from traffic areas, so that children on swings do not endanger other children.

If building from scratch, bear the above in mind. Do not cut down trees or lay cement until decisions are made about what trees should remain and which areas should be maintained as soft surfaces. Also, put up the fence last, so that equipment can be trucked in easily.

There should be a large sandbox (6 feet square or larger), ideally made of poured cement or concrete blocks rather than wood, and sunk below ground level for the most part. The sandbox should have a cover that is easy to attach and remove, to protect it from animals and bad weather. Ideally, the sandbox should be located in the corner of the play area farthest from the entrance to the building, so that the amount of sand that children bring into the building on their bodies and clothing will be minimized. Also, the children should be taught to shake the sand out of their shoes and off of their bodies and clothes before leaving the sandbox. It is also convenient to have low, covered storage cabinets (which may also serve as benches) for sand toys near the sandbox.

Large-muscle playground equipment should be located on grass or another soft surface if possible. Where budgets permit, some of the newer types of outdoor equipment are worth purchasing. Thus, in addition to the traditional slide and jungle gym, you might consider tubes that the children can crawl through, tires, chain or rope ladders, and other kinds of obstacle course type equipment designed to resemble forts, ships, and so on. Outdoor water-play equipment is another possibility, although it is generally more troublesome and less valuable and useful than the items already mentioned. Portable water tables are useful for blowing bubbles, bathing dolls, sailing boats, and so forth.

The cement or other hard surface should be large enough for group circle games and for play with wheeled toys such as wagons, scooters, tricycles, and Big Wheels. To minimize confusion and possible injury, traffic patterns should be established to regulate the children's movement of wheeled toys so that they travel in a circle or other one-way patterns. Cross traffic should be minimized, and head-on collisions should be prevented entirely. Instructions about the use of wheeled toys should be reinforced by painting lines indicating traffic lanes and arrows or signs indicating the direction of movement. Furthermore, by using one color of paint to indicate traffic patterns for wheeled toys and another color for game markings such as circles, bases, and boundary lines, the hard-surface area may be laid out to facilitate large-group activities.

Wheeled toys should be stored in a weatherproof shed located on or near the hard surface where the toys will be used. This shed should have large sliding doors that are easy to open and close, allowing the children to remove and replace equipment themselves. Pictures or symbols on the back wall of the shed and/or lines or markings on the floor should be supplied to help the children remember where and how equipment items are properly stored. If the shed is large enough, doors can be made in each end and it can be situated in a traffic lane so that it functions as a tunnel for the children to ride through. Alternatively, such a shed can be used as a castle, fort, or on another basis for imaginative group play.

In addition to the large-muscle toys mentioned above, outdoor play should sometimes include small trucks or other vehicles (either used on the hard surface or in the sandbox), plastic horseshoes or ring-toss games, beanbags (both for throwing through holes in standup plywood targets and for games such as "hot potato"), and balls. Balls should be of the light, plastic type, and of relatively large diameters (6 to 12 inches). Young children can throw and catch such balls successfully, whereas they have trouble with smaller

Outside play areas need not be restricted to traditional commercial equipment. This is part of an obstacle course fashioned from wood, rope, and tires. The same play area includes a rope ladder similar to the rigging on a sailboat, a homemade fort, and a shaded quiet area.

127

balls such as baseballs and tennis balls and with odd-shaped balls such as footballs.

Some types of outdoor equipment are dangerous and should not be used with preschoolers except under conditions of careful and continuous supervision. Especially dangerous are high slides and other equipment that allow a child to climb high enough to injure himself seriously should he fall, trampolines, and swings. Swings are not particularly dangerous for the child who is swinging, but it is very common for another child to get kicked in the face or head or hit with the swing itself because he wandered too close to the swings without realizing it. If swings are present, the children should be carefully trained to stay clear of them, and the swings should be plastic (or the improvised tire type) rather than wood or metal. All in all, swings are not very useful. They take up too much space and provide little exercise or opportunities for imaginative play compared with other types of outdoor play equipment.

Other types of equipment are inappropriate for the preschool because the children are not yet old enough to use them appropriately or effectively, and they are more likely to frustrate than to please preschoolers. Included here are football, baseball, and basketball equipment, roller skates, peewee golf, and tiddly winks. The children will enjoy these when they are older, but preschoolers lack the size and coordination for them.

Ideally, the outside play area should exit onto a paved surface covered with an awning or some other protection. This area will be shaded from the sun and window glare, and at the same time will provide an outside area that can be used for activities in bad weather.

FURNISHINGS AND EQUIPMENT

The ideal preschool classroom in operation looks very different from the traditional elementary school classroom. First, the furnishings are much smaller, scaled to the sizes of the children. Second, although tables are present and are used for some activities, many activities take place on the floor. Third, the children seldom do things in unison or function as a single large group. More typically, they work and play singly or in small groups in the various activity centers that dot the classroom. Preschool activities are generally more informal, more individualized, and more action oriented than activities in elementary schools.

Like any good classroom, the ideal preschool classroom should have good lighting, good ventilation and temperature control, good sound absorption, and ample storage space. It should contain one or more bathrooms outfitted with toilets and sinks scaled to the size of the children in the room. Since so many activities take place on the floor, most of the floor should be carpeted (most teachers prefer to leave at least part of the room uncarpeted for activities such as art and meal times, which often involve spills). If a single large carpet is not available, smaller throw rugs or area rugs should be used in places where children typically play on the floor. Such smaller rugs should be of the nonskid variety, of course, to avoid accidents.

The room should be located on the ground floor, near an entrance. It should also be convenient to the outside play area and the cafeteria (if the children eat outside the room). The room should be free of heavy wooden desks and tables, and of traditional student desks or desk chairs. Instead, it should be furnished with light plastic tables and chairs that can be easily moved around or stacked.

Light, easily portable equipment of this sort allows the teacher much greater flexibility in using the available space to meet immediate needs than would be possible if stationary or heavy, bulky equipment were present. Unless there is an abundance of space, even the teacher's desk should be removed if it is of the large, heavy type that takes up space without providing much functional usefulness. Instead of such a desk, the teacher can use cabinets or shelving built along the wall for storage, and can keep a small table with a few drawers for writing and record keeping.

Everything in the room should be planned with the ages and sizes of the children in mind. This means child-sized sinks and toilets, small chairs and low tables, and shelving and cubbyholes for storage that extend down to the floor. Most of this storage space should line or be built into the walls, although it should be supplemented with portable bookcases and cubbyhole shelving that can be used as dividers between activity areas. Tables come in various sizes and shapes, and should be selected according to the sizes of the children and the type of program used by the center. In general, rectangular tables seating one child on each end and three or four along each side are best for general purposes, but triangular or crescent-shaped tables might be preferable for certain kinds of programs. The latter tables can be combined to make semicircular or even completely circular seating arrangements with the teacher seated in the middle, in position to interact directly with each child seated around the table without getting up. This arrangement can be very convenient when a single teacher must serve food to a large group of children or when the children are doing table work that requires periodic help or inspection from the teacher.

The room should be stocked with a quantity of good quality educational toys and manipulative equipment. Although preschoolers can benefit from and should be exposed to stories and verbal instruction, they learn primarily from experience, from actively manipulating objects in their environment. Thus, the toys and manipulative equipment available for the children should be selected with care, because in a very real sense these items represent the basic curriculum of the preschool. The ideal kinds of toys and equipment to purchase are those that:

1. Are interesting and enjoyable to the children
2. Are safe (no glass, sharp edges, lead-based paint, pieces small enough to invite swallowing and choking, or other potential safety hazards)
3. Are sturdy and durable
4. Are flexible enough to be used for a variety of purposes, thus inviting repeated use and fostering creativity in play
5. Invite active manipulation and provide for automatic self-correction, so that the children learn as they play
6. Are useful in teaching recognition and discrimination of size, shape, color, number, texture, and other basic concepts or sensory aspects of objects.

A great variety of toys meet all or most of these criteria, and most of them are relatively inexpensive. Figure 6.2 lists representative toys and equipment appropriate for children of different ages.

The usefulness of a toy or equipment item depends upon the degree to which it meets the criteria outlined above, not its price, novelty, or the amount of advertising it receives. Many quite expensive toys, including most of the new ones introduced each Christmas season, can be used in only one way. Such toys might be popular for a short time, but once the novelty wears off, they usually gather dust on the shelf. Meanwhile, more flexible toys such as blocks, formboards and pegboards, dolls and puppets, and small vehicles will be used continually throughout the year. Thus, how often and in what ways the children use it are usually the best clues to the value of a toy or equipment item. However, some toys may not be used often because they are unfamiliar to the children. In these cases, unfamiliarity rather than the toy itself might be the reason that the toy is not used. To find out, demonstrate to the children how the toy is used and encourage them to use it on their own. If they are interested in the toy, they will begin to use it once they know what to do with it.

Large-muscle toys ordinarily should not be kept in the classroom, although where possible there should be a large room or lobby that can be used for large-muscle activities on rainy days. This can be done by getting out balance beams, exercise mats, climbers, and so on.

In any case, large wheeled toys, rocker boats, seesaws, balls, and the like should be used outside, but not in the classroom where they are likely to produce unsafe and disruptive play. Although the preschool classroom should stress active manipulation of equipment and learning by doing, this should not extend to running, climbing, and other large-muscle activities that require more open space and are best reserved for outside play periods.

The room should also be equipped with a phonograph and/or a tape recorder, and with a variety of records suitable for use in musical activities with the children. If the children are members of an ethnic or racial minority

FIGURE 6.2

Representative toys and equipment appropriate for 3-, 4-, and 5-year-olds.

A. Sensorimotor development

3-year olds	*4-year olds*	*5-year olds*
Montessori Self-corrective Equipment	Puzzles	Puzzles
Blocks	Beads	Lego Blocks
Simple Puzzles	Large Parquetry Blocks	Tinker Toys
Beads, Snap Blocks	Picture Matching	Lincoln Logs
Number Sorter	Dominoes	Blocks
Form Boards	Blocks	Matching and Discrimination
Matching Objects	Water Table	Inch Cube Blocks
Water Table	Sand	Water Table
Sand		Sand

B. Fantasy play

3-year olds	*4-year olds*	*5-year olds*
Adult Dress Up Clothes	Props, Costumes for Role Play	Props for Grocery Store
Costumes, Uniforms	Doll Houses	Props for Fire or Police Stations
Kitchen Corner	Garages, Airports, etc.	Barbie Dolls and Props
Play Animals	Doctor, Nurse Sets	
Dolls	Puppets	
	Dolls	

C. Verbal, school skills

3-year olds	*4-year olds*	*5-year olds*
Songs and listening games	Magnetic letters, numbers	Cuisenaire Rods
Records	Chalkboards	Printing name
Simple picture books	Books for teacher reading	Books for independent use
Show and tell	Very simple table games	Card games
	Finger plays	Simple table games
	Tape recorder listening center	Riddles, jokes
		Finger plays
		Tape recorder listening center

D. Gross motor

3-year olds	*4-year olds*	*5-year olds*
Tricycles	Big wheels	Roller skates
Wagons	Wagons	Tools, wood scraps
Climbing bars	Climbing bars	Climbing bars
Slides	Slides	Slides
Sand play	Sand play	Balls and ball games
Bean bags	Scooter	Scooter
	Tumbling	Tumbling
	Balls and ball games	

E. Arts and crafts, music

3-year olds	*4-year olds*	*5-year olds*
Easels, paint	Easels, paint	Easels, paint
Crayons	Crayons, felt pens	Crayons, felt pens
Finger paints	Finger paints	Finger paints
Rhythm instruments	Musical instruments	Musical instruments
Play dough	Play dough, clay	Play dough, clay

group, songs and dances reflecting their cultural heritage should be included. With older children, audio equipment can be supplemented with earphones and used in listening centers that contain activities planned to foster language development and direction-following abilities.

With the sophisticated children's programming available today, a television can be a valuable asset in preschool classrooms, provided that it is judiciously used. It should be situated a few feet from the floor, so that the children do not have to crane their necks or squint in order to see it. Also, it should be used only during specific time periods to watch selected programs if it is to be maximally useful. If turned on haphazardly or left on continually, it will cease to have much usefulness as an educational tool, functioning instead simply as background noise or even as a substitute for the teacher.

Each child in the class should have his own hook for clothing and his own cubbyhole for storing possessions. Both of these should be low enough so that the child can use them without help. Each should be marked with the child's name, partially to promote quick identification and partially to encourage and reinforce name recognition by the child. In addition, the room should have adequate storage space, which is always at a premium in preschool classrooms. Shelving and cubbyholes along the walls, supplemented by portable shelf space used as area dividers, can be used to display equipment meant for the children's use. These must be close to the floor and otherwise sufficiently accessible so that the children can remove and return toys and equipment on their own. In addition to this storage space for equipment used by the children, teachers should have storage space for extra supplies, equipment not presently in use, cleanup and maintenance equipment, and personal belongings. These items can be stored on shelves or in cabinets placed high enough along the walls to be out of the reach of the children or in cabinets or closets that can be locked for safety.

Other items always at a premium in a preschool are containers and materials for use in arts and crafts projects. Teachers should develop the habit of saving such materials, and should ask the children's parents to save them also. Containers and other objects that ordinarily would be thrown away can be put to good use in classrooms. For example, metal cans, berry baskets, and cigar boxes all make excellent containers (especially if they are painted or decorated with contact paper to make them attractive as well as functional). Styrofoam meat trays can be painted on or broken into pieces for collages. Similarly, string, rubber bands, nails, wood scraps, sandpaper scraps, old paint brushes, pieces of ribbon, spools, cardboard tubes from bathroom tissue and wax paper rolls, and other candidates for the household garbage can should be saved and brought to preschool where they are needed and useful as arts and crafts equipment.

Free supplies can also be obtained from commercial sources. Ice cream

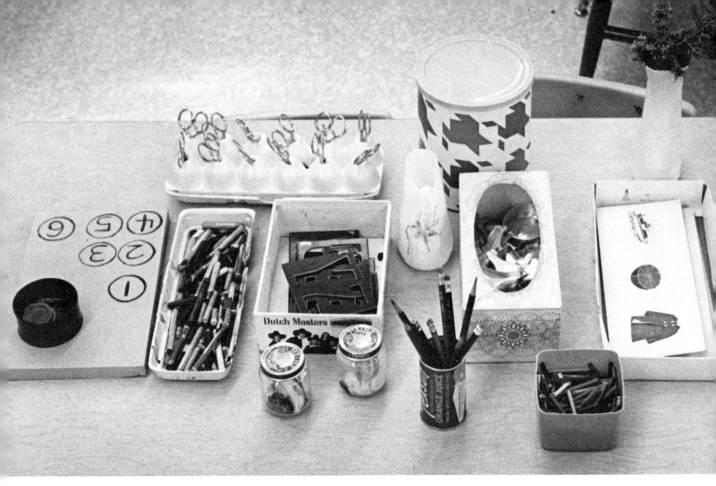

Examples of how household containers can come in handy in the preschool are shown on the table.

stores usually give away large ice cream containers, which make excellent wastebaskets and containers for items such as blocks. Large quantites of wood scraps are usualiy available for the asking at lumberyards. Boxes and containers of all kinds can be obtained from a variety of stores and businesses. The wise teacher will take advantage of these resources and enlist the help of the children's parents in supplementing the equipment and supplies budget in this manner.

Certain other suggestions about furnishings and equipment will be made in the following section when individual learning-activity centers are described.

ACTIVITY CENTERS

The preschool looks strikingly different from the traditional elementary school, in which much classroom space is taken up by desks or tables where the children work on assignments. The preschool does contain tables and chairs for use by the children during certain activities, but most activities will be conducted individually or in small groups in learning centers located

133

An open-space arrangement; note how shelves and other dividers are used to create identifiable activity areas along the walls and in the center of the room.

around the classroom. Usually, the children will not be assigned to a particular desk or place at a table and expected to stay there. Instead, they will be given opportunities to use equipment located in all parts of the room (subject to minimal, necessary rules), so that their location at a given time will depend on what activity they have chosen to pursue.

A well-designed and equipped preschool classroom is divided into functional activity centers. When this is done properly, the result is immediately obvious even to the casual observer. Dividers, area rugs, portable shelving, and other items that define the boundaries within and between areas are arranged so that the observer sees a room in which the available space has been arranged to create a variety of separate and easily identified activity centers. The impression gained is one of an orderly, well-planned environment differentiated into functional subunits, not simply a large space randomly or haphazardly filled with equipment. The number and size of the activity centers within a given classroom will depend upon the size of the room and the number and ages of the children. Some or all of the following should be included.

Small-Group Activity Areas　These areas should be set up for activities in which the teacher works with a group of children. Where systematic instruction is involved and the teacher wishes to minimize distractions to the children in the group, this area should be located in a quiet corner of the room and partially enclosed by bookcases, shelves, cabinets, or other dividers. These should be tall enough to prevent the children in the group from being affected by events taking place in other places in the room, but not so tall as to prevent the teacher from being able to monitor what is going on all around the room while working with the small group. The area should contain a table large enough to accommodate the number of children ordinarily taught within it, as well as enough chairs (if extra chairs are not available, they will have to be brought into this area for activity periods). A small bookcase or table should be placed near the teacher's chair to keep materials handy and ready for use during instruction times. The seating arrangement should be such that the teacher faces the rest of the class and can keep an eye on what is happening around the room, while the children in the group sit facing the teacher with their backs toward the rest of the class, lessening the chances of their being distracted. If more than one teacher is present and more than one small group is active at the same time, an additional small-group area will be needed. In this case, the two areas should be in opposite corners or at least on opposite sides of the room. This will minimize the degree to which the two activities interfere with each other, and it will also place one teacher on each side of the room, making it easier to handle management and control problems quickly and nondisruptively (see Chapter 12).

Book Area

Books, magazines, and other materials for the children to look through should be placed in this area. Ideally, the materials should be on a display rack so that their covers, not just their spines, are easily visible. This feature is necessary if the children are to be able to quickly and easily find the books they are looking for, since preschoolers (who have not yet learned to read) use the colors, sizes, and covers of books to identify them. If a display rack is not available, order one or have one constructed (they can be cheaply and easily made from plywood). In the meantime, record racks, bookcases, or small tables may be used as substitutes.

The book area should be made as appealing as possible. Books should be displayed attractively and rotated frequently. In addition to perennial favorites, books on display at a given time should include those concerned with relevant holidays, current events, and topics currently being discussed or investigated in classroom activities. Relevance of this sort will help produce interest in the books, and the books will help reinforce and expand the knowledge gained in other activities.

The book area is a quiet area and should be set up next to a small-group area, to help minimize the probability of distracting noise. In addition to the books themselves, the book area should contain furniture designed to clarify its status as an independent area. It should be a functional area designed for use, not merely a bookrack set against the wall. In addition to stocking the bookrack with appropriate books and displaying them attractively, teachers can make the area inviting by including chairs and a small table or a small rug that the children can sit or lie on when looking through books. Rocking chairs are especially useful in book areas.

Encouraging independent use of this area often can be reinforced by having the teacher conduct story time in the book area. The children can be seated on chairs or on the floor while the teacher reads a book selected from the bookrack. Use of the area can also be encouraged by teachers or other adults in the classroom who take time to come to the area themselves and question children who are looking through books, or who pick out a book themselves and begin to go through it with interested children. This type of modeling is likely to increase independent and self-initiated use of the book area by the children. For some books (especially the very popular ones), it is useful to have two or more copies. This not only will minimize squabbles over who gets to use a given book first; it will also allow two or more children to look through the same book simultaneously, an opportunity which often heightens interest and leads to much discovery learning.

Manipulative-Play Areas

The room should contain several areas where the children can play or work with various kinds of toys and equipment. For example, one area might contain equipment ordinarily used at a table, such as puzzles, pegboards, beads, or formboards. This area should contain bookcases or shelves containing the equipment, as well as a table and some chairs for the children to use while playing. If the table and chairs cannot be located in the area itself, they should be as close to it as possible in order to minimize the distance between the place where the equipment is stored and the place where it is ordinarily used.

Equipment such as blocks, trucks, nested boxes or bowls used for making towers, and any other equipment that is heavy and/or usually used on the floor, should be stored on low shelves where it can be easily taken out and replaced by the children. Very large equipment such as blocks or boxes can be stacked on the floor, although the storage place should be clearly marked. Again, such equipment should be stored as near as possible to the place where it is ordinarily used. Area rugs should be provided (if the area is not already carpeted) for equipment that is usually used on the floor.

Symbolic-Play Areas

The room should contain one or more symbolic-play areas where children can make believe or act out roles. For example, this area could contain clothing items and simple costumes. Almost any kind of clothing can be useful, since the children will enjoy dressing up in clothing that they do not ordinarily wear (particularly adult clothing). However, uniforms that make for ready identification and role playing (fireman, policeman, astronaut, cowboy, nurse, doctor, gasoline station attendant, bride and groom, soldier, etc.) are especially useful.

Adult role taking can be fostered by providing a housekeeping area containing a stove, refrigerator, table, dishes, and utensils. This setting and associated props promote not only role taking of adult behavior at meal times, but adult role taking generally. Such activity can help a child to fulfill some of his wishes symbolically, to work through some of his fears and negative emotions, and to reduce his egocentrism by allowing him to assume the perspectives of persons other than himself.

Another good setting for role playing is a store outfitted with items to purchase (canned goods, cereal boxes, etc., for a food store) and a checkout counter with a cash register. Older children can apply numerical concepts here by using play money and counting out change.

Other role-play settings can be established less elaborately with the use of a few simple props. A desk with a telephone, some policemen's badges and hats, and an area designated as a lockup can serve as a police station, for example, and other sets of props and make believe can be used to create fire stations, barber shops, beauty parlors, medical and dental offices, and other settings that are familiar and/or interesting to the children. Sometimes just a few simple suggestions from the teacher will be all the children need to create the setting and act out the drama on their own. The appropriateness of settings, of course, will vary somewhat with age. Younger children usually are more interested in settings with which they are familiar, such as the home and the store. Older children, in contrast, might be much more interested in playing spaceship.

Arts and Crafts Area

An area should be set aside for art work involving paint and for crafts projects that require cutting, pasting, modeling with clay, or other activities that might become messy. Ideally, this area should be situated near a sink, so that needed cleanup materials are handy. It also should be located in an uncarpeted part of the room, since the inevitable spills associated with this area will ruin a carpet. If there is no sink in the room, a bucket of water and a sponge or rag should be available whenever are projects likely to create immediate cleanup needs are in progress. In addition to shelf space for paints, brushes, paper, scissors (with blunted ends), paste, and other art or construction materials, the area should include smocks (mothers' old blouses are ideal) for the children to wear over their clothing when painting. Easels to paint on will be needed, and unless the room is large and the art area protected from traffic, the easels should be collapsible so that they can be stored out of the way when not in use.

Problems due to accidents can be minimized by using foresight in the purchase of materials for this area. Paints should be restricted to watercolors and other paints that are completely washable; clay or play dough should be stored in airtight containers so that its pliable texture can be maintained; art equipment should be scaled to the children's sizes and physical needs (for example, young children can handle thick crayons and thick-handled paint brushes, but will have trouble using equipment with very thin handles); and paste or glue used should be the type that dissolves easily when washed. Also, young children should not be given projects that require sustained and precise cutting (because of their limited development in fine motor movement and eye–hand coordination, using scissors with precision is extremely difficult for them).

Display Areas

The room should contain one or more areas with materials for the children to inspect or manipulate. These would include such things as animals and fish, rock collections, plants (perferably individually planted and cared for by the children themselves), leaf collections, models or displays of automobiles, trains, airplanes or rocket ships, and the like.

With older preschoolers, display areas can be set up as math, science, or nature areas. Ideally, these should include objects for the children to inspect or manipulate in order to discover mathematical or scientific knowledge for themselves. A lesson or some form of structured introduction to the use of the center may be needed in order to familiarize the children with its possibilities, but once they clearly understand how the center can be used, they should be encouraged to do so on their own.

Large-Group Activity Area

One fairly large area of the room, preferably not covered by a rug, should be reserved for games, music, dancing, group exercises, and other activities in which all of the children might participate together. To facilitate certain games, it might be helpful to paint circles, dots, or lines on the floor, or to use tape for such outlines. In any case, group games, dancing and musical activities, and large-muscle group activities should be included in the program, and a section of the room will be needed that is large enough for these activities to take place. If the room is too small to maintain a large-group activities area on a permanent basis, try to arrange it so that an area can be constructed very quickly by moving a few tables or other easily portable furniture or equipment items.

Special Learning Centers

In addition to the above, which should be found in all or most preschools, certain preschools may have the equipment to provide special kinds of learning centers, especially if they are dealing with older preschoolers. For example, listening centers can be set up using language masters or tape recorders with headsets for the children to listen to recorded information or instructions, perhaps in conjunction with some form of exercise that gives them an opportunity to practice or apply what they are learning as they listen. Other special learning centers can be set up through multimedia displays on a topic of interest to the children. As with every learning center, the ideal setup includes objects or equipment that the child can physically manipulate to get feedback and experiment with for himself, rather than merely things for

A special discovery area resulted from a class visit by a father who worked for the telephone company. These boys are enjoying exploring some telephone parts the father lent to the teacher after the visit.

139

him to look at. Remember, preschoolers learn best when they get direct, firsthand experience, especially when it involves manipulating or experimenting with objects in their environment.

Other Classroom Areas   Additional areas exist in the classroom which are not centers as such, but which are regularly used for a particular purpose at certain times during the day. These include eating areas (if eating is done in the classroom), sleeping or resting areas, isolation areas to be used when children become disruptive or aggressive enough to warrant their removal from the group (see Chapter 12), teachers' desks or tables, and the like. The size and appearance of these classroom areas will vary with the ages of the children, the type of program, and other variables, but the principles described in the section below should be kept in mind in determining where these areas are located in relation to one another.

PLACEMENT OF ACTIVITY CENTERS AND OTHER CLASSROOM AREAS   It has already been mentioned that the classroom should be clearly differentiated into recognizable areas and centers to help provide an organized, structured environment for the children. There is no single ideal classroom arrangement, even for classrooms of identical design. However, several useful principles can be put forth to aid teachers in planning their classroom arrangement for maximal safety and efficiency.

1. Classroom traffic should be minimized, and the traffic that does exist should flow freely.

The major method for minimizing traffic is to locate storage facilities for toys and equipment items as close as possible to the classroom areas in which they are ordinarily used, thus minimizing the distances that children must move the equipment when they take it out or return it. Freely flowing traffic is maintained largely by avoiding cross traffic and by eliminating obstacles from traffic lanes. Undesirable cross traffic would be created, for example, if two large groups of children situated on opposite sides of the room were asked to switch places at precisely the same time by moving across the same floor space. Bumping, jostling, and possibly more serious disruptions would be virtually certain to occur under such circumstances. Such problems can be avoided by staggering the flow of traffic from one location to another and/or by having children use alternate, indirect routes to move from place to place so that their paths do not cross directly.

Frequently used traffic lanes should be wide enough so that the children do not regularly bump and jostle one another or bang into classroom furniture. Traffic lanes leading to doorways, washrooms, drinking fountains, or other heavily used pathways should be free of obstacles. Narrow passageways that cause children to bump into each other should be widened. If this is not possible, a one-way pattern of traffic flow should be designed and taught to the children, so that cross traffic in these narrow passageways can be eliminated. It may be useful to reinforce this teaching by putting up signs and arrows, especially when the children are first learning the traffic pattern.

The main rationale for concern with traffic patterns is safety and efficiency. If problems in either of these areas arise, traffic patterns might be a contributing factor. For example, if jostling and bumping is a continual problem in the class, it is likely that undesirable patterns of cross traffic and/or narrow passageways are involved. Similarly, if certain equipment keeps getting lost or frequently gets spilled, it may be that the equipment is stored too far away from the area where the children usually use it (also, the containers may be inappropriate). In any case, careful planning to insure optimal traffic patterns can help maximize efficiency and minimize injuries.

2. The noise levels typically generated in a given activity center or area should be taken into account in determining where it is placed in the classroom.

For example, if more than one teacher is present, it frequently happens that both teachers simultaneously lead activities with different groups of children. The activity centers should be separated from one another, preferably in diagonal corners of the room, to minimize interference. Also, activity centers that are typically noisy, such as the block/construction area or the role-play/make-believe area, should be kept away from centers that involve activities demanding close concentration by the children. Activity centers that do not involve as much noise, such as the book area or various discovery centers, should be located near activity areas that demand high levels of concentration. Placement of centers with these principles in mind will help maximize each child's independence and help minimize the frequency with which teachers must stop to warn noisy children to quiet down. Needless to say, sound-absorbent walls and ceilings are also very helpful in minimizing the disruption caused by the inevitable noise that active children create.

3. Teachers should always be situated so that they are facing the room and can monitor activities other than those in the immediate group with which they are working.

This is especially important in activity centers involving teacher presentations to small groups of children. At these times, the teacher's back should face the wall, so that she can see what is going on all around the classroom. Meanwhile, the small group of children should be seated with their backs to the rest of the class, facing the teacher, thereby minimizing the frequency of distraction and inattention.

4. Storage facilities and cleanup equipment should be located with an eye toward maximum efficiency and independence on the part of the children.

Equipment should be easy to take out and replace, and should be located close to the area in which it will be used. Arts and crafts projects or other messy activities should take place near the sink if there is one in the classroom, and preparations for any activity likely to involve significant cleanup should include appropriate cleanup materials as well as the equipment for the activity itself. In general, maintaining a neat and clean classroom environment should be a continuing responsibility. If both teachers and children learn to replace regularly any equipment taken out before moving on to new activities or taking out new equipment, and to clean up any spills or accidents immediately after they occur, classroom maintenance will be a relatively minor and painless activity rather than an onerous chore.

5. Lighting should be taken into account in locating classroom areas.

Ideally, of course, all areas of the classroom should be adequately lit. Where this is not true, however, be sure to locate activity areas requiring careful visual inspection or discrimination near windows or lights, locating areas which do not require such fine visual discrimination in the darker areas of the room.

6. The flooring should promote maximal safety and quiet.

As noted previously, most of the classroom floor should be covered with carpeting or at least with nonskid area rugs, although most teachers prefer to schedule such activities as arts and crafts projects, meals, and large-group activities in uncarpeted areas. Uncarpeted areas should be cleaned and well cared for, but extremely slick surfaces likely to produce falls should be avoided. Rugs or carpeting are especially important for muffling noise. Large wooden blocks banging on a hardwood floor can be irritatingly disruptive, whereas these same blocks are not nearly as noisy on a carpet or area rug.

7. Use furnishings to help border and define activity centers and areas.

In general, activity centers should be located along the walls of the room, leaving the center open for traffic and for use in large-group activities. Wall space in a preschool classroom is a precious commodity, and its use should be carefully planned to insure that the teacher gets the most out of the available resources. Creation of activity centers is vastly simplified if shelving or cubbyholes are built into the walls or along the walls, since here all that is required to create centers are occasional dividers (portable bookcases, desks, tables, etc.), along with natural borderlines such as doorways, sinks, and drinking fountains. Where centers cannot be set off with portable bookcases or other physical barriers, area rugs are useful to provide a boundary line for a given center. Such rugs will help give the centers some physical definition in the eyes of the children, and, if the children are encouraged to stay on the rug when using the area, will help prevent the area from spreading or spilling over into adjacent areas. Schematic representations of preschool classroom designs that embody the above principles are presented in Figures 6.3 and 6.4.

OTHER SAFETY AND EFFICIENCY CONSIDERATIONS

In addition to the points already mentioned, there are several steps that teachers can take to maximize efficiency and safety and promote independence on the part of the children in their everyday classroom activities. First, any situation that produces crowding should be avoided; these include: standing in lines, "funneling" of children into dead-end spaces where they have to turn around and push their way back again, obstructions preventing easy access to cubbyholes and other storage spaces frequently used by the children, and so forth. Whenever the entire group has to do the same thing, try to arrange a staggered schedule so that lines and waiting are avoided. For example, if the group is to clean up the classroom and go to the restroom before leaving for a meal, it is usually best to involve everyone in the cleanup and have the children go to the restroom one or two at a time. This is better than lining up the group outside the restroom where they must idly stand waiting their turns (these "dead time" situations often produce rowdiness and disruption), or trying to send everyone to the restroom at once.

Sharp corners, low-hanging or jutting objects, or any other safety hazards of this sort should be eliminated. Shelves or other features of the walls that protrude at the children's eye level are particularly dangerous and should be eliminated. Also, care should be taken not to place tables or other large, heavy objects in traffic lanes where children are likely to bump into them.

If it is necessary or desirable that the children line up (for example, lining up at a door in preparation for leaving the room), be sure that the line does not block important traffic lanes and is generally out of the way of the other children who are not yet ready to join the line. Thus, it would be ideal to have the children line up along a wall or in front of an activity center that is not in use at the moment, whereas it would cause problems if they lined up in front of restroom doors or cubbyholes where other children would have to break through the line in order to enter the restroom or get at their cubbyholes. It also helps if the children are taught simple locomotion rules, such as keeping to the right in halls and passageways and lining up in convenient and efficient ways. It may help to draw or tape a line along the floor for the children to use as a marker when they get in line. Although teachers should not lose sight of the fact that forming lines and other school customs are merely means to achieve efficient and safe movement of groups of children under crowded conditions, it is important to train the children to form

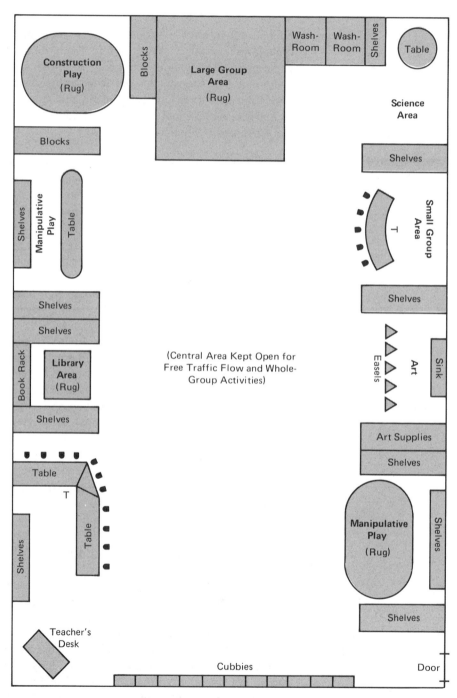

FIGURE 6.3
A rectangular classroom plan.

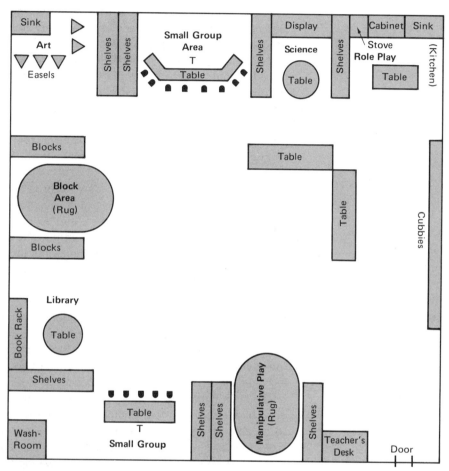

FIGURE 6.4
A smaller, more-crowded classroom. (The center area can be used for whole-group activities, moving large tables if necessary.)

the habit of walking rather than running in halls and moving in single- or double-file lines rather than expanding to fill the hallway. Lines are a necessary evil to help prevent the injuries that result when large numbers of children are milling around and/or running in hallways. Lines are especially important for preschoolers in schools where older children attend, as the likelihood of an injury is greater. An older and much larger child could severely injure a small preschooler simply by accidentally running into him in a hallway. During field trips or other situations where the group is moving in unfamiliar environments, it is important to keep the children close together and to see that the teacher aide or some other responsible adult stays at the end of the line to keep children from straggling behind or getting lost. Getting lost in a strange place can be a very traumatic experience for a preschooler, and it should be prevented if at all possible.

Safety can also be promoted in the way that equipment is stored. Heavy objects should be stored on the floor or on the bottom shelves, so that they do not have to be lifted and carried by the children. Containers should be light and small, and should not have sharp corners or edges or hard-to-remove covers. Any equipment that the children are expected to work with on their own should be stored on shelves or tables low enough for them to get at without reaching or straining upwards. Accidents are especially likely when children are forced to reach up over their heads to take out or replace an equipment item. Safety hazards such as sharp scissors, paper cutters, sharp knives, poisons (this category includes many common cleaners), permanent stains or inks, and so on, should be stored where the children cannot reach them. If children are allowed to handle scissors, they should be taught to hold them with the points facing downward and the scissors enclosed within their fists to minimize the dangers of dropping the scissors or of injuring someone with them.

**PROMOTING
INDEPENDENCE**

Several aspects of classroom arrangement and equipment storage help promote independence in the children by allowing them to handle most of their needs on their own without help from the teacher. This is also efficient from the standpoint of saving the teacher's time, of course, but its value in promoting the child's independence is also worthy of comment.

The main consideration involved is making sure that furniture and facilities are child sized and that equipment is stored low enough for the children to be able to take it out and remove it safely and easily. This means child-sized toilets, sinks, tables, and chairs, as well as low blackboards, easels, and lots of bookcases and shelving that extend to the floor. Toys and equipment should be neatly placed on the shelves, spaced sufficiently apart so that a glance at a given shelf or bookcase immediately reveals an orderly arrangement rather than an impression that the items have been haphazardly piled on the shelf. Each toy and equipment item should have its own specific place for storage, preferably marked with words and/or symbols to help the children remember. It may also be helpful to paint lines or use tape to subdivide shelves into areas for specific items. These visual aids will help remind the children that each item has its place and will make it easy for them to locate desired equipment and replace it in its proper place when they finish using it.

Small items such as beads, inch cubes, parquetry blocks, crayons, and the like should be stored in several small containers rather than one or two large ones. This will simplify sharing of the materials and will minimize spilling accidents and squabbles over access to them, which often occur

In the picture above, we see blocks and toys stored neatly and safely, encouraging the children to replace items properly. Below, the same shelves are shown in disarray. Their sloppy appearance is likely to tempt the children to replace items carelessly, and some aspects are potential hazards.

when several children are asked to share materials stored in a single large container.

Meals and snacks should also be planned so that the children can function as independently as possible. Ideally, they should serve themselves or carry their trays to a central serving place. They should be able to handle the rest of the meal on their own, including eating, cleaning up, and disposing of utensils and dishes after the meal. Children should also be encouraged to handle snacks independently as soon as they are able. Athough it may be necessary or advisable in a given group to have a standard snack time, many teachers have achieved gratifying results when they allowed the children to get their snacks individually on their own when they felt like it (after setting up rules about the number of snacks that the children may eat in one day, of course).

Be alert for ways to change your behavior to help further the children's independence. Two clues to areas where improvement might be needed are the frequency of accidents and the frequency with which children come to you for help. If certain kinds of accidents happen repeatedly, it is likely that an adjustment in classroom-traffic patterns or equipment-storage procedures will help reduce the accident rate. Similarly, if children repeatedly are coming to you with the same request for help with a task, you may be able to devise a procedure that will allow them to handle the problem partially or completely on their own. In fact, if they cannot do so, it may well be that the task is beyond their present capabilities and somewhat inappropriate for them.

CLASSROOM DECORATION

Classroom decorations are largely a personal matter, in which the teacher uses creative talents and personal taste to produce an attractive "home" for the class. Since the specifics of classroom decoration are largely a matter of the teacher's taste and personal creativity, there is little to be said about them. However, there are several general principles that should be kept in mind in decorating a classroom, regardless of what particular kinds of decorations are used.

1. Although there is a place for purely decorative items, classroom decorations should be functional as well as esthetically pleasing.

For example, the decorations in a given classroom might include artwork done by the children and put up for display, pictures of items that children are presently learning about, displays stressing letters, numbers, colors, shapes, animals, birds, or other categories or concepts that the children are learning, and the like. Displays that combine words with pictures or cutouts are especially useful for helping children learn to recognize letters and words and associate them with their meanings.

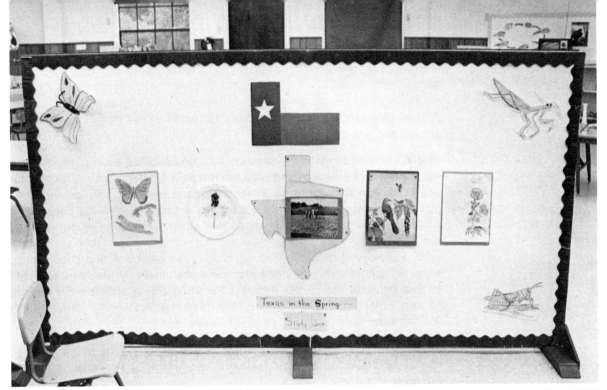

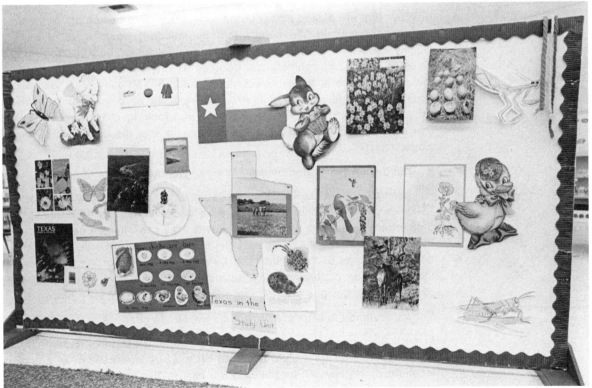

The picture above shows a well-designed and well–spaced wallboard display. The picture below shows how the effect of the display is lost when the wallboard is cluttered.

149

2. Wall displays are most attractive and functional when they are properly spaced and uncluttered.

Displays should be distinctly separate from one another, so that the intervening wall or other background area serves as a frame to set off the display and helps call the children's attention to it. This effect can be enhanced by using borders to surround the display. Contrasted with these uncluttered, well-framed displays are decorations that cover virtually an entire wall and run into one another so that they are not easily recognizable as discrete units. People in general and young children in particular find it difficult to focus on such displays, and the functional usefulness that is intended might be lost because the clutter distracts the child and makes it more difficult for him to focus on a single item. Thus, wall displays should reflect quality and not quantity.

3. Any wall displays that are meant to be inspected closely by the children should be placed at or near their eye level rather than higher up, at the eye level of an adult.

Displays that are placed higher up on the walls should be cutouts or pictures that do not contain fine details that the children would have to inspect closely to see and appreciate. Easels, the backs of bookcases, and the sides of desks and cabinets can be used as display areas to help increase the display space at the eye level of the children. You can get an idea about what a display looks like to the child simply by walking around the room on your knees or by sitting on the floor and looking at it. If you find that you cannot see what you want the children to see, the display is probably placed too high.

4. Wall displays can often be used to identify activity areas.

For example, housekeeping pictures could be placed on the wall above the housekeeping area, and cutouts showing books above the book area. With older children, the wall space in an activity area can often be used to convey information, such as the number of children allowed in the area or an indication of the kinds of things that can be done with some of the equipment in the area (using pictures or pictorial directions for making things with construction toys, designs that can be constructed with parquetry blocks, etc.).

5. Bear in mind the safeness of your classroom decorations.

In particular, beware of potted plants and similar decorative items that can easily topple over on a child if placed on top of a bookcase or in a similar location where they can be pulled down easily. Also, mobiles or other hanging decorations should not extend down far enough to pose a hazard to children.

Following the above guidelines as much as possible, teachers should decorate their classrooms according to their personal interests and tastes. You will often find it enjoyable and rewarding to involve the children in this enterprise by, for instance, planning an arts and crafts project that will produce decorations to be hung up on the walls when completed. These activities not only provide the children with a sense of accomplishment, but also allow them to take part in the planning and implementation of the decoration of their classroom. This helps instill a sense of pride in and identity with the classroom, and will probably also help build a sense of responsibility for maintaining it.

Also, teachers should pay attention to the way they themselves are dressed. Clothing should be attractive as well as functional (children usually like bright, cheerful colors), and teachers should model clothing and grooming habits that they would like to teach the children.

OVERCOMING PROBLEMS So far we have been discussing an ideal preschool classroom, speaking at times as if the teacher were designing the classroom from scratch. This is rarely the case, of course; most teachers are assigned to classrooms that are already constructed and equipped, and many of these are a far cry from the ideal delineated above. Even so, no matter how far removed your classroom may be from the ideal, there are always many steps that you can take to improve it if you are oriented toward change and willing to expend the necessary time and energy.

First, with regard to any particular change that you see as desirable or necessary, begin by asking your supervisor if the change can be made. In many cases you will be able to get changes made simply by asking for them. Where this is not possible, there are still many things that an individual teacher can do to improve the classroom. Some of these are suggested below.

If storage space is insufficient, low bookcases or shelving to go along the walls can be obtained or constructed cheaply and quickly. You may be able to enlist the help of one or more fathers of children in your group for this task; a talented carpenter or handyman can construct simple shelving or bookcases easily and quickly. Such shelving is very cheap when made from wood scraps or unfinished wood. Although it may not be as attractive as more expensively constructed shelving or built-in shelving, it is just as functional and effective. Attractiveness can be enhanced by covering the shelves with masonite paper or similar material.

Storage problems can be eased through methods other than adding shelf space. One way is to create a storage corner in the room by blocking off space with other furniture. Crowded rooms can be made to appear much less crowded by storing infrequently used items in such a blocked-off storage area where they are out of the way and not cluttering up precious shelf space. Similarly, items not used very often or items that are rotated in and out of the room at varying periods can be kept in storage space outside the room. This may entail some inconvenience, but it is preferable to having a cluttered room. Although not useful for children, high shelves (5 feet or more off the floor) can be attached to the wall for storing teachers' items and/or children's items not presently being used. However, beware of using these shelves for heavy items or sharp objects that could fall and injure the children.

If there are too many doors and not enough wall space, nonfunctional doors can be blocked off and, in effect, treated as part of the wall (this must not be done with functional doors or fire exits, however). One simple method is to place a bookcase, bulletin board, or shelf across the door and create an activity center. Another way to get more out of the available space is to use flexible tables that can be easily moved to suit current needs. For example, tables can be moved together for eating and then moved to different parts of the room for use in activity centers. The sides and backs of bookcases and shelving can be used as display areas to supplement the display areas on the walls.

If there is no sink in the room, be sure to have a bucket with sponges, a mop, and soap. Train the children to refill the bucket and use it on their own. If there is a sink in the room, but it cannot easily be reached by the children, add a riser that will allow them to get at it more easily. Risers can be used similarly for high toilets and blackboards that usually would be difficult or impossible for the children to reach.

If you are short of bookcases and shelving or other more ideal dividers, use area rugs to define activity areas or use substitute dividers such as bulletin boards, blackboards, or easels.

If the classroom is poorly lit, locate the book area and other areas requiring close visual concentration near the windows and avoid putting decorations on the windows.

If you are short of containers, save boxes, baskets, cans, cigar boxes, and other containers. Decorate them with paint or contact paper and label them or add pictures showing their contents.

In general, inventory the assets and liabilities of your classroom and then take steps to remedy any defects you have noticed. First, try to get the school to fix or change any aspects that will cause problems. Where this is impossible, or where you must wait awhile before changes can be made, ask yourself what adjustments you can make to eliminate or minimize the problem. Try to maintain an active, problem-solving orientation in which you view classroom design and equipment problems as obstacles to be overcome, not as permanent factors that simply must be accepted. Even on a limited budget, determination and creativity can produce important classroom improvements leading to a more pleasant environment for both teacher and children.

SUMMARY

The well-planned preschool is designed to provide the young child with an environment that offers him a rich variety of stimuli and experiences likely to foster his general development. Furthermore, it is designed so that this can be accomplished with maximum safety, provision for group living, and promotion of independence.

Safety considerations include attention to transportation and pickup and delivery arrangements, careful delineation of policies and exchange of information with parents, maintenance of a well-equipped dispensary and clearly established policies for dealing with emergencies, and avoidance or elimination of hazards to the children's health and safety.

Provision for successful group living and promotion of independence can be fostered through child-sized furniture and equipment; storage places that the children can reach and use on their own; meal arrangements that minimize the children's dependence upon teachers or other adults; selection of equipment appropriate to the children's developmental level; demonstration of such equipment to children who do not know how to use it; use of containers likely to minimize spills and accidents; provision of many sets of toys or equipment items stored in separate, small containers rather than stored in a single, large container; planning of traffic patterns that minimize cross traffic and crowding; and scheduling of activities so that everyone can spend as much time as possible involved in productive activities and as little time as possible standing and waiting.

The outside play area should include both a hard and a soft surface, and each of these areas should be equipped with a variety of durable, enjoyable toys and equipment. The equipment inside the classroom will vary with the nature of the program, but in any case the classroom should be clearly divided into separate activity areas or centers and not just randomly or haphazardly filled with equipment. Each center should have well-defined boundaries and should have any relevant equipment items stored in or near it, so that it is a functional subunit of the classroom. Lighting, noise levels, traffic patterns, and other relevant considerations should be taken into account in placing the classroom activity centers relative to one another. Wall displays placed above each area or center can help identify it, although these should be attractive as well as functional.

Regardless of how far a given teacher's classroom may be from the ideal described in this chapter, there are always steps that can be taken to improve it. Undesirable furniture or equipment can be removed; shelving, bookcases, and certain equipment items can be purchased or constructed easily; many containers and items useful for learning activities can be collected in homes or stores from among items that otherwise would be discarded; and creative application of paint, contact paper, cutouts, wall displays, and other decorations can do much to brighten any classroom. Whenever teachers become aware of obstacles or undesirable features of their classrooms or their preschools in general, they should begin to make inquiries or plans to change these problems rather than simply adjust to them.

1. If you were asked to describe four factors that are of most importance in designing a successful physical environment for the preschool, what features would you name?

2. Visit three different preschool locations and sketch the physical setup. What specific suggestions would you make for improving the physical environment in each of these three preschools? Be specific.

3. Visit three preschool programs and observe the outdoor play area. What suggestions can you make for improving the use of existing space? List any dangerous or inappropriate equipment that you see on the playground and explain.

4. Plan a special learning center. Describe the learning goals of the center, the particular age of the children it is designed for, and the specific materials that will be utilized.

5. Explain in your own words how the physical environment determines in large measure the frequency and quality of independent-play activities that children can engage in.

6. Your classroom is crowded. You can't make it any larger, but you might be able to reduce crowding by making some changes. What are five ways to reduce crowding?

7. Once you know the ages and number of children you will teach, the equipment that will be available, and the room you will use, you can make plans for equipment display and rotation. What principles will you use?

8. Suppose an equipment item isn't being used much. Is this because it is not appropriate for the children, or because they do not know how to use it (or how to use it in new ways)? How could you tell? If the item were appropriate, how could you motivate the children to want to use it more often? Is this worth the trouble?

9. Review catalogues from equipment- and school-supply companies. Check prices and quality of items. What expendable supplies would you need to order? Make an order for expendable material for a year with a class of 25 children.

10. Assume your supervisor tells you to reduce this list by 25 percent. What items would you delete? What criteria would you use?

11. Review resources for providing ideas for simple nutritious snacks and

lunches. Outline a one-week plan for snacks and lunches. How can children be involved in food preparations?

12. Plan an outdoor play area. Include equipment that would be used. Design a specific area that would satisfy the minimum needs of 3-, 4-, and 5-year-old children.

13. Devise lists of suitable books to have available for 5-year-old children (books which can be read in groups; books grouped according to folk stories, science, social studies; or books useful for specific units—color, transportation, shape, numbers). Present your plan to the class with justification for selection.

14. Explain how learning centers can be changed according to the children's needs, interests, and concerns. Be specific (e.g., how often should a center be changed?).

15. Plan a wall display: define a topic, explain your selection of material (will you use children's work?), suggest the center in which it will be displayed, and so on.

16. During observations in preschools, note: (a) Are adequate materials on hand (in use and reserve)? (b) Is space provided for a variety of activities? (c) Is the equipment child sized? (d) Is there equipment for large-muscle development as well as equipment for small-muscle development (manipulative equipment)? (e) Are there materials and activities for creative expression? (f) Are there opportunities for both active and quiet play? (g) Are the facilities well-integrated in the overall planning?

17. During an observation, choose one area or piece of equipment and record observations of its use by several children. How was it used by each? Note other possible uses. What did its purpose seem to be? How did use of the equipment vary? If possible, start a usage record on a piece of equipment on the first day it is introduced and observe the pattern of its usage for a week. Are there any systematic changes with time?

18. List ten ideas for obtaining or making free or very inexpensive equipment (besides those listed in the chapter). Make enough copies so you can share your list with all your classmates.

19. Go through the lists and eliminate duplications. Then, reorganize the ideas into those that you can or should implement right now, those that you should implement in the weeks before you start teaching, and those that are useful only after you have begun teaching.

20. Suppose that nap or rest time is your major time for planning and activity preparation (it shouldn't be, but many nursery school situations are far from ideal), and you have three children who obviously do not need or want a nap. What could you do? Discuss various suggestions with classmates.

21. Using easily available materials, make an item for the classroom (container, activity prop, toy or game, educational activity). Make a list of the materials needed and instructions followed and make copies for distribution to classmates.

22. George runs into a pole and is stunned by a blow to the head. He is wobbly at first, but seems all right five minutes later. What should you do?

READINGS

Association for Childhood Education International. *Equipment and supplies: tested and approved for preschool/school/home.* Washington D.C.: Association for Childhood Education International, 1968.

————. *Housing for early childhood education.* Washington D.C.: Association for Childhood Education International, 1968.

————. *Learning centers: children on their own.* Washington D.C.: Association for Childhood Education International, 1970.

Baker, K. *Let's play outdoors.* Washington D.C.: National Association for the Education of Young Children, 1966.

Blitz, B. *The open classroom: making it work.* Boston: Allyn & Bacon, 1973.

Kritchevsky, S., Prescott, E., and Walling, L. *Planning environments for young children: physical space.* Washington D.C.: National Association for the Education of Young Children, 1969.

New York State Education Department. *Equipment for children in kindergarten.* Albany, N.Y.: New York State Education Department, 1960.

7
GETTING OFF TO A GOOD START

By getting off to a good start, a solid basis can be established for a productive and enjoyable year for both teachers and children. Problems that occur because of a poor start at the beginning of the year may be difficult to overcome and may seriously undermine the quality of the program and the benefits that the teachers and children derive from it throughout the year. Thus, although the specifics will differ according to the type of program and the ages of children enrolled, it is essential that each class get off to as good a start as possible.

PREPARING THE PARENTS

The parents should be prepared, as completely as possible and as early as possible, by being provided with information about the program and instructions about things they will need to do before their child begins participation in it. At minimum, this means their filling out an application form that will give the school information about the family and the child, and your preparing a sheet that will give the parents important information about the school.

The application form should include, among other things, the child's full name and nickname; any relevant health information, particularly allergies; the name, home address, and phone number of the nearest neighbors; the name and phone number of the child's doctor; the child's birthday; the child's special interests or talents; the child's status with regard to toilet training and any other relevant self-care behavior; and information about the child's general adjustment and strengths and weaknesses as seen by the parents.

The information sheet for parents (Figure 7.1) should include a brochure or data sheet giving information about the highlights of the preschool program. In addition, it should inform the parents about any required vaccinations or other health requirements; provide instructions concerning items that the

157

FIGURE 7.1
A Sample Information Sheet for Parents

General Information

Jackson Heights Preschool   1529 Parkside, Chicago, Ill. 60651   Phone 459–7863
Mrs. Sharon Phillips, Director

Hours: (3-year-olds) 8:30 A.M. to 11:30 A.M.
(4-year-olds) 8:30 A.M. to 11:30 A.M., or 8:30 A.M. to 2:30 P.M.

School will be open Monday through Friday, from September 1 through June 10, except for the holidays listed on the attached sheet. Children may be dropped off between 8:00 and 8:30 A.M., and should be picked up between 11:30 and 11:45 A.M. or 2:30 and 2:45 P.M. Please make every effort to observe these hours, to avoid inconveniencing the teachers or worrying your child.

Fees: Half day, $45.00 per month; full day, $85.00 per month.

The school is planned and operated to serve children enrolled on a *continuing* basis. Thus, only children enrolled for one month or more are accepted. We cannot provide drop-in care on a daily or hourly basis. The first month's fee should be paid when you register your child. Later payments should be made on a monthly basis, unless other arrangements are made with the director.

Teachers: Room 1 (3-year-olds) Mrs. Donna Kapche
Room 2 (3-year-olds) Miss Dianne Wilson
Room 3 (4-year-olds) Mr. Robert Williamson
Room 4 (4-year-olds) Mrs. Carol Latham
Room 5 (4-year-olds) Mrs. Janet Honea

Car Pools: The attached list of names, addresses, and phone numbers of every family with one or more children enrolled is provided for your convenience in arranging car pools.

Pickup Authorization: If your child is to ride home with someone other than his usual ride, please call or send a note giving us the name and description of the person picking him up. We will not release a child to unauthorized persons.

Illness: Do not bring your child to school with a cold, sores, discharging eyes, rash, fever, or if he has had an upset stomach in the past twenty-four hours. Please notify us if he has exposed other children to a contagious illness.

Clothing: All clothing should be plainly marked with name tapes or iron-on tape. Since our program emphasizes activity and freedom of movement, we prefer washable play clothes. Also, clothing the child can manage without adult help in dressing is preferred. An extra change of clothing should be left at school for use if your child should get wet or soiled.

Field Trips: You must sign the attached permission form so that we can take your child on field trips. Also, please let us know if you will be available at any time to help drive and supervise the children on field trips.

Birthdays: Children like to have their birthday party here at school. We are happy to have you bring refreshments for your child's group to celebrate his birthday here if you wish. Please let us know a day or two ahead however, so we can prepare for it.

Please be sure your child gets a good night's sleep before school days and that he eats a good breakfast. Any time anything happens at home to upset your child's normal routine or emotions, please give us a call or send a note along with him telling us about it. Remember, our first concern is the happiness of your child, so feel free to call on us any time we can be of help. Please read carefully any notes that are sent home with your child. Please return the attached field-trip permission sheet, medical form, and general-information form as soon as possible.

---

child will have to bring to school (an extra change of clothing, for example); provide specific information about times and methods of delivering and picking up the children; provide information and relevant forms for medical and travel releases; provide class lists giving the names, addresses, and phone numbers of all children and parents enrolled in the school (not just the child's class), as an aid to parents who wish to form car pools; suggest guidelines regarding breakfast, bedtime, or other home activities that may affect the child's school behavior; list the teachers and phone number (or numbers) of the school; recommend procedures to follow when the child will be late or absent; and provide suggestions about what to tell the child about school if he will be attending for the first time.

Each of these sheets should be prepared in relevant languages if non-English speakers are involved in the program, and they should be reviewed orally and filled out by a staff member if the parent is known or believed to be illiterate or semiliterate. Parents should be encouraged to keep these information sheets containing important phone numbers near their phone where they can be located quickly when needed.

Home and School Visits

If at all possible, a teacher visit to the home, or a visit by the child and one or both parents to the school, should be arranged before the first program day begins. Such visits are crucial in helping the teachers become acquainted with the parent and the child. This is much easier to do in the atmosphere of a private visit than during snatches of conversation carried on amid the hubbub of an ongoing preschool program, so that individualized visits should be scheduled, if at all possible, before the beginning of school. Your primary goal in such visits is to become acquainted with the child and parent during an informal chat. This may or may not include filling out the application form and/or going over the parent information form mentioned above. In any case, items of mutual interest should be discussed with the parent to help establish and cement a good teacher–parent relationship. Also, some time should be spent with the child to help him get to know you as an individual and to like you as a person.

If the interview takes place at the school, it should be done in the classroom in which the child will spend his time, and you can give him a conducted tour of the room to help him become familiar with the school environment. This kind of familiarity, along with a warm, close relationship established during such a visit, can reduce or eliminate problems that often occur when a young child is separated from his mother as he enters school for the first time. It makes a big difference to a child whether his mother is leaving him in the care of a person he knows by name in a room with which he is already familiar, as opposed to being left with a stranger in a strange room with strange children.

If you perceive that the child is inhibited or afraid of you during the visit, make an extra effort to relax him by talking to him and engaging him in pleasurable activities. It is wise to have one or more attractive and interesting toys prepared for the child, so that he will begin to perceive you as someone who will provide him with positive experiences and interesting stimulation. It is also important to take time to explain to the child in some detail exactly what is going to happen at the school, describing events *in order of sequence* for him. This will help him establish a firm set of expectations that, as they unfold during the day, will reassure him and make him feel more comfortable with you and with the idea of being in school away from his mother. Young children do not understand and cannot respond very favorably to expectations presented in *time units* ("You will stay here for an hour and a half and then we will have a snack"), but they can understand *sequences* of events ("*First* we will have a play time when you can take something from the shelves over there and play with it; *then* we are going to have music time when we will march around and sing some songs; *then* we will go outside to play on the monkey bars and the other things out in the playground; *and then* we will come in and have a snack"). The child who might not understand time units will understand that outside play time comes between music time and snack time, and when he sees these events unfold as described, he will be reassured that the teacher is telling him the truth and can be believed about other things, too.

THE FIRST DAY

The first day of school should be a very special day that is planned in detail. Your major goals on this day are to make each child feel comfortable in the school setting and to deal with any school-adjustment problems that may arise. If possible, arrange to stagger the arrival of the children so that you can greet each child individually and spend a few moments with him to get him engaged in some activity. To help you remember names, have name tags ready to be fastened to each child's shirt for quick identification. Put on the name tag as the child comes into the room, bend close to him to greet and welcome him, and move him as quickly and smoothly as possible away from his mother and into an activity. Have several popular activities available and ready for use by the children as they enter the room. Activities that involve physical manipulation, such as puzzles, construction toys, and the like, or fascinating stimuli, such as aquariums or animals, are especially useful in directing the child's attention to things in the classroom, getting him engaged in classroom activities, and helping him to forget about his mother. Whenever feasible, it is usually best if the mother leaves the child with the teacher and makes a quick exit, commenting that she will be back to pick him up when school is over. The exception is the child who obviously fears school and/or the teacher and cannot yet tolerate such an abrupt break

When a bashful boy resists leaving his mother, the teacher gives him special attention and concentrates on getting him actively involved in an enjoyable activity. The mother remains in the room as long as the boy appears to be concerned about her, but she stays in the background and lets the teacher engage the child.

161

from his mother. In such cases as this, the mother may have to stay around until the child is more reassured and becomes involved in classroom activities.

In any case, you, not the mother, are primarily responsible for helping the child in overcoming any separation problems he may have and learning to be comfortable with you and the school situation. The child may feel better if his mother spends time with him, but this will not help him adjust to you or to school. Only you can gain his trust and acceptance. Thus, as quickly and smoothly as possible, "take over" the child from the mother. This is usually done most easily if the mother stays nearby (but in a passive role) and if you involve the child actively in some activity that captures his interest. In short, attempt to *distract the child from his fears by involving him in school-related activities;* do *not* attempt to deal with his fears directly, since mention of fears is only likely to increase them. Even well-meant attempts at reassurance ("Don't worry, Johnny, your mother will be back later and I'll take good care of you while she's gone") are more likely to increase rather than decrease worry in a child experiencing separation anxiety. Teachers report greater success with the distraction method, in which the separation from the mother is not even mentioned, and the child is engaged in play with a toy that interests him. Acceptance and trust of the teacher will come as a byproduct of such activities, since the teacher will be spending time with the child, showing him how to use a toy or making comments about his play, and thus communicating in subtle ways a combination of warmth, friendliness, interest, stimulating ideas, and other positive overtures. These will appear automatically in the process of sharing an enjoyable experience with the child, so that they will not have to be expressed in more direct (and perhaps more forced and less convincing) ways.

This same basic method should be applied to persistent cases of separation problems, although in many cases it will be necessary to have the mother remain nearby, and perhaps even in some cases to spend time with the child, in order to keep him calm. We stress again, however, that it is primarily up to the teacher to "convert" the child in these situations; the mother could not do very much to change the child's attitude even if she wanted to. The main method for overcoming such fears is for the teacher to arrange to share positive experiences repeatedly with the child and gradually build an image of being a positive, warm, and trustworthy person, so that the child will gradually be able to tolerate increasing amounts of time spent with the teacher away from the mother. Building credibility by describing events that will occur in sequential order, as described above ("First, you will play, then we will sing, then we will go outside, then we will have a snack") is especially useful in helping the child build trust in the teacher's word. Gradually this can be extended to include the whole day, so that he can feel secure and know when his mother will return ("and then we will play with the toys some more, and then we will clean up, and then your

mother will come and pick you up and take you home"). Repetition of descriptions of what to expect, coupled with confirmation of these expectations
as the day progresses, will gradually show the child that he can depend
upon the teacher's word.

ESTABLISHING RULES   Although this must not be overdone to the point of taking the fun out of
the preschool program, it is important to establish and maintain classroom
rules right from the beginning of school. School is a group experience, and
it requires rules that are not necessary for children who are playing at home.
Some will carry over from home, but many will not. In fact, many rules
necessary in school are contradictory to what the child experiences outside
of school. For example, running around and making noise are two very common activities that young children engage in and are seldom admonished
for in their play in and around the home. Also, many children have never
had to learn to share toys and materials. However, in the interest of classroom safety and efficiency, these activities must be regulated in school. Thus,
the young child must make the difficult discrimination between situations
in which an activity is permissible and situations in which it is not.

*The most important factor determining the teacher's success in establish-
ing rules is that the rules be demonstrated and rehearsed rather than just
verbalized.* Procedures regarding removing, using, and replacing toys and
equipment should be practiced by the children so that the teacher can get
a chance to observe them actually doing it themselves and to give any corrective feedback that is necessary. In these situations, and in presenting rules
generally, the teacher should adopt a totally positive approach, simply stating and showing how things should be done and communicating the expectation that the children will do so. There should be no hinting that the children
might not do so, such as by threatening punishment if the rule is broken ("You
have to do it this way; if you don't, you won't be able to play with the toy").
Most children are quite willing to follow rules as long as they know what
to do, so that your primary task in establishing rules is to make sure that
the children do know what to do and can do it successfully on their own.
Failure to observe rules usually will be due to forgetfulness rather than to
deliberate misbehavior, and the teacher's reactions should reflect this fact.
In the early weeks, all failures to follow rules should be met with rule reminders and corrective action to see that the rule is followed, but not with threats
or punishment. Such incidents can be minimized if teachers alertly monitor
the class so that they can spot potential problems early and nip them in
the bud (see Chapter 12).

It may be helpful, especially with very young children, to use certain stock
signals and phrases that will make it easier for them to recognize situations
in which particular rules apply. For example, when you want quiet in the
room, it is advisable to use a single, consistent method. Some teachers prefer

a bell, buzzer, clicker, or some other signal, while others prefer a verbal phrase ("Attention, children," "Listen, children," etc.). The particular method used is not as important as the teacher's *consistency* in using it. A quiet signal is most effective when it is used for *one purpose only* (to obtain quiet) and when it is used *the same way every time.* Ideally, the teacher should give the quiet signal loudly enough so that everyone hears it (but not overly loudly), wait a second or two for the children to stop their activities and look at the teacher, and then proceed to give instructions. The short wait is important, since the children will need a few seconds to turn their attention from what they are doing to the teacher's instructions. At the same time, the pause should not be too long, since some children are liable to resume activities or begin some new activity rather than wait for instruction. Consistent application of the above principles will teach the children that the teacher means business when calling for quiet and will give instructions two or three seconds after giving the quiet signal.

Other classroom rules should be established according to the ages of the children and needs of the particular classroom. To the extent that the children are able, they should participate in the establishment of rules. In this case, the teacher establishes rules by eliciting them from the children, rather than by presenting them in declarative or imperative form. The problem that requires solution should be explained and/or demonstrated to the children, and suggestions about rules or procedures that would solve the problem should be elicited. After some discussion, agreement on a rule should be formalized and the rule can then be expressed verbally and repeated by the group.

Rather than having a large number of very specific rules, try to have a relatively small number of general rules that apply to many situations. Thus, rules such as "no running in the room," "replace toys and equipment that you are using before getting out anything new," "one at a time in the washroom," "we will be friendly with one another and share things together," and a few others should suffice (perhaps along with a few special rules regarding special equipment, procedures in the lunchroom, etc.). Basically, rules and limits are ways to protect the children's rights and physical well-being, and to insure that equipment is used and maintained in an orderly manner. Try to enforce rules *on the spot.* For example, if you see a child leave a tricycle without putting it away, remind him *immediately; do not* wait until he has begun a new activity. During early stages when rules are only partially internalized, it will be helpful to have the children repeat them out loud and to reinforce them by giving demonstrations or else having the children demonstrate how things should be done.

In addition to presenting rules in a positive way without threats or punishment, do not neglect to *reinforce the children for following rules appropriately.* Teachers, and adults generally, have an unfortunate tendency to pay more attention to children's misbehavior than to their good behavior. As a general policy, and especially early in the year when you are trying to establish rules, be sure to notice and comment upon children's behaviors that show conscious attempts to follow the rules. Ideally, these should be individualized comments that convey warmth and pleasure as well as recognition and appreciation of the child's efforts, rather than more public pronouncements that hold the child up as an example to the other children (this can boomerang by making the child "teacher's pet").

EQUIPMENT DEMONSTRATION

It is generally advisable to limit the amount of toys and equipment available early in the year, especially with children new to school. As the children become familiar with available equipment and learn to share and care for it, new items should be introduced gradually.

Most of the toys and equipment in the classroom will be new to the children, and the teacher will have to demonstrate how to use and care for them. Often these can be group demonstrations, although sometimes individual demonstrations will be needed for complicated equipment, equipment involving very small pieces, or equipment that must be used individually. *In demonstrating equipment, it is important to show each separate step, moving slowly and emphasizing key words, pointing to aspects of the equipment that you want the child to look at as you go.* If only one or a small number of steps is involved, the entire process can be demonstrated at once. When something more complicated is being demonstrated, the process probably should be divided into two or more subparts to be mastered in stages. Something as simple as how to use a book may require demonstration (i.e., don't throw it, step on it, or tear it; carry it closed, not open; turn pages slowly and carefully; use it in a well-lighted area; go through the book from front to back to get story sequence).

Each demonstration or stage of a large demonstration should involve an initial presentation by the teacher in which appropriate parts of the equipment are labeled and in which the teacher "thinks out loud" while going through the motions of using the toy or equipment item. Motions should be slow and exaggerated so the children can follow them. Key words should be emphasized, and pointing, gesturing, and holding up should be used to make sure that attention is directed to the appropriate aspects of the equipment at the appropriate time. After the teacher has demonstrated the item once or twice, a child should be asked to do the same thing while the teacher and the other children watch. The demonstration can be further reinforced while the child works if you describe and label what he is doing as he does it. If he succeeds, praise him and invite another child to try it; if he runs into trouble, help him out by giving him hints or showing him what to do.

In general, if materials are to be handled and used appropriately, everything at school should be demonstrated to the children, or at least to some of them. This includes not only each toy or equipment item in the classroom,

The teacher notices a girl who is inhibited or confused about how to use the equipment. She responds by first *showing* the girl how to remove the pegs from the pegboard and then sitting down with her and *showing* her how to use them. She continues until the girl is able to continue on her own.

but also auxiliary skills needed for use of pencils, crayons, and scissors; opening jars; using glue and paste; eating and drinking; toileting and washing; carrying things so as to minimize dropping and spilling; returning items properly; and many others. In each case, the teacher should show the children what to do, following the principles mentioned above, and then give them an opportunity to practice the actions themselves, providing praise and encouragement, corrective feedback, or both, as needed. Children vary greatly in the kinds and quality of experiences that they have had before coming to school, and this background of experiences will relate to the amount of demonstration (and repetition of demonstration) that they need. Some children will already know how to do certain things before they come to school; others will pick up the essential points with just one or two demonstrations; still others will need repeated demonstrations with individualized corrective feedback. Again, it is essential to bear in mind that difficulties in this area are almost always due to lapses of memory and to the children's lack of previous experience with the equipment or behavior in question, and rarely to deliberate or calculated misbehavior. Thus, it is important to be prepared for slow learning and failures, and to respond to any such difficulties with patience and additional demonstrations and not with anger, disgust, frustration, or punishment. If a child is not doing something correctly, simply continue showing him how to do it until he does do it correctly.

**PROMOTING
INDEPENDENCE**

Establishment of classroom rules and demonstration of the use of toys and equipment are necessary to provide common ground rules and a base of experience from which children can operate. However, once the child has shown that he has mastered the fundamental uses of a given toy or equipment item, he should then be encouraged to use it independently and creatively. For example, it would be unrealistic and frustrating to ask a child to draw a picture when he does not know how to hold a crayon. This child needs demonstration and practice in holding and using crayons, along with eventual practice in such fundamental tool skills as drawing straight lines, curved lines, and other controlled strokes. Once he has mastered these basic skills, however, he is ready to use them to create drawings or pictures of his own choosing, and should not be restricted to filling in coloring books or tracing lines.

The general principle here is to find out where each child stands in his ability to use a given toy or equipment item, and then move him along to higher steps. If he is still at a stage where he has not mastered the fundamental manipulation of the item, he will need demonstration, practice, and feedback. If he has acquired such mastery, he may need only suggestions about things he can do with the item and perhaps a little help in getting started.

Similar principles apply to toilet training, spills, cleanup, classroom management, and the like. Children having problems in these areas should be worked with *patiently.* Demonstrate the correct way to do things, using a voice tone, facial expression, and gestures that communicate positive expectations that the child will succeed (although not necessarily immediately). With children who do not have problems in these areas, instruction is unnecessary. Sometimes they can be used as classroom helpers, if they have mastered certain classroom-management skills well. Thus, for example, children capable of opening milk cartons without dropping or spilling them can be asked to open them for the class or for some of the other children who are still having difficulty.

The teacher's crucial task in this area is to strike the vital balance between providing praise and encouragement to children who achieve success while at the same time not overdoing it by making certain children "teacher's pets" or otherwise calling undue attention to their success. The key here is to praise each child for progress in moving forward from his own level, whatever that level might be. Thus, one child might receive praise for opening a milk carton without spilling it, while another might be encouraged for opening all the milk cartons and distributing them to the class for snacks. Similarly, one child might deserve praise for being able to follow a straight line with a crayon, while another might be commended for making a rather sophisticated and artistic drawing. It is important that *both* children in each of these examples get recognition and praise for their behaviors. You should constantly bear in mind the expectation that children will show great individual differences in their abilities and progress, and should verbalize this expectation to the children so that the more successful ones do not acquire an unhealthy sense of elitism or superiority, and the less successful ones do not acquire an unhealthy inhibition or low self-concept: "All of your are different; some of you are good at some things and some of you are good at others, and you are all good at many things. If you are good at something, try to help your neighbor if he needs help. Let's all share and help one another."

**PLANNING AND
SCHEDULING**

Advance preparation of carefully planned schedules is always important to effective teaching, but never more so than in the early weeks. Whether or not your preschool is using a planned curriculum, it is essential that each day be scheduled in detail. If necessary, the schedule can be written on the board or typed and posted in an easily accessible place for reminder.

In making out a schedule, begin by blocking out those times that are fixed (starting time, snack time, lunch time, rest time, time to clean up the room and prepare for dismissal). In some schools, fixed times might also include trips to the washroom, other mealtimes, and outdoor play times (in large schools where the outdoor play space must be shared with other classes).

Within these limits forced by the fixed elements of the schedule, plan and schedule other activities for the remaining time periods. Schedule individualized or group activities early in the year, with group activities being short and confined to small groups of children as much as possible. In general, it is a good idea to schedule lessons or other activities demanding high concentration early in the morning and reserve low-concentration activities for later in the day. It is also advisable to alternate individual activities with group activities, lesson activities with free-play activities, and quiet activities with more active activities. These and other principles of scheduling were discussed in more detail in Chapter 5.

As the early weeks progress, you can move more from individual to small-group activities and from small-group to large-group activities as the children get used to school routines and to working together. You can also gradually increase the length of activities as the children's attention spans increase. These changes should be made gradually and on an individual basis. Some teachers make the mistake of attempting to hurry this process too quickly, because working in groups is more efficient and easier to schedule than work with individuals, but attempts to get individual children to function as group members and/or to sustain participation in an activity beyond their present attention span will be self-defeating. Instead, in the early weeks concentrate on those children who seem to need extra help in adjusting to school, until they demonstrate sufficient adjustment to school routines to be scheduled along with other children, without any special attention or individualized work.

Bear in mind that any extra time and effort spent in establishing appropriate classroom-management procedures early in the school year will be well worth the effort in the long run, since this will minimize disruptions and management problems throughout the year. Continually remind the children of the rules and redemonstrate the expected behaviors that they have not yet mastered, and continually project positive expectations that they will do so. Express confidence that the child is a "big boy" or "big girl" capable of behaving properly. You might also point out that privileges and opportunities to participate in certain activities will be granted as soon as the child proves himself ready for them (this should not be overdone, however, since it may backfire and the child may begin to disrupt such activities deliberately if he feels that he is being frozen out of them).

As the children become accustomed to the school routines, you can considerably reduce the amount of time that you spend giving demonstrations and rule reminders. Directions can be faded out, both in frequency and in length (for example, "All right, it's time to put our things away and get the room cleaned up so that we can line up and get ready to go," can be shortened to "Time to clean up and get ready to go," and then to, "Cleanup time."). The children can help with everyday classroom-management responsibilities by serving as monitors. Development of a monitor system will not only reduce the amount of time that you need to spend doing everyday tasks personally; it will also give the children a chance to assume responsibilities that they will enjoy and take pride in. Monitor assignments should be rotated so that different children get different responsibilities, although a given job might have to be removed from the responsibility of a particular child because he is not doing it properly. If this happens, give the child another chance at a later time.

Be sure that you have lots of backup activities planned for use in the early weeks at times when weather or other uncontrollable conditions prevent you from carrying out the activities that you had scheduled. During this time, when many children are still not yet accustomed to school routines, it is very important that they be actively engaged in productive activities as much as possible, and that waiting time or other "dead time" be avoided. Both fear of being in a strange environment and classroom-management problems that occur due to disruption or aggression will be minimized when the children are involved in absorbing activities. The opposite will be true when children have nothing to do or find themselves standing around waiting for something to happen. Thus, in general, but especially in the early weeks, schedule activities and have materials prepared so that everyone can be almost continually involved in some form of activity and so that transitions between activities can be smooth and quick. This kind of a rich, fast-paced schedule, along with patient and continuing demonstrations and rule reminders, will be sufficient to enable the vast majority of preschoolers to adjust quickly to their new school environment with a minimum of difficulty.

SUMMARY

Things generally go smoother, and many potential problems are prevented, if you get the year off to a good start. One aspect of this is preparing the parents, both by gathering information from them that will be needed or useful in dealing with their child, and by providing them with needed information about the school. The latter should include a sheet containing information about pickup and delivery of children, the school phone number, and other important items. If possible, teachers should arrange a private visit with each family, either in the home or at the school, before school begins. Some giving and collecting of information will be involved, but the primary purpose of this visit is to become acquainted with the family and especially the child, and to make the child like you and feel comfortable being with you.

You and the parents can help prepare the child for school by developing positive expectations that will make him look forward to going. Unless the child cannot tolerate it, the mother should leave quickly after bringing him to school on the first day. In any case, the teacher has the main responsibility for helping children cope with problems of mother separation; this is best done by distracting the child through involving him in enjoyable activities with the teacher. Fears will rapidly fade away if teachers establish themselves as interesting, likable persons who provide interesting experiences and whose word can be counted on.

The first few weeks, and especially the first day of school, require especially complete planning and preparation. Begin with only a limited amount of toys and equipment, but select items that are particularly engrossing and popular. Demonstrate how each item is used if the child does not already know, and spend some time with him to get him started using the item and to make some suggestions about what he can do when you leave. Be sure to have backup activities planned in case weather or other unforeseen problems prevent you from carrying out your scheduled activities.

Concentrate on establishing rules for classroom behavior and on getting the children accustomed to school routines in the first few weeks. Establish a few general rules that will be taught to the children and insisted upon. Handle other problems with instructions given on the spot. In any case, bear in mind that in most instances children new to school fail to follow rules because of unfamiliarity with the situation or equipment involved, and not because of deliberate defiance. Thus, although it is necessary to insist upon conformity to rules, establishing rules will require great patience in repeatedly restating the rule or demonstrating the correct procedure to the child and in avoiding punitive or threatening behavior. Be sure that the children understand the reasons for rules, not just the rules themselves.

In addition to presenting rules and equipment demonstrations in a positive way, adopt a positive attitude in your reinforcement activities. Praise or express appreciation when you see a child following a rule or taking care to handle or use equipment properly, and in general stress the positive. Avoid reacting in ways which teach the children that they can get attention through misbehavior.

Remember that rules are just tools that you use to promote safety and provide for group living; they are not ends in themselves. Thus, rules that are no longer needed should be discarded, and the children should be encouraged to move toward independence as soon as they are able to handle it. Rules can be faded out, and the children can be allowed greater self-determination, as they become accustomed to school routines. Also, the length of scheduled activities can be gradually increased as the children's attention spans increase.

In summary, the keys to getting off to a good start include: preparing the child and the family for school ahead of time; carefully planning and preparing activities in the early weeks; presenting rules for classroom behavior clearly and consistently; demonstrating how to do things correctly (patiently repeating as many times as necessary); and insuring that the children are almost always involved in productive and enjoyable activities, so that the problems that frequently arise during "dead times" are minimized.

QUESTIONS

1. If you were sitting in a preschool room on the first day of class, how would you know if the room got off to a good start or not? That is, what precise things would you observe? Why these things?

2. This chapter assumes an ideal situation, in which the teacher has had a chance to visit with parents and get information on forms before school begins. What should you do if you must begin teaching without this information and parental contact?

3. What is meant by the statement that the teacher should "take over" the child from his mother as soon as possible?

4. Classroom rules and procedures (verbal versus mechanical attention-getting signal, etc.) vary with the ages of the children, school policy, and *teacher preferences*. How can you discover your own preferences? What rules and procedures work best for *you*? How will you find out? What should you do if your preferences conflict with school policy?

5. Some children have difficulty adjusting to school because they are not accustomed to listening carefully to adults for information and directions. Such children may ignore you or appear not to hear you. How should they be handled?

6. What should you do about children who lack basic self-care skills (eating and drinking without spilling, getting clothes on and off, bowel and bladder control, etc.)?

7. Role play a demonstration of equipment as the teacher would at the beginning of the year. What provisions would you make for concrete experience and direct feedback? Take turns at this with classmates, giving and receiving constructive reactions.

8. Devise a monitors' or helpers' chart.

9. The day is not over, but you have completed all scheduled activities. What do you do? Plan "filler" activities that could be used almost anytime. Be sure they are valuable experiences, not just "busy work."

10. How would the first-day schedule differ from the regular schedule? Why?

11. How would geographic and climatic conditions affect scheduling and activity planning? Is there a greater need for "filler" activities in January for a program that is located in Florida or Michigan? Why? Why not?

12. On the first day of school, Becky is brought by her mother. Her mother leaves, thinking Becky is okay. Moments later, Becky bursts into tears. What do you do?

READINGS

Blitz, B. *The open classroom: making it work*. Boston: Allyn & Bacon, 1973.
Evans, F., Shub, B., and Weinstein, M. *Day care: how to plan, develop, and operate a day care center*. Boston: Beacon, 1971.
Read, K. *The nursery school*. Philadelphia: Saunders, 1966.

8
MAKING AND ADJUSTING SCHEDULES

The schedule of any preschool program should be designed primarily to serve the needs of the children rather than the needs of the staff or the center. Too often, teachers forget this basic principle, and the result is a schedule that looks quite efficient on paper, but does not take into account some of the basic principles of how children learn. While every teacher has to work around a certain number of fixed, daily events, there are still a large number of other options that the teacher can consider in trying to individual-ize the schedule and the program. In the following section we shall discuss some general considerations and principles for making decisions about scheduling, how to schedule for large blocks of time (such as a week), and how to plan for smaller units of time (such as one day).

BASIC CONSIDERATIONS
One of the first considerations that affects the kind of schedule you will develop is the number of hours children attend the preschool program. This can vary from a half-day (three-hour) program, to a full-day program of ap-proximately six hours, to a total day-care program that usually consists of eleven hours. The operating hours of the center will definitely affect the kinds of services that will be offered to the children; for instance, the number of meals served, the amount of time needed for naps or resting, and the kind of custodial care that must be combined with the educational program. Where full-day care is offered (eleven hours), state and local regulations must be observed carefully. These regulations usually determine the number of adults needed for supervision, the number of meals to be served, and the quality of the caretaking facility. All of these factors will affect scheduling.

Another consideration is the kind of facility in which the program is housed. The greatest degree of scheduling flexibility will be possible in pro-grams self-contained in their own buildings. In this situation, the problems of sharing restrooms, playground facilities, or eating facilities with other

173

groups of children are usually minimal. A program housed in its own facility can schedule events in total consideration of the children's needs. Very often, however, a preschool program is housed in a larger facility where it is part of a public school or neighborhood center. Since there are a number of other ongoing activities that must be considered in scheduling, the teacher's planning must always take these external constraints into account. Very often, events such as meals and playground time are scheduled at a fixed time, and while the teacher has no control over these events, they must be considered in planning the rest of the schedule.

Special problems arise when facilities are shared. It is not unusual for a preschool program housed in a neighborhood center to share its classroom facilities with other center programs that meet late in the afternoon or in the evening. When this occurs, the preschool teacher must be prepared to put away most of the equipment at the end of every day and to put the materials out again in the morning. Another unique kind of scheduling problem arises when a preschool program uses multiple rooms. For example, all motor activities might occur in one room, all manipulative activities in another, all role playing and dramatic play in another, and so forth. Very often these programs adopt multi-age groupings and team teaching, which create unique scheduling problems. To be effective, planning must be a mutual effort of the entire staff.

The number of resource people available also will affect the kind of schedule that can be developed. When planning, the classroom teacher must consider the number of adults that will be in a room at any one time, who these adults are, and how much time they will actually spend in the classroom. These adult resources will affect the grouping strategies that can be used, as well as the number of planned activities that can be presented to the children.

There are certain invariant events that every teacher must include in schedules. These events include meals, snacks, restroom time, nap time, outdoor play, and transportation schedules. These are events over which the teacher has very little control, yet they affect the scheduling of other events throughout the entire day.

The final basic consideration affecting scheduling is the time of year. The schedule that a teacher plans at the beginning of the school year will be quite different from the schedule in effect toward the end of the year. The children's needs when they first come to school are considerably different from their needs later in the year. Children's attention span, their ability to work independently, and their ability to work in small and large groups will change greatly over time. As their abilities change and their level of functioning matures, the schedule must reflect this developmental growth.

Figure 8.1 shows one example of how teachers could schedule some of the invariant events over which they have no control. This is the first step

FIGURE 8.1
A Daily Schedule

8:30–8:45	Children arrive	11:45–12:00	Lunch
8:45–9:00		12:00–12:15	Lunch
9:00–9:15		12:15–12:30	Nap
9:15–9:30		12:30–12:45	Nap
9:30–9:45		12:45–1:00	Nap
9:45–10:00	Restroom	1:00–1:15	Nap
10:00–10:15	Snack	1:15–1:30	Restroom
10:15–10:30	Playground	1:30–1:45	
10:30–10:45	Playground	1:45–2:00	
10:45–11:00		2:00–2:15	
11:00–11:15		2:15–2:30	Playground
11:15–11:30		2:30–2:45	Playground
11:30–11:45	Restroom	2:45–3:00	Dismissal

in planning a specific schedule. While the time of these events will vary from one preschool to another, the process will be the same for every teacher. To briefly review, teachers must consider the following factors as they begin to block out schedules:

1. Hours of operation.
   a. A half-day program.
   b. A full-day program.
   c. A total day-care program.
2. Kind of facility.
   a. Self-contained building.
   b. Housed in a public school or neighborhood center.
   c. Shares room and other facilities with other programs.
   d. Program housed in multiple rooms; team teaching and multi-aged grouping.
3. Number of resource people available.
   a. Teacher aide only.
   b. Teacher aide and parent volunteers.
   c. Other resources such as college students or high school students.
   d. Any combination of above.
4. Invariant conditions.
   a. Meal times.
   b. Restroom facilities.
   c. Playground activities.
5. Time of the school year.
   a. Early in the school year.
   b. Midpoint.
   c. End of year.

The following section examines some of the principles that should be considered in scheduling large blocks of time, such as a week. The scheduling principles focus on the kind of planning that must be related to the educational component of the program.

WEEKLY SCHEDULING

Selecting Objectives

Scheduling a large block of time efficiently requires careful attention to the objectives that will be covered within that particular period. We will assume that the teacher has covered all of the steps described in Chapter 5 which are necessary for converting learning goals to learning experiences. The teacher and aide select the particular objectives they wish to attain, and list these objectives, along with the particular learning activities that will be presented for achieving them. A useful technique is to list the objectives by skill or content areas, so that the teacher and aide can get an overview of the different kinds of activities planned for the week.

Related Learning Experiences

Next, the teacher and aide should discuss other kinds of learning experiences that might support the planned activities. These would include field trips, stories, special kinds of learning materials for independent work or role playing, a visit from an outside resource person, or a tour in the neighborhood. The teacher and aide can use this planning time to brainstorm ideas and to review any special needs the children might have. In addition to related activities and learning experiences that meet special needs, the teacher and aide might decide to leave blocks of time open for those spontaneous events that will allow them to capitalize on the children's interests.

Estimating Time

The next step is to review the number of planned activities and related activities and determine how children will be grouped in order to obtain maximum benefit from participation in the learning experiences. Some activities lend themselves well to a total-group presentation, some to a small-group presentation, others to a one-to-one interaction. The nature of the objective determines, in large measure, the sort of grouping that must be used. For example, if the objective deals with a motor skill such as coordination of large muscles, a game approach with total-group participation would probably be effective. However, if the objective is mastery of a language skill that requires interaction and verbalization between the teacher and child, a small group would probably be most effective. At this point in the planning and scheduling process, the teachers should have an overview of all of the learning activities that will be scheduled during a particular week, as well as the number of groups with which they will work.

**Who Will Teach and
Supervise the Various
Learning Activities and
Experiences?**

Once decisions have been reached regarding the selection of objectives, related activities, and the amount of time that will be needed to cover the particular objectives, the supervising teacher and the aide can decide who will assume responsibility for each activity. The teacher and aide need to consider volunteers, such as parents or students, who might be available to assist them during the week. Next, the supervising teacher must assign specific responsibility for teaching or preparation to each available adult. If resource people other than the teacher's aide are to be assigned particular tasks, it is the supervising teacher's responsibility to notify those people and assist them with planning and preparation. Major responsibility for instruction usually rests with the teachers, however. The supervising teacher will generally assume responsibility for presenting the more complex types of learning experiences, and will assign less demanding tasks to the aide. As the school year progresses, however, the teacher aide should learn to present many different kinds of activities.

Just as the planned learning activities are assigned to various people in the classroom, other kinds of responsibilities are also assigned. These responsibilities include observing the children as they work independently, interacting with them on the playground, preparing snacks and supervising snack time, and providing help to those children who have special kinds of needs.

**Pacing and Spacing
the Schedule**

Once decisions have been made regarding the number of planned activities that will be presented in any week, the sizes of groups required for each of these activities, and which adult will have the responsibility for any scheduled event, the teacher and aide are ready to consider some principles of pacing and spacing. They must consider not only the needs of the children, but also the needs of the adults in the classroom. Under no circumstances should the teacher or other adults in the classroom overload themselves by assuming too many demands on their time in any one day. Just as children cannot learn when they are tired or when excessive demands are made of them, adults cannot teach effectively when they have not paced or planned their time wisely.

The length of the school day largely determines the number of activities that can be scheduled for a given week. As a rule of thumb, those working in full-day programs should schedule no more than three planned activities in any one day. The assumption here is that these activities will be presented to small groups; for example, the teacher will present each activity three times, once to each of three groups, in any one day. The teaching load should be divided between the teacher and aide, with the teacher usually taking major responsibility for two planned activities, and the aide for one. At least one and preferably two related activities should be scheduled daily.

These would include stories, music, art, or any other special kind of activity the teacher believes appropriate for that particular week. If the children attend school for only a half day, then no more than two planned, directed learning activities should be scheduled for any one day. Related activities for a half-day program should not generally exceed two per day. It is important to remember that children need a balance between the ratio of direct instructional learning experiences and those that are child selected or child directed. Children need time to assimilate and accommodate new information, to practice new skills, and to explore their environment independently. Teachers also need time to work with the children enthusiastically and with zest. By avoiding overloading a weekly and daily schedule, both teachers and children can maintain the level of motivation needed to master new skills and acquire new information.

Pacing should be considered as the teacher schedules lessons for successive days. If the direct learning activities are such that practice is required before moving to the next level of skill mastery (e.g., a motor skill that the children must practice), at least one day should be skipped before scheduling the next activity. The in-between day can be used for practicing the new skill. Many other kinds of objectives require practice on the part of the children or the opportunity for them to experiment with the new skill on their own.

Many times it is necessary to demonstrate a particular piece of equipment that will be used for a planned learning activity. When these demonstrations must occur, the teacher should schedule the equipment demonstration prior to presenting the particular planned lesson.

Once the teachers have determined how many planned lessons will be presented in any one day, how many related activities will be scheduled, the number of equipment demonstrations necessary, and the number of days that will occur between successive activities, they can begin to fill in the weekly schedule with specific information (see Figure 8.2). The teachers have already considered, in their earlier schedule, some of the invariant conditions over which they have no control, such as meals, restroom time, playground time, and naps. As they fill in the weekly schedule with detailed information, they are ready to move to the next step of planning and scheduling.

Preparation of Materials

After the specific activities for a whole week are scheduled, the teacher and aide are ready to examine the planned activities, related activities, and other kinds of learning experiences that will require special materials or preparation. The teacher and aide should review what is needed, and each should assume responsibility for special preparations. Sometimes a lesson requires that the teacher bring items from home; other times preparation requires cutting out pictures or preparing some manipulative items. By listing what will be needed, the teacher and aide can anticipate and avoid problems

FIGURE 8.2
A Weekly Schedule

	Monday	Tuesday	Wednesday	Thursday	Friday
A. M.	Language arts: concept of family (small groups)	Equipment demonstration (Number Sorter) (small groups)	Science: concepts of hot and cold— cooking activity (total group)	Matching numerals (small group)	Filmstrip: families (total group) Small-group discussions
	Sensory-perceptual: sorting by size	Language arts: my family (small groups)			
	Story: *The Three Bears*	Story: *The Three Bears*	Art: groups B and C Story: role playing (small group A)	Language arts: comparing families— experience chart (small groups)	Art: groups A and B Story: role playing (small group C)
P. M.	Music: total group	Motor: imitating body movements	Music: total group	Art: groups A and C Story: role playing (small group B)	Music: total group

that might arise if they attempted to work with the children without careful preparation beforehand.

Classroom Environment

The final step in planning a weekly schedule is for the teacher and aide to review the complete schedule and to make some decisions regarding the total classroom environment. Many times a decision will be made to change the wall displays so that they relate to some of the topics that will be presented to the children. At other times it might be appropriate to set up a new learning center. For instance, if some of the planned activities deal with concepts related to health, one of the learning centers could be set up as a medical clinic. Clothing items and other toys that would support role playing and dramatic play on the part of the children might be placed in the center for that unit of study. Another special consideration in planning the classroom environment relates to the kinds of equipment and learning materials that the teacher and aide want to place around the classroom. Special puzzles related to the unit topic, more complex manipulative items, or unusual collage materials might be placed on the shelves if the teacher or aide feel that they will contribute to and support the theme of the week.

**Planning for
Other Resource People**

If other resource people will be available to work in the classroom during the week that is being planned, the teacher and aide must consider this as they complete their detailed scheduling. If they have done their job well, they have listed the specific activities that will be presented as well as the people who will be working directly with the children. If resource people such as parents, volunteers, or students will be available in the classroom, then the teacher or aide must prepare guidelines for these adults to follow. Simple instructions written on index cards can be prepared and filed on the teacher's desk. When the volunteers come, it will be a simple matter for the teacher or aide to hand them a card with suggestions of activities that they can then present to the children or use as guidelines for interacting.

This kind of planning can be extremely time consuming, especially at the beginning of the school year when the teacher and aide are still trying to get to know the children in their classroom. However, as the school year progresses, if the teachers have done their job well and if they have kept careful records on the progress made from week to week, planning time will be greatly reduced. Weekly scheduling is only an interim step. This kind of planning occurs once a week, and will usually take about an hour to an hour and a half. The planning task is not ended when the weekly schedule is completed, however. The next step in the process involves daily planning and preparation.

DAILY SCHEDULING

As the teacher and aide worked through the process for scheduling for a week, they selected the objectives that would be covered, they listed other activities that would be appropriate to include, they estimated the number of planned lessons and related activities, they decided who would have major responsibility for presenting particular activities, they made tentative decisions regarding the pacing and spacing of the planned activities, and finally they reviewed any special materials that they would need to prepare or equipment that they would have to bring into the classroom. Every bit of this information is needed for developing the daily schedule.

There are a number of factors to be considered as teachers plan for a particular day. The physiological needs of the children are a major consideration. The young child is most alert early in the day. The teacher must consider this factor in planning and scheduling any activity that requires intense concentration early in the day. For example, a learning experience requiring the child to remember or reproduce a sequence of specific sounds should be scheduled earlier in the day than a musical game-type activity that focuses on gross body movements. As a general rule, the first hour to hour and a half of the school day can be used to greatest advantage for more cognitively directed activities. The teacher should consider this in scheduling for different kinds of objectives or learning goals.

Many factors related to pacing within a particular day should be considered. The first of these is whether or not the activity requires the child to be active or passive. Some activities, such as story time, require that the child function in a passive role. While he might answer questions concerning the story, he will most probably spend 10 to 15 minutes sitting quietly and listening to the teacher. Other kinds of learning experiences, such as a project in one of the role-playing areas, require that the child be active physically as he participates.

Another factor to consider in pacing is whether the learning experience is teacher directed or child selected. It is extremely important that a well-balanced program include opportunities for the child to select activities on his own, as well as particular learning experiences that are selected and directed by the teacher or other adults in the classroom. An appropriate and reasonable balance must be maintained. Again, the teacher and aide must consider this factor in planning the daily schedule.

Varying and interchanging the particular adults who interact with the children is another consideration for pacing within a school day. Each child should have opportunities to interact with all of the adults who work within the program. This would include not only the teacher and aide, but also any volunteers, parents, or students in training who might be assigned to the classroom. Positive experiences with many different adults who are capable of interacting in a supportive manner help the child learn to trust and relate openly to adults.

The teacher has the option of scheduling small-group, large-group, or tutorial sessions for the children. Again, this factor should be considered in designing a schedule that will assist the teacher in holding the children's interest. Certain kinds of objectives lend themselves to presentation in a particular size of group. For example, if the objective deals with expressive language skills, and the teacher is anxious to allow the children many opportunities to respond verbally to a series of questions, the most appropriate group would be a small one. If, on the other hand, the objective is focused on singing and playing an action game designed to enhance language development, the teacher could very appropriately work with the entire class.

During many parts of the day, the teacher has the option of scheduling activities either indoors or outdoors. Many teachers tend to conduct most of their activities indoors, simply because it has been traditional to do it that way. If at all possible, teachers should take advantage of good weather and capitalize upon the outdoors as an appropriate and proper learning environment for young children. For example, a learning experience that deals with changes in seasons can be conducted very effectively outdoors, sitting under a tree. The concept of transportation can also be presented in a realistic setting by taking the children outdoors and letting them observe the different kinds of vehicles that travel down the street. The teacher can prepare an experience chart as the children observe different forms of transportation common to their neighborhood. The environmental setting should be capitalized upon in terms of pacing the daily program.

Planning the Daily Schedule   Keeping in mind the factors mentioned in the previous section, the teacher is now ready to consider planning the daily schedule. The first step involves blocking out time for routine events that occur daily. These would include meals, snacks, toileting, rest, outdoor play, and cleanup. In most cases, the times for these events are determined by the director or principal of the school, and teachers must work around these assigned schedules. Next, the teachers schedule the planned activities that will be presented on that particular day. They review the group size appropriate for the activity, and determine how many times a particular activity will have to be presented. Next, the teacher and aide schedule the related activities they feel will be appropriate for that particular day, as well as art, music, and free-exploration time.

When the teachers have completed the schedule for the day, they should review the events planned and check for internal consistency. Have they observed the basic principles of pacing and spacing known to be helpful in motivating young children in their learning? The following questions should all be considered:

- Have they scheduled the most demanding tasks early in the day?
- Have they alternated activities demanding a high level of concentration with those demanding lesser concentration?
- Have they alternated teacher-directed with child-selected learning experiences?
- Have they rotated the children from large to small to individualized kinds of grouping situations?
- Have they varied the number of adults who interact with the children during the day?
- Have they used indoor and outdoor environments to the greatest advantage?

The final consideration as the daily schedules are worked out involves how the children will move from one part of the day to another. These are practical considerations that are often overlooked by an inexperienced teacher. For example, if the children are to work on a collage project during the day, they must be given sufficient advance warning and time to clean up before they can be expected to move to another planned activity. This can be handled in a simple manner if the teacher or aide agree that they will alert the children five minutes before the activity is scheduled to end. Another potential problem likely to be overlooked by the inexperienced teacher involves planning in such a way that the children are required to stand and wait between activities. It is unreasonable to expect young children to stand in line, or wait a long time for a turn, without becoming extremely restless or disruptive. These situations can be avoided with proper planning. For instance, children can be dismissed in small groups and allowed to wash in preparation for lunch. One teacher can stay with the children in the restroom while the other supervises them in the classroom. As the children wait for the entire class to complete this preparation, the teacher in the classroom can read a story, lead them in a song, or play a familiar language game with the group. Careful planning helps the teacher avoid situations likely to cause the children to break rules. Handling transitions between activities should be considered as part of daily planning and scheduling. By the teacher's paying careful attention to possible transitional problems, disruptive behavior can be minimized.

Figures 8.3, 8.4, and 8.5 give examples of sample schedules that might be developed for a half-day program, a program that extends for six hours a day, and a full day-care program. Each of these schedules assumes that a teacher and at least one other adult is present in the classroom to work with the children. While the schedules are quite different, each considers the basic principles of planning and scheduling discussed above.

Is This Kind of Planning and Scheduling Really Necessary?

There is no doubt that good planning takes a great deal of time. Many teachers might feel that they cannot afford the time necessary to plan according to the guidelines and principles that we have discussed. Teachers must ask themselves, however, whether or not they can afford to develop a program where this kind of planning does not occur. How is it possible to individualize a curriculum, to meet the needs of every child in a classroom, and to provide special help when necessary, if the teacher and aide do not plan carefully? Teachers who cannot find the time for this task cannot possibly work together as a team and present a cohesive program. Unless the adults in the classroom clearly know what they *want* to happen, they cannot make appropriate decisions about when or why to deviate from the planned schedule. A classroom can be equipped with expensive toys and learning materials, but if the adults in the classroom have not considered carefully how they will use this equipment effectively, nothing but haphazard interactions can occur.

Maximizing the quantity and the quality of adult–child interaction is critically important for the success of any preschool program. Careful planning can create an environment in which this kind of interaction is possible. Without planning, those children who are most demanding or most appealing will monopolize the time and attention of the adults in the classroom. Too often, the child who is quiet, who is not demanding, or who cannot communicate his needs will be overlooked by the adults and will never receive his fair share of their time and attention.

FIGURE 8.3

A Daily Schedule

Time: 8:30 A.M. to 12:00 P.M.
Half-Day Program
Services: Snack

8:30–8:45	Children arrive
8:45–9:00	Greeting, circle time, review of plans for the day
9:00–9:45	Small-group activities (15 minutes each, three groups rotate) Teacher: language arts Teacher aide: sensory-perceptual Independent activities: self–selected
9:45–10:45	Restroom, snack, playground
10:45–11:30	Story: *The Three Bears* } 2 groups rotate Art: collage
11:30–12:00	Music: entire group
12:00	Dismissal

FIGURE 8.4

A Daily Schedule

Time: 8:30 A.M. to 2:30 P.M.
Full-Day Program
Services: Snack and Lunch

8:30–8:45	Children arrive
8:45–9:00	Circle time: greeting, review of plans for the day
9:00–9:45	Small-group activities (15 minutes each, three groups rotate) Teacher: language arts Teacher aide: sensory-perceptual Independent activities: self-selected
9:45–10:45	Restroom, snack, playground
10:45–11:30	Story: *The Three Bears* } 2 groups rotate Art: Collage
11:30–11:45	Restroom
11:45–12:15	Lunch
12:15–1:15	Nap
1:15–1:30	Restroom
1:30–1:45	Music: entire group
1:45–2:30	Independent or self-selected activities
2:30	Dismissal

FIGURE 8.5
A Daily Schedule

Time: 7:30 A.M. to 5:30 P.M.
Full Day-Care Program
Services: Breakfast, Snack, and Lunch

7:30–8:00	Children arrive
8:00–8:30	Snack/Breakfast
8:30–9:00	Circle time: greeting, review of plans for the day
9:00–9:45	Small group activities (15 minutes each, three groups rotate) Teacher: language arts Teacher aide: sensory perceptual Independent activities: self-selected
9:45–10:45	Restroom, snack, playground
10:45–11:30	Story: *The Three Bears* ⎫ Art: Collage ⎬ 2 groups rotate
11:30–11:45	Restroom
11:45–12:15	Lunch
12:15–1:45	Nap
1:45–2:00	Restroom
2:00–3:00	Self-selected activities
3:00–3:15	Snack
3:15–4:15	Playground
4:15–4:45	Music: entire group
4:45–5:30	Self-selected activities
5:30	Dismissal

Most early childhood educators would agree that the child's cognitive and affective development cannot be separated. Teachers working in a preschool classroom must be sensitive to the needs of the whole child. These needs will vary from day to day, from week to week, and from one kind of learning experience to another. Careful planning means careful monitoring. As the teacher and aide review the events of each day, revise the daily schedule, and modify the plans for the week, they must take into account the progress made by each child in the process. Constant awareness of the effects that the day's activities have had on the child's performance reminds the teacher of special needs that must be met. From the moment the teachers step into the classroom, if they have planned and prepared for the day, they can focus on the children, their interactions with them, and the "teachable moment" as it arises. A teacher who is ill prepared, who cannot control the children, or who has no idea where they have been or where they are going cannot possibly respond to the whole child or recognize those spontaneous moments that must be capitalized upon for teaching experiences. Too many teachers pay lip service to the concept of a free and unstructured environment without ever assuming the responsibilities that go with the supervision of such an environment. The less structured the situation appears, the more time and preparation the teacher has to commit. The master teacher has learned this lesson well and knows the importance of planning and scheduling for the well-being of both the children and the other adults who work in the classroom.

CONCLUSIONS

Very few teachers will argue with the *concept* of the importance of planning and scheduling. The problem, however, arises in regard to *the amount of time that must be committed to the task*. Many teachers argue that this time simply does not exist. Very often their working day extends from the moment the children arrive in the morning until the time they leave late in the afternoon. Too often, the center where they are employed does not schedule any time at the end of the day for the teacher and aide to plan or modify plans for the following day. Ideally, twenty to thirty minutes at the end of the day is the most appropriate time for planning and scheduling. During this time, the teacher and aide can review very briefly the events of that particular day and can make decisions regarding preparation and plans for the following day. In schools or centers where this time is reserved, the most efficient planning can occur.

What does a teaching staff do when time is not provided at the end of the day for planning and scheduling? There are other options that teachers can consider. Regardless of the program model being implemented, every school day includes some time devoted to rest or nap. The teacher and aide can meet quietly in a corner of the room while the children are resting, and do their planning for the following day. Another option is to ask a parent or volunteer to supervise the children for twenty to thirty minutes, allowing the teacher and aide time to plan. Another option, far from ideal but better than no planning whatsoever, involves having the teacher plan independently, either late in the afternoon or early the following morning, and then posting the revised schedule and plan for the aide. In the morning, the aide can quickly scan the revised schedule and raise questions before the day's activities begin.

While the options discussed above are less than ideal, they are far better than omitting the process completely. Teachers who claim that they do not have time to plan and to schedule are being derelict and neglectful of their professional responsibilities. Priorities always can be reordered if the teacher feels that planning is an important task. The success of the instructional program depends, in large measure, on the time and the effort the teacher is willing to invest in the planning process. Without these essential ingredients of planning, little but haphazard teaching and, even worse, insufficient learning will occur.

QUESTIONS

1. Explain the value of the schedule. Why should teachers make a schedule? One goal of scheduling is to maximize the quantity and quality of adult–child interaction. What other goals or advantages that occur when scheduling is done appropriately are lost when scheduling is not done well?

2. If someone handed you a weekly schedule, could you determine its appropriateness? What three or four basic things would you look for?

3. Some writers have suggested that nap time or other very quiet periods should be scheduled immediately after outdoor play or other boisterous activity. Is this wise? Why or why not?

4. What kinds of activities should be scheduled immediately after meals and snacks? What kinds should be avoided at these times?

5. Many teachers like to start the day with a whole-group greeting period and/or end it with a whole-group review-discussion-reinforcement period. What are some advantages and disadvantages of this? Do *you* intend to use either or both of these activities? Why or why not?

6. Plan a daily and weekly schedule for a nursery school similar to the one you expect or hope to teach in. Which parts are fixed, and which are flexible? What are some alternative arrangements for use of the time that can be scheduled flexibly? Are these arrangements equally profitable? What are their comparative advantages and disadvantages? Is any one plan clearly the best?

7. Plan activities for a rainy day that could be altered for use with almost any unit of work.

8. During observations, notice how the teachers have planned so that the children do not have to stand idly or wait in line for excessive lengths of time. (Or have they planned?) Notice movement between activities: how much confusion is there? How much wasted time? What could be done to help make transitions between activities less confusing and time consuming?

READINGS

Association for Childhood Education International. *Equipment and supplies: tested and approved for preschool/school/home.* Washington, D.C.: Association for Childhood Education International, 1965.

Grotberg, E., ed. *Day care: resources for decisions.* Washington, D.C.: Office of Economic Opportunity, 1971.

Hymes, J. *The child under six.* Englewood Cliffs, N.J.: Prentice-Hall, 1963.

Kritchevsky, S. "Physical settings in day-care centers." In E. Prescott and E. Jones, eds. *Group day care as a child–rearing environment: an observational study of day care programs.* Pasadena, Calif.: Pacific Oaks College, 1967.

Moore, S. and Richards, P. *Teaching in the nursery school.* New York: Harper & Row, 1959.

Read, K. *The nursery school,* rev. ed. Philadelphia: Saunders, 1966.

9
GROUP INSTRUCTION WITH YOUNG CHILDREN

We have emphasized repeatedly that the preschool child learns most efficiently through individual activities involving manipulation of concrete objects. Thus, regardless of the type of program or the children enrolled, good preschool programs involve as many of these kinds of opportunities as possible, ideally with tutoring or at least with the opportunity for occasional individualized interaction with the teacher or another adult.

However, there will be many occasions in which you will be conducting a formal or informal lesson activity with groups of children. Here we refer to an activity that has specific learning objectives or goals; in other words, one that attempts to teach certain information, concepts, or skills to the children. The remainder of the chapter will present a variety of suggestions for group instruction that are applicable to almost any group situation, either formal or informal.

MINIMIZE GROUP SIZE

The reason for teaching children in small groups in the first place is efficiency. Much of the teacher's time can be saved if the same lesson can be taught to several children at once rather than to each child individually through tutoring. However, there is a trade-off here between savings in the teacher's time and dilution of the effectiveness of the activity. Tutoring is maximally effective because the teacher can focus full attention on the child and adapt the activities to meet his individual needs. This becomes much more difficult to do when more than one child is involved in the activity, and the difficulty increases with each additional child.

Thus, one important rule to bear in mind is that preschool children should be taught in groups small enough to allow the teacher to monitor each individual in the group carefully and respond to his individual needs. Small groups are better than large groups in general, but it is especially important

188

to have small groups when the learning objectives are difficult for the children, when they involve concentrated activity and detailed feedback, or when the children are young and not yet able to maintain sustained attention to group lessons. Five-year-olds and most 4-year-olds can maintain such attention for twenty minutes, but younger children require shorter lessons taught in smaller groups.

This will often mean presenting a ten-minute lesson or activity three or four times to groups of four or five children each, rather than presenting it only once to the entire class. The repetition involved in this approach will be more than compensated for by the dramatic improvement in the quality and effectiveness of the learning experience. Observations of teachers who try to teach large groups of preschool children show that even the most talented teachers *rarely* can make such presentations work effectively. Instead, they spend much of their time fighting for attention, and the children spend much of their time being bored and restless. The primary reason is that the children do not get enough individual attention and opportunities to respond; even if the lesson provides for frequent response opportunities, the group size will impose constraints that cause each child to spend most of his time passively watching while the teacher talks or other children respond. Such prolonged passivity makes for boredom and disruptive acting out.

Thus, strive to minimize the size of your activity groups, being especially careful to minimize group size with very young children or in situations where the material to be taught is difficult and demanding. Instead of presenting a single lesson to the whole group, teach it two or more times to smaller groups while the other children are involved in free play or some other activity. Arrange your schedule so that your groups rotate from one activity to another, thus insuring that each child will be included in the lesson group at some time during the day.

GETTING AND HOLDING ATTENTION

It is important to get the lesson off to a good start by immediately getting and holding the children's attention. Several techniques can help to insure this. First, be sure that you have all the materials that you plan to use during the activity prepared in advance and stored in an easily accessible place. Ideally, they should be on a shelf or in some other storage area within reach of where you will be sitting or standing during the lesson, so that you will not have to move in order to get materials. Any required preparation (cutting out figures, punching holes, preparing formboards, etc.) should be done in advance, unless demonstrating the process is part of the lesson. The point here, of course, is that you are virtually certain to lose the attention of the children if you make them wait while you prepare materials or while you leave the lesson area to get something that should have been within reach to begin with.

It is also important to prepare the children. By using direct instruction and socialization as well as indirect cues such as facial expressions and voice tone changes, teach the children that they are expected to pay careful attention to lessons. This means teaching them that certain activities which are ordinarily permissible (leaving one's seat to move around the room, playing with self-chosen materials, talking with other children, etc.) are not acceptable during lesson times, when children will be expected to pay attention to the activity. As with other expectations for classroom rules, maintain a positive note here. Bear in mind that you are asking the children to make a somewhat difficult discrimination between when certain activities are permissible and when they are not, and that there is nothing inherently wrong with the behavior that is being forbidden during the activity; it is not accepted simply because it interferes with the lesson.

Combining the previous two considerations (preparing your lesson materials and preparing the children), we conclude that you should not attempt to begin a lesson until all materials are ready and all the children included in the group are seated and ready for participation. When these conditions are met, begin crisply and get into the lesson quickly. Most teachers find that the children respond best to some kind of standardized signal that tells them "It's time to stop talking and pay attention to the lesson now." The particular words are not especially important; any sentence or phrase that communicates this meaning to the children will do ("Pay attention now, children," "O.K., let's begin"). However, you should use the same signal every time, because it will be easier for the children to recognize and understand.

A good strategy is to begin by holding up or otherwise showing some interesting object or picture likely to draw the children's interest and attention. This will be more effective, of course, if you keep your "lesson starter" out of sight before the activity begins, so that your showing it will have a surprise or novelty effect in addition to its inherent interest value to the children.

In addition to having such a "starter" ready for use, be sure to prepare a sequence of statements and questions that you plan to use in conjunction with this object. This will constitute your introduction. Continue to direct attention by holding up or pointing to objects that you want the children to watch, or by giving demonstrations (with concurrent explanations as you go) for them to observe. These techniques are especially useful at the beginning of the year when you are teaching the children to pay attention.

If you have gotten off to a good start, holding the children's attention is primarily a matter of good pacing and insuring the continued participation of all the children. Suggestions on how to do this will be given in the following sections. However, in cases where the children's attention does wander, it is important to regain their interest as quickly as possible, before minor inattention spreads and leads to a more major or sustained disruption.

One good way to direct attention at the beginning of an activity is to hold up and/or point to an object or picture (be sure everyone can see, though!).

191

Many group activities occur on the floor, in a small circle. Here, teachers should position themselves close to the children, so that all are within reach. This makes it easier to catch wanderers quickly and to eliminate distraction through touch and gesture (see below). Also, in positioning the children for such activities, avoid placing them near distracting objects such as puzzles and blocks, and have them face a corner or wall rather than toward other activity centers or other children.

Although inattention should be eliminated as quickly as possible, this must be accomplished without disrupting the activity and ruining its pace. Ideally, you should not even call attention to the child's inappropriate behavior. This can be done by casually tapping or touching him, moving closer to him, or calling on him to respond or take a turn. If it is not possible or convenient to eliminate the problem this way, try to do it as briefly and nondisruptively as possible. Simply call the child's name and indicate that he should pay attention with a look or gesture, or add a very brief comment such as, "Look here."

If more than one child is inattentive, or if you do not wish to call attention to a child individually, give a general rule reminder ("Remember, we all pay careful attention during lessons"). In any case, do *not* overdwell on the child's misbehavior ("John, I see what you and Mike have been doing over there; you stop that whispering and giggling") or express exasperation ("John, why is it that I always have to call on you to pay attention? What's the matter with you, anyway?"). Such nagging ruins pacing, switches the attention of the other children to the misbehaving child, and is perceived by the misbehaving child as rejection. All of these are unnecessary and undesirable outcomes.

In addition to the above, a technique that helps to maintain attention and that is especially useful for insuring that children attend to the appropriate stimulus is to include transitional and connecting words and phrases when switching from one part of an activity to another. Transitional statements, like "O.K., now let's see if you can do it," or "Now we'll add some red paint and see what happens," help restimulate attention and alert the children to the fact that the activity is moving into a new phase.

INSURING EVERYONE'S ACTIVE PARTICIPATION

One common mistake that even experienced teachers often make is concentrating their attention on only a few children in the group rather than making sure that everyone participates actively. This is a trap that is easily fallen into, because by spending most of their time with the children who are eager to participate, teachers can both keep these children happy and insure that the majority of questions and response demands are met successfully. To the untrained observer, such activities often seem to be very successful, perhaps even ideal. However, closer inspection reveals that the teacher is really dealing successfully with only three or four children while the others are passively sitting or perhaps actively attending to something else. Thus, the activity, while perhaps successful for the few active participants, is a failure if its intended objective was to teach the concept or skill involved to *all* of the children.

We do not mean to suggest here that participation should be as exactly equal as possible. It is not only easy, but to a certain extent it is productive to allow the eager children to participate more often than the more reticent ones. This will provide the eager children with the attention and response opportunities that they seek, and will help insure that the reticent ones are not put on the spot in situations in which they are either unable or so unwilling to respond that attempts to make them do so would be undesirable. It *is* important, however, to be consciously aware and *in control* of the response rates of the different children in a group. Too often teachers are simply *reactive* to the differential press for response opportunities that different children present, when instead they should be *proactive,* maintaining awareness of these individual differences in the students and making sure that they are not unduly influenced by them (Brophy & Good, 1974). Teachers should determine when and how often each child should respond on the basis of judgments concerning what is best for him individually (see Chapters 11 and 12), and should avoid creating situations in which response opportunities are gained by jumping up and down, waving hands, shouting, or other undesirable and unnecessary behaviors.

In addition to maintaining a general awareness of each child's participation rates and making considered judgments about the frequency and type of participation that is best for him, the teacher can do several specific things to insure that every child in the group participates actively, whether or not he is responding at a given moment. First, form the habit of continually monitoring the entire group, so that the children know that you are regularly checking their attention and participation. This will not only reduce the likelihood of inattention, it will also enable you to observe and to take action to correct confusion and errors more quickly than you might otherwise. Stay as close as possible to the children, and have them seated facing you so that eye contact can be established easily with all of them. Do not have any children seated behind you or to the side of you where you cannot notice them easily. Each child should be able to see you, and you should be able to see him, without difficulty.

Introduce the activity and conduct the demonstration with positive expectations and enthusiasm. Be sure that each child in the group can clearly see what you are doing. Help direct attention by underscoring key words and pointing or gesturing where appropriate. During activities that involve individual responses or actions, you can encourage the other children to watch the child who is presently responding by making comments about his performance or asking them to comment on it. Also, reassure the other children that they will get their chance ("Mike, you're doing fine; Susy, John, and Mary, you'll get a chance soon").

Where possible, provide multiple supplies for activities that involve individual turns, so that the children can all work simultaneously rather than having to spend a lot of time watching and waiting. For example, if the activity involves work sheets, a small group can be seated around you and can all begin work together after you have given an initial demonstration or set of directions. The children should be close enough so that you can monitor their progress individually and give corrective feedback or other help where necessary. If the activity does require that all children except one watch and wait while the remaining child performs, help the onlookers to watch thoughtfully and actively by making comments to stimulate their interest or curiosity.

GROUP OR CHORAL RESPONSES

One way to save time and allow everyone to participate simultaneously is to use group or choral responses. Because of their efficiency, they should be used where appropriate. However, they involve disadvantages which dictate that their use be restricted to certain situations. First, group responding is unnatural, and often produces unnatural, sing-song responses from the children. Second, children need opportunities for individual responses to develop their expressive skills and confidence in their ability to perform individually in public situations. Third, and most important, group responses make it difficult to monitor the progress of individuals because the teacher may not notice in every instance if a child does or does not respond correctly. This makes it possible for a child to fail to acquire the concept or skill being taught without the teacher realizing it, or even for the child to acquire an erroneous idea or response because his error was never detected and corrected by the teacher. Thus, it is essential to spend at least some of the time having children respond individually, so that you can carefully monitor their mastery of the concept or skill involved.

Group responses are good for concepts that are very easily learned, such as labels (for example, when introducing any new object, routinely hold up the object, give its name, and then ask the group to repeat it a few times out loud). Group responses are also especially good when the concept or skill being taught is one that is learned only very slowly and in very small steps (for example, physical abilities and other motor learning, or learning to speak English without an accent). However, if the lesson involves a clear-cut behavioral objective that is deemed crucial for all children to master immediately, or if it involves a difficult concept or skill that usually is not learned without careful and continuing adult monitoring and correction, individual responses are essential. One especially useful technique for responding to individual differences here is to dismiss from the group the children who have mastered such concepts or skills and work with the remaining children on a more intensive, individual basis. Also, such situations are best handled if the children are taught in several groups, with each group being as small as the available time and personnel will allow.

STRUCTURE AND PACING OF ACTIVITIES

The younger the children, and the less experienced they are in school, the more that watching and waiting time should be minimized. Activities should be subdivided into steps or segments so that the children's memories will not be taxed by long, involved demonstrations and so that they can achieve success at each step without unreasonable difficulty.

In general, this will mean a minimum of sustained teacher talk and a maximum of child responses. Once you have introduced the activity with whatever teacher demonstration is necessary, move quickly to child responses that give the children a chance to perform the relevant tasks themselves. Meanwhile, help them to conceptualize and learn the relevant vocabulary for tasks they are doing by describing them and making comments about them as they work. This will help sustain attention and build conceptual and verbal schemas in the onlookers as well.

Children should be taught new skills to the point of *overlearning,* meaning that they consistently respond correctly and give every evidence of having thoroughly mastered the concept or skill. However, this should not be carried to the point of unnecessary and meaningless drill on material that the children have overlearned long since.

When children make mistakes, *tell them so.* One frequent and unfortunate tendency in adults is a fear or distaste for telling children when they have made mistakes. This is no favor to the child. First, children commonly make mistakes and commonly are corrected for them by their peers. Spend a few moments watching one child giving another child instructions on how to do something, and you will see all mistakes pointed out immediately and correction given without apologies or comments intended to soothe the child's hurt feelings. The reason is that the child doesn't have any hurt feelings; except in unusual situations, children are quite accustomed to making mistakes in the process of learning something new, and it does not bother them. Thus, when a child makes a mistake, simply point out the mistake to him and proceed from there. In some cases, this will mean redemonstrating the whole operation and having the child begin again. In other cases, simply indicating the nature of the mistake will be enough to allow the child to correct it and continue on his own.

The child should be allowed to do as much as he can on his own, but he should *not* be allowed to persist in mistakes or be protected from learning about his mistakes. Allowing a child to persist in mistakes will only reinforce bad habits and make change more difficult for him. The net result will be that, in addition to having to learn a new concept or skill, the child will have to unlearn an inappropriate one which he has learned. For example, if a child is having trouble because he is holding a pencil, a fork, or a pair of scissors in a way that makes it difficult or impossible for him to use the tool properly, show him the correct way rather than let him continue fumbling in frustration.

Misguided attempts to protect the child by refusing to acknowledge errors or by labeling them as something else will do no good and might do some harm. First, as mentioned above, children do not need this kind of protection, since they will not be bothered by their errors. Second, such behavior on the part of the teacher might change the child's concept of making a mistake from a simple recognition of a reality that occurs dozens of times daily (this is what making a mistake means to most young children) to a feeling that he has done something terrible for which he should be ashamed. Children develop their knowledge about the meanings of events from watching the reactions of adults. If adults react to mistakes as if they were terrible events that cannot be mentioned or discussed, the children will acquire this same idea themselves.

Thus, activities with young children should be series of demonstrations followed by opportunities for the children to perform, with any error being corrected immediately through redemonstration. Following correction of the error, the child can be allowed to continue with the task (if it is a continuing task), or the teacher can move on to someone else and come back to the child later (if he has simply missed a one-word answer response or similar short task). On the one hand, the teacher needs to be very conscious of children's errors, in order to concentrate on those children who most need individualized help. On the other hand, though, *errors should be treated as normal, expected events* that regularly occur in the process of learning things. Unless the material is purely verbal, be sure that your correction includes *showing* the child what to do as well as telling him.

The nature of the lesson may differ in different groups, depending upon needs and interests of the children. If the material is completely new to all or most of the children, the time should be spent exclusively or primarily on practice and work with the new concepts and skills involved, to the point that the children achieve mastery at the level of overlearning. On the other hand, if the children already seem to know the concepts or skills, or if they learn them quickly and easily, the activity can be expanded. Rather than have the children continue practicing something that they already have mastered, expand the activity by moving to higher levels in the same task progression or by relating the material to the children's experiences or to other knowledge or skills. If the activity involves some kind of tool skills that can be used for a higher-level purpose, the expansion might involve applying the skills to such a purpose rather than merely practicing the skill itself. For example, once children have learned to handle paints and paint brushes, they should be encouraged to attempt to paint particular pictures. Again, the general principle is to see that *each* child learns a given concept or skill to the level of overlearning, but that once this point is reached, further practice of the same skill should stop and the activity should terminate or else be expanded to apply the skill to some higher-order purpose.

ENDING ACTIVITIES

As the activity progresses, the teacher will have to make the key decision at some point of whether to continue with the entire group or to dismiss part of the group. A decision will also have to be made about when to stop. The decision about persisting with the entire group versus breaking up the group should be based upon the range of differences in responses that you observe among the children. If all are learning at about the same rate and seem to be finding the activity to be about equally difficult, continue with the whole group, insuring that everyone gets frequent chances to participate and that everyone learns each step as you go along. On the other hand, if it becomes clear that part of the group already knows or can very easily learn everything involved, while the other part is going to need individualized and extensive work, it might be better to break up the group by taking the first subgroup through to the end of the activity and then dismissing it, thus saving the remaining time for more intensive work with the remaining subgroup.

If this is done, it should be done in a low-key, matter-of-fact manner. Praise the children who have mastered the concept and dismiss them from the group, perhaps with some instructions about what they can or should do next. Then simply return to the remaining children and resume the lesson ("Billy, George, Mary, and Joan, I see that you are all finished with your pictures. They're very pretty. Take them over and hang them up on the bulletin board, and then get something to play with. O.K., Ralph and Linda, let's see how you're doing. . . ."). Do not overdo your praise of the departing children or criticize those that remain, because either action might foster an unhealthy elitism in the successful children or an unnecessary stigmatized feeling for the children who remain. Instead, treat such instances as just another example of the general principle that some children excel at some things and other children excel at others, and the dismissal of some children from the group is not particularly noteworthy or important.

With children remaining in the group for more work, or in any situation where children are having difficulty learning, several principles should be kept in mind. First, as mentioned above, point out any errors immediately and redemonstrate or allow the child to continue on his own from there. Second, form the attitude yourself (and teach it to the children) that mistakes and difficulties in learning are to be expected and dealt with as a matter of routine, without expressions of frustration, disgust, pity, or rejection. Third, allow (insist if necessary) the child to do as much as he can on his own, without doing it for him yourself. At the same time, however, avoid pointless pumping of a child who does not know the answer to your question and is unlikely to think of it unless you give him some help. This child needs help in the form of redemonstration or some kind of clue, not just more encouragement to respond. Where repeated failure is encountered, do not simply persist with the identical demonstration and instructions that have so far failed to be successful. Try to analyze the child's problem and identify the particular reason for his difficulty, and try to teach the concept or skill in a somewhat different way. This should be done immediately if possible, although you may have to take time to think over the problem and come back to it the next day. Sometimes, due to idiosyncratic vocabularies or other individual factors, a child will fail a task under one set of instructions but succeed when the instructions are slightly altered. Other children will not be able to succeed on a task if it is too long, but they can gradually achieve success if the task is broken into subtasks that they can take one at a time and build on as they master each successively. Suggestions for dealing with problems in learning will be treated in more detail in Chapter 11.

Regardless of whether or not the entire group is still together or whether only a subgroup remains, at some point you must decide to terminate the activity for the day. The schedule will provide general guidelines here, but it should not be adhered to so strictly that it becomes an end in itself rather than simply a means to assist you in meeting your goals. Several considerations are involved in deciding when to stop an activity. First, a good general rule is always to *stop early rather than late.* Teachers regularly report that children are eager to resume an activity that was interrupted while they were still highly interested in it, while the opposite is true regarding activities that persisted long beyond the point that the children had lost interest. Unless there is some easily identifiable and correctable reason for the children's disinterest, do not persist with an activity when the majority of the group is obviously no longer interested in it. There is little to be gained from the standpoint of learning, since the children are unlikely to retain much of the material to which they are exposed under such conditions, and there may well be some deleterious effects if they acquire a negative attitude towards the topic or skill involved. Thus, if an activity is dragging or the children are clearly restive and bored, it is almost always better to abandon it and switch to some other activity, resuming later in the day or on the following day.

Also, when such things happen, analyze the reason for them and make any necessary adjustments. If the children were distracted or restless for reasons having nothing to do with the activity itself, simply postponing it until a more opportune time may be sufficient. However, if the activity produced a clearly negative response in the children because of something inherent in it, an adjustment should be made. Perhaps it was too difficult and frustrating and needs to be postponed until later in the year, or even until the children are older. Perhaps it needs to be divided into two or more smaller parts that are more realistic in their objectives. Perhaps the topic was completely foreign to the children's experience, so that it should either be abandoned or made more concrete through the use of objects, pictures, or some other concrete stimulus that would make the content more meaningful for them. Perhaps it involved too much passive waiting and watching, and therefore needs to be adjusted to eliminate this problem. In any case, when an activity obviously does not work, and there is no apparent reason why the children might have been distracted from it, an analysis and some corrective action is in order before it is repeated.

When activities have gone well, they should end when all of the children have mastered the objectives. This may or may not coincide with the time allotted for them in the schedule. If the objectives are successfully mastered before the allotted time is up, you should take one of two courses of action: either expand to areas beyond the objectives already mastered, or terminate early and allow the children to return to free play or some other activity. Do *not* persist by pointlessly repeating questions and response demands that the children obviously have overlearned.

OBTAINING AND REACTING TO CHILD RESPONSES

Your questions and response demands should be designed to proceed in *sequences* systematically and gradually from the known to the unknown and from the easy to the difficult. Make it clear to the children whether they are expected to respond together or whether the question or response opportunity is intended for a specific individual. One important rule to teach the children, and to insist upon at all times, is that an individual's opportunity to respond be respected (i.e., no calling out answers or bragging that you know the answer; each child is entitled to time to think without being distracted by other children or losing his response opportunity because someone else calls out the answer). Also, be sure to *get a response* from each child, whether or not he knows the answer to your question or is able to fulfill your response demand. Teach the children to say "I don't know" rather than to remain silent when they don't know an answer. Show them that you are willing to wait patiently and to give them time if they want time to think about an answer or about how to solve a problem, but also make it clear that they can and should tell you that they don't know in cases where they are stumped.

When a child cannot respond correctly, either give him the answer or give him some help and have him try it again. Do *not* have some other child answer for him, because this will tend to foster competitiveness in the group (children calling out "I know, teacher, I know," whenever a child doesn't respond almost immediately). If the question involves arbitrary cultural knowledge (e.g., a color label, community helpers) or other information that one either knows or does not know and cannot reasonably be expected to figure out for oneself, simply give the child the answer and come back to him later with the same or another question. On the other hand, if the response demand calls for something that the child could reason through for himself on the basis of what he already knows plus some help that you could give him (in the form of a clue or a rephrasing of the question), give him the help and then provide him with a second response opportunity.

GIVING FEEDBACK

In addition to making certain that you receive a response to each question or response demand, be sure that you give the child feedback following each response or failure to respond. Children in general, and young children in particular, often do not know whether or not their response has been correct unless they are specifically told by the teacher; yet, some teachers frequently fail to give such feedback (Brophy & Good, 1974). Feedback, especially feedback following correct responses, need not be extensive; any words or actions that clearly indicate the correctness of the child's response to him will suffice. Thus, feedback can frequently be restricted to nodding the head up and down, winking, repeating the answer, saying "Yes," "That's right," and so forth. Feedback following incorrect responses should be as specific and prescriptive as possible, indicating the exact nature of the error and perhaps also providing the correct answer or some form of help that will make it easier for the child to get on the right track.

It does *not* appear to be especially important or even particularly useful to praise the individual correct answers of children. Teacher praise of individual correct answers is uncorrelated or sometimes even negatively correlated with student learning gains (Brophy & Evertson, 1973), and extensive praise of individual answers may amount to little more than distracting interruptions rather than rewards or reinforcements. In general, seeing that the child receives feedback to every response, and that this feedback is as specific as possible, is more important than praise for individual successful responses. This does *not* mean, of course, that the teacher's warmth and a close teacher–child relationship are not important. Quite the contrary. However, recent research is suggesting that it is the *general* quality of the teacher–student relationship as developed and maintained in the total context of the preschool experience, rather than the teacher's praise of isolated successes, that is really important. If the teacher has created a solid relationship with each child, praise of his specific individual responses is neither important nor expected (unless the expectation is built up by frequent praise in such situations). By the same token, if the teacher has alienated and/or frightened the children, praising them for responding successfully is unlikely to do much to improve the generally undesirable relationship. A solid relationship is based upon knowledge of and appreciation for the child's individual characteristics, not on praise of a few isolated correct answers.

It is a good idea to praise the group if the group as a whole did very well, or to praise individuals for their general progress during private interactions. In either case, *praise should be specific, identifying precisely the actions that are being praised.* Such specific praise shows the child that you have been paying attention to and are appreciative of his progress, and is probably going to be much more effective than nonspecific, empty-sounding praise. *Also, praise should be individualized and based on each child's progress at his own level,* rather than on absolute standards that might not be applicable to many of the children. Thus, a child who is just learning to ride a tricycle should be praised for his success in learning to maneuver it forward and backward in a straight line, while a child who is experienced in riding a tricycle might be praised for more advanced skills.

Criticism and rejection in response to failure to respond or to incorrect answers are unnecessary and destructive and *should be avoided.* Such behavior serves no teaching function, since it does nothing to help the child correct his mistake, and it is virtually certain to undermine the teacher–child relationship and harm the child's self-concept. It should be unnecessary to say much about this, but the fact is that observation in classrooms frequently reveals teachers criticizing children who do not answer questions or meet response demands successfully. Often this is because the teacher has an inappropriate role definition. It is important for teachers to remember that their job is to instruct children (particularly children who have less ability and/or knowledge and thus are more in need of instruction), not simply to get children to make responses and then label them as correct or incorrect. In fact, the true essence of the teacher's job, and the place where the best teaching skills are specifically called for, is in dealing with mistakes and failures. This probably all seems quite self-evident, yet many teachers behave as though they have forgotten it.

Another inappropriate response often observed in teachers is the tendency to feel rewarded by the children's answers and successes and punished by their incorrect answers and failures (Good & Brophy, 1973). Many teachers apparently have this attitude, even though upon reflection it is seen as clearly inappropriate. First, there is no reason for teachers to celebrate or otherwise overreact to correct answers and successes. Often a child will succeed because he already knew the answer or skill involved before an activity ever began. In these cases, the child's success had nothing to do with the teacher at all. Even where the teacher is responsible for a child's success, there is no need or reason for overly zealous celebration. After all, this is the

Here the teacher takes time to pay attention to and make a specific comment about a child's drawing. She not only praises the child, she *specifically* points out something noteworthy about the picture.

teacher's job. By the same token, there is no reason for teachers to overreact negatively to a child's failure. Such failure is usually not the teacher's fault, so there is no reason for her to respond as if it were. Instead, teachers should discipline themselves to learn to respond to child failure as a challenge and an indication that diagnosis and reteaching are in order (see Chapter 11). Blaming or rejecting the child for failure will only punish him unjustly and at the same time make your job more difficult. Thus, success should be acknowledged with an attitude of quiet satisfaction and appreciation, and failure should also be acknowledged and reacted to with an attitude of "Let's diagnose the problem and find out what the child needs in order to succeed." Intense evaluative comments and other strong personal reactions are inappropriate in both cases.

Certain kinds of criticism are appropriate in some situations, however. Such situations would include repeated and deliberate disruptive or inattentive behavior, repeated refusal to respond, and impulsive responding that shows that the child has not attempted to think about the question seriously. In such cases, it would be appropriate to give the child a warning indicating that you are aware of his behavior and that you want him to stop, adding a description of the behavior that you want him to show instead ("John, don't be in such a hurry to answer the questions. Listen to the question and think about it before you answer. I would rather that you took your time and gave me a good answer than just give me the first answer that comes to your mind"). Warnings should be brief, as in the example just given. Any extended discussion of a more serious problem should be dealt with individually, since a longer disruption of an activity would ruin its pacing and focus the attention of the entire group on the offender instead of on the topic at hand. Methods of handling more serious problems will be discussed in detail in Chapter 12.

**MAKING TIME
FOR RETEACHING**

All teachers, but most especially those working with a packaged curriculum, have the problem of making time for individualized reteaching with slow learners. We have several suggestions in this regard. First, remain continually aware of this problem. Some teachers simply forget about the problem of reteaching slow learners, or develop an attitude of indifference toward them, so that little or nothing is done to meet their special needs. Obviously, this is not appropriate.

More specifically, there are several things you can do to make time for reteaching. First, as mentioned previously, within a given activity, children who achieve the objectives clearly can be released to free play or other activities so that you can continue with a smaller group and thus have more time for individualized tutoring. If necessary, reteaching days can be scheduled periodically to help the slower children catch up. On such days, the children who do not need reteaching would be allowed to engage in free play or specially planned activities, while those children who do need reteaching would be given individualized or small-group instruction in those concepts and skills in which they were deficient.

Slow learners can also be helped by suggestions or special preparations in the areas of free play or special projects. For example, children having difficulty with pencil work because of problems in holding and manipulating a pencil can be encouraged to spend some of their free-time activity in work with small-muscle manipulative materials such as pencils, crayons, chalk, and so on. Children with motor problems can be encouraged to use equipment or engage in exercises designed to help develop those motor areas in which they need work. Reinforcement and reteaching can also be accomplished by setting up appropriate learning centers and/or designing individualized projects for independent work by children who need practice with certain kinds of activities. Thus, language master or listening-center activities can be designed especially for children who have problems in the language area, a variety of activities involving counting can be designed for children who need practice at counting, and so forth.

An especially important and effective method of reteaching is *tutoring* by an adult. In general, teachers should make as much time as they can to do such tutoring themselves with children most in need of it. However, tutoring can also be done by volunteers, parents, older children, or even peers who have already mastered concepts. This is one method and resource that teachers should take every opportunity to use. Any teacher working in a preschool connected with an elementary school should request that fifth or sixth graders be assigned to come to the classroom to work individually with children who need tutoring. The elementary school children will enjoy this job and are capable of doing it well, and this plan allows the teacher to see that children who need tutoring get it without having to do it personally. As studies suggest, elementary school children respond very favorably to the responsibility that tutoring entails, and this experience leads them not only to do the best job they can in tutoring the younger child, but also to improve their own attitudes towards school and their own work habits. Thus, this form of tutoring appears to be one method in which everyone involved gains.

Occasionally, a child will deliberately fail in order to get individualized attention from the teacher or tutor. If you suspect that this might be happening, do not move too quickly before you are certain of it. Take every opportunity to observe the child to determine whether or not he truly is failing deliberately to get attention in individualized contacts before you talk to him about it. If you determine that he is doing so, tell him that you can see what he is doing and ask him to stop, explaining that tutoring time is limited and you want to see that it is used with the children who need it most. Do not get angry at the child or reject him for his behavior, because such behavior signals that the child is desperately in need of attention and is probably not getting enough, at home and/or at school. Make a point of seeing that he gets considerable individualized attention and warmth in the future so that he no longer feels the need to get attention through deliberate failure or other attention-getting mechanisms.

 This problem is especially likely to occur if your tutoring involves only reteaching rather than expansion. Such problems may develop among the more-advanced children who never get tutoring because they learn easily without it. Arrange for tutorial-enrichment sessions with those children, so that they do not come to feel neglected or to seek individual tutorial attention by deliberately failing.   *Tutoring for reteaching*
enrichment

MISCELLANEOUS SUGGESTIONS

Below are a few additional suggestions about group instruction with young children.

First, with children who persistently behave disruptively and who are slow to become socialized to school routine, two techniques are particularly useful. First, separate children who tend to create trouble when they get together. Keep them in separate groups and in general try to arrange class-room schedules so that they do not get much of a chance to create disruptions together. If the problem persists continually, you might consider facing them with it directly in a private conference, pointing out that the two (or more) of them have been causing disruption and breaking classroom rules when they get together and warning them that if they don't do better they may have to be kept apart regularly.

Do not force a child to attend an activity if he seems ill, upset, or otherwise unwilling or unable to participate actively. Like everyone else, young children sometimes have short periods of depression in which they need time to be alone to think. Thus, in general it is a good idea to take a child at his word if, upon occasion, he says that he does not want to participate in an activity and just wants to go somewhere and lie down. Try to be sure to get back to him as soon as you can in order to find out what the problem is if he is willing to talk about it. If he isn't, leave him alone (although you may wish to mention the problem to the parent).

This should not happen on a regular basis, of course. If it does, it means that something is seriously wrong with the child in his home and/or school relationships. A talk with the child about this, and perhaps also a talk with the parents, is in order. If the child's behavior is motivated by some kind of severe problem at home over which you have no control, perhaps the best that you can do is attempt to reason with the parents about it and make suggestions about how they can change their behavior; meanwhile, go along with the child when he expresses a need to be left alone.

On the other hand, if the child's behavior appears to be a form of resistance to participation in the class activity and/or a form of defiance of you, obviously he needs an opportunity to ventilate his feelings and you need to take steps to repair a deteriorated teacher–child relationship. This may mean admitting several things to the child and/or making several changes in the way the child is treated. However, in such cases the child should not be allowed to continue to sit out activities and pout. Talk with him until you reach some kind of agreement about what kinds of changes should be forthcoming on both of your parts, but among changes to be forthcoming from the child, be sure to include the stipulation that in the future he will participate in group activities.

Teachers working in early education programs, especially former elementary school teachers who are used to the idea that one must finish the entire curriculum during the school year, should beware of overconcern about covering the curriculum completely. Obviously, it is all to the good if the children fully master all of the objectives contained in the year's curriculum. However, teachers need not be overly concerned if they don't. In fact, it is better that the children fully master (i.e., master to the point of overlearning) some fraction of the curriculum objectives than that they rush through the curriculum without really mastering any of it. Concepts and skills that are fully mastered to the point of overlearning stay with the child, but those that are "covered" but not really mastered will be lost before long. *Thus, individual children and the class as a whole should be moved along at as rapid a pace as they can handle, but no more rapidly.* If they cannot finish the entire curriculum made available to a teacher, the teacher should not attempt to push them to a false achievement.

Cognitive stimulation is important at this and any age, but for preschool children the single most important factor is their relationship with the teacher. If the children like and respect their teacher, and if they learn such things as achievement motivation, positive attitudes towards school and school tasks, and a positive self-concept, they are off to a good start. However, children who learn objectives only because they were force-fed through drill activities and similar tactics are unlikely to retain and build on what they have learned if they have not acquired positive attitudes towards teachers as individuals, schools as institutions, and themselves as learners.

Thus, bear in mind that all of the specific suggestions made in this chapter carry the implicit understanding that the teacher is building and maintaining healthy relationships with each child in the class. If this is not true, teachers who follow the suggestions will have a useful bag of teaching tricks, but they will be unlikely to truly succeed with the children, even by their own standards. It is important to teach young children and it is important to do it well, but it is absolutely essential that it be done in an atmosphere of warmth, encouragement, and respect.

SUMMARY

This chapter presented suggestions for effectively teaching preschool children in small groups. The techniques discussed are particularly useful for formal group instruction involving a specific, planned activity, although most are also relevant for informal use by a teacher who recognizes a "teachable moment."

One major principle is to minimize the size of the group. This allows for faster pacing and better monitoring of children's responses, and it minimizes the amounts of time that the children must spend waiting and watching.

It is also helpful if the teacher begins group activities in a standardized way, so that the children will recognize that an activity is beginning and that they should be alert and paying attention. This involves using a standard signal or phrase to get attention, pausing a few seconds while the children turn their attention to you, and then briskly getting into the activity. In a typical activity that begins with some kind of demonstration, have an interesting stimulus to show the children and cue their attention through pointing, holding objects up for them to see, and modulating your voice and making gestures as appropriate attention-maintaining signals.

Once into the lesson, insure participation by monitoring the group regularly to keep track of their attention and by keeping everyone continually involved in an active way. Provide frequent opportunities for the children to respond or take turns and minimize the time that they must passively watch and wait.

If everyone is able to keep up with the activity without difficulty, keep the group together until the planned objective is accomplished. At this point, either terminate or expand to higher-level activities. If the levels of understanding and success in the group are very uneven, it may be best to proceed through the end of the planned objectives with those children who are mastering the objectives easily and then to dismiss them from the group, saving the remaining time for more intensive work with the children who had difficulty. In any case, each child should learn each key objective to the point of overlearning, meaning that he can achieve success regularly and without hesitation or error.

It is important to get some kind of response every time you ask a question or make a response demand, even if the response is "I don't know." Do not allow the children to resist or withdraw from responding habitually. Where a child fails to respond or makes an error, give him the answer and have him repeat it (if the question deals with some new material you were introducing and/or if it deals with a matter that the child is unlikely to be able to figure out through reasoning). In contrast, if there is a good possibility that the child might be able to figure out the answer for himself, it is usually preferable to encourage him to try to respond or to provide some kind of help rather than simply to give the answer. In any case, be sure that each response demand yields some kind of response from the child. Within this scheme, try to get the highest-level response that the child is capable of giving.

Be sure to give feedback following each response. Although effusive praise is not necessary (and perhaps inadvisable), let the children know that they are correct when they give a correct response. Also, let the children know when they are wrong, but be sure to do this in a matter-of-fact way that does not suggest that being wrong is something to be ashamed of. Never criticize or reject a child for failing to respond correctly (although sometimes you may have to warn a child who is not responding correctly because he is not paying attention).

Children who are having difficulties with a particular activity will have even more difficulty with higher-level activities of the same type unless you provide for reteaching through tutorial activities, learning-center activities, or other methods of giving the child practice on skills in which he is weak. Reteaching should be initiated as soon as possible after the activity, and it should continue until the child has mastered the objective to the point of overlearning.

QUESTIONS

1. Why teach the same thing to several small groups when you could teach it once to the whole group?

2. What determines a "teachable moment?" Is it something inside the child that you have to wait for, or can you create it yourself?

3. What factors should you consider in assigning children to groups? Which are the most important? How many groups should there be? Should the same children be in the same groups for different activities? Why or why not?

4. How can you tell whether or not all of the children have been able to follow a presentation (i.e., master the objectives of the activity)? What should you do if one or more of them do not understand?

5. What does overlearning mean? How can you tell when a child has achieved it? Why should he achieve it?

6. Role play small-group activities with a few classmates, taking turns. Concentrate on getting *responses* from *everyone* at *each* stage, on giving *feedback* to *each* response without ruining your *pacing,* and on *praising effectively*. Give and receive helpful criticism and suggestions.

7. Many writers and teachers believe that children will learn everything of importance (at least in the preschool years) through naturalistic discovery during play. Is this wholly or partly true? If so, why bother with group instruction and planned curricula? Discuss these issues with classmates, trying to separate *facts* from *unproven assumptions.*

8. Prepare a fifteen-minute lesson for 4-year-olds. What are your goals? What questions would you ask? How would you know if you were successful?

9. Observe actual teaching or watch tapes of small-group lessons. Was the teaching effective or ineffective? Some of the dimensions you might consider would include: attention-getting techniques; control of group—techniques for regaining attention; response modes of the children; feedback to correct and incorrect responses. Which ones seemed to be successful? Are mistakes pointed out? If they are, how do the children respond? Do the children usually respond when called on? What kind of reinforcement is used? How are groups handled when some of the children need further help?

READINGS

Blank, M. *Teaching learning in the preschool: a dialogue approach.* Columbus, Ohio: Merrill, 1973.

Brophy, J. and Good, T. *Teacher–student relationships: causes and consequences.* New York: Holt, Rinehart & Winston, 1974.

Evans, E. *Contemporary influences in early childhood education.* New York: Holt, Rinehart & Winston, 1971.

Good, T. and Brophy, J. *Looking in classrooms.* New York: Harper & Row, 1973.

Hess, R. and Bear, R. *Early education: current theory, research, and action.* Chicago: Aldine, 1968.

Kounin, J. *Discipline and group management in classrooms.* New York: Holt, Rinehart & Winston, 1970.

Parker, R., ed. *The preschool in action.* Boston: Allyn & Bacon, 1972.

OBSERVATION
AND ASSESSMENT

Observing the children and assessing their progress in mastering stated goals are two crucial aspects of the teacher's job. Without accurate information, which has been carefully and systematically collected, teachers cannot stay abreast of each child's interests, progress, and needs. Such information is vital, not only because it helps teachers keep track of their progress in meeting their own goals, but also because it is absolutely necessary if the preschool experience is to be truly individualized to meet the children's particular needs.

Observation and assessment are discussed together in the present chapter because we view them as essentially the same operation. Whether a teacher collects information by observing a child working on a task or playing with his peers and then records notes in a notebook, or whether instead the class is administered some kind of test, the basic process is the same: The teacher is systematically collecting and recording information about the children. There are various subcategories of observation and testing. Some of these are most useful for some purposes and some for others.

In a sense, all observation is the same: The teacher watches a child or a group of children and makes mental notes of one or more items of information. Observation methods differ, however, in the degree to which the observation process itself and the process of recording the information observed is systematized and standardized. At one extreme is haphazard observation in which the teacher simply attempts to notice and remember whatever is most interesting or salient at the moment. This process can be made more systematic if the teacher keeps a notebook, recording critical incidents or other items of information that might be important for future planning or decision making. An even more systematic method of observation might be to record information on a standardized checklist while observing each child in the class as he individually completes a standardized task.

Testing, or formalized assessment, involves the use of standardized information-gathering instruments. It is important to recognize that testing does not differ in any important way from other forms of observation and information gathering. Tests should be viewed simply as information-gathering devices, and should be kept in proper perspective. Their importance should not be magnified to the point that they inspire fear or awe in either teachers or children. Further, although they function as accountability devices to the extent that they measure the degree to which teachers and children have mastered stated goals, bear in mind that *tests are merely means that teachers use in helping to reach those goals, and are not goals in their own right.* The comments made earlier in Chapter 9 about responding to failure and incorrect answers apply also to poor test performances. Test performances should be used in a realistic, matter-of-fact way to identify strengths and weaknesses and to make decisions about the best ways to help children overcome any areas of inadequate learning that do show up. There is no need to protect the children from knowledge of such weaknesses, so long as the teacher takes the proper attitude towards them.

NORM-REFERENCED TESTS

Norm-referenced tests are so called because they have been standardized on a (usually) sizable sample of children in order to obtain *norms,* which are standardized performance scores based on chronological age. Such norms are used to describe a child's performance relative to that of other children of the same age. For example, if children from the standardization sample who were aged 4 years, 6 months scored an average of 52 total points on a particular test, this information would be the basis for reasoning that any child who obtained a total score of 52 on this particular test had a performance equal to that of the "average" child of 4 years, 6 months of age. Similarly, if children from the sample in their third month of first grade scored an average of 76 on the test, a total score of 76 might in the future be translated into a "grade-level equivalent score" of 1.3 (first grade, third month).

These are just two examples of the same basic process or logic that underlies all norm-referenced tests: (1) administer the test to a sample of children differing in age; (2) identify the average total score for children at each age or grade level included in the sample; (3) working backwards from these data, compose a table that can be used to translate any child's total score on the test into some standardized norm score (mental age, developmental age, grade-level equivalent, age equivalent, percentile score, etc.). Sometimes the conversion process is complicated by additional tables, especially when raw scores are converted into mental-age scores or developmental-level scores. In this case, the converted norm is entered in another table that also takes into account the child's chronological age, so that an intelligence quotient (IQ) or developmental quotient (DQ) is obtained.

Although the specifics differ in the various examples given above, the basic underlying logic and the processes involved in converting the child's raw score into some kind of standardized-norm score are the same. The net result is also the same: In the end, you have a score that says how the child's performance compares to that of other children *his age*. Thus, norm-referenced tests provide a way to convert raw scores into relative scores that tell you whether the child is below average, average, or above average in his performance on the test, compared to other children of *the same age*. This is useful information for some purposes (especially for assessing the child's general readiness for a curriculum and for predicting his probable success relative to the other children), although in many cases, especially with regard to IQ scores, it has been treated as if it were far more important than it actually is.

There are two major advantages to norm-referenced tests. First, the tests themselves are standardized, and the administration booklet comes with tables that allow you to quickly convert a child's raw test score into a standardized-norm score, providing a convenient comparison of the child with other children his age. This is an advantage that cannot be matched by teacher-made tests on material that has not been normed or standardized. To take an extreme example, suppose you make up a test of ten items and find that every child in the class easily achieves all ten items. Does this mean that the class is very bright or has done very well? Without norms, you simply do not know. It might be that *all* children of this particular age would also pass these ten items, and that, therefore, the performance of the class was not particularly noteworthy and the test was not particularly useful. Thus, one major advantage of norm-referenced tests is that their norms provide you with expectations about how children of various ages *should* perform.

A second advantage of norm-referenced tests, especially of individually administered intelligence and achievement tests, is that the scores they provide are usually reliable and stable, and generally are good predictors of future performance on similar tasks (usually the best predictors available). Apparently, this is because such tests are the best measures of general intellectual abilities, even though their accuracy may be affected by such factors as rapport with the examiner, test-taking attitude, familiarity with the test or similar tests, vocabulary or language problems that might prevent a child from passing an item that he would pass if he could understand the instructions, systematic error sets or perseverative responses (see Chapter 11), and many other factors. Because so many factors can enter the picture, scores from norm-referenced tests should not be accepted blindly or without question, especially if they involve an individual child, if they conflict with expectations based on performance in everyday school activities, and/or if they occur in cases of children who speak English as a second language or who are part of a minority subculture that differs from the mainstream American culture in ways that might affect test performance. Assuming that one or more of these factors is not operating to invalidate the test results seriously, information from norm-referenced tests provides a good indication of the relative general abilities and probable future achievements of a *group* of children. Thus, they are useful in providing convenient indexes of the general-ability levels of a group of children. Also, along with general knowledge about child development, they may be useful in program planning for particular groups.

Along with the two important strengths already discussed, norm-referenced tests contain several significant weaknesses. Many of these are connected with the sources of invalid test scores listed above, although these problems occur with any kind of test. A particular problem that is especially identified with norm-referenced tests, however, is their failure to provide diagnostic information that would be useful in planning individualized treatments for each child (see Meeker, 1974). An IQ or grade-level equivalent score is a convenient index allowing comparison of a child with other children his age, but it says absolutely nothing about his individual pattern of strengths and weaknesses. Two different children can obtain precisely the same total score on a given norm-referenced test, but they might have strikingly different patterns. In an extreme case, it is conceivable that one child might pass only items that the other failed, and vice versa. These would be two completely different children from the viewpoint of their patterns of strengths and weaknesses and their needs in the classroom, even though they got precisely the same test score.

Thus, on balance, there is little reason to administer norm-referenced tests to preschoolers unless this is required by funding agencies. Such tests do not provide diagnostic information useful in planning specific instructional strategies (in contrast to the criterion-referenced assessment devices discussed below), and usually they are not even necessary as a general index of the ability of the group. In the vast majority of cases, IQs or other scores from norm-referenced tests merely certify what teachers already know on the basis of knowledge of home-environment conditions and observation of the child at home and at school. Occasionally a norm-referenced test will identify a child who is much brighter than was previously realized, but this does not happen very often and is at least as likely to occur through the administration of a criterion-referenced test as through the administration of a norm-referenced test. Thus, unless the test provides subscale scores or other pattern data useful as diagnostic cues, or there is some external pressure to do so, we see no reason for teachers to administer norm-referenced tests to preschool children. Such tests will not provide useful information in most instances, and they have the potential of producing harmful effects if they induce negative expectations or defeatist attitudes in the teachers. The various kinds of criterion-referenced measures discussed in the following section are much more valuable.

CRITERION-REFERENCED MEASUREMENT

The term *criterion-referenced tests* was coined to contrast with the previously established term *norm-referenced tests*. Whereas norm-referenced tests convert a child's raw score to a standard score based on age norms, criterion-referenced tests are designed to measure the degree to which the child has mastered a set of instructional goals or objectives (criteria) previously specified by the teacher, curriculum planner, or other test user. Consider the ability to count from 1 to 20. On a norm-referenced test, children's scores would be based upon the average age at which children learn this particular ability. In contrast, a criterion-referenced test is designed to discover whether or not the child has mastered this task; and, if he has not, to specify as precisely as possible those aspects that he has mastered and those that he has not. Thus, the term criterion-referenced tests refers to the familiar and traditional measuring device most typically called *teacher-made tests*.

By criterion-referenced tests, we mean any measurement device that a teacher uses to assess whether or not a child has attained specific criteria. The measurement device need not be a test in the usual sense at all; it can be some kind of observation method or checklist. Even if it is a test in the usual sense, the items may call for the child to make responses such as pointing, providing a verbal label, or performing some kind of physical action (in contrast to the pencil-and-paper tests that are typical in elementary school). In fact, assessment at the preschool level is most typically of this type. Since few preschool children have learned to write or even print (except for their names and perhaps some letters), items requiring written responses are clearly inappropriate at this age level.

The usefulness of a criterion-referenced test depends on two major factors: (1) the appropriateness of the objectives (criteria) for the children to be tested; (2) the degree to which the test measures mastery of these objectives accurately and reliably. The first factor is based on the program objectives rather than the test itself. These objectives must be matched to the developmental levels of the children and otherwise suited to their particular needs. If they are too difficult, the test will only confirm this by showing that everyone failed. If they are too easy, everyone will pass most or all items, and the test will not be very useful for diagnosis. Thus, the usefulness of a criterion-referenced test depends in part on the match between program objectives and the abilities, interests, and needs of the children.

The second factor is the test itself. Items should be *standardized* so that scores for every child are equivalent and comparable. Also, items should be truly *criterion-referenced* in the sense that they *directly test objectives of the program;* in other words, only objectives that are an explicit part of the preschool program should be included. These may be simple memory items (Can the child repeat a fact or skill that he was taught?) or more complex transfer or generalization items (Can the child recall the fact or skill when the problem is presented in a new way or when he is asked to apply it in a new context?), but they should all be items that assess mastery of concepts or skills included in the program. Other items may provide information about a child's general abilities or background of experiences, but not about his progress in mastering program objectives.

In sharp contrast to our previous statement that norm-referenced tests are not very useful, we strongly stress the importance of a program or systematic criterion-referenced assessment, using measurement devices that meet the requirements stated above. This is the only way that teachers can get an objective record of the progress of each child and of the class as a whole in meeting established goals (criteria), and this information is invaluable in planning individualized instruction for children who need special work in particular areas. Simple random observations are sufficient for keeping track of general differences among the children, but only careful records based on systematic criterion-referenced measurement can provide the specific and detailed information necessary for adequately planning individualized instruction. In addition, such information provides teachers with an objective record of their own relative success in meeting criteria. Without systematic measurement, it is all too easy to fall into the trap of noticing only successes and ignoring or overlooking failures. This appears to be a very common human weakness, and teachers are as prone to it as anyone else. However, it can be prevented through systematic measurement capable of identifying areas where the class in general is not meeting specified criteria, so that additional planning and reteaching can be undertaken. Thus, systematic measurement is essential.

Although we can stress the importance of systematic measurement and provide some guidelines about the features that a good measurement system should have, we cannot precisely specify the goals or criteria that should be measured. This is because a good criterion-referenced measuring system is keyed to the specific goals of the particular program with which it is being utilized. Thus, a measurement system that would be optimal for one program might be completely inappropriate for another. In short, *criterion-referenced assessment involves measuring the degree to which a program is accomplishing its stated goals,* so that these goals (and their various subgoals) must provide the basis for the items to be included in the measurement system. In addition to this fundamental characteristic, the following factors are important in constructing an optimal criterion-referenced measurement system.

1. Assessment must be standardized, so that scores from different children will be comparable.

This will be discussed in the following section.

2. Assessment should be carried out at frequent intervals.

If the program involves a sequenced curriculum, this might mean tests given weekly or at the ends of units. In less-structured curricula, assessment might be carried out less frequently, but it still should be done either at regular intervals or at points in the school year at which it is logical to assess progress towards criteria central to the program. Frequent assessment allows for frequent checks on progress and helps to identify problem areas earlier so that appropriate action can be taken before the problem becomes more serious.

3. Assessment should include affective and behavioral goals (where appropriate), in addition to cognitive and linguistic goals.

If a program has intentions of fostering development in the affective or social-emotional area, it should take steps to measure its progress in doing so. This will probably mean some form of systematic observation of children in free play or semistructured behavioral situations rather than traditional tests, since affective goals are difficult to measure with much validity or confidence using traditional interview or testing techniques. There is nothing wrong with this; in fact, structured behavioral observations ordinarily would be more valid, and therefore more appropriate measurement devices, than traditional interviews or tests, even though many teachers don't think of observation as simply another form of assessment. It is, however; observational data are just as valid and useful as data from formal tests, provided that the observation situation is standardized and the data are recorded objectively.

4. Assessment should obtain continuing measurement on all major goals stressed by the program.

This is related to the previous point. Sometimes only selected program goals are measured while others are not, often because a standardized test is available that happens to measure these goals. Bear in mind that all facets of the program should be measured, and that the measurement devices used should be selected or designed because they are appropriate for measuring the goals taught by the program, not simply because they happen to be available and handy. Thus, if a norm-referenced test or other standardized test is available that is particularly appropriate for measuring aspects of your program, go ahead and use it. *However, do not use a standardized measure that is inappropriate, no matter how convenient and inexpensive*

*it might be. Instead, make up your own criterion-referenced measurement
devices that will measure your success in meeting your program goals.*

*5. Assessment should include items of varying difficulty levels, and in par-
ticular stress higher-level objectives.*

If you were to test every single concept or skill included in a program, you
would probably have to spend as much time testing as you spend teaching,
and obviously this would be needless overkill. You can solve this problem
by *sampling,* testing a small subset of goals from each major area of the
program. Although you could select such goals at random, this is not the
best way to proceed. Many subgoals will have become trivial and useless
as test items because they are low-level skills that have been overlearned
for some time. There is no point in including such items on a test, since
all of the children will pass the items; you will simply waste time without
gaining any useful information.

It pays, rather, to concentrate your testing on the end points or final goals
of a series of activities or experiences in the program, in order to see if
the program has achieved the end product that it set out to reach. Measurement should not be restricted solely to such high-level or end-point goals,
however, because this might make the test too difficult and frustrating for
certain children. Thus, certain subgoals should also be included, particularly
those that have diagnostic value and would be useful in yielding information
about the kinds of reteaching that a child might need if he has failed to
master a series of goals in a given area. Thus, the ideal test would be one
that contained a mixture of final goals and subgoals and which would be
expected to yield a fairly high percentage of success (a class average of
70–80 percent of the items passed). Such a test would be a well-balanced
assessment instrument in that it would provide a high proportion of success
experiences for the children while still allowing for enough failure to identify
specific children and/or program objectives that require reteaching, and it
would also provide some clues concerning the form that such reteaching
should take (this will be discussed in a later section).

For example, a good color-knowledge item might require the child to
match, sort, and then label several color samples successfully. General success rates on this item would reveal your general success in teaching these
color discrimination and labeling abilities. Also, individual success or failure
patterns would provide useful diagnostic information. A child who can match
and sort only needs further teaching of labels, but one who had difficulty
matching or sorting would require more fundamental reteaching stressing
color identification and discrimination.

Test Construction

Using the principles outlined above, develop items for tests (or observation
checklists, etc.) that will appropriately sample the children's mastery of im-

portant objectives in each major aspect of the program. In order to make test scoring as simple and objective as possible, be sure that your test items and scoring criteria are phrased in strictly behavioral terms. This is most easily accomplished, of course, if the program objectives themselves are clearly stated *behavioral objectives.* In contrast to more abstract or vague goals, behavioral objectives are explicit descriptions of specific, observable behavior. Because of their specificity and the fact that they involve description of overt behavior, behavioral objectives are useful tools for helping teachers to know what to look for and to observe accurately when assessing children's mastery of program objectives.

For example, story comprehension and language development are examples of goals that many preschool programs espouse. However, they are too general to qualify as behavioral objectives. An example of a behavioral objective that involves both of these more abstract and more general objectives would be the following: "When asked 'Why did the dog run away from Billy?' the child both will provide the correct answer (the dog had learned to fear sticks, and Billy had a stick in his hand at the time) and will respond in one or more complete and grammatically correct sentences." Behavioral objectives such as this make test scoring easy. For example, the response "He ran because he was afraid of the stick," would be scored as correct because it meets the criteria. In contrast, "He was afraid," would not be correct, because, although it is a complete and grammatically correct sentence, it does not give the full reason for the dog's behavior, while the response "the stick," would not be correct because it does not constitute a complete and grammatically correct sentence. Behavioral objectives can and should also be used in the affective area. For example, sharing is one social behavior that most preschool programs value and attempt to instill in the children. It is relatively easy to measure in an objective way by setting up a standardized sharing situation and scoring the child for whether or not he meets the behavioral objective: "When asked to share his blocks with the second child, the first child will do so without protesting or expressing hostility towards the second child."

The above are just two examples of useful behavioral objectives. For a complete and very readable account of behavioral objectives as they apply to both curriculum development and test construction, see Mager (1962). With regard to assessment, the main point to bear in mind is that any objectives included on a test or other measuring device should be expressed in behavioral terms whenever possible, so that they can be easily and objectively measured. Another factor of importance in considering a test item is its *validity.* That is, does the item actually measure what you want it to measure? If an item is supposed to measure a particular program objective, you should be satisfied that it does in fact measure that objective before including it in any test. This is relatively simple if the item involved is a straightforward repetition of a task that has been included in the program. In this case, all that is required to insure validity is that the item is presented in the test in precisely the same way it was presented in the program. Exactly the same materials and equipment should be used, and the wording of questions or response demands should be identical. In the case of bilingual programs, test items should be administered in the same language in which the behavioral objective being measured was taught in the first place.

The problem of insuring validity becomes more complex in cases where you want the child to do something more than simply repeat or show that he remembers something previously taught. Sometimes you will want to see if the child is able to *transfer* or *generalize* a concept or skill learned in one situation to the demands of a different situation. Test items involving transfer or generalization are important, because they help you establish whether the child has truly understood a concept or whether he has merely memorized a verbal response or a chain of physical actions without really understanding what he is doing or why he is doing it. The child who truly understands will be able to generalize his concept or skill and use it under different circumstances or apply it to different purposes. In contrast, the child who does not truly understand what he is doing and is responding purely out of rote memory will be able to succeed only when he is asked to do exactly the same thing that he has been asked to do before, and asked in the same way as he has been asked before. He will become confused and probably will fail if changes are made in the words used in the instructions or in the stimuli to which he is to respond, or if he is asked to transfer or generalize his learning by applying it to a new situation or problem. Transfer and generalization items help you to guard against mistakenly thinking that a child has truly mastered a concept or skill when in fact he has only memorized a particular response to a particular stimulus.

Transfer and generalization items must be carefully prepared, however, in order to guard against the opposite problem: mistakenly thinking that a child has not really mastered a concept when in fact he has. This can happen if the instructions for the item contain words that the child does not understand, or if the difference in the level of response demand between the original behavior and the transfer item is unreasonably great. In such situations even children who have really mastered a concept or skill will fail a transfer item, in the first case because they do not understand the directions, and in the second case because the transfer item requires mastery of a large complex of related skills and not merely the single skill that the child has mastered so far.

For example, suppose that the child has mastered the concept that one must open a jar or can in order to find out what is in it. An appropriate transfer item might ask him what one must do to find out what is in a similar can or jar, or perhaps another container such as a box or chest. Assuming that he had mastered the concept "You have to open up a closed container to find out what is inside," the child could reasonably be expected to transfer or to generalize his learning to these new situations. However, it is unlikely that the child would have the vaguest idea of what to do if he were asked "What preparatory steps would be required in order to ascertain the contents of this receptacle?" Use of such inappropriate vocabulary would cause most children to fail the item even though they had mastered the concept. Similarly, a child might fail an item, even if he understood the directions and knew what he was supposed to do, if you gave him an object that was so difficult and complicated to open that even adults were unable to open it.

Some items that meet the criteria discussed so far are nevertheless inappropriate for other reasons. One is *convenience*. Unless there are strong reasons for doing so, there is little point in planning to use a test item that calls for hard-to-get materials or for time-consuming and difficult preparation. *Ease of administration* is also relevant. Some tasks make good test items but are tricky to administer properly because they make unrealistic demands on the teacher or child. Again, avoid such items unless they are really crucial and no simpler way to get the information can be devised.

In summary, good test items are stated in objective behavioral language that makes for easy scoring; are valid in the sense that they measure mastery of objectives taught in the program; are not confined solely to repetition or memory items; and are easy and convenient to administer. In constructing transfer or generalization items, however, it is important to be sure that the instructions are understandable to the child and that the transfer task is one that he can reasonably be expected to perform on the basis of having mastered the objective taught in the program.

Given the limited attention spans of young children, it is wise to test individually or in small groups and to confine tests to ten or fifteen minutes at a time. Testing individually or in small groups will enable you to observe the processes children use in responding to items, and thus to distinguish true failures from confusion about directions, perseverations, and so on (see Chapter 11). Tests should be kept short to maximize validity. If you exceed the children's attention spans, you will get mostly guesswork on the later items. Thus, frequent short tests are much better than infrequent long ones.

TEST ADMINISTRATION   Once an appropriate test or other measurement device has been constructed, steps should be taken to insure its standardized administration, meaning that the test is given in exactly the same way to all of the children, so that their scores are comparable to one another and equally meaningful. The specifics of optimal testing conditions will vary somewhat for different programs, but the following factors should be considered.

In giving a test, the teacher makes sure that the child is listening to and can understand the instructions (top left), watches carefully to note her physical response (top right), questions her to get a verbal response (bottom right), and then gives a friendly word of encouragement to help keep the girl relaxed and the setting informal (bottom left). In this way, teachers can make tests enjoyable both for themselves and the children, while at the same time they systematically obtain assessment data.

1. Distractions should be eliminated or at least minimized.

Ideally, children should be tested individually in a separate room, free of noise and distraction by other children. Where this is not possible, the child should be tested in a quiet corner of the room, seated with his back toward the rest of the class so as to minimize distractions. Furthermore, steps should be taken to hold the noise level down and in general eliminate distractions as much as possible during test times. There is no need to insist on absolute quiet or other unnatural behavior, but loud and boisterous activities, or activities which are so popular that the child will have difficulty concentrating on the test because he is missing out on them, should not be scheduled to coincide with testing times.

2. Label tests for what they are; do not attempt to camouflage them or to protect the children.

As mentioned previously, children experience failure many times every day and are not bothered by it unless they are led to believe that it is something to be ashamed of. Thus, don't be afraid to call a test a test. If you don't like the word "test," refer to it as a "review," or use a phrase like "Today we are going to see if you can remember some of the things that you have been learning." The particular word or phrase that you use is not especially important, but it is important that you make it clear to the children that testing times are designed to find out how well they can do some of the things that they have been learning in school, and that they will be expected to pay close attention and try to do their best.

3. Conduct the test in a relaxed, low-key manner and attempt to make it an enjoyable experience for the child.

This is one time in which the child will be sharing a prolonged personal contact with you, and he very likely will enjoy it if you remain relaxed and enjoy it yourself. Insist that the child pay close attention and listen to the instructions before making a response, but present the items in positive ways by challenging the child and by provoking his curiosity and interest. Even this, however, should be done only to the degree that it is necessary. If a child is well-motivated and attentive, proceed briskly through the test, saving your "motivators" for situations where they are needed. Where a child is becoming restless or inattentive, rekindle his interest with comments like "Oh, this next one is a hard one. I wonder if you can do it." Be sure to do this for *all* children, not just those that you expect to succeed.

4. Provide encouragement to the child to the extent that he seems to need or want it.

This can be done whether the child is generally successful ("Wow, you really know how to do these things, John!") or generally unsuccessful ("These are really tough, aren't they? . . . But you are doing a good job and trying really hard. Keep up the good work").

5. Where testing conditions permit, you can often help motivate the child by commenting on his successes and failures directly or by responding to his own appraisals of his performance.

However, most teachers find it more convenient not to comment directly on success or failure with single items, for two reasons. First, the test might be readministered to the same child at some time in the future, and such direct feedback about success and failure on particular items would bias the results of the second testing. Second, the children will naturally talk to one another about the test, and if they are tested individually or in small groups, those who are tested earlier might give their answers to those who are tested later if you give specific feedback during the test. If either or both of these factors apply to your situation, it would be wise to avoid giving specific feedback about whether the child got an item right or wrong. Instead, encourage the child with comments suggesting that he is generally paying good attention, doing his best, doing well, and so on, without specifically stating whether he has gotten a specific item right or wrong. If neither of these items applies to your case, you may wish to give specific feedback to the children as you go through the test. Most teachers prefer not to, because they find it useful to review the test with groups of children later and also find that reviewing might make a difference in performance on future items that are related to the item being reviewed.

Also, if the child is attentive and well-motivated, it is often wise to proceed briskly through the test rather than take extra time to give feedback and run the risk that his attention and motivation will begin to deteriorate later. However, this is largely a matter of the teacher's preference and judgment based on her knowledge of the children. When there is no reason to believe that giving feedback might invalidate the meaningfulness of later items on the test or of a readministration of the same test, you may find it convenient or preferable to give specific feedback to each item as you go along.

6. Be sure that each item is administered in standardized fashion to all children.

Instructions for each item should be written or typed, so that they can be read to the child. Experience in test administration has shown that this is necessary to insure that each child gets precisely the same instructions on each item. Nothing less will do; even the most dedicated and determined teachers have found that they do not administer tests appropriately unless they *read every item to every child.*

Other precautions are also needed to insure standardization. Teachers should practice administering a test a few times before actually using it with the children, both to learn to deliver each item smoothly and to eliminate any tendencies toward undesirable behavior that would *cue* the children to give or not to give certain responses. Item instructions should be read in such a way that the child is not cued to make the correct response (or any particular response, for that matter). Children can pick up cues through changes in voice tone, eye or facial expressions, hesitation or changes in speed of speech, hand movements or pointing, the way that the teacher arranges the various objects involved in an item, or through any of several other methods of indirect and implicit communication. For example, if the item calls for the child to pick the correct word from a list of five or six words, the teacher may unintentionally cue the correct response by hesitating before the correct word, by pronouncing it more loudly, or by otherwise emphasizing it when reading the word list. Similarly, if the item calls for the child to point to the correct one of a set of pictures or objects, the teacher might inadvertently cue the correct answer by hesitating longer when pointing to the correct picture or object or by looking at it (children often will carefully inspect the teacher's face and expression before answering a test item). In a complex item such as constructing a puzzle, teachers might inadvertently provide extra help by nodding their heads or showing some kind of perceptible approval response when the child picks up the right piece or begins to put the piece in the slot properly.

All cuing of this sort should be avoided entirely, since it nullifies the validity of the test results. If all children are cued on a certain item, the item is in fact much easier than it was intended to be, and the children's scores might therefore be deceptively and inappropriately high. If cues are given to some of the children but not to others, the test scores of different children will not be truly comparable. Also, such behavior suggests expectation effects (the teacher may be subtly helping children expected to do well and/or discouraging children expected to do poorly; for more on this, see Brophy & Good, 1974). Thus, to insure that the test actually measures what it is intended to measure, and to insure that different children's scores are truly comparable with one another, be sure that the test is administered in a standardized way to each child and that behaviors that might cue the children toward certain responses are avoided.

7. Before testing, thoroughly prepare the test area and materials and plan appropriate activities for children who are not being tested.

All materials needed for testing should be placed in the testing area prior to testing. They should be in ready-to-use form, and should be stored where they will be out of the way (and out of sight, where this is relevant), but nevertheless easily accessible for use when needed. Ideally, they should be in drawers or on shelves where they can be reached without your having to get up or leave your seat.

Have a variety of interesting but relatively quiet activities planned for the children who are not being tested at any one time. If other adults are in the classroom, they should take responsibility for keeping the children profitably occupied and reasonably quiet while you are busy testing. Arts and crafts activities and special projects are especially good for testing days. When selecting children for testing, try to pick ones who are between activities rather than ones who are in the midst of an engrossing project. In any case, assure the child, if necessary, that he can return to his project or activity shortly.

USING TEST INFORMATION

Tests should be tools actively used to improve teaching, and not merely instruments to gather information that is then filed away and forgotten. Test information is useful for making decisions about the kinds and levels of curricula appropriate for different children, about how different children can or should be grouped, about the teacher's general success in meeting stated objectives, and about individual differences in the children's success in meeting objectives.

Assessing Entry Level

Criterion-referenced test data are especially important at the beginning of the year in programs in which the children are going to be grouped for instructional purposes. This data will allow the teacher to group the children intelligently on the basis of similar patterns of mastery of the various objectives taught in the early part of the school year. Such grouping is *potentially* very helpful, since a homogeneous group of children with a similar pattern of abilities and needs can be taught more easily than a heterogeneous group with a sharply contrasting pattern (other things being equal). Thus, a good criterion-referenced test administered very early in the year may help the teacher decide how many groups should be formed, what should be the basis for forming such groups, what is the general level of the children's readiness for the program, and how great is the general degree of homogeneity or heterogeneity in background readiness among the various children in the classroom.

Although grouping based upon test performance can and should improve instruction for all children, typically it does not (Good & Brophy, 1973). One reason is that teachers often do not take advantage of grouping by teaching different groups differently. It is common to observe teachers attempting to teach the same curriculum at the same rate and with the same methods to each of several different groups that were originally formed on the basis of their being different from one another! Thus, one implication of grouping on the basis of test patterns is that the different groups will be taught differently.

A second problem is that grouping is often oversimplified and overgeneralized, to the point that it becomes an end rather than a means. It is not at all uncommon for teachers to state that their groups have remained constant throughout the year, or that they have switched only two or three children from one group to another. This is completely inappropriate; such behavior will only impede rather than foster successful teaching. First, children have different ability levels and degrees of background in various curriculum areas, so that they can and should be grouped differently for activities in each of those areas. Second, although data from IQ tests and other norm-referenced tests show that in some cases abilities in different areas tend to be correlated, so that it makes sense at times to speak of general ability or general intelligence, this factor must be kept in proper perspective. Very few children have equal abilities in different areas. Instead, it is more common for children to be well-developed and skillful in some areas but relatively slow in others.

Thus, good language development does not necessarily guarantee good development in the area of mathematical knowledge and reasoning, and both of these general areas are largely independent of development in perceptual-motor skills. Examples could be multiplied, but the point is simple and clear: Any grouping for instructional purposes should be done on the basis of performance on criterion-referenced tests—which provide a profile of the child's readiness or abilities in the various areas stressed by the program, and not on the basis of norm-referenced tests—which yield only a single general score. This means that the children will be grouped differently for different curriculum areas, and that grouping will be fluid, with frequent changes of children from one group to another, based upon their rate of progress and present performance. Where these conditions do not exist, grouping should be abolished. It is better to have no grouping at all than to have rigid, inflexible groups that serve no positive instructional purpose and may well do damage by creating negative teacher expectations and/or undesirable attitudes of competitiveness or elitism in the children (Good & Brophy, 1973; Rist, 1970).

Groups formed because they are different should be taught differently. Children who have not mastered the fundamentals of an area should be given repeated instruction and practice in these fundamentals until they master them. Meanwhile, children who have mastered the fundamentals should be allowed to move on to higher-level activities or to apply these fundamentals to now uses, rather than continue with needless repetition of exercises that they have long since overlearned. One caution: it is better to err on the side of overteaching than underteaching, since concepts and skills mastered to the point of overlearning will stick with the child permanently, while concepts and skills that are not securely mastered are likely to be forgotten. Thus, it pays to be certain that the child has fully mastered a concept or skill before moving him on to something else.

Be especially careful about exempting children from participation in activities when you are not certain that they have mastered them. Even though a child may do very well on a test given early in the year in a particular area (language development, for example), it is possible, and in fact likely, that there are certain gaps in his learning. Thus, rather than exempt such a child from all language-development activities judged to be below his level, it would be safer to take the child through the activities but to move as briskly as his abilities and readiness allow. It is likely that in the process of doing this you will discover some areas where the child needs a bit of concentrated work, even though in general he may be considerably ahead of his classmates. If such learning gaps do turn up, involve the child in activities that will allow him to work on these areas of weakness, meanwhile exempting him from participation in activities designed to improve areas in which he is already quite well-developed.

Analyzing Test Results

Proper analysis of test results will give you feedback about your own relative success in meeting goals as well as about the relative success of each child in the class. In discussing interpretation of test results in this section, we are assuming that a well-constructed and properly administered test (according to the criteria above) has been used.

The first step in analyzing test results is to compose a summary sheet or scoring grid showing each child's performance on each test item (see Figure 10.1). You should sum across and down the page in order to obtain total scores for each child and totals for each item reflecting the number of children who passed it. Armed with this information, you are now ready to assess your own performance and that of the children.

You can judge your own performance by comparing the children's actual scores with those that you expected based upon your knowledge of their previous performance and the probable difficulty of the test. If the children's performance was clearly above or below your expectations, some investigation is in order. If scores were unexpectedly high across the board, this suggests that you are underestimating the performance of the children in everyday activities and/or that the test was easier than you thought it was. In contrast, if the scores were generally much lower than you expected, either the test was more difficult than you thought or, more probably, you have been misjudging the children's performance by crediting them with a greater degree of learning than they actually have attained. We say "more probably" here because, as mentioned previously, teachers, like anyone else, are prone to notice success more readily than failure. Thus, to the extent that a teacher is in error in predicting the performance of a class, unwarranted optimism is more likely than undue pessimism.

Where test scores have been disappointing, resolve to pay more careful attention to the children's responses in future lessons and activities, especially to make sure that all children are called on and that all children who do not understand are repeatedly and sufficiently retaught until they do. If you are surprised with unexpectedly low test scores several times in succession, and especially if the children missed items that you were sure that they knew, it is likely that in your everyday teaching you either are answering questions for them or failing to notice when they are not responding or responding incorrectly.

Whatever the general level of performance, analyze the pattern of errors that appear. Are the errors randomly scattered among children and across items on the test, or are there individual children who scored lower than the rest of the group and/or certain items that were especially difficult for the children? Any such patterns that you can identify will be useful in planning reteaching.

For example, Figure 10.1 shows both types of error patterns. Items 5 and 7, which both involve labeling (vocabulary), were especially difficult for the class as a whole. This indicates that objectives in this area were not met

FIGURE 10.1

A Sample Test-Score Summary Sheet

Items	Andy	Betty	Brenda	Carl	Drew	Edward	Kelly	Kim	Louis	Robert	Sharon	Sammy	Vickie	Walter	Yolanda	Total
Motor																
1. Balance beam	O	X	X	X	X	O	X	O	X	X	O	X	X	X	X	11
2. Hopscotch	O	X	O	X	X	X	X	X	X	O	O	X	X	X	X	11
3. Scissors use	X	X	X	O	X	X	X	X	X	O	X	X	O	X	X	12
Vocabulary																
4. Color words	O	X	X	X	X	X	X	X	X	O	O	X	X	X	X	12
5. Animal words	O	O	X	O	O	O	X	O	X	O	O	X	O	O	O	4
6. Occupation words	O	X	X	X	X	X	X	X	X	O	O	X	X	X	X	12
7. Clothing words	O	O	O	X	O	X	X	O	O	O	O	O	X	O	O	4
Number																
8. Count to ten	O	X	X	X	X	X	X	X	X	O	O	X	X	X	X	12
9. More/Less	X	X	X	X	X	X	X	O	X	O	O	X	X	X	X	12
Auditory																
10. Follows directions	O	X	X	X	X	X	X	X	X	O	X	X	X	X	X	13
11. Loud/Soft	X	X	X	X	X	X	X	X	X	X	X	X	X	X	X	15
Social																
12. Sharing	X	X	X	X	X	X	O	X	O	X	X	X	X	X	X	13
13. Helping	X	X	X	X	O	X	X	X	X	X	O	X	X	X	X	13
Total	5	11	11	11	10	11	12	9	11	4	4	12	11	11	11	

as successfully as objectives in other areas. Also, note that Sharon, Robert, and Andy had low scores relative to everyone else in all cognitive areas (they did well on affective items). These three children will need intensive reteaching, requiring that you plan individualized activities to help them improve their weaknesses in academic skills. You may also wish to consider teaching these three children as a special group at times, to give them additional instruction beyond that which they receive with their classmates.

Planning Reteaching and Readiness Work

Use your analysis of error patterns in the children's test scores as the basis for planning reteaching and readiness work to strengthen areas of weakness. If all or most of the class missed a given item or cluster of items, this curriculum area needs to be retaught to everyone. If a certain subgroup in the class consistently missed a certain type of item (for example, motor items), this group can be brought together as a group for activities designed to strengthen this area and to help these children develop to the point where they can master the objectives in the test.

Sometimes the pattern analysis will not reveal particular kinds of items that were missed by the class as a whole or by an identifiable subgroup in particular, but it may identify one or more children who generally scored poorly. This pattern suggests that these children need much individualized tutorial reteaching and specialized assignments, since they are obviously considerably behind their classmates. In a sense, this is the most serious kind of problem, and steps should be taken immediately to provide these children with the assistance that they so badly need. This topic will be discussed at greater length in the following chapter.

Where teachers are implementing a planned curriculum with sequential objectives, it is crucial that test results be analyzed immediately and reteaching be undertaken before the class moves on to new material. Very often, where success in one set of lessons depends upon having mastered previous sequences of activities, children fall hopelessly behind if weaknesses and learning gaps crucial to the curriculum are not eliminated by appropriate reteaching and other instructional activities. Several days of *reteaching should be scheduled,* in which the teachers work with the individuals who need specialized activities or in specially prepared enrichment or expansion activities. Unless such actions are taken, children who are failing today are virtually certain to fail with even greater frequency and regularity in the future.

If the program does not involve sequenced activities that build directly upon one another, immediate reteaching will be less crucial, although still important. Under these conditions, the main goal of the teacher should be to plan reteaching and readiness activities to be as individualized as possible, basing both group and individual experiences upon the child's patterns of strengths and weaknesses as shown in the criterion-referenced tests. Thus, some children should work primarily on cognitive development, although they may be subdivided into a group stressing linguistic development, a group stressing visual perception, a group stressing listening skills and direction following, and so on. Other children may need work in motor development and physical coordination. Still other children may do well in cognitive and motor activities but need work in affective and social development areas. To the extent that time and resources allow, plan your follow-up activities to provide these children with the kinds of learning experiences that they appear to need most, and recheck their (and your) progress by administering additional criterion-referenced tests to get at the same general objectives (but not necessarily the same specific ones) in the near future.

SUMMARY

In order to make intelligent and effective decisions about meeting each child's needs, teachers must carry out a regular program of observation and assessment to determine individual progress in mastering program goals. Assessment can be done through relatively informal behavioral observations or through formal tests; *how* it is done is not as important as doing it frequently and accurately and gearing it to the particular goals (criteria) established for the program.

Although norm-referenced tests might be of limited value, the most useful assessment involves criterion-referenced tests or observation devices. These should be standardized, should be administered at frequent intervals, should include affective and behavioral goals as well as cognitive ones, should be keyed to program goals, and should be at a level of difficulty appropriate for revealing strengths and weaknesses in individual children and in various aspects of the program. Standardization means explicit behavioral objectives, standardized test-administration procedures, and avoidance of cuing or other activities that might make the task easier or more difficult for a particular child than for his classmates.

Early in the year, tests are useful to assess entry-level skills of the children as part of the procedure for grouping children with similar patterns of strengths and weaknesses. Grouping of children on this basis should facilitate teaching; however, it will do so only if different groups are taught differently in accordance with their particular needs. Both the basis for grouping and the assignment of individual children to different groups should be re-evaluated frequently to make sure that the groups still are needed and are functioning as intended.

Test scores or other assessment data should be systematically analyzed to discover clusters of items that the children have difficulty with or clusters of children who had difficulty with all or parts of items. Identification of patterns of this sort will aid planning of prescriptive reteaching and individualized follow-up activities geared to eliminate the weaknesses shown on the test.

QUESTIONS

1. Observe a testing situation. Are all of the criteria for effective test administration met?

2. Devise an observation sheet for measuring goals in the social-emotional area. Design a standardized situation that would provide a basis for observations.

3. Practice writing objectives in behavioral terms. Do your objectives lead easily and directly to evaluation procedures? If not, why not?

4. Plan *transfer* and *generalization* evaluation exercises (based on activities planned from behavioral objectives stated above).

5. Devise a simple observation sheet to record the behavior of a child during a test situation. What important behaviors would you code? Why? What would you do with this information once you had acquired it?

6. How would you interpret a child's progress to his *parents?* What kinds of information would you use?

7. Give three sets of examples of how information about a child from tests and observations could be communicated to parents: (a) in language that would be appropriate and helpful; (b) in language that could not be misunderstood and/or cause needless problems for you, the parents, or the child.

8. Given an opportunity, would you like to get norm-referenced IQ or readiness test scores for your children? Why or why not?

9. If such information were available to you, how could you use it appropriately? How could you misuse it?

10. Suppose you make up a criterion-referenced test to find out if the children have mastered some important objectives stressed in the previous month. You expected about an 80 percent average score, but the children averaged only 29 percent. What does (could) this mean? How could you find out?

11. Given that 50 percent of children are always going to be "below average," why should we concern ourselves with assessment at all?

READINGS

Almy, M. *Ways of studying children.* New York: Teachers College Press, Columbia University, 1969.

Brandt, R. *Studying behavior in natural settings.* New York: Holt, Rinehart & Winston, 1972.

Buros, O., ed. *Sixth mental measurement yearbook.* Highland Park, N.J.: Gryphon, 1965.

Gordon, I. *Studying the child in school.* New York: Wiley, 1966.

Johnson, O. and Bommarito, J. *Tests and measurements in child development: a handbook.* San Francisco: Jossey-Bass, 1971.

Mager, R. *Preparing instructional objectives.* Palo Alto, Calif.: Fearon, 1962.

Rowen, B. *The children we see: an observational approach to child study.* New York: Holt, Rinehart & Winston, 1973.

Wright, H. *Recording and analyzing child behavior.* New York: Harper & Row, 1967.

Eight tests frequently used with preschool children are described below. The list is representative but selective; many other instruments could have been listed. We have selected the most widely used tests simply because teachers are most likely to encounter them if their school has a testing program.

Readers will note that no affective (self-concept, social-personal development) instruments are listed. This is not because we do not think that this area is important; it is because no well-validated and widely used tests in these areas exist at present. However, much research and test development is going on, and it is hoped that these efforts will yield useful affective measures for young children in the near future. For the moment, however, the few measures that are in use are still being pilot tested and validated, so that we cannot recommend any tests in these areas for immediate use by teachers.

Individualized IQ Tests

• Stanford-Binet Intelligence Scale, rev. ed. (Boston: Houghton Mifflin, 1960).

This is probably the best-known individual measure of IQ, and the standard against which other IQ tests usually are compared in assessing their validity. It is administered individually and requires the child to respond to a large number and variety of tasks. Testing time varies but will average from about forty-five to sixty minutes, and considerable skill and training in testing techniques is required. Although it is perhaps the best test of IQ, it is not very practical for preschool teachers because of the time and training necessary for its administration and because it is not particularly useful as a diagnostic device for planning individualized instruction.

• Wechsler Preschool and Primary Scale of Intelligence (New York: The Psychological Corporation, 1967).

This test, commonly known as the WPPSI, is a comprehensive, individually administered test of general ability or IQ. Like the Stanford-Binet, it assumes considerable testing experience and training for test administrators, it must be individually administered, and it takes forty-five to sixty minutes (on the average) to administer. It is somewhat more useful diagnostically than the Stanford-Binet, because it is divided into a number of subtests that provide a profile of the child's relative strengths and weaknesses across the tasks measured. However, because of the testing expertise necessary and the time required to administer it, it is not practical for use by the ordinary preschool teacher unless a school psychometrist is available to administer and interpret it.

Language Tests

• Illinois Test of Psycholinguistic Processes, rev. ed. (Urbana: University of Illinois Press, 1970).

This test, commonly known as the ITPA, involves several subtests of the child's receptive language (What can he understand?) and expressive language (How well can he communicate his thoughts and concepts?). Because it does involve several different subtests, it provides a diagnostic profile that can be useful for planning experiences to help the child improve in areas of weakness. However, the test is time consuming, must be individually administered, and requires considerable care and skill for proper administration. Thus, it is not very useful for the typical preschool, unless a psychometrist is available to conduct the testing and review the results with the teacher.

- The Peabody Picture Vocabulary Test (Minneapolis: American Guidance Service, 1959).

This test, commonly called the PPVT, is intended as a brief estimate of general intelligence through assessment of the child's receptive vocabulary. The child is shown sets of four pictures at a time and asked to point to the one which is a picture of the thing that the examiner has just named. The test proceeds from simple to more difficult items, continuing until the child misses six of eight consecutive items. Although it is of some usefulness as a general screening instrument, and does not assume special testing expertise, this test is subject to considerable measurement error because the child easily can guess correctly (there are only four choices). Also, its validity for low SES and/or minority-group children has been questioned in several studies.

Knowledge and Concept Inventories

- Boehm Test of Basic Concepts (New York: The Psychological Corporation, 1968).

This test is an individually administered inventory of basic concepts that the preschool child usually possesses. The test can be administered by preschool teachers without any special training, and, although testing is done individually, it takes little time. Thus, this test is a useful diagnostic tool.

- The Caldwell-Soule Preschool Inventory (Princeton, N.J.: Educational Testing Service, 1967).

This inventory, similar in many ways to the Boehm test, is an individually administered instrument designed to measure whether or not the child possesses vocabulary, concepts, and basic skills common to children of preschool age. Although some norms are available, its major use is as a diagnostic instrument to indicate areas in which the child needs special work. Although it is administered individually, it can be done relatively briefly (perhaps fifteen minutes) and does not require special testing expertise, so that it is practical for most preschool teachers to use.

**Norm-Referenced School
Readiness Tests**

• Lee-Clark Readiness Tests (California Test Bureau, 1962).

Like the Metropolitan Readiness Tests described below, the Lee-Clark Tests attempt to predict school readiness (and, more generally, school achievement in the early grades). However, these tests are briefer than the Metropolitan tests and thus quicker and easier to administer. They also can be administered to groups, although the groups should be as small as possible and the children should be closely monitored to see that they understand and follow the directions. The tests are excellent for predicting achievement in the early primary grades, but they are of limited diagnostic usefulness for the preschool teacher.

• Metropolitan Readiness Tests (New York: Harcourt Brace Jovanovich, 1965).

The Metropolitan Readiness Test battery consists of six subtests: word meaning, listening comprehension, perceptual recognition of similarities, recognition of alphabet letters, number knowledge, and perceptual-motor control. It is designed to measure skills related to early language-arts instruction, and is intended for children of kindergarten age. The children must be able to follow instructions and have sufficient writing skills to take the test meaningfully. The test is made for administration by teachers with no special training in psychometric testing, and it can be administered to groups of children. However, as always, the group should be as small as possible so that the teacher can monitor the test-taking behavior of the children and be prepared to take note and/or intervene if a child seems to misunderstand the instructions. The Metropolitan battery takes longer to administer than the Lee-Clark, but it is somewhat more useful as a diagnostic tool. Both tests, however, are designed primarily as predictors of achievement in the early elementary grades.

11
DIAGNOSTIC TEACHING

Teachers cannot expect to achieve success, especially with young children, if they merely present something once or twice and assume that this is sufficient to enable all of the children to learn. This is an obviously unrealistic and inappropriate expectation on the teacher's part, which, among other things, fails to take into account the vast individual differences that are to be found in any group of children. Yet, many teachers teach as though they really do expect the children to learn from such minimal instructional activity.

This will not happen, of course, even if the curriculum is ideally suited to the group and even if the teacher makes an outstanding initial presentation of a concept. Even in a group selected to be as homogeneous as possible, there will be some children who already have mastered the concept or skill, some who have not yet mastered it but who can easily pick it up as they participate in the learning experience, and some who will not successfully master it in a single activity because they need readiness work and/or time to practice the new skill until they master it to the point of overlearning. The present chapter is concerned primarily with the latter group, that is, the children who do not learn a concept or skill when taught with methods that succeed with most or all of the other children.

DIAGNOSIS

This chapter is entitled "Diagnostic Teaching" because the key to successfully reteaching children when they have failed to master a concept or skill the first time around is to diagnose accurately the nature of their difficulty. Accurate diagnosis of a lack of readiness, vocabulary problems, conceptual confusion, or some other difficulty that is preventing the child from mastering the new concept or skill is essential if the teacher is to plan effectively to reteach with materials and methods most likely to enable the child to succeed.

235

The term *diagnosis* is borrowed from medicine, and it is used here because the process the teacher must go through in attempting to discover the nature of a child's learning difficulty is similar to the process that a doctor goes through in determining the cause of a patient's symptoms. To treat a patient rationally and effectively, a doctor not only must observe the symptoms accurately but must diagnose the cause correctly. For example, suppose a patient complains of a headache. A doctor would be successful in a good percentage of such cases by simply prescribing aspirin and rest, since many headaches merely reflect temporary physical distress and require only the administration of pain killers until the source of the problem runs its course and the body returns to its normal state. However, some headaches result from brain concussions, brain tumors, or other serious injuries or diseases. Failure to diagnose properly in these cases not only will result in inadequate treatment of the headache, but might also result in serious illness or even the death of the patient. In these cases, it is vital that the doctor diagnose accurately and do much more than prescribe a mild analgesic and rest.

To a teacher, learning failure presents a problem analagous to the problem that the patient's headache presents to the doctor. On the surface, the symptom is relatively easy to recognize: The child fails to respond or responds incorrectly, and in general he fails to master the concept or skill being taught. However, useful diagnosis requires more than a simple success–failure observation. Why did the child fail? Inattention? Failure to understand the directions? Unfamiliar vocabulary? If the child fails for any of these reasons, the teacher would have to take steps to help him attend to and/or understand the instructions. But what if the child understands the instructions and still fails? In this case, the reteaching effort will have to be different. Here the problem is more fundamental and will probably require more intensive effort to overcome, since the child apparently lacks mastery of some important subpart of the task or needs time to practice the new skill until he can perform at satisfactory levels. These examples illustrate the vital role of diagnosis as the basis for planning reteaching. If the problem is diagnosed accurately and appropriate reteaching is undertaken, the child will probably achieve success. However, if the problem is that the child lacks some subskill and requires readiness work, but the teacher thinks that he has failed only because he didn't understand the instructions, her reteaching efforts will fail repeatedly. In such a case, the child knows what he is supposed to do but is unable to do it, and continued attempts by the teacher to get him to do it without providing him the reteaching help that he needs will be a frustrating and useless exercise for both teacher and child.

KEEPING RECORDS

Successful diagnosis in the classroom depends partly upon well-developed observational skills and partly upon knowledge of how children learn, especially of the kinds of difficulties that can confuse or impede them in their efforts to learn. Thus, training and practice in either of these areas will help improve your diagnostic skills. Both of these skills take time and experience to acquire, and you should work continually at developing them.

You can greatly improve the ease and accuracy with which you diagnose children's learning difficulties, however, regardless of your levels of knowledge and experience, if you keep systematic records on each child's patterns of success and failure. This is done most easily, of course, in sequenced programs that use criterion-referenced tests, which can serve as a running record of each child's progress in meeting the objectives included in the program. If you do not have the advantage of such ready-made tests, design your own (again, remember that when we use the word test, we refer not only to formal assessment devices, but also to observation and other informal methods of collecting and recording information on the children). In the cognitive area, such records should include notations about each child's patterns of success and failure in each of the areas of the curriculum. When recording failures, be sure to record your best estimate as to *why* the child failed, using some of the distinctions discussed below. In the affective area, record keeping should include some systematic data collection on relevant behaviors (attention span, sharing, group participation, ability to get along with other children, etc.) as well as notation of critical incidents (traumatic experiences, major events in the child's life, or other happenings that appear to have great importance for the child and that might be useful for understanding the child's subsequent behavior and making decisions about how best to meet his needs).

Some of the more common sources of learning difficulty are discussed below. Practice until you have learned to identify each of them accurately when they occur, because this will greatly simplify planning and increase efficiency in situations where children have failed to learn and must be retaught.

FAILURE TO UNDER-STAND DIRECTIONS

One set of learning difficulties includes the problem of failure to hear or understand a question or direction. This can happen for many different reasons, as listed below.

Inattention

Where only a single response is involved, a child's failure may be due to simple *inattention*. Here all that is required is that you repeat the question or instructions. If a child is chronically inattentive, you will need to work on this problem in its own right (see Chapter 12) in addition to handling individual instances of the problem by repeating the question or instructions. However, save intensive work on inattention for private conferences as much as possible; during group activities confine yourself simply to repeating the question or instructions and getting a response from the child who has been inattentive. If inattention is a chronic problem with many of your children, it may mean that you are improperly pacing activities, moving too slowly or failing to keep all of the children actively involved. If reviewing Chapters 9 and 12 does not enable you to diagnose the problem or problems on your own, get help from your supervisor or another adult who can observe you during the day and attempt to identify the reasons for the children's inattentiveness.

Vocabulary Problems

Sometimes children attend to an instruction or question but do not understand it because they do not understand one or more key words. This often happens with young children because of their spotty vocabularies, and it is a continuing problem with bilingual children, especially if they are being taught in their second language. In these cases, it is necessary to rephrase the question or instruction in language that the child can understand and/or to provide needed definitions or translations. This particular problem is difficult to diagnose by simply observing the child, so it pays to train your children to inform you whenever they do not understand a word or an instruction. Encourage them to ask "What is ———?" or "What does ——— mean?" and similar questions which will indicate to you that they have not understood. Nonverbal cues with which the child may indicate his lack of understanding include failure to respond when he has obviously been paying attention and a confused or indecisive facial expression. Faced with this behavior, it is usually best either to simply repeat the question or direction and continue to observe the child or to ask him directly if he understands.

Correcting a vocabulary problem might involve anything from simply supplying a definition or translation to digressing from the activity in order to teach the new word and its associated concepts. This will depend on the importance of the word to the objectives of the activity and on the inherent difficulty of teaching the meaning of the word. If the word and the concept for which it stands are central to the activity, it will be necessary for you to take the time to teach the children its meaning if the objective is to be mastered successfully. On the other hand, if the word is not at all crucial (for example, if it appears in an example that can easily be substituted with another example that contains words the child understands), it might be best to explain briefly and then move on.

Also, some words are inherently more difficult to teach than others. Labels for concrete objects are particularly easy to teach, since you can point to the object, give the label, and then have the child repeat it a few times. Usually this is all that will be required. However, if the word stands for some difficult or abstract concept, particularly one that cannot be easily demonstrated or pointed to, it may be much more difficult to teach. For example, relational words like "bigger" or "middle" usually will require a series of examples to insure learning. Whether or not it is worth interrupting the presentation in order to teach such a concept thoroughly depends upon whether or not the concept is crucial. If it is crucial, and especially if several of the children seem confused, it might be better to abandon the original plan and instead teach the concept causing confusion (reserving the original plan until the children have mastered the more fundamental concept).

Thus, *the objectives of an activity must be taken into account in making decisions about problems of confusion or gaps in vocabulary.* Sometimes it will be worth changing the original plan in order to teach the subconcept; at other times it will be best to skip over the problem and continue with the activity, coming back later to the child who is confused to deal with him individually.

Sometimes a child will be confused not merely because he lacks knowledge of an important word phrase, but because he has some kind of positive confusion about it. That is, he thinks that "up" is "down" or that "left" is "right," or he confuses terms like "taller" and "bigger." Such confusion usually cannot be detected at first, because the child thinks he understands you and confidently proceeds to answer or starts to follow directions. It is only as he gives the answer or begins to try to carry out the task that it becomes clear that he does not understand. When you suspect such confusion, begin by *asking the child to restate the question or instructions in his own words.* This will let you know whether or not the child has heard you correctly. If he is able to restate the question or directions correctly but obviously misunderstands them, question him to try to narrow down and pinpoint the exact nature of his confusion. What aspects of the question or directions does he understand correctly? Where does his confusion lay?

For example, if you ask the child to give you a "tall, red block," and he gives you a short, red block, you need to find out whether he simply didn't hear or pay attention to the word "tall," or whether he has confused the terms "tall" and "short." Find out by asking him to restate the instructions, and then proceed accordingly. If he did not attend to the word "tall," inform him that he didn't get the whole set of instructions, caution him to listen carefully, and then repeat. If he is confusing "tall" with "short," you will have to clarify these terms for him.

Confusion of terms is particularly frequent with polar opposites (tall–short, big–small, hot–cold, ask–tell, etc.) and with terms that are indirectly related to one another because they are parts of a more general concept or dimension (colors, numbers, letters, animals, etc.). Confusion is also frequent with terms that are difficult for a young child to differentiate (shape–size, blocks–beads, books–magazines, husband–father, city–state, etc.). Usually such misconceptions can be cleared up with relative ease, although the ones that are more abstract and difficult to demonstrate can take longer. Again, the desirability of taking time out from the planned activity in order to clear up such confusion depends upon the importance of the concept involved to the objectives of the activity. The concept should be taught where it is important to the objectives. Where it is not, go on with the activity and return later to the confused child to help clear up his confusion.

Perseveration

Another common cause of mistakes in young children is *perseveration*. Perseveration refers to the tendency to persist or continue with a given behavior *after it is no longer appropriate*. Perseveration is often seen in young children's attempts to trace, copy, or print letters, where they may have difficulty in stopping at the end of the line and may continue until they reach the edge of the page. This would be an example of *motor perseveration*. Another kind of perseveration may occur when a child has been responding appropriately to one type of question but fails to adjust his mode of response when the type of questioning shifts. For example, suppose you have been asking questions about counting and numbers, so that the child becomes accustomed to the idea that the correct answer is a number. You then point out five pencils to him and ask, "What color are these pencils?" and the child says "five" instead of "yellow." When you encounter this kind of perseveration, caution the child to listen carefully to the question and then repeat it, giving him a second chance to respond. Usually this will be enough to correct the problem, both in the immediate situation and in general. For those few children who show persistent perseveration problems, you should point out in a private talk that it is more important to listen carefully to the question and answer the question after thinking about it than to be the first one to respond. Special assignments involving listening skills and direction following might also be useful here, including work in a listening center if one is available.

Error Sets

Another major source of problems is what Marion Blank (1973) calls *error sets*. An error set is a habit of responding in a particular way whether or not it is appropriate at the moment. It might be something as simple as always answering "yes" to yes–no questions or always picking the middle choice when given a choice of three objects, or it might be something more complex, such as alternating "yes" and "no" answers or responding in some other kind of pattern that has nothing to do with the content of the question. Similar kinds of error sets occur when the child is asked to choose left-versus right-side choices, where again he may choose always left or always right, alternate regularly between the two, or develop some more complex pattern.

The key here is a *pattern* to the child's responses that has nothing to do with the question asked. Teachers must be alert to spot such patterns if they are to diagnose error sets of this kind correctly. It is important to do so, because a child operating with such an error set can completely confuse a teacher who is assuming that he is responding rationally to questions and who may develop erroneous diagnoses of his problem as a result. For example, a child's pattern of responses, if taken at face value, might suggest that he doesn't understand a particular word in the directions. However, if he is responding with an alternation error set (picking the left choice one time and the right choice the next), the actual situation may be that he is not really listening to the question or attempting to deal with it at all, and that this, rather than vocabulary, is the crux of the problem.

Another type of error set is *impulsiveness.* Many children, in their eagerness to respond, will blurt out the first answer that comes to mind as soon as they have any idea about the kind of answer you want, rather than listening carefully to the entire question and thinking before responding. These children need to be cautioned to listen and to think before responding. In dealing with such children, call attention to and praise their careful listening and their responding appropriately, rather than simply rewarding a quick or correct response. In other words, concentrate on stressing the appropriate *processes* to use in responding to questions, not merely the attainment of the correct answer. At times it is also helpful to ask such children to *explain* their answers in order to help them focus on their own thinking processes and to help reinforce the idea that you are interested in how they got the answer as well as the fact that they did answer correctly.

If error sets and perseveration are frequent problems in your class, you may be partially causing them by overemphasizing quick responses or "Who knows the answer?" and underemphasizing the use of good processes such as careful listening and consideration of alternatives before making a response.

INABILITY TO FOLLOW DIRECTIONS

So far we have described situations in which children could not understand the directions or were not listening to them. However, there are times when the child does understand the question or direction in the sense that he knows what you want him to do, but he is unable to do it. This can happen for any of several different reasons, and accurate diagnosis requires that you be able to distinguish among these reasons and to see how these situations differ from the previous ones involving failure to attend or to understand the directions.

No Response

The situation that is the simplest for the teacher to recognize, but often the most difficult to deal with, is the one in which the child makes *no response.* That is, the child clearly pays attention while you ask a question or give a direction, but he does not respond when you finish. He merely stares at you, looks at the floor, or looks uncomfortable or uncertain. Teachers are often threatened by this situation, because they find silence very disconcerting and often are afraid that the child will be painfully embarrassed or otherwise undesirably affected by this kind of experience. This is usually not true, although it may be in certain instances. Teachers must use their knowledge of individual children in making judgments about how to react in these situations.

In general, if the child remains passive for several seconds without giving any clues about whether or not he is thinking about the answer or is likely to make a response, try repeating the question or direction. As an alternative to repeating the entire question or direction, give a brief prompt to find out if the child is intending to respond ("Do you know?" "Well?" etc.). This will remind the child that you are waiting for him either to make a response or indicate that he is unable to do so, and will usually produce a response of some kind.

If the child remains silent and passive even after such a probe or repetition of the question, observe him very carefully and try to *decide the reason for his silence*. In particular, try to decide whether his problem is one of knowledge or of motivation. Is the child willing to respond but unable to do so because he is not sure about what to do, or is he unwilling to respond because of fear or defiance? To help find out, give the child the answer and then ask him to repeat it. This will take him off the hook if he is confused or inhibited, and it will do no harm if his problem is defiance. Asking him to repeat the answer will help you to discover whether or not he is defiant. If the child refuses to repeat the answer, and especially if he communicates anger or defiance through nonverbal gestures, it is likely that he is actively resisting you for some reason. This suggests that he is emotionally upset and angry with you, and that you should have an individual conference with him as soon as possible (see Chapter 12).

Occasionally a child may not respond to a request to repeat an answer because he is afraid. These children will stare at the floor, shuffle their feet, or look nervous rather than appear angry and defiant. Alternatively, they may begin to form a sound with their lips but be unable to carry it through to a verbal response. Or, they may respond in a low whisper or soft tone. In any case, behavior of this sort indicates that the child's problem is fear or lack of confidence. Try to help by encouraging him to speak up ("That's it, say it out loud so that we all can hear it"). Praise or otherwise reinforce the child when he does speak up, and make it clear that you expect him to respond appropriately and are confident that he can and will do so. If he persists in fearful inhibition despite such encouragement, he may need more concerted individual treatment (see Chapter 12).

If the child shows neither fear nor defiance and readily repeats the answer that you gave him after initially failing to respond, it is likely that his initial failure was due to confusion and inability to respond rather than to any motivational or attitudinal problem. Have him repeat the answer once or twice again to help him remember it, especially if he is learning something new. In any case, this child simply needs more teaching, especially additional response opportunities. He may also need some reteaching of earlier material that he may not have learned or some special individualized work in the areas in which he is weak. However, the main thing to do in this case is to minimize your attention to the child's initial failure to respond and to move on briskly, praising his successes and ignoring his failures.

If a child habitually remains silent when he does not know an answer, train him to *tell you that he is confused* or to ask you for more information rather than staying quiet. If silence of this sort is a widespread problem in your classroom, you may be unconsciously contributing to it by being overly critical when children fail to respond or when they respond incorrectly. This kind of behavior can inadvertently teach them to remain silent unless they are sure that they are correct. It is also possible that the kinds of questions you are asking or the kinds of response demands you are making are too sophisticated for the children at this time, so that they are continually baffled or confused. Try to diagnose the situation and take appropriate steps, either by simplifying the curriculum to make it more appropriate for the children's levels and/or by making a concerted effort to avoid critical remarks and to attend to and praise children's successes rather than their failures.

In summary, if a child does not respond initially to questions or directions, you should first repeat the question or direction to show that you expect him to respond and are waiting for him to do so. If he still does not respond, give him the answer and ask him to repeat it, observing him carefully to decide whether his problem seems to be confusion or inability to respond, fear or inhibition, or anger and defiance. According to your diagnosis of the reasons for his silence, follow up with individualized work (if needed).

Hesitant and Clumsy Responses

Often a child will know what you want him to do and will do it, but he will do it only very slowly, clumsily, or in a disorganized way. If he is working on a task that involves use of his hands, he may make clumsy hand movements, take a long time to do the job, or make many errors that he has to correct as he goes along. In problems requiring verbal responses, he may take a long time to think of an answer, may make mistakes and then have to correct them, or may use only partially correct words or phrases.

These problems are common and natural in the learning of young children, especially when they are learning something for the first time. We all tend to proceed slowly and clumsily when we are learning something new. If you consider your own behavior when you first learned to roller skate or drive a car, for example, you will remember how disorganized and unsure of yourself you were and how clumsily you performed all of the actions that you later learned to do smoothly and effortlessly. Children confronted with the task of learning brand new material, especially complex motor responses that must be practiced repetitiously in order to achieve a smooth, coordinated response, have much the same problem. Even when all the children start from the same developmental point, there will be great individual differences in their rate of learning. All of this is completely normal and to be expected.

Your main problem in these situations is to make sure that the child does in fact understand what he is supposed to do. If he does not, and especially if he has developed an incorrect way of responding so that he is, in effect, practicing errors, intervene as quickly as possible. Demonstrate the correct way to respond and have the child practice until you are satisfied that he knows what to do. At this point, success is largely a matter of seeing that the child gets as much individualized practice as he needs, bearing in mind that some children will need relatively little and others will need a great deal in order to achieve the same level of mastery. *If the child's response is correct in the sense that he is using the right process but is simply slow or clumsy, all he needs is practice and encouragement.* Point out his progress to him and express your confidence that he will improve with practice. Where necessary, communicate your satisfaction with his progress and reassure him if he is worried that he may not be doing as well as other children. Impress upon him that he will learn to do as well as his peers if he practices regularly.

For children with problems in the language or direction-following area, assignments that will allow them to practice these skills (such as work in a listening center) are especially useful. With children who have difficulty discriminating or understanding relationships, provide examples and elicit responses until you have taught them the relevant concepts to the point of overlearning. For problems of muscle coordination or motor problems involved in controlling a pencil or a pair of scissors, provide repeated opportunities for the child to practice and perfect his skill.

Learning Gaps

Sometimes a child will fail on a task because he has not yet mastered some subtask fundamental to it. *In this case, the child needs practice not only on the task itself but also on the subtask that he has not mastered.* For example, a child cannot meaningfully succeed at any task involving counting if he has not yet mastered the more fundamental relationship of one-to-one correspondence (that is, the idea that you count out one number for each object and stop counting when you run out of objects). By careful observation and repeated questioning of the child during numerical tasks, you eventually can determine that he is not merely guessing or perseverating, but is making errors because he lacks a fundamental understanding of this concept. In this case, the child needs individualized work with one-to-one correspondence, so that activities involving counting will take on a new meaning for him as he gains a fuller grasp of the counting process. Similarly, many children will have difficulties completing planned arts and crafts projects because they have not yet mastered such fundamental skills as cutting or pasting. Such children may well enjoy participation in arts and crafts activities even though they do not produce a very esthetic product, but they will benefit from some specific instruction in cutting and pasting and, in the long run, will probably gain more satisfaction from their obvious increase in skills.

Confusions and Misconceptions

Sometimes a child's problem will be more complex than simple unfamiliarity with the concept: The child may confuse two or more concepts that he has learned at the same time. For example, the first time he was introduced to the light–heavy distinction, he may have confused these terms with small–large. Thus, if you ask him to hand you the heaviest object, he may regularly hand you the largest one, or, if all of the objects are the same size, he may be completely confused by the question. Many examples of this kind of confusion in young children's thinking have been discovered by Piaget and his colleagues. For example, a child may think that a group of five beads or M&Ms is larger than a group of nine if the five are spread out and the nine are very close together. Or, he may confuse unique names with the words that they stand for or with a more general class of objects. For example, if a child has only seen one phonograph in his life, he may think that it is a unique object and may not understand that a similar but not quite identical object is also a phonograph. Pictures or schematic representations of real people or objects may also cause trouble, especially when they are not scaled to actual size. For example, if you are using pictures of dogs and elephants, the child may be seriously confused by questions involving "bigger" or "smaller" if the dog in one picture is larger than the elephant in another picture. Many children will say that the dog is larger than the elephant because of the difference in the pictures. This is especially probable if the child has never seen a real elephant and does not know through firsthand experience just how large elephants are (and many disadvantaged children never have seen a real elephant). For example:

Teacher Which is bigger, a dog or an elephant?
  Child The dog.
Teacher The dog is bigger? [The teacher should note here that the child
      says "the" dog, not "a" dog.]
  Child Yes.

Teacher How do you know?

Child Look! [Points to the two pictures.]

Teacher I see; the picture of the dog *is* bigger than the picture of the elephant. But these are just pictures. Have you ever seen a *real* elephant?

Child No.

Teacher Well, *real* elephants are very big—bigger than a car! [Teacher gives concrete referent here.] So, even though you can't tell it from these pictures, an elephant is much bigger than a dog—even a big dog. You'll see when we go to the zoo.

Confusions of this sort are difficult to detect and must be distinguished from errors such as random guessing or perseveration. Observe the child carefully and look for patterns in the way he responds. Ask questions or give directions to identify the exact nature of the problem. It is especially helpful to ask the child to explain the reason for his responses, since these explanations may reveal the source of his confusion. Once the confusion has been identified, teach the child the correct concept or skill to the point of overlearning, so that you can be sure that the confusion is eliminated entirely.

Learning Disabilities

Sometimes the problem may be more serious than simple confusion or learning gaps. The child may have sensory-perceptual or motor difficulties that interfere with his ability to perform a task. For example, he may confuse left with right, up with down, or right side up with upside down. He may confuse "b" and "d," "P" and "F," "p" and "q," or "6" and "9." He may have problems in distinguishing between a square and a rectangle or between a circle and an oval. He may have difficulty keeping a pencil on a line if you ask him to trace or copy something. He may have general perceptual-discrimination problems that make it hard for him to distinguish between two things that are similar but not quite the same.

These and similar problems are often referred to as *specific learning disabilities* or *lack of readiness.* Most of them disappear with time, whether or not special instruction is given to the child. However, most problems of this kind can be eliminated with proper corrective teaching and opportunity for practice. Furthermore, the problem may get worse with time if left untreated, because the child may continue to practice his incorrect mode of response until it becomes more firmly established and more difficult to eliminate. Also, the child may lose interest and confidence if he experiences continual failure. Thus, we recommend that you take immediate action to help a child overcome problems of this sort when you diagnose them, using some of the techniques described below. If such techniques do not appear to be working and if the problem appears to be stubbornly resistant to change, it may be worth having the child tested at a special education diagnostic clinic or similar facility capable of assessing the specific nature of his problem and making suggestions about treatment.

PRESCRIPTIVE TEACHING TECHNIQUES

So far in this chapter we have discussed the importance of accurate diagnosis of the causes of learning difficulties and have described some of their more common symptoms as observed in young children. In the remainder of the chapter we will make suggestions about how teachers can respond to these learning difficulties with specific techniques likely to succeed in helping the child overcome his problem.

Problem Prevention

The best technique of all, of course, is to prevent a problem from occurring or to nip it in the bud before it becomes entrenched. Problems are minimized by doing a good job of presenting an activity in the first place, and this in turn is accomplished by careful preparation, good pacing, smooth technique, and careful observation of the children's responses during teaching. More specifically, the key to preventing problems lies in seeing that each child gets many opportunities to respond and in observing the children carefully as they do respond.

The importance of seeing that each child gets frequent opportunities to respond is probably obvious, but, nevertheless, the failure to do so is one of the most common bad habits observed in teachers at all levels. Observational studies of the classroom have repeatedly revealed that teachers spend far more time talking than they may realize, while the children passively listen rather than respond in more active ways. Much of this, of course, is necessary, since young children need instruction and demonstration. However, the amount of teacher talk observed in the classroom is usually much in excess of what is needed, and learning is much too often a matter of passive listening rather than active discovery or practice.

The need for child response is important at any level, but it is especially crucial in working with young children. As we have mentioned before, developmental research has indicated that young children learn largely by *doing,* and their relatively short attention spans limit the amount that they can learn through passive listening and watching. Thus, it is vital for teachers working with young children to conduct activities at a brisk pace, providing whatever introductory information and demonstration is needed, but then moving quickly to having the children answer questions or begin to practice the skill being taught. Thus, once you have introduced an activity, most of the remaining time should be spent questioning the children and/or giving them opportunities to respond, as well as providing them with feedback about how they are doing.

Also, be on the alert for the child who is not responding or is confused;

don't fall into the trap of hearing only the correct verbal responses and noticing only the correct physical ones. Some of the more common self-defeating behaviors that have been observed in teachers include:

- Too often having the children respond chorally rather than individually, so that children who do not respond or who respond incorrectly go unnoticed.
- Failing to wait patiently for a child to respond (showing impatience or frustration, calling on someone else, allowing other children to call out the answers, answering the question yourself).
- Asking rhetorical questions that are not really questions at all.
- Asking too many yes–no and either–or questions that encourage guessing and often lead the teacher to believe that the child knows something when he does not.
- Giving fewer, rather than more, response opportunities to the children who are having difficulty and therefore are most in need of practice.
- Deluding oneself into believing that a child has mastered a new concept or skill on the basis of a lucky guess or a successful response achieved by imitating the teacher or another child rather than by figuring out the answer independently.
- Giving children having difficulty only very easy questions or very simple tasks, or providing them with more help than they need, or moving in too quickly to help when the child might have succeeded on his own if allowed more time.
- Trying to teach too many children at once, rather than using subgroups.
- Failing to keep accurate records on child progress.
- Failing to follow up with children having difficulty by providing tutorial assistance or other reteaching that will prevent them from falling further and further behind their classmates.

In short, many learning difficulties can be nipped in the bud if teachers systematically provide adequate child-response opportunities, provide response opportunities at the right level of difficulty, provide response opportunities that allow for observation of each *individual* child's mastery of the concept or skill being taught, wait patiently for each child to respond rather than prematurely giving up on him or providing help, insure that each child's response opportunity is respected by refusing to allow other children to call out the answer, concentrate particularly on the children who have difficulty as the lesson progresses, and follow up with appropriate reteaching activities with children who appear to need them. All of this is much easier to do if children are taught in small rather than large groups. The smaller the group, the more opportunities each child gets to interact with the teacher and to respond individually.

Probably the key decisions to be made in teaching an activity are when to provide the child with help and what kind of help to provide. These decisions depend in large part upon the nature of the concept or skill being taught. Where the question requires the child to provide a label, a place name, an item of cultural knowledge, or any other isolated factual information item that one either knows or does not know and cannot reasonably be expected to figure out on one's own, it is best to give the child the answer if you have given him a fair amount of time and he does not appear likely to answer (or if he says that he doesn't know the answer). In situations like these, where being able to provide the correct answer depends on whether or not the child has memorized it rather than upon his ability to arrive at the answer through thinking and problem-solving processes, there is little point in encouraging the child to continue thinking or in repeating the question. Here the child does not know the answer and is not likely to come up with it on his own, no matter how much time you give him. Thus, supply the answer and ask him to repeat it, and then come back to him later to see if he has retained it.

On the other hand, if the question or problem is one that the child can reasonably be expected to think through on his own or with the help of a clue or a rephrasing of the question on your part, it is usually best to provide him with this help and encourage him to try to get the answer on his own rather than giving him the whole answer yourself. This procedure provides the child with practice in thinking and problem solving, which he will not get if you give him the answer immediately.

Thus, in general, wait a reasonable time for the child to make a response or to indicate that he is unable to do so. If he cannot respond on his own, either give him the answer (if the problem is one that he cannot be expected to think through on his own) or provide help by rephrasing the question or giving a clue (if this is likely to be enough to enable him to continue thinking to reach a solution to the problem). In all cases, insist that the other children respect the child's right to respond and that they do not call out answers or make derogatory remarks while he is trying to think.

Complex, continuing tasks present the problem of deciding when and how to provide help if a child is making mistakes. Again, the nature of the help that you should provide will vary with the task. If the child is working with Montessori equipment or other self-correcting equipment, you may not need to provide any help at all. Provided that the child knows how to use the equipment, he should be able to correct his own mistakes eventually without any help from you.

You will need to provide some kind of help in situations where the equipment or task does not have built in self-corrective mechanisms. Again, questions of how soon and how much to help will vary with the task. In short tasks, such as copying letters or putting together puzzles that have only four or five pieces, it is usually best to leave the child alone unless he becomes fixated upon an inappropriate strategy. Thus, for example, if the child is generally successful in copying the letter or putting together the puzzle, but is working in a slow or clumsy fashion, it is likely that encouragement and continued practice is all he needs. However, if the child persistently has trouble copying the letter because he is holding the pencil too high, or has difficulty with the puzzle because he is putting the pieces in upside down, you should intervene and show him the correct way to hold the pencil or place the puzzle pieces. Continuation of such clearly self-defeating behavior on the child's part will only lead to frustration and may lead to the acquisition of bad habits that might have to be unlearned later.

In a long or complex task involving a series of substeps, the kind of help you should give will depend upon the nature of the child's error and the place in the sequence in which it occurs. For example, if the child can't even begin the task properly because he doesn't really understand what to do, you will need to redemonstrate the entire task, or at least redemonstrate how to begin. In contrast, if the child has done 90 percent of the task correctly and starts to become confused only at the last step or two in the sequence, it is usually best to give him time to try to work it out on his own rather than to intervene prematurely. Difficulties between these extremes require intermediate responses from the teacher. In general, your guiding principle should be to let the child do as much as he can when he can reasonably be expected to work the problem out on his own, but to intervene when the child obviously does not know what to do or has become fixated on an error that he keeps repeating over and over again.

Be especially alert to watch each child and demonstrate carefully before you allow any of them to begin tasks that require them to start in a precise manner. For example, in tasks involving cutting with scissors, it sometimes is absolutely necessary to begin cutting at a certain place if the task is to be completed successfully. In this case, be sure that each child holds the paper or material to be cut properly and has his scissors positioned at the right place before beginning. Similarly, mazes and other pencil activities require that the child start with his pencil point at a certain place. Here again, you should insure that each child has his pencil placed properly before allowing him to begin.

Some problems can be prevented by asking questions as you are introducing the activity. In particular, if the activity combines objectives from earlier activities, or if it assumes certain knowledge or skills on the part of the children, you should question them to make sure that they have adequate command of the knowledge or skills required at the start of the new activity. If one or more children lack the prerequisites, you should delay beginning the activity itself until you review or reteach them.

PRINCIPLES OF RETEACHING

The techniques listed in Chapter 9 and in the preceding sections of the present chapter should enable you to deal successfully with learning problems as they come up during lessons or activities. However, some particularly difficult or stubborn problems cannot be completely solved during the activity itself, and will require some follow-up reteaching. The following sections suggest some reteaching activities that can be used for some of the more common learning difficulties that you will encounter in young children.

The Child Only Needs Additional Practice

In many cases, the child will have achieved understanding of what he is supposed to do and will be able to do so to some degree, although he may work too slowly or too clumsily. This is the classical learning pattern when anyone (not just a child) is learning a complex, new skill for the first time. Two main factors are involved in mastering such skills to the point of overlearning: (1) mastering each of the basic, fundamental steps involved in the process; and (2) practicing these steps, individually and in coordination with one another, until they can be done effortlessly and automatically. When a child's clumsiness is due solely to the newness of the activity and not to the use of some inappropriate process, all he needs is more practice, not more instruction.

The basic reteaching strategy here is to provide a large number and variety of examples and to give the child frequent response opportunities and practice. The basic method of dealing with mistakes or inability to respond is to provide the correct answer and then have the child repeat it or imitate it. This should continue as the child gradually increases his speed and accuracy.

Almost any complex motor response fits into this category (puzzles, block building, bicycle riding, roller skating, etc.). Once the child masters the fundamentals, he knows what to do; he now needs only practice to sharpen his ability to do it. Where a child shows a notable weakness in a particular area, plan to provide practice activities for him that will allow him to develop his skills in that area. These may well include exercises in the classical sense, although ideally they should consist mainly of game-like activities that the child will enjoy and which will allow him to practice the motor skill involved as a byproduct of his participation in the games.

Also included in the category of child learning that usually requires only additional practice rather than additional instruction are vocabulary words, names for people and objects, isolated bits of cultural or factual knowledge, and other informational items that simply must be committed to memory. Here the child merely needs sufficient repetition of the answer (along with having the teacher ask him to repeat it aloud himself) until he has memorized it to the point of overlearning. A child who is just learning information of this sort cannot arrive at the answer through reasoning processes, and it is simplest just to repeat the answer and have him repeat it back to you until he learns it rather than to try to wait until he remembers on his own. Often this will require repeated practice distributed over several occasions; few new things are firmly learned in one session.

It should be noted that *informational items of this sort are usually inappropriate for young children,* particularly if they involve concepts or content that the child cannot really understand yet or is not yet interested in. Young children can learn to memorize almost anything, but unless the learning is meaningful and in some way related to their concrete experience, the vast majority of what they memorize will soon be forgotten, and even that which is retained will not be very meaningful to them. Thus, as a general rule, teachers should insist that children memorize specific items of factual information only when these are crucial or are items of importance that all children should know.

The Child Lacks a Key Concept or Subskill

All children have gaps in their learning patterns, so that occasionally they will lack a concept or skill that a particular activity assumes as a prerequisite. In this situation, the child will be unable to answer a question or follow a direction because he will not be able to understand part of it. In order to deal with his confusion, you must first discover the concept or skill that he lacks and teach it to him, then go on to the higher-level concept or skill you originally planned to present.

Difficulties of this sort can occur with such basic concepts as colors, numbers, or shapes, but they appear more often in connection with relational words (biggest, middle, bottom) or prepositions (on top of, beneath, outside). A main principle to bear in mind in these situations is to teach by giving the child *many examples* of the concept or skill he does not know. Further, *show* the child; don't just tell him. Give as many *different* examples of the concept as you can, presented in rapid succession. Many times this alone will be enough to get the idea across to him. Thus, to convey the meaning of the concept "middle," show several sets of three different objects or pictures and let him point out the middle one.

Where relevant, *describe the key features when showing examples.* When trying to teach the concept of a square, for example, point out the four corners and trace the four sides with your finger. Better yet, have the child do it himself. During tracing, stress the perpendicular edges by making sharp turns at the corners. If you are trying to differentiate a square from a rectangle, demonstrate that all four sides are the same length by rotating the square between an upright and a side position to show that it looks the same either way, while the rectangle looks different depending on which side it rests upon.

After introducing and teaching new concepts to the point of overlearning, contrast positive examples with examples that do not fit the concept. At first, these should be extreme examples that will help the child focus his attention on the relevant attributes of the main concept, so that he does not become confused. Thus, a good contrast for a square would be an extremely oblong rectangle rather than a slightly rectangular one that looks almost like a square. The sharp contrast between the square and the very oblong rectangle will help the child to see that the square has equal sides and looks the same no matter which side is up. Another good contrast for a square would be a circle, to show that the square has straight lines and sharp corners.

In using contrasts between examples, bear in mind that your purpose is to teach the child the basic concept (the square in this case), and not to teach him labels for many different concepts. If you try to teach him too much at one time, you will only confuse him. Therefore, when teaching the concept of a square, for example, ask questions like "Is this a square?" and "Which is the square?" These questions focus on the square to the exclusion of other examples, and they direct the child's attention to this particular concept. As the child begins to succeed regularly on questions like these, begin asking him to explain his answers ("How did you know?"). Continue this until the child can recognize a square *every time* and can explain the properties of a square to your satisfaction (if this is part of your objective).

In contrast, do *not* ask questions like, "What is this?" (while pointing to a circle) or, "Which one is the square and which one is the circle?" This makes the task much more difficult for a child who is still unclear about the concept of a square. Now, instead of trying to teach him merely about squares, you are teaching him about squares and circles at the same time when he is still unsure about squares. Also, terms like "square" and "circle" may become confused if they are presented together when the child has not yet learned either one clearly. This is even more likely if you say things like "This is a rectangle. A rectangle is just like a square stretched along two sides." This not only makes it harder for the child to keep the concept of a square firmly in mind, but it also makes it very likely that he will confuse the terms "square" and "rectangle."

If the child has not attained the concept after seeing several examples and having the distinctive features pointed out and discussed, a more thorough and systematic lesson will be required. This may involve preparation of special equipment to *eliminate distracting elements* or to *help the child focus on the key characteristics* of the concept. It usually helps to move from the verbal or perceptual level to the level of physical action where possible. Thus, a child who is confused about the shape of a letter of the alphabet, for example, can be given cardboard cutouts of the shape of the letter and asked to feel and trace the outlines with his fingers. He can also be given exercises requiring him to trace the outline with a pencil, first by tracing over printed examples and later by copying them himself. Here again, the child should learn the shape of a given letter by itself before you try to teach him to compare it with shapes of other letters, most especially with other letters that are similar to it.

Physical action is usually required to demonstrate certain relational concepts. In fact, it is often impossible to show relational concepts in isolation from other things, so that they must be taught by comparing two things that differ on the relevant attribute. Ideally, the contrast should be very strong when you first introduce the concept. Thus, concepts like "tall" and "taller," for example, should be taught with pairs of items that are similar except in length (such as a very long and a very short pencil or a tall and a short tree). People of similar size and age but different heights might also provide good examples if the height difference is great enough; however, avoid pictures of parents and children, because at first the child might confuse "taller" with "bigger" or with "older."

After selecting appropriate examples to teach a concept, be sure to emphasize the relevant attributes through voice and gesture as you demonstrate. For example, slowly run your hand up the taller example and say "Look how *tall* this one is! It goes *all the way* up to here. It is *very tall.*" Then switch to another example and say "This one isn't tall at all. The other one is *taller.*" Remember, your goal in this example is to teach "tall" and "taller," and not to teach the contrast between "tall" and "short."

Relational concepts like "inside" must be taught by repeated physical demonstrations of putting one thing inside of another. This should be done slowly, demonstratively, and with stress on each key word: "Watch. I am going to put this ball *inside* the box. See where I am putting it? Now it's *inside* the box. Now I am going to take it *out*. Now there is nothing *inside* the box. See?" This could be followed up with statements like "Put the ball inside the box," "Is there anything inside the box now?" and "See if there is anything inside this other box." All of these questions will help the child to learn the concept of "inside." They focus his attention on this concept alone, to the exclusion of competing concepts that might confuse him. Another technique is to have the child actually get inside a room or container. Remarks like "Is the ball inside the box or outside the box?" or "Tell me all of the things that are inside the box" should be avoided at this stage, because they are much more complex and involve much more than an understanding of the concept "inside." They can be taken up later, once the child has firmly mastered the concept of "inside."

Reteaching of this sort, aimed at filling a learning gap that prevents a child from succeeding in a lesson, should continue to the point of overlearning (i.e., the child can succeed without error or difficulty). The child should have a firm grasp of the concept before moving back to the higher-level lesson that requires him to *use* this concept. If you move on too quickly, before he has firmly mastered the subconcepts, you may still confuse the child in the more difficult lesson.

The Child Confuses Two or More Concepts

Children often confuse polars or opposites (left–right, tall–short, ask–tell) or concepts that are difficult to keep separate because they frequently occur together (tall, big, heavy; mother, wife, lady; bigger, older, taller). To eliminate such confusion, you must get the child to focus on the *separate* meanings of these terms. To do this, teach *one* of the terms in isolation from the others, using the techniques described above. Then teach the other term without reference to the first one. *Only when both terms have been mastered securely* should you try to teach them together and compare and contrast them. Continue comparing and contrasting until the child clearly masters the distinction between the terms (even a single error in a series of eight or ten trials is evidence that some confusion remains and further reteaching and practice are needed).

Similar reteaching principles apply if the child is confusing letters and numbers, especially those that are either mirror-image reversals or spatially rotated variations of one another. It is best not to teach these letters and numbers together while trying to point out similarities and differences. Instead, teach them separately, letting the child feel, trace, and copy each one by itself. For example, the child must learn to recognize the letters "b" and "d," and to associate the separate sounds that go with them. It is not important, and it may even be harmful, to point out the similarities between the letters and to show how one is a mirror reversal of the other. Instead, it will usually be much easier for the child if you teach the two letters separately, so that the chance of his confusing them is slimmer. Introduce one and teach it to the point of overlearning, so that the child recognizes it every time and can label it without hesitation, and then introduce the other.

Bear in mind then, that although it is usually helpful to point out relationships (similarities and contrasts) between concepts, in the cases of *similar concepts or stimuli* the potential for confusing children with this method may be very great. Only if one concept is very familiar and has been thoroughly mastered can the child learn a new, similar concept more quickly by comparing and contrasting it with the familiar one. Otherwise, if neither concept is familiar, or even if the more familiar concept is not yet securely mastered, comparison of the two may confuse the child more than help him. The child will associate the new concepts together in his mind, but he may not clearly understand what each one means separately. As a result, he may learn that "ask" and "tell" are related, but he may begin to use the words interchangeably rather than using each in the sense appropriate to its true meaning.

**Memory or Integration
Failure**

Sometimes a child can do each subtask required in a higher-level task but will not be able to put the subtasks together and do the entire high-level task on his own. This may be just a problem in memory. That is, the child may have difficulty remembering all of the instructions while performing the earlier subparts of the task, so that he has forgotten what he is supposed to do by the time he gets to the later subtasks.

Failure of integration is a related problem. Here, the child can do the separate subparts required for a task, but he cannot put them all together or connect them in a way that will enable him to succeed at the more difficult level. For example, if you ask him to give you red beads or blue beads, or large beads or small beads, he may succeed regularly. However, if you ask him for large, red beads or small, blue beads, he may begin to fail.

Problems of memory or integration failure are overcome primarily through repetition and practice. However, the child may need more than practice alone. *Complex objectives that require a sequence of steps may need to be broken down into a number of subobjectives* that the child can practice separately and master before he tries to integrate them to perform the more complex task.

If a child has not developed an appropriate problem-solving strategy on his own, you will have to explain one to him ("Remember, you have to look for two things. If I ask for a big, red bead, look and be sure that the bead you give me is a big one and that it is colored red"). If instructions and practice of this sort do not work, you may have to simplify the task even further by having the child divide the beads into small and large ones and then subdivide these piles into color groups. Then you can ask him to give you beads from each group until he learns to do so without error, and then begin to mix the beads and ask the original task of him again.

When children show a memory or integration failure, be sure that they master the subtasks you create for them to the point of overlearning before you ask them to combine those subtasks into more complex tasks. Remember when you first learned to drive a car? If your instructor had told you everything about driving the first time you sat behind the wheel, rather than dividing the task into small substeps taken a few at a time, you would have forgotten much of what he had said by the time he had finished his lecture. Children having difficulty because of memory and integration problems face a similar situation. The difficulty is not with the individual parts of the task, since the child can master all or most of these in isolation. However, when he is asked to put them all together into a complex sequence of behaviors, the task of remembering the directions and integrating and sequencing all of them properly is too much for him to handle at one time. Thus, he needs to take the task in smaller steps until he masters each of them and gradually is able to do the entire task as a single operation. This will take time, however, and often considerable tutorial assistance.

For example, in learning to print his name, the child needs to have mastered the various motor skills involved in handling a pencil and controlling it as he makes marks on the page, needs to know how to make each of the individual letters involved in his name, and needs to be able to put them together in the proper order and with the proper spatial rotation (i.e., none of the letters backwards or upside down). For the child who knows these things, the request to write his name is a simple one that he can respond to with ease. However, a child who has difficulty in all three of these areas may need considerable teaching and practice before he can learn to write his name without difficulty. If he is not gripping the pencil properly, or even if he is holding it properly but is still unused to pencil work and is making clumsy hand movements due to simple unfamiliarity, any kind of practice at using the pencil will help him to write his name as well as any other kind of pencil work. Thus, the child can benefit from tracing and drawing activities as well as from direct practice at making letters or attempting to print his name. If he is not holding the pencil properly, he should, of course, be taught how to do so.

If the child is having trouble with one or more letters, he will need practice with them. This may mean simply providing the child with a model and having him copy it many times, making sure that he makes the right pencil movements (starting the letter at the right place and staying with the proper sequence of movement to make the letter most efficiently and appropriately). If he has great difficulty in doing this, you may have to supply extra help by providing dots or broken-line outlines of the letter that will make it easier for him to visualize it and help him form a spatial concept of its outline in his mind before asking him to copy a model without any such help. In any case, the child cannot really learn to print his name without effort until he has learned to print each letter in his name without hesitation or difficulty.

Even after he has mastered each letter, the problem remains of putting the letters together in the proper order and printing his name appropriately on the page. He may need to be taught to start at the left side of the page, to stay on the line, to move from left to right, or other basic skills of this sort. If he has difficulty remembering the order of the letters of his name, you might have to give him practice here by having him first write the first letter, then the first two letters, then the first three letters, and so on, until he learns to print his entire name in the correct order.

Whatever the skill area, the basic principle for dealing with memory and integration failures is to break down the task into parts that the child can handle, and then build back up to it as he achieves mastery.

Reteaching Through Tutoring

The optimal way to teach a child who is having difficulty is through tutoring by yourself or by some other adult who may be available. If adults are not available, older elementary school children or even peers who are capable of instructing the child in the relevant skill or concept can be used as tutors. In fact, sometimes children are better than adults at tutoring peers or younger children, since they seem to approach the task more directly and naturally, and with less hesitation (Thomas, 1970). Adults often waste much time in tutoring by worrying about whether the child is enjoying the activity, making sure that he is not upset when he makes an error, and the like. These behaviors are unnecessary, as observation of children tutoring one another will show. When children tutor one another, they get right down to business and stay on the task, since both children understand implicitly that the child who knows the task is supposed to teach it to the one who does not. There is no anxiety involved, because both children accept this definition of the relationship and neither child is particularly upset by failure because neither child expects instant and total success. Adults, in contrast, are often upset by failures and afraid that the child is going to dislike them or lose interest in the task if he does not master it immediately. Often they create these kinds of responses by communicating such failure expectations through direct verbalization or through indirect cues of voice tone and gesture.

Thus, bear in mind that, when you tutor a child, patience and informality are in order. The tutoring should be carried out as a special, personal interaction between you and the child, which you expect the child to benefit from and enjoy, and not as some kind of disgraceful ordeal that the young child is being subjected to because he is somehow inadequate. Remember, young children will take their cues from you in learning to react to classroom events. Thus, if you treat learning failures as expected, everyday occurrences and simply react to them with reteaching activities designed to overcome the child's weaknesses, the child will not be upset by failure and will learn to expect and probably enjoy participation in such reteaching activities. In contrast, if the child learns (by watching your expressions and listening to your reactions) that failure is some kind of disgraceful or terrible thing, he is likely to begin to react to it much differently. This type of child will show evidence of shame or inhibition when he is unable to respond, or he may begin to become emotionally upset in the face of failure. If this happens with any regularity, you need to do two things. First, check your own teaching to find out whether or not you may be communicating inappropriate attitudes about failure to the children through your own behavior. Second, in addition to tutoring to reteach the concepts or skills involved, use the techniques described in Chapter 12 for working to improve the confidence of anxious and inhibited children.

SUMMARY

This chapter provided suggestions for reteaching materials to children who were unable to learn them initially. The key to successful reteaching is accurate diagnosis: identifying the precise reason for the child's learning difficulty. Accurate diagnosis is achieved by carefully questioning the child and observing his responses in order to identify a pattern that reveals the processes that the child is using to deal with the problem. Once you know what concepts and skills the child has, what ones he does not have, and the kinds of processes that he is using to work on a problem, you are in a position to plan reteaching activities tailored to the child's particular needs. This is much easier to do if you habitually keep records on the children, noting the patterns of success and failure that they show in their various activities and indicating the reasons for difficulty when it occurs.

One fundamental distinction to make in diagnosing is determining whether a child has understood the question or response demand but is unable to do it, or whether the failure has occurred because he has not heard or understood the question or response demand. The latter problem may occur because of inattention, vocabulary problems, perseveration, or error sets. Once you have diagnosed the particular reason for failure to hear or understand the directions, take steps to see that the child understands by insuring that he pays attention, explaining the meaning of any words that he doesn't understand, or countering his perseverations or error sets (whichever is appropriate).

Situations in which the child has heard the instructions but is unwilling or unable to follow them require different responses. If the child makes no response, repeat the question or instruction, observe the child carefully, and try to decide whether he is thinking about the problem and getting ready to answer, is inhibited or afraid to answer, or is defiant and unwilling to answer. If he still does not respond, give him the answer and have him repeat it or imitate it. If he refuses to do so and is generally showing defiance, deal with him individually as soon as possible.

Where the child does make a response but the response is incorrect or inappropriate, observe carefully to determine the processes that he is using in responding. If the child is using the correct processes, so that he is merely hesitant or clumsy rather than confused about what to do, all he needs is more practice. However, if he is using an incorrect process because he is confused or is inexperienced with the materials involved in the problem, take corrective action by eliminating the confusion and/or demonstrating how materials should be used. Often a simple demonstration or explanation will be enough to clear up the problem and enable the child to proceed on his own. However, if the problem is more serious, especially if it involves memory or integration failure (the child can do isolated parts of the task but cannot put them together to do the whole task), you will have to help by dividing the task into parts that the child can master one at a time and then gradually build up to the original task again. This may require some tutorial reteaching of the concept or skill involved in several different ways, and the presentation of a large number of response opportunities or examples.

At this age children learn more by seeing and doing than by listening to verbal explanations, so that a variety of examples and opportunities to practice will often be required to overcome the child's confusion. These re-teaching activities should be reinforced by involving the child in games or learning-center activities that will allow him to practice the relevant skills or deepen or broaden his knowledge of the concept. Be sure that the child has learned to use the right process, however, or such practice may do more harm than good. If a child knows what process to use, practice will help sharpen and refine his skill. However, if he is using an incorrect process, simply providing practice opportunities without correcting the process amounts to allowing the child to practice errors, making a bad habit worse.

QUESTIONS

1. Explain how different children could receive the same poor performance score for different reasons (for example, when only three of the ten mastery problems were done correctly). Provide specific examples, and explain how the teacher should react to each type of failure.

2. What is diagnosis? How does the collection of systematic data relate to diagnostic action?

3. Teachers have goals other than children's mastery of academic skills. Suggest a *specific* goal drawn from such general areas as social behavior or self-concept development, and explain what records a teacher might collect in order to assess progress and provide assistance when necessary to help children attain affective goals.

4. Role play your response to a child's perseveration problem. Define the problem clearly, and then demonstrate the specific language and techniques that you would use in dealing with it.

5. Observe someone teaching one small group of children an academic unit. That is, observe all instruction with a particular group of children on a particular unit. On the basis of your observation, predict the performance of the *group* and each individual child on the mastery test. On the basis of mastery test results and *your observational information,* design and teach a remedial unit for those children that did not achieve mastery.

6. There are many ways that teachers can help a child overcome weaknesses in addition to direct reteaching. One way is by involving the child in play or individual activity that fosters development in his weakness area. Give examples of how this can be done for a child weak in a cognitive area and for a child weak in an affective area. Discuss your ideas with classmates.

7. A few children have difficulty copying their names on drawings. What steps should you take in deciding how to help them?

8. Develop *free-time activities* that would help children who are slow or lacking in skills and/or concepts—eye–hand coordination, small-muscle control, auditory discrimination, visual discrimination, recognition of and naming of letters and numerals, classification, serial ordering, colors, shapes.

9. Devise or discuss appropriate activities that could be developed into individualized projects to work with a particular child with minimum teacher assistance.

10. How would you handle peer tutoring? Assume you have available fifth and sixth graders. Discuss their responsibilities and how you would include them in your planning and scheduling. Would they be used for reteaching and/or enrichment?

11. Make a survey of several preschool classrooms and identify the evaluation and grouping procedures that are utilized.

READINGS

Blank, M. *Teaching learning in the preschool: a dialogue approach.* Columbus, Ohio: Merrill, 1973.

Good, T. and Brophy, J. *Looking in classrooms.* New York: Harper & Row, 1973.

Guszak, F. *Diagnostic reading instruction in the elementary school.* New York: Harper & Row, 1972.

Hunter, M. "Tailor your teaching to individualized instruction." *Instructor* (March, 1970), 53–63.

Kephart, N. *The slow learner in the classroom.* Columbus, Ohio: Merrill, 1960.

Montessori, M. *Dr. Montessori's own handbook.* Cambridge, Mass.: Bentley, 1964.

————. *The Montessori method.* New York: Schocken, 1964.

Popham, W. and Baker, E. *Planning an instructional sequence.* Englewood Cliffs, N.J.: Prentice-Hall, 1970.

12
CLASSROOM MANAGEMENT

This chapter presents suggestions on how teachers can establish and maintain a good classroom atmosphere. By *classroom management* we mean teacher behavior concerned with promoting the children's interest and cooperation in the classroom. This includes both the positive aspects involved with stimulating curiosity and interest as well as the more negative aspects involved with keeping order, maintaining discipline, establishing control, and the like.

Very little definitive research on classroom management by teachers in preschool settings is available. Consequently, in making suggestions we usually will be extrapolating from studies of the effects of parental child-rearing behavior or of classroom-management behavior by elementary school teachers. We have consistently kept this in mind, however, so that the suggestions, while not demonstrably definitive, should be appropriate and effective for preschool teachers.

PREVENTING PROBLEMS

Research by Kounin (1970), among others, has shown that the keys to successful classroom management are preventing problems from beginning in the first place and preventing the problems that do arise from spreading or becoming more serious. Kounin discovered this by comparing a group of teachers who were recognized as excellent classroom managers (i.e., they seldom had any discipline problems) with another group of teachers that continually experienced severe discipline problems. Reasoning that comparison of differences in how these two groups of teachers handled discipline problems would provide information about what to do and what not to do in such situations, Kounin observed how the teachers handled discipline problems and made comparisons between the groups. Much to his surprise, there were no consistent differences. In other words, teachers who were very successful and teachers who were notably unsuccessful in managing their classrooms handled discipline problems in pretty much the same way.

This surprising finding led Kounin to reanalyze the data, following up on some hunches developed about variables other than those included in the original coding. The reanalysis showed striking differences between the two groups of teachers that were closely related to the frequency of discipline problems that they experienced in their classrooms. These key differences were *not* in teacher behavior *in response* to disobedience, disruption, or other management problems, but instead they involved teacher behavior that *minimized* such problems. The effective classroom managers were successful because they prevented problems from occurring in the first place and handled the problems that did occur so that they were eliminated before they became disruptive. The major techniques that the teachers used in minimizing problems will be discussed in the remainder of this section. However, bear in mind that the key to successful management is *problem prevention,* not punishment or other methods of dealing with problems *after* they occur. Every teacher will experience some problems and will need to develop techniques of dealing with them. However, if you master the techniques suggested in the following sections and take a positive, prevention-oriented approach to classroom management, discipline should not be an important problem in your classroom. On the other hand, if you take an authoritarian, threat-and-punishment approach to classroom management, you are asking for trouble.

Essential Teacher Attitudes   Before making any specific suggestions, we wish to stress a few general attitudes and orientations toward young children that we believe are essential if teachers are to succeed in managing classrooms effectively. The suggestions in the following sections all presuppose that teachers have these attitudes. If these attitudes are not present, the suggested behaviors will be reduced to "gimmicks" and probably will not succeed. First, teachers must like children and respect them as individuals. On the negative side, this means avoiding such behaviors as nagging, threatening, shaming, rejecting, and the like. More importantly, there are several positive attitudes and behaviors involved here. First, if teachers genuinely enjoy children and teaching, they should *look like it.* They should smile easily, show interest and enthusiasm when children are relating events or showing off their creations, be able to express affection physically to those children who seem to want or need it without inhibition or embarrassment, and be able to work closely with children naturally and comfortably, especially in situations that call for behavior like getting down on the floor with them or gathering them together in a close group in order to tell a story or play a game. There is no need to "ham it up," but the teacher should be comfortable and approachable in working with children, and the children should show no hesitancy or embarrassment about coming to the teacher for interaction.

Such behavior will form the basis for developing close and rewarding personal relationships with each child. This will promote the children's affection for and identification with the teacher, which in turn will make them much more likely to want to please the teacher and be willing to follow classroom rules without resentment or rebellion. Thus, in addition to all of the other benefits that result from it, the establishment of a warm and mutually respectful relationship makes it much easier for a teacher to deal with a given child in a problem situation.

Teachers must also establish and maintain their *credibility*. That is, they must say what they mean, mean what they say, and practice what they preach, if they expect the children to take them at their word. Teachers should never make a promise or a threat unless they have every intention of carrying it through, and if it proves impossible to carry through for some reason, the reason should be explained to the children. Also, teachers must model in their own behavior the behavior that they are trying to get the children to practice. Teachers cannot successfully instill politeness, good manners, and respect for others, for example, if they do not practice these virtues themselves in their interactions with the children. Although they do not know the word for it yet, even preschoolers can recognize hypocrisy when they see it.

In addition to its importance in establishing the teacher as a likable and respectable person, teacher credibility helps to provide the children with needed structure and dependability. When children know that teachers can be taken at their word, they can be secure in their knowledge of the expectations and limits that apply to them, and they are much less likely to engage in "testing" forms of misbehavior calculated to discover whether or not teachers mean what they say. Also, teacher credibility makes it more likely that the child will assume responsibility for his own misbehavior. If the teacher has been consistent in explaining and enforcing a particular rule, a child who breaks that rule will have no one to blame but himself. However, where the teacher has been inconsistent, the child might justifiably feel that he is being picked on if he gets punished when someone else has "gotten away with it."

Thus, to help establish and maintain credibility, teachers should carefully think through classroom rules and procedures. What behaviors are absolutely forbidden? What behaviors are allowed in some circumstances but not others? What will be done when two or more children want to use the same equipment item at the same time? Will children sometimes be channeled into differential activities or given differential rights or privileges? If so, what are the reasons for these decisions, and how will they be explained to the children? Teachers must have answered such questions to their own satisfaction and be prepared to explain them to the children if they are to maintain credibility.

In summary, the techniques discussed in the following section are useful, but none will succeed for very long if used in isolation by a teacher who has inappropriate basic attitudes towards children or teaching. They are meant to be used *within a relationship* characterized by mutual affection and respect, by teachers who have established their credibility with the children by being consistent in their words and deeds and by practicing what they preach.

Establish Clear Rules Where Rules Are Needed

Certain recurring daily routines may require formal rules that all of the children will be expected to learn and follow. Specific needs will vary with the teacher's preference and classroom conditions, but examples of situations that typically call for explicit rules include procedures for use of restrooms, behavior towards classroom visitors, storage of personal belongings, sharing or taking turns, activities that can be done at will versus activities that require specific permission, and behaviors permissible during rest periods for those children who do not need or want to rest.

For any situations important enough to require a specific rule, *teach the rule* to the children and *explain the rationale* for it. Do not assume that the reason for the rule will be obvious or that the children will understand it without explanation. Some children may be totally unfamiliar with much of the equipment or situations that your rules cover, and consequently they may not have the slightest idea about why a rule is important. Providing an explanation not only gives them a learning experience but also shows them that you are setting up the rules for their own good rather than for some arbitrary or unknown reason. A child who knows the reason for a rule is much more likely to follow it. Also, remember that sometimes classroom rules put restrictions on behaviors ordinarily not restricted outside the school. For example, running around, roughhousing, and noisy play are normal, everyday activities for young children, and they are allowed or sometimes even encouraged outside the school. However, considerations of safety and group living require limitations on such activities within the school. This rule is likely to strike some children as unreasonable and unfair, or at least as puzzling and inconsistent, unless it is carefully explained to them.

To the extent that they are able to do so, the children themselves should participate in the process of establishing rules. This activity will help stimulate their thinking and get them to see the need for a rule and the rationale that underlies it. Like anyone else, children are more willing to follow rules they have established themselves than rules imposed by someone else. Rules should be stated in a short, easy-to-remember form, and the children should repeat them aloud several times as an aid to memory. Also, some rules and procedures will require a physical demonstration in addition to a verbal explanation. For example, in teaching the children how to take out and return equipment, store their personal belongings, or carry out some other physical activity, do not merely tell them what to do. Instead, *show* them by demonstrating the expected behavior and providing opportunities for them to practice and get corrective feedback if they need it.

Rules should be held to a minimum and should be clearly needed. If there is no obvious and convincing reason for a rule, the rule should be eliminated or revised. Do not allow rules to become obsolete or overgeneralized. For example, it is often necessary to establish a rule about the use of a new equipment item when it is introduced, because most of the children want to use it. However, after the item has been in the classroom for a few weeks, the rule usually will no longer be necessary because the demand for the item has lessened. Also, avoid overgeneralized or restrictive rules which make demands upon the children that are not really necessary to accomplish the goals that the rules were established for in the first place. For example, all-day programs will usually have a rest or nap period scheduled, typically shortly after lunch. Some restrictions will be required here, in order to insure that the children who want or need a nap are not prevented from getting it by the others. However, it is unrealistic and overly restrictive to require that all children nap or remain absolutely silent throughout the period. As in most other areas, children show great individual differences in their sleep and rest needs, so that a given class is very likely to contain some children who need a nap and others who do not want a nap and do not need one. Rather than force the latter children to squirm unhappily and strive to remain silent during the rest period, allow them to engage in quiet activities such as looking through books, coloring, playing with quiet games and toys, and so forth. Thus, a rule like "everyone must rest during nap period" would be inappropriate, while a rule like "during nap period children who are awake should talk softly and play quietly so as not to wake up the children who are sleeping" would be much better.

Let the Children Assume Independent Responsibility

Teachers should not do things that the children can do for themselves. Although in some cases specific instructions and demonstrations may be needed at first, the children can generally be expected to take out and replace equipment, handle food and containers, use the restroom, move chairs, form lines, and carry out other routine activities of this nature on their own. This will free both teacher and children from having to endure needless rituals, such as when the children must sit and wait while the teacher names them one by one to get in line or to carry out some other routine function. Early in the year, it may be necessary to assist the children with specific directions and to instruct them just a few at a time (but not just one at a

Children can handle tasks like serving juice on their own if they are given proper instruction and are provided with safe, easy-to-use containers.

time) when undertaking an activity, so that they can be monitored and any individual needs for corrective feedback can be observed. However, these temporary measures should be abandoned as soon as the children have internalized the relevant rule or mastered the particular procedure. At that point, it will be necessary to use only general and brief instructions and provide rule reminders for the children who forget or regress.

Minimize Delays and Disruptions

Many management problems begin because children are bored and restless during periods of inactivity or because the teacher is busy dealing with a problem in another part of the room. This tendency for disruption to expand and multiply once started is the major reason that prevention is the key to successful classroom management. There are many things that teachers can do to hold disruptions and distractions to a minimum.

Thorough planning is important; many problems begin because the teacher breaks the flow of an activity in order to get an equipment item or prepare a demonstration that should have been readied earlier. When this occurs, the children will be waiting passively, and this often leads to disruptive behavior.

Similarly, planning and scheduling should minimize (eliminate entirely if possible) situations in which the children have to stand and wait in line or otherwise passively wait for something. For example, before lunch it might be necessary to have the children clean up the room, go to the restroom, and line up at the door to prepare to leave for the lunchroom. A ritual-oriented teacher could spend thirty minutes or more on these activities by first involving the entire class in a cleanup operation that continues until all cleanup work is finished, then having the class go one by one to the restroom, and then having them line up one by one at the door as they emerge from the restroom. However, the same goals could be accomplished, in much less time and without a lot of needless standing and waiting, if the teacher staggers the children and conducts activities simultaneously (some children go to the restroom while others clean up, and as those children emerge from the restroom they join in the cleanup process; children are not asked to line up at the door until the cleanup is completed or almost completed).

Similarly, if teachers follow the guidelines in Chapter 6 for storing toys and equipment so that the children can obtain them themselves, they will save much time needlessly spent dispensing these Items. With proper planning, the teacher can minimize the time that she spends passing out supplies that the children could get themselves if the items were stored where they could reach them, supervising the use of items stored in one large container that could have been stored in several small ones, and so on. In general, therefore, plan your classroom arrangements and instruct the children so that they can handle as many routine matters as possible on their own, thus minimizing their standing in lines. This kind of planning and preparation will serve the double function of promoting independence and self-management skills in the children while at the same time minimizing disruptions and other management problems that arise when children are forced to wait passively for something.

In addition to making it possible for children to operate independently by providing equipment appropriate to their interests and abilities and storing it so that it can be easily taken out and returned, you must consciously work to develop independence and personal responsibility in the children. After the first few days of school, when the children have become familiar with the classroom equipment and have seen demonstrations of how it is used, they should be encouraged to select and use equipment independently. Few rules are necessary to accomplish this. In fact, the general rule that a child must put something back the way he found it before he takes out something new, plus perhaps a few rules regarding the sharing of high-demand items, may be enough.

Where possible, it is usually best to allow a child to play with whatever he wants to play with. You may have to limit a child's time to play with a given toy because other children also want to play with it, but do not feel that you need to discourage a child from playing with a toy simply because he enjoys it and plays with it often. Teachers sometimes worry because a child likes to play with the same toy day after day for a period of several weeks. This is perfectly normal; young children typically go through periods or stages in which they become intensely interested in particular activities and enjoy repeating them over and over again. Thus, unless there is something about the child's play that gives you specific cause for concern (such as symbolic play that is cruel or sadistic or that indicates some kind of severe problem in the child's home life), do not assume that there is something wrong because the child continues to prefer a particular toy over an extended period of time. You might encourage him to try new things through modeling, demonstration, and suggestion, but do not go beyond this by attempting to force him to play with other things or to stop playing with his favorite toy. Eventually he will tire of the toy and move on to new things; in the meantime, unless there is something about his play that is disruptive to the rest of the class or that is apparently unhealthy to the child himself, let him play with the toy as often as he wants to.

Some children will need quite specific encouragement toward independent use of classroom equipment, especially those who wander aimlessly around the room or who take out equipment, look at it or fumble with it awhile, and then return it. These children probably need demonstration and some individualized instruction in the uses of equipment items, as well as some suggestions about what to do during times when they appear to be aimlessly wandering. If they come to you seeking suggestions or directions, provide them, but work to help them gradually learn to make choices and decisions on their own rather than to depend on you to tell them what to do.

With children who have trouble getting started with or completing projects, begin by giving specific instructions and setting specific goals. Ideally, you should sit down with the child and work with him, cooperating or giving instructions as a few activities are completed, and then leave the child with a suggestion or two for additional activities to be done on his own. Continue to provide such children with individualized suggestions and goals for as long as they need it, but try to phase out this activity gradually by encouraging them to use equipment items purposively and constructively on their own.

Ideally, then, all children involved in free play or self-chosen activities should be capable of independently deciding upon what they want to do and carrying through with doing it. This will leave the teacher free to conduct and organize an activity or lesson or to roam around the room giving individualized attention, according to the dictates of the program.

CUING AND REINFORCING APPROPRIATE BEHAVIOR

So far we have discussed preventing problems by providing a supportive environment and establishing and maintaining appropriate rules. However, rules will not handle all situations, so that teachers need to know how to give effective instructions on the spot when they are needed. Also, teachers must know how to specify clearly and to reward desirable behavior so that the children know what to do and are positively motivated to do it.

Stress Positive, Desirable Behavior

Learning is easier and more pleasant when we are told *what to do* than when we are told *what not to do*. This is why most planned learning experiences begin with a demonstration or explanation that the children watch and then imitate. Teachers would not try to teach addition by naming all of the numbers that $2 + 2$ does not equal, for example. In general, learning a skill or concept directly is easier than learning it by trial and error. Teachers usually are aware of this when dealing with cognitive learning, but they, as well as parents, often forget when it comes to misbehavior. Too often we tell children "don't," and emphasize what they are doing wrong rather than explain or demonstrate what they should be doing. This is inefficient from the teaching standpoint; in addition, it often creates problems of anxiety or resentment. Thus, try to give rules and instructions in positive terms, such as in the following examples:

Positive Language	*Negative Language*
Close the door quietly.	Don't slam the door.
Try to do this all by yourself.	Don't cheat by copying your neighbor.
Quiet down; you're getting too loud.	Don't make so much noise.

Sharpen your pencil like this (*demonstrate*).	That's not how you use the pencil sharpener.
Carry your chair like this (*demonstrate*).	Don't make so much noise with your chair.
Sit up straight.	Don't slouch in your chair.
Raise your hand if you think you know the answer.	Don't yell out the answer.
When you finish, put the scissors back in the box and put the pieces of paper on the floor into the wastebasket.	Don't leave a mess.
These crayons are for you to share—use one at a time and put it back when you finish so that others can use it too.	Stop fighting over those crayons.
Open your milk carton like this (*demonstrate*).	Don't spill your milk when you open it.
Go to the toilet and wash your hands.	Don't wet your pants.
When you put the blocks back on the shelf, sort them out and put them all in the places where they belong.	Look at how sloppy you have left those blocks—what's the matter with you?

Praise Desirable Behavior In addition to giving specific, positive instructions about what to do, praise the children when they do it. This may seem obvious or trite, but classroom observations usually show that positive behavior is seldom praised and that the praise that is given is often very general, lacking in credibility, or otherwise inappropriate.

Young children look up to and identify with adults that they like and respect, and they are very pleased when they receive praise from such adults. Thus, the teacher's praise functions as both a behavior-control mechanism and as a way to reward children and foster their self-esteem. Therefore, teachers should praise frequently, but appropriately.

It is important to praise frequently for several reasons. First, getting into the habit of doing so helps keep the teacher oriented toward positive rather than negative behavior. As much as possible, teachers should keep an eye peeled for examples of positive, praiseworthy behavior and should praise individual children or groups of children when they see such behavior. In addition to rewarding desirable behavior and making the children feel good, a positive attitude helps the teacher establish and maintain a role as a warm, loved, and sought-after adult. In contrast, a teacher who seldom praises and often criticizes will be seen by the children as a nag or a warden, and will induce fear or rejection rather than love and respect in them.

Another important reason for praising frequently is that some children need this kind of positive attention very badly, and they will act out in undesirable ways in order to get attention if they do not get praise for desirable behavior. Teachers who praise children often will have few problems with attention-getting behaviors. This will be especially true if the teacher praises appropriately, particularly by specifying the desirable behavior being praised and ignoring attention-getting mechanisms.

In addition to praising *frequently*, teachers need to praise *appropriately*. Some guidelines for praising appropriately follow.

1. Praise should be simple and direct.

It should be delivered in a natural voice, without gushing or overdramatizing. Even very young children will see such theatrics as phony.

2. Praise is usually more effective if given in straightforward, declarative sentences.

It is better to say "That's very good; I never thought of that before," than to gushingly exclaim "Wow!" or to ask rhetorical questions like "Isn't that *wonderful!*" The latter are condescending and are more likely to embarrass the child than to reward him.

3. The particular behavior or accomplishment being praised should be clearly specified.

Also, any noteworthy effort, care, or perseverance should be recognized: "Good! You figured it out all by yourself. I like the way you kept at it until you found out how to do it." Praise of this sort is probably much more effective than something like "Good, you did it right." Be especially alert to take note of and to praise any new skill or accomplishment that a child acquires, especially one that he has been struggling with for some time.

4. Use a wide variety of words and phrases when praising.

Do not lean on a single, stock phrase to the point that it becomes meaningless to the children and begins to sound insincere or to give the impression that you have not really paid much attention to them. Teachers sometimes do this by continually praising with exactly the same words and in exactly the same tone ("Very good, Jeff . . . Very good, Heather" . . . etc.).

5. Verbal praise should be backed with nonverbal communication of approval.

"That's good, Billy," is not very rewarding if it is said with a deadpan expression, a flat voice tone, and an air of apathy. The same phrase is much more effective if delivered with a smile, a tone communicating appreciation or warmth, or a gesture such as a pat on the back.

6. It is especially important to specify what you are praising when you use a phrase like "You were very good today."

Young children hear so much about being a good or bad boy or girl that the words "good" and "bad" are often linked in their minds with obedience and disobedience. Thus, unless you specifically state that you are telling a child that his work is good or that he has made a good block tower or some other good product, he may think that you are praising him for compliance or some other kind of "good" *behavior* rather than for some *accomplishment*.

In summary, children will be encouraged by teachers and motivated to work well and obey them if they know that the teachers see and appreciate their efforts and progress. Teachers can foster this attitude by making a concerted effort to praise children's efforts and progress, using natural, genuine language and describing the behavior being praised in specific terms.

GETTING AND HOLDING ATTENTION

So far we have discussed general teacher qualities and behaviors that can establish a good classroom atmosphere and make it likely that children will view teachers positively and spend most of their time in profitable activities. In this section we will suggest techniques for dealing with problems of minor inattention and disruption due to boredom, fatigue, distractions, and the like. Kounin's (1970) research suggests that the best way to handle this kind of inattention or distraction is to prevent it from happening, or, if it does happen, to check it before it spreads and becomes more serious. Several techniques for doing this are discussed below. The basic principle underlying them is for the teacher to behave in ways that make the child attend at *all* times, not merely at times when he is being asked to answer a question or make a response.

The techniques below are particularly appropriate for use during planned activities in which you are working with a *group* and in which *concentration on the activity* is vital to its pacing and general success. Where concentration and close attention are less important, or where you are working with individuals, other techniques may be more appropriate.

Focus Attention When Beginning Activities

Before you begin an activity, make it clear that you expect each child's full attention at all times, including times when other children are taking their turns or answering questions. First, be sure that you have the children's attention before you start. Do not try to launch into a lesson by shouting over the din and waiting for it to die down. Instead, give some kind of attention signal first, wait a few seconds for attention, and then begin (this is discussed in detail in Chapter 9).

Keep Lessons Moving at a Good Pace

Once you get attention and start an activity, don't lose it by spending too much time on minor points or by causing the majority of the children to wait while one responds individually at length, while equipment or supplies are passed out, while you leave to get something that you should have prepared earlier, and so on. If necessary, group the children for differential activities of a similar nature, each planned to match difficulty level to the children's experience and ability levels (for example, in a pattern-matching task, give different pattern cards to different children). In general, avoid "dead time" during activities, in which all or most of the children are passively sitting and waiting.

Monitor Attention during Activities

Throughout an activity you should regularly scan the group that you are teaching. The children are much more likely to keep their attention focused on the activity if they know that you are monitoring them regularly, both to see if they are paying attention and to observe any signs of confusion or difficulty. In contrast, if you bury your nose in a manual, rivet your eyes on the blackboard, or look too long at one particular child who happens to be answering or responding, you are asking for trouble.

Show Variety in Asking for Responses

You should continually reiterate that you expect all children to pay full attention during activities and to master any concept or skill that you teach. If your teaching pattern is completely repetitious and predictable, some children are likely to become inattentive during times when they know you are not going to call on them.

Thus, ask a variety of questions and make a variety of response demands; do not become overly predictable in your pattern of calling on children (for example, avoid always going from left to right down the group, without exception, every day); make comments about the activity of a child who is making an extended response in order to help stimulate the interest and attention of the group; occasionally ask a child to comment upon an answer or response just made by another child; ask questions before naming a child to give the answer instead of vice versa; insure that everyone participates in the activity whether or not he volunteers; and, in general, use variety and unpredictability in order to stimulate and maintain interest and attention.

Stimulate Attention

Sometimes you can stimulate attention directly or indirectly by cuing children. Changes in voice tone and deliberate emphasis of key words are ways to cue the children to the fact that something new is happening. Another way is to use transitional signals such as, "All right," "Now," and so on.

In addition to these more subtle, indirect methods, you can cue the children more directly with statements like, "Now here's a really hard one—let's see if you can get it," or "Let's see, who will I call on next?" When the topic or type of response demand changes, the children can be cued directly with a statement like, "All right, you know your colors. Now let's see if you can figure out what will happen when we mix some of the colors together."

Where attention problems are confined to one or two individuals, you can subtly cue their attention by directing such remarks to them: "Cheryl, I wonder if you know this one." "I'm going to try to fool you now with this next one. Do you think I can fool you, Joe? Well, let's see."

Model Appropriate Behavior

During times when the children are supposed to be paying attention to one of their peers who is making a response or to some stimulus presentation, model the appropriate behavior by paying alert, close attention yourself. If necessary, reinforce this by thinking aloud, making comments about what you think is going to happen or might happen, or describing or commenting on the child's response as he makes it. Such comments model for the children the kinds of observations and other mental operations that they should be making while watching one of their classmates perform.

Know When to Stop an Activity

The attention span of young children is limited, even for the most interesting activities. As a general rule, it is better to end an activity too early than too late. When activities go on past the point at which they should have been stopped, more and more of the children become bored and restless. Rather than fight for attention and force the children to attend when they no longer can, it is usually better to end the activity early and resume it at some more opportune time.

Also, watch out for unnecessary and repetitious subparts of longer activities. For example, unless you are working with a small group, it is probably unnecessary and may be harmful to ask every child in the group to repeat a word or perform some minor response that everyone already knows how to do. This puts the children in the position of having to wait their turns for a long time, and this kind of waiting breeds restlessness.

Recitation and show-and-tell activities are especially likely to become boring after a while. Thus, it is usually unwise to have each child participate in show and tell on one day. Instead, have a few children participate each day, and arrange for participation on a rotating basis so that everyone gets an equal opportunity.

DEALING WITH MINOR INATTENTION AND MISBEHAVIOR

As previously noted, the key to successful classroom management lies in establishing good relationships with the children and in preventing problems from occurring, using the techniques described above. However, there will be times when problems do occur, and the remainder of the chapter contains suggestions for dealing with such problems. The present section concerns minor problems of inattention and minor misbehavior. The techniques suggested all share a single general principle: Eliminate the problem as quickly and with as little distraction of other children as possible.

Monitor the Entire Classroom Regularly

Form the habit of standing or sitting so that you are in position to see the entire classroom, and regularly scan the classroom to keep abreast of what is going on. This will enable you to observe potentially disruptive problems in their early stages and to stop them before they become more serious. It will also cut down on the amount of misbehavior, since children are less likely to act out if they think that they will be seen than they are if they think they can "get away with" something.

Ignore Minor Misbehavior

In cases of brief inattention or minor misbehavior that is not disruptive, it is usually best to ignore the behavior rather than to call attention to it. This is especially important in the case of *attention-getting mechanisms,* behavior that some children use in a deliberate attempt to provoke a teacher to react. Calling attention to such behavior by some kind of direct intervention only reinforces the behavior and distracts the other children.

Thus, when misbehavior is brief and nondisruptive, it is usually best to simply ignore it. However, especially in the case of children who frequently use attention-getting mechanisms, be sure to provide positive attention or praise as soon as the child does something praiseworthy. If the problem is so disruptive that you must intervene, or if it appears to be about to spread to other children, try to eliminate it as quickly and nondisruptively as possible, using one or more of the techniques described in the following section.

Nondisruptive Intervention

When minor misbehavior is repeated or intensified, or when it appears likely to become disruptive or to spread to other children, you cannot simply ignore it. However, in dealing with it, your main goal is to stop it as quickly, effectively, and nondisruptively as possible. Ideally, you should do so without disrupting the pace of your activity. Useful methods include the following.

1. Use eye contact.

If you can establish eye contact with the child, this in itself often will be enough to stop the misbehavior, although you may want to add a nod of the head or some other gesture to help communicate your message. You will get more opportunities to use this method if you form the habit of monitoring the classroom regularly, since children who know that their teacher regularly scans the room are more likely to look up to see if the teacher is watching when they begin to misbehave.

When an inattentive child is close by, the teacher can regain his attention by casually touching him, thus avoiding more time-consuming and disruptive methods that distract the other children and break the pace of the lesson.

277

2. Use touch and gesture.

If you are working with a small group or are otherwise close to an inattentive or misbehaving child, you can simply use a touch or gesture to get his attention rather than wait until you can establish eye contact. Even when children are across a room, if you have eye contact you can often communicate effectively with them by pointing, touching your finger to your lips to indicate quiet, or using some other suggestive gesture.

3. Use physical closeness.

If you are moving around the room at the time, it is easy to cut off misbehavior by simply moving near and standing close to the misbehaving child or children. In this way you can insure that they are aware of you, and, at the same time, can get across your message without overtly saying anything to anyone.

4. Ask for task responses.

Rather than mention a child's misbehavior directly and call attention to it, where possible a better procedure is to distract him from it by redirecting his attention to the activity or to productive involvement in some task. If a group activity is in progress, simply calling on the child will serve the double purpose of stopping his misbehavior and returning his attention to the activity. If he is causing problems during a free-play period, you might approach him directly and suggest that he involve himself with a particular toy or equipment item. This avoids calling direct attention to the child's misbehavior, and, at the same time, gives him some direction about what to do.

5. Praise desirable behavior.

In addition to praising desirable behavior as part of your general teaching style, you can sometimes use praise as a behavior-control technique. If the opportunity arises, praise the neighbor of an offender for engaging in appropriate behavior. This avoids directly calling attention to the offender's misbehavior, and, at the same time, it gives him an idea of what he can do in order to earn your attention and praise. Thus, praise a child for persisting rather than criticize his neighbor who has given up; praise one who has finished his assignment rather than criticize his neighbor who has been wasting his time; and praise one who has carefully straightened his area rather than criticize his neighbor who has not.

If you use this technique, be sure to follow up by observing the offender to see if he responds by imitating the child who has just earned your praise. If he does, be sure to praise him also. This helps reinforce the idea that the children will get your attention and praise through positive rather than negative behavior, and it helps dispel any notion that you are playing favorites or that certain children are your "pets."

DEALING WITH PROLONGED OR DISRUPTIVE MISBEHAVIOR

So far we have discussed only techniques for preventing problems and for dealing with minor problems. Consistent use of these techniques will hold problems to a minimum, but there still will be some problems. We now suggest ways of dealing with behavior that is sufficiently serious or disruptive to require more direct and forceful intervention.

Stopping Misbehavior Through Direct Intervention

When misbehavior is dangerous or seriously disruptive, stop it quickly by calling out the name of the child involved and correcting him. Since such intervention is itself disruptive, use it only when it is needed.

There are two basic ways to intervene directly. First, you can demand an end to the misbehavior and follow this by indicating the appropriate behavior. Your message should be short, direct, and to the point. Name the child, identify the behavior that must stop, and tell him what to do instead. Speak firmly and loud enough to be heard, but do not shout and nag. When the child or children who are misbehaving obviously know what they are doing wrong, there is no need even to label the misbehavior. Instead, simply tell them what to do ("Mike, finish your work," "Karen and Don, look here").

A second technique is to remind the children of relevant rules where their misbehavior is in violation of a previously established rule. Do not sermonize; give your rule reminders briefly but firmly. Rule reminders are especially useful when several different children have been misbehaving or when you do not want to call attention to individuals. In this case you can simply phrase the rule reminder as a general statement applying to all ("Children, you are getting too loud; remember to speak softly").

Stopping misbehavior through direct intervention or through rule reminders should be done only in situations where the children are quite aware of what they are doing wrong and of what they should be doing instead, and where no information is needed from the children. These are situations where the nature of the misbehavior is quite obvious: laughing and talking instead of paying attention, knocking over or throwing blocks, and so forth. If the situation is more ambiguous and you are not sure about what is going on, instead of simply and directly intervening as suggested above, it might be better to investigate the incident before making judgments about how it should be handled. This is especially important in fights and arguments between children where you have not seen how the problem got started and are not sure who is in the right and who is in the wrong. Ambiguous situations like these will require some investigation.

However, in cases where it is quite obvious what the child is doing, confine yourself to rule reminders and instructions about what to do. *Do not ask questions.* Questions are not needed if the situation is clear and your goal is simply to return the misbehaving children to productive activities. Thus, there is no need for an investigation. Also, the kinds of questions that teachers ask in such situations are often meaningless rhetorical questions that have the effect of badgering or nagging the children rather than gathering information ("What's the matter with you?" "Why haven't you finished your work?" "How many times do I have to tell you to stop running around?").

In addition to avoiding unnecessary questions in these obvious kinds of misbehavior situations, *avoid threats and appeals to authority.* Simply tell the child how you want him to behave; this will not only give him some direction, but it will communicate the expectation that you expect to be obeyed. However, if you add a threat, you put yourself in conflict with the child and, at the same time, indirectly suggest to him that you are not sure that he is going to obey you. In particular, avoid threatening children in a way that puts them on the spot and makes them lose face. Such threats not only convey uncertainty about whether or not the child will obey you; they virtually dare him to defy you in order to save face.

In addition to inappropriate questioning and unnecessary threats, *avoid nagging* (overdwelling on the misbehavior itself). Do not describe the misbehavior in detail or recite all of the times that the child has misbehaved in this way during the last week, month, or year. This does no good and may well do harm if the child gets angry and decides to retaliate. Even if children don't get angry at such nagging, they may begin to see it as funny and may begin to misbehave in ways calculated deliberately to provoke it. Remember, when faced with misbehavior, your task is to eliminate it, not to describe it or nag the children about it. Frequent nagging in a classroom is a sign that the children are controlling the teacher, and not vice versa.

CONDUCTING INVESTIGATIONS

So far we have been discussing intervention in misbehavior situations that are clear-cut enough to allow the teacher to react without collecting additional information. However, sometimes it will be necessary to question children to find out what has happened in situations that are unclear. Knowing how to conduct an effective investigation will help you deal with the misbehavior efficiently and appropriately.

First, any questions that you ask should be genuine attempts to gather information, and not rhetorical questions of the type described previously. They should be direct and to the point, and should concern matters of *fact* that a child can answer. Do not ask questions about children's *intentions* unless you actually want and need this information ("Why did you leave the room?" "Why did you throw the paint in the garbage can?") Such questions about intentions may help establish why the student did what he did. However, do not berate the children with rhetorical questions like "Did you think you could get away with it?'' or confuse them with questions that they cannot really answer, like ''Why didn't you remember to be more careful?''

When dealing with a fight or a serious dispute, it is usually best to remove the children from the room, or at least get them away from the rest of the group, so that you can conduct an investigation in private. This will minimize face-saving maneuvers, and other problems that are likely to arise when you try to settle a dispute in front of the entire group. Question the children one at a time, insisting that any others be quiet, letting each say his piece, and reassuring all of them that everyone will get his chance. Hear each child out and ask questions to satisfy yourself about the actual sequence of events before making snap judgments or taking any follow-up action. Make it clear that you expect the children to tell the truth. Where discrepancies between stories appear, point them out and ask questions to get clarification, but be sure not to ask them in a way that prejudges the truthfulness of a particular child's version of the story. Unless you have *seen* (as opposed to *heard* through second-hand report) contradictory evidence, do not tell a child that you do not believe him or cannot accept what he says.

If it does become clear that one or more children is obviously lying, express sorrow, disappointment, and the expectation that this will not happen again. Where this is a repeated behavior pattern, you may have to threaten or use punishment (see below). However, be careful not to overreact here. Young children do not easily distinguish between lying and telling the truth. This is partly because they have a general orientation towards telling valued adults what they think the adults want to hear, and partly because their moral development (and cognitive development generally) has not yet proceeded to a point where they can distinguish lies from truths and exercise moral judgment in the same way that an adult can. Thus, although it is important for you to work continually at getting children to tell the truth when they do not do so habitually, do not expect immediate or spectacular results; this is simply unrealistic for a teacher working with preschool children.

If your investigation reveals a clear-cut explanation of what happened and why it happened, follow up by taking appropriate action. In most cases, this should be confined to rule reminders or to on-the-spot decisions about what should be done, based upon previously established rules or general guidelines for behavior in the classroom. Do not use punishment unless the offending child has done the same thing repeatedly and has been warned about it.

Often, your investigation will not lead to a clear-cut version of the incident, because one or more of the children involved is not telling the truth. In such cases, it is better to leave the disputed points unsettled than to side arbitrarily with one or more children against one or more of the others when you are not certain about the truth of the matter. Here, rather than to accuse someone arbitrarily (and perhaps incorrectly), it is better simply to express sorrow and disappointment that the incident occurred in the first place, and that one or more of the children is not telling the truth, in the second place. Then, explaining that there is nothing you can do about the situation since you do not know who is telling the truth, ask the children themselves to suggest solutions. If possible, choose one of these solutions, particularly if it is a solution that all involved parties accept.

Again, avoid punishment if possible, since it is unlikely to do any good. Do not be concerned about the fact that the child or children who lied may have "gotten away with" something. If you have done a good job of expressing your disappointment at their behavior, they probably will feel guilty or ashamed, and will be unlikely to repeat such behavior in the future. This is just one instance of the general principle that long-term goals take precedence over short-term objectives in the area of moral or ethical training. General factors such as modeling, demanding desirable behavior, and establishing good relationships with the children are far more important in determining your success in dealing with moral problems than the way you handle any single, isolated incident.

EFFECTIVE PUNISHMENT

Punishment should be avoided as much as possible, but in certain instances it is necessary and appropriate. To use it effectively, however, you must know when and how to punish. Ineffective use of punishment does more harm than good.

When to Punish

As a general rule, punishment is appropriate only for *repeated* misbehavior. It is a treatment of last resort, to be used only when children persist in the same kinds of misbehavior despite continued warnings. It is a way of exerting control over a child who is unwilling to control himself for the moment.

Punishment should be used only as the last resort, because it signifies that neither the teacher nor the child can cope with the problem. It is an expression of lack of confidence in the child, telling him that the teacher thinks that he is not trying to improve or that his misbehavior is deliberate. This can damage the child's self-concept as well as diminish the chances for permanently solving the problem. This is why punishment is not appropriate for isolated incidents, no matter how severe. In an isolated incident, there is no reason to believe that the child acted deliberately or, at least, that he will repeat the act in the future. Your expression of concern and instruction about how to behave in the future are appropriate here, but punishment is not.

Even in cases of repeated misbehavior, punishment should be avoided when the child seems to be trying to improve. Any approximations of desirable behavior should be rewarded, and the teacher should give children the benefit of the doubt by assuming their good will in trying to improve and by expressing her confidence in their ability to do so. In contrast, punishment tells the child that he has failed to respond and that the teacher has lost confidence in his will and/or ability to do so.

What Punishment Does

The effects of punishment are limited and specific. Make sure that you are clear about what punishment does and does not do, so that you can use it properly and avoid deluding yourself about its effectiveness. A great body of research evidence (reviewed in Bandura, 1969) shows that punishment is primarily useful only for controlling misbehavior, not for teaching desired behavior. Further, punishment affects the expression of behavior, but not the desire or need for that expression. *Punishment can reduce or control misbehavior, but by itself it will not teach the child desirable behavior or even reduce his desire to misbehave.* Thus, punishment is never a solution by itself; at best it is only part of the solution. However, it will temporarily stop misbehavior, and thus it is appropriate when misbehavior is repeated and serious enough to require its use.

Using Punishment for the Right Reasons

If you do punish, you should do so consciously and deliberately, as part of a planned treatment for repeated misbehavior. Punishment must not be used as a way to get even with a child or to "teach him a lesson." Punishment of this sort is really just an attack upon the child, and he will respond, like anyone else, with anger, resentment, and the desire to strike back. This will only make the problem worse.

It is easy to see when a teacher is using punishment to deal with frustrations or anger rather than as a deliberate control technique. Such teachers make statements like "We'll fix your wagon," or "We'll show you who's boss." These are not manifestations of effective punishment; they are emotional outbursts indicating poor self-control and emotional immaturity on the teacher's part.

Types of Punishment

Different kinds of punishment have different effects. Among the more common kinds, we recommend exclusion from the group and limitation of privileges; we do not recommend severe personal criticism or physical punishment. Severe personal criticism or personal attacks on the child are never appropriate. They have no corrective or control function and cannot be justified on the grounds that the child needs them. They will only depress and/or anger the child and the rest of the children, compounding the teacher's problems.

Physical punishment is sometimes useful, especially for very young children. However, we do not think that it should be used in school. First, it is difficult to administer objectively and unemotionally. By its very nature, it puts the teacher in the position of attacking the child, physically if not personally. This can cause injury, and in any case it will almost certainly impair the teacher's chances of establishing and maintaining a workable relationship with the child. Also, physical punishment is usually over quickly, and it has an air of finality about it. Because it is so intense, attention tends to be focused on the punishment rather than on the misbehavior that led to it. Thus, it usually serves no corrective function, tending instead to induce only anger and resentment. It usually fails to induce guilt or personal responsibility for behavior in the offender, who is much more likely to be sorry for having gotten caught than for having misbehaved.

Finally, physical punishment is only temporarily effective at best. Children who come from homes where their parents beat them regularly or otherwise rely heavily on physical punishment to discipline them tend to be the children who most often cause problems because of aggressiveness and hostility. Criminals convicted of violent crimes almost always show home backgrounds in which physical punishment was the primary socialization "technique." In general, it seems that physical punishment teaches people to attack others when angry; it does not teach them appropriate behavior.

How to Punish Effectively

The way punishment is presented to the child is more important than the type of punishment used. It should be made clear to the child that punishment is being used as a last resort because he has left the teacher no other choice. The child should know that his own behavior has brought the punishment on him, and that the teacher is not doing it to get even or to pick on him.

Tone and manner are very important here. Avoid dramatizing the situation ("All right, that's the last straw!" "Now you've done it!") or making statements that turn the situation into a power struggle ("I guess we'll just have to show you who's boss around here!"). Instead, the possibility of punishment should be raised in a soft, almost sorrowful voice. Your tone and manner should communicate a combination of deep concern, puzzlement, and regret over the child's continued misbehavior.

Whether or not you actually state it in words, your implied message should be: "You have continually misbehaved. I have tried to help by reminding you about how to behave and telling you why it is so important, but you still misbehave. I don't know why you do it, but I am worried about it and I still want to help. However, I cannot allow this misbehavior to continue. If it does, I will have to punish you. I don't want to do this, but I will if you leave me no other choice."

If warnings such as these are not sufficient, you will have to follow through with punishment. Ideally, the punishment should be closely related to the offense. For example, if a child misuses materials, it is most appropriate to restrict or suspend his use of them for awhile. If he continually gets into fights and arguments, he can be isolated from other children for awhile. Whatever the punishment, be sure to specify clearly the reasons for it and the actions that the child can take to restore his normal status. Make a distinction between your attitude toward his unacceptable behavior and your overall acceptance of him as a person. The child should know that he is being punished solely because of his misbehavior, and that he can regain his status by changing that misbehavior.

Withdrawal of privileges and exclusion from the group should be tied closely to some remedial behavior whenever possible. This means telling the child not only why he is being punished, but also how he can regain his privileges and rejoin the group. The explanation should stress that the punishment is only temporary, and that he can redeem himself by showing clearly specified desirable behavior: "When you can share with other children without fighting," "When you can pay attention," "When you can use the crayons without breaking them." This will focus the child's attention on positive behavior and give him an incentive for changing.

In contrast, avoid the prison-sentence approach: "You have to stay here for ten minutes," "No recess for three days." This fails to provide a positive focus and to place responsibility for change on the child, and it gives him plenty of opportunity to build up anger and resentment against you. Similarly, avoid the authoritarian, "I am the boss" approach: "Stay here until I come and get you," "No more crayons until I give you permission." This approach also fails to give the child responsibility for changing his own behavior, and it places you in the position of "bossing him around." *In summary, punishment will be most effective if it is closely related to the offense, if it follows closely after the offense, if it is presented in such a way that the child has no one but himself to blame for it, and if conditions are specified so that the child can remove it by improving his behavior. Also, the less frequently you rely on punishment or threat of punishment, the more effective it will be.*

Exclusion from the Group   Exclusion from the group (often called isolation) is an effective punishment technique if handled properly. However, teachers sometimes misuse it in a way that actually makes it function as a reward instead of a punishment. When this happens it is usually because the child has not been truly isolated from the group and has been placed in a position where he can get attention by acting out.

Ideally, the place used for isolation should be located so that a child sent there will be excluded from the group psychologically as well as physically. He should be out of sight of the rest of the children and out of contact with them. He should not be in a position to disrupt activities or distract the attention of the other children. Also, he should be instructed to think about his misbehavior and not be allowed to play with anything. Such isolation, combined with the techniques for explaining the punishment described above, will insure that exclusion actually will be experienced as punishment and will have the desired effects on the child's behavior. We hope this sounds distasteful to you, because it is! For punishment to be maximally effective, it should *be* distasteful; it should be something that neither you nor the child wants, which has become necessary because the child has left you no other alternative.

Teachers who learn to punish in this manner will not have to punish very often, because children will find the experience to be thoroughly distasteful and to be avoided in the future. Also, your own distaste will impress upon the child the seriousness of his misbehavior, and, assuming that you have worked to establish the kind of relationship described earlier, the child probably will be strongly motivated not to allow this to happen again.

In contrast, if you actually enjoy punishing children, or if your "punishments" are not really punishments, so that you don't find them distasteful, you probably will not punish effectively. In the first case, enjoyment of punishment suggests that you may be doing it for the wrong reasons (to get even with a child who irritates you, to vent your own frustrations, etc.). The child will correctly perceive that you are picking on him, and he will develop revenge motives and a desire to "get even" rather than guilt and a desire to repent. If you should find that this is a general problem, you should get help immediately. A teacher who actually enjoys punishment on a regular basis will do no good and is capable of doing great harm to young children.

If you do not enjoy punishment but don't exactly find it distasteful either, primarily because your "punishments" are not really punishments, you probably have a serious credibility problem. Perhaps you are continually making threats that you do not carry out, or perhaps you are dispensing "punishments" that the children don't mind or actually enjoy, so that they actually function as rewards for the children. In any case, this situation is inappropriate. As mentioned previously, punishment is something that should be done only as a last resort and only after careful deliberation. When handled properly, it produces a truly distasteful experience not only for the child but also for the teacher.

If it does become necessary to exclude a child from the group, the child himself should be allowed to indicate when he is ready to behave properly and return. If he does not say so spontaneously, go to him occasionally and ask if he thinks he is now ready to participate in the group and behave as expected. The child's word should be taken at face value here; he should not be subjected to nagging about earlier misbehavior or to a "grilling" in which he is required to make specific promises: "You'll stop knocking over blocks?" "You'll stop hitting Judy?" "You'll be quiet and listen when I ask you to pay attention?"

When the child requests readmittance, responds in a way that clearly tells him that he is accepted back into the group. Avoid vague phrases like "Well, we'll see." Give the child a brief statement to show him that you have heard and accepted his intention to behave appropriately, and then instruct him to join the group: "Well, Roger, I'm glad to hear that. I hate to have to exclude you or anyone. We're getting ready for a snack now—come and join us!"

Occasionally you may have to reject the word of a child who gives you a half-hearted or tongue-in-cheek pledge to reform. Do this with caution, however, since it is better to give the child the benefit of the doubt than to risk undermining his reform efforts if they should be genuine. However, if the child has a history of failing to live up to his promises to reform, you may have to extend his punishment. In this case, be sure to make the reasons clear to him, so that he sees that you are acting on the basis of his behavior: "I'm sorry, but I can't accept that. Several times recently you have promised to behave and then have broken your promise as soon as you came back to the group. I don't think you realize how serious this is. Go back to your chair and stay there until I get a chance to come and talk to you about this some more."

Punishment as a Last Resort

We cannot stress too strongly that punishment is a measure of last resort to be used only when absolutely necessary. It is appropriate only when a child persists in disruptive misbehavior despite the teacher's continued attempts to encourage desired behavior and to explain the reasons for it. It is a temporary measure to curb misbehavior in students who know what to do but refuse to do it. It should not be used when the child's misbehavior is not disruptive or when the problem exists because the child doesn't know what to do or how to do it. In these situations the child should be given instruction, not punishment.

There are several reasons for minimizing the use of punishment. First, it places undue attention and emphasis on undesirable instead of desirable behavior. Second, it reduces work involvement and raises the level of tension among all of the children in the room (Kounin, 1970). Thus, the use of punishment in response to one problem may generate several other problems. Third, punishment interferes with the establishment of a close, personal relationship with the child, and in the long run the quality of the teacher–child relationship is more important than the outcome of any single, isolated incident. Thus, a teacher who unnecessarily and unwisely uses punishment to "teach that child a lesson" may win the battle but lose the war.

In summary, punishment is a last-resort measure that should be avoided whenever possible and used minimally and with great discretion when it becomes necessary. When so used, it probably will be an unpleasant experience for both the teacher and the child, so that it is unlikely to have to be used again in the near future. Finally, bear in mind that the key to successful management lies not in effective punishment, but in effectively motivating the children and planning and carrying out appropriate activities so that the need for punishment seldom arises. You won't have to cope with problems that never arise because you prevented them ahead of time.

COPING WITH SERIOUS ADJUSTMENT PROBLEMS Some children have serious and continuing emotional or personality disturbances that will require special, individualized treatment. Although different kinds of problems require different treatments, several general considerations apply.

1. Do not isolate a child or label him as a unique case.

Expectations and labels can act as self-fulfilling prophesies, so avoid labeling a disturbed child as someone special or different from the rest of the class. Discussions with such a child about his behavior should be as private as possible, and should not be conducted in front of the rest of the class. Also, do not label the child in negative ways to the other children, or they will begin to expect undesirable behavior from him and to treat him in ways that tend to produce it.

2. Stress desired behavior.

This is especially important for children with persisting problems. Such problems are harder to eliminate once they have become labeled as characteristic of the child, because the label places undue attention on his particular form of misbehavior and tells him that the teacher and his classmates expect him to misbehave in particular ways. Be especially careful to avoid nagging or other overdwelling on the misbehavior of such children, and concentrate particularly on stressing your hope for their improvement and progress toward desirable behavior. Phrase your expectations in positive language, so that the child will have a goal to strive for and a gauge to use in measuring his progress. Observe and take note of his successes in approximating desired behavior, so that the child will be aware of his movement even though he is still relatively behind his classmates. Be patient and ready to provide encouragement when the child shows regression or loss of control. Even though these will be irritating times for you, they will be even more frustrating and discouraging for the child if he has been making a genuine effort to improve. Encouragement at times like these can be vital in giving the child the determination to persist in striving to improve. In contrast, if you take a negative approach featuring threat and punishment, the child is unlikely to improve, and it is very likely that a discouraging cycle of misbehavior and punishment will become established and persist throughout the year.

3. Focus on the child's school-related behavior.

Sometimes children have serious problems caused by home difficulties that you cannot control. Depending upon your relationship with the child's parents, you may or may not be able to improve the home situation. However, no matter what the child's home situation, you can always work with him on a personal, one-to-one basis concerning his *school* behavior. Unless the child is so disturbed as to be in need of professional treatment, he should be able to achieve a reasonably good adjustment at school, no matter how serious his home problems may be. It may be necessary to make special arrangements for some children (allowing them to sleep if part of the problem is that they don't get enough sleep at night; allowing them to spend time alone cooling off and working things through if their parents have just had a terrible argument, etc.), but in general they should be expected to act the same way as other children. In other words, at school they should be treated as are the other children, not as special cases to be coddled or pitied because they come from poor home backgrounds. Often such children need to be treated as *normal* children more than anything else, and attempts to give them special help that are condescending or based upon pity may only depress the child and further compound his problems. Thus, although it is important for teachers to be aware of home situations that are causing problems for children, and sometimes even to attempt to deal with these home problems directly, it is most important that they provide such children the experience of being treated as normal, accepted, "first-class citizens" in their roles as members of the school group.

4. Build a close relationship with the child, and use it to learn his point of view.

The child's failure to respond to a reasonable and patient teacher's behavior signals that some special problem is operating that requires special treatment. Even a young child may have enough insight to be able to reveal some of the reasons for his emotional disturbance, but he is unlikely to do so unless he likes, trusts, and respects the teacher. Teachers can establish such relationships primarily by being the kinds of persons that we have described previously. However, in the case of particularly disturbed children, make it a point to spend time with them individually discussing whatever the child seems to want to talk about. You may have to be relatively indirect at first in trying to find out the roots of his problems; direct probing might confuse or annoy the child. However, if you do succeed in establishing a close relationship in which the child looks forward to spending time talking with you, it is likely that he will begin to reveal the nature of his problems of his own accord without much probing from you. Thus, build a relationship by showing interest in the child and concern about him, and by being a person that he enjoys spending time with. In time, such contacts may produce information useful for diagnosing or providing individualized treatment. If the child is clearly incorrect in his assumptions, try to show him this by giving him insight in language he can understand. For example, if he feels that you dislike him because you do not allow him to continually tag along after you in the classroom, try to make him see that your behavior is necessitated by your need to care for all of the other children in the room in addition to him, and that it is not a rejection of him.

In addition to these general procedures that should be used in dealing with any child who has a recurring problem, there are certain special techniques that are especially useful for particular problems. These will be discussed below.

Defiance

Occasionally a child will defy you by vehemently talking back, swearing at you, or refusing to do as he is told. When faced with such defiant children, your first consideration should be to remain calm and avoid being drawn into a power struggle. Most adults tend to get angry in these situations and to strike back with a show of force. This may succeed in suppressing the defiance in the short run, but in the long run it may involve harmful effects, especially if teachers lose their temper or if children are publicly humiliated.

If you do succeed in remaining calm and suppressing your tendency to react with immediate anger, you will be in a good position to deal with the defiant child. Defiant acts make everyone in the room fearful and uneasy, especially the child who is acting out. The other children know that the act is serious and may bring serious consequences, and they will be on edge waiting to see what is going to happen. You can gain two advantages by pausing a moment before responding here: (1) You will gain time to control your temper and think about what to do before acting; (2) the mood of the defiant child is likely to change from one of aggression and anger to one of fear and contrition during this time. When you do act, act decisively, although in a calm and quiet manner. If possible, remove the defiant child from the class for an individual conference. If this is not possible, or if the child remains defiant and unwilling to leave, tell him that the matter will be discussed later. Do this with a tone and manner that communicates serious concern but without implying any threats or promises. This will indicate to both the defiant child and his classmates that some action will be taken, but it will leave your options open regarding what kind of action this will be. An appropriate response here would be: "I can see that something is the matter, and we'd better talk about it. Please wait for me by the door—I'll be with you in a minute." An alternative would be: "Please sit down and think it over during the rest of the period—I'll discuss it with you later."

It is vital that defiance be handled in a private conference. First, the fact that it occurred at all signals that something is seriously wrong with the child and possibly also with the teacher–child relationship. This calls for private discussion and resolution. Second, if the problem is discussed in front of the class, where the teacher's authority has been threatened by an angry outburst, both the teacher and the child will find it difficult to avoid face-saving gestures that only make the problem worse.

Acts of defiance usually are the culmination of a build-up of anger and frustration in the child. Difficulties at home or in relationships with peers may be part of the problem. However, the teacher is almost always part of the problem too. Students are unlikely to defy their teachers unless they are resentful or feel that they are being picked on. Thus, in discussing defiance with a child, be prepared to hear him out. He will likely accuse you of treating him unfairly, and you must be prepared to entertain the possibility that he is right. If you have made mistakes, admit them and promise to change your behavior in the future.

Encourage the child to say everything he has on his mind (to the extent that he can verbalize his feelings) before attempting to respond to one or more of the points he raises. This will help you get the full picture as the child sees it, and will allow you some time to think about what you are hearing. If you attempt to respond to separate points as the child mentions them, the discussion might turn into a series of accusations and rebuttals that will leave him feeling that he has been "answered," but that he still was right in accusing you of general unfairness. Regardless of the specific points raised, be sure to express your concern for the child and your desire to treat him fairly. This general reassurance will be more important than your particular responses to his accusations.

It may be necessary to review the teacher's role with some defiant children. The child should understand that you are primarily responsible for caring for him at school and are not interested in ordering him around or playing policeman. Show him that your exertion of authority is done for good reasons having to do with the needs of group living and the general good of the class. Even serious cases of defiance usually can be handled with one or two sessions like these, if you are honest in dealing with the child and if you follow up the discussion with appropriate behavior. Although unpleasant, such incidents present you with a blessing in disguise. They bring out into the open problems that have been smoldering under the surface for a long time. Also, the defiant act itself usually will have a cathartic effect on the child, releasing much of the tension that has been built up and leaving him in a more receptive mood for developing a constructive relationship with you. You can take best advantage of such a situation if you remain calm, show concern for the child, be willing to listen to him, and follow up with appropriate behavior.

Aggression

Undesirable behavior should be ignored where possible, but this is usually not possible with aggressive children because they may hurt others or damage classroom equipment. This, of course, cannot be ignored or allowed. When such behavior appears, demand an immediate halt to it. If the child does not comply, do not hesitate to restrain him physically. If he responds by straining to get away, making threats, or staging a temper tantrum, simply hold onto him until he regains self-control.

While restraining the child, speak to him firmly but quietly, telling him to calm down and get control of himself. Reassure the child that whatever he is upset about will be discussed and dealt with, but not until he calms down. If he insists that you let go of him, tell him firmly that you will do so as soon as he stops yelling and squirming. Reinforce this verbal assurance nonverbally by gradually relaxing your grip as the child tones down his resistance. When you are ready to release him completely, do so quietly and informally. If you do it in a more formal fashion ("Are you ready to be quiet now?"), the child will likely feel the need to make face-saving gestures as soon as you let him go.

Restraint may also be needed if children are fighting and do not respond to demands that they stop. Restrain one of them, preferably the more belligerent, by pulling him back and away from his opponent so that he is not hit while being held. This will effectively stop the fight, although it may be necessary to order the other child to stay away. At this point it is helpful to do a lot of talking generally aimed at getting the children to calm down and explaining that the matter will be dealt with as soon as they comply. It is vital to take charge, since the children are likely to continue to exchange threats or other face-saving actions. Humor is helpful here, since threats and face-saving actions are only effective if taken seriously. Thus, a smile or a little remark to show that you consider them more funny or ridiculous than serious ("All right, let's stop blowing off steam") is likely to put a stop to them quickly.

Once an aggressive child is calmed down, remove him from the class and talk to him individually. If two children were fighting, talk to both together. As usual, begin by hearing the child out. It is important to help aggressive children see the distinction between feelings and behaviors. *Feelings* should be accepted as legitimate or at least as understandable, but aggressive *behavior* must be forbidden.

If angry feelings are not justified by the facts, explain the situation in a way that does not deny the reality of the child's feelings but, at the same time, does not legitimize them: "I know that you want to be first, but remember that others do, too. They have just as much right to be first as you have. So there is no point in getting angry at somebody just because he went first. You'll just have to learn to get used to waiting your turn. If you try to be first all of the time, other children will think that you are selfish and won't want to play with you."

If the feelings are legitimate, they should be accepted expressly, but the misbehavior that went with them should not be. State clearly to the child that he will not be allowed to hit others, destroy property, or otherwise act out angry feelings in destructive ways, and that he will be expected to control himself and confine his responses to acceptable behavior.

Habitually aggressive children will require some resocialization to teach them new ways of dealing with their frustrations and anger. They must learn that frustrations and anger do not justify aggressive behavior. Tell them that they must learn to express their feelings verbally rather than by acting out physically, and *give specific instructions about how this should be done.* For example, the child who "hits first and asks questions later" needs instruction on handling frustrations and conflicts. Urge him to inhibit his tendency to strike out and teach him how to resolve conflicts through discussion and more appropriate actions. Teach him to ask classmates what they were doing or why they were doing it, instead of simply assuming that they were deliberately attacking him. Instruct him to express his feelings verbally to whoever has caused him to become angry, since the "offender" may have acted unwittingly and may not even realize that he has made the other child angry. The "Magic Circle" technique (Bessell & Palomares, 1967) and other methods designed to teach the Golden Rule and to help children learn to put themselves in the place of someone else are especially valuable with aggressive children.

Where a squabble has resulted over a situation covered by a classroom rule, remind the children about the rule and their obligation to follow it. Where no rules exist, some kind of decision or perhaps a rule for use in the future might be required. In conflicts over who goes first or who gets to use what equipment, for example, some procedure to insure that everyone has an equal turn would be appropriate. For single events, a random method such as a coin toss might be appropriate. Where the situation is more complex, give-and-take reasoning and bargaining might be introduced. Thus, if one child gets to go first at a given game, some other child would go first at the next game, and so on. Often the children can settle disputes of this sort by making up fair and equitable rules on their own if encouraged to do so.

Where aggression results primarily from a child's failure to deal properly with a specific situation (inability to share, inability to wait his turn, overreaction to teasing or accidental physical contact by another child, etc.), help him work on the problem by making specific suggestions and providing encouragement. Express sympathy with his frustration, but at the same time insist upon prosocial behavior. Again, stress the Golden Rule here. Help the child see and understand how he would respond if he were treated the way he treats others.

In more serious cases where the child has a self-image of being a "tough guy," professional treatment may be required. Often such children come from brutal or sadistic home environments, so that a true solution to the problem will require family intervention rather than treatment of the child alone. However, even with these very serious problems, there are many things that teachers can do. First, as with any aggressive child, try to help the child see how his behavior is self-defeating because it leads to punishment and to rejection by his classmates. Also, be especially careful to avoid labeling such a child or reinforcing any undesirable labels that he may apply to himself. Do not refer to the child as a bully or announce that he must be separated from other children because he "can't keep his hands to himself." Such actions imply that the child is different, that there is something permanently wrong with him, or that he cannot control himself. Instead, take action and make statements that will help build the child's confidence in his ability to learn to behave acceptably.

Whenever possible, arrange for the aggressive child to play positive roles in his interactions with classmates. It might be especially helpful for him to be used as a tutor or to be allowed to teach classmates skills that he has learned. In role-play situations, assign him parts that feature kindness, friendship, and helpfulness towards others; he would be ideal for the part of an ogre that everyone fears and dislikes until they find out that he is really good underneath.

Acknowledge and praise cooperative and helpful behavior by aggressive children whenever you see it. Also, head off any potential conflicts as early as possible. Turn potential fights into cooperative situations by making specific suggestions about how the children can handle them. Then praise the children for doing so if they follow your suggestions successfully.

Some children show a complex of behaviors involving restlessness, difficulty in maintaining concentration on a single activity, and, sometimes, aggression or destructive behavior. Such children are sometimes described as *hyperactive* or *hyperkinetic,* with the implication that their behavior is the result of a malfunctioning nervous system and/or a hormonal imbalance. We have chosen not to use these terms because they carry what we believe to be unnecessary and unfortunate connotations. Although it is certainly possible that many children showing such behavior do have malfunctioning nervous systems and/or hormonal imbalances, the relationships between these neurophysiological conditions and classroom behavior are poorly understood at best.

In any case, it is clear that bodily conditions of this sort can only be contributing or predisposing causes, not complete explanations for such behavior, especially not for aggressive or destructive behaviors. Whether or not a particular child has a malfunctioning nervous system and/or a hormonal imbalance, it remains necessary for the teacher to work with the child to help him learn to expand his attention span, increase his concentration, and decrease his undesirable behaviors. The techniques that teachers should use will be the same regardless of whether or not the child has some physiological problem contributing to his behavioral problem. Either way, the child will require the kinds of special attention and techniques described above.

Of late, many children labeled hyperactive or hyperkinetic have been treated with drugs. Early reports on this practice were so favorable that it became something of a fad for a time, but more recent studies have concluded that the evidence does not justify widespread and indiscriminate use of drugs for treating behavioral problems in children. Even when improvements in behavior are noted after the beginning of drug treatment, the data usually are ambiguous and do not conclusively show that the drugs are actively changing the child (administration of the drugs may change the expectations of the child, his parents, and the teacher, and these changes in turn may produce child-behavior changes, independent of any effects of the drug). Further, even if drugs are effective, no one knows yet why they have the effects that they do, and there remains the danger of undesirable, and in some cases unknown, side effects.

Thus, teachers should beware of the temptation to overreact to labels such as hyperactive or hyperkinetic by assuming that all of the child's problems are physical and that drugs or some other physical treatment is required to change them. This is a convenient and appealing concept, because it seems to "explain" the problem and provide a "solution." However, children with interpersonal behavioral problems need *behavioral* interventions instead of, or in addition to, treatment with drugs. This is a classical example of an undesirable self-fulfilling prophecy, in which the child is labeled and then treated in such a way (because of his label) that he is unlikely to improve and very likely to worsen in his undesirable behavior.

We have given several suggestions about how teachers can deal with aggressive children. Before leaving the topic, we wish to discuss one frequently advocated technique that we specifically do *not* recommend. This is the practice of providing substitute methods of expressing aggression, such as telling a child to punch a pillow instead of another child, or telling him to act out aggression against a doll while pretending that the doll is the teacher or another child. Such practices are often recommended by psychoanalytically oriented writers who believe that angry feelings must be acted out in behavior. Such writers believe that anger will deepen unless it is acted out, so they advocate such practices in order to allow harmless acting out of angry feelings (which presumably has a cathartic effect on the child by reducing or eliminating his anger). This suggestion has wide appeal because of its face validity, particularly the notion that acting out feelings leads to a cathartic effect. Most of us do experience catharsis if we "get if off our chests" or "have it out." Expressing angry feelings verbally is probably a good thing, provided that it is done in such a way that we do not provoke anger in the listener. However, this does not mean that angry impulses need to be acted out behaviorally.

Encouraging a child to act out his anger against a substitute object will only increase or prolong the problem, rather than reduce it. Instead of helping the child to learn to respond more maturely to frustrations and to learn more acceptable ways of acting when frustrated, this method: (1) reinforces the idea that his emotional overreactions are expected, approved, and "normal"; (2) reinforces the expectation that whenever he gets angry he will need to act out his anger behaviorally; (3) provides an inappropriate model for the other children, making it likely that the problem will spread to them, too.

The problem here is that the connection, "I need to act out angry feelings—I can release them through catharsis," is merely the end point of a chain of reactions. The connections "frustration—angry feelings" and "angry feelings—act out" precede the cathartic end point. Thus, every time the end point of the chain is repeated and reinforced, the entire chain leading up to it is repeated and reinforced. As a result, the child is reinforced not only for expressing anger harmlessly, but also for building up extreme anger in the first place and for believing that the presence of such anger requires or justifies acting out in behavior.

Thus, teachers are not doing children a favor by encouraging them to act out hostilities against substitute objects. They are merely prolonging and reinforcing immature emotional responses. If this persists, the treatment will produce an adult who is prone to having temper tantrums at the slightest frustration, and who spends much of his time building up and then having to release hostile feelings. This sort of person is neither very happy nor very likeable; he is emotionally immature. Thus, instead of telling children to act out inappropriate emotions, help them to distinguish clearly between emotions and behaviors, and also between appropriate emotions and inappropriate emotions. Inappropriate emotions (unjustified anger or other overreactions) should be labeled as such, and the reasons why they are inappropriate should be explained. Behavior that is simply unacceptable must not be tolerated, no matter how strong the child's emotions or how strong his impulse to act out. Acceptable and more effective alternatives should be explained and insisted upon. You should consistently and continually communicate the expectation that the child can and will achieve mature self-control. Avoid suggesting that he is helpless in the face of uncontrollable emotions or impulses.

The Show-off

Some children continually seek attention from teachers or classmates by trying to impress or entertain them. This can be enjoyable at times, but often such children are exasperating or disruptive. Your basic method of dealing with them should be to give them the attention and approval that they seek, but to confine it as much as possible to their appropriate behavior. Their inappropriate behavior should be ignored. When it is too disruptive to be ignored, avoid doing or saying anything that will call attention to misbehavior or make the student feel rejected. Thus, say something like "Pay attention now," rather than "Stop acting silly."

If a show-off seeks individual attention at an awkward time, delay him rather than refuse him. Tell him that you will take up the matter with him later, at a specific time. When praising such a child, praise only appropriate behavior and be sure to specify what is being praised. This will motivate him to repeat these behaviors in order to gain further approval from you, and will help to subtly reinforce the idea that he can get your approval through appropriate behavior and does not need to clown or go to elaborate lengths to get your attention. In general, show-offs need constant reassurance that they are liked and respected, and you should try to fill this need. However, your specific praise and rewards should be reserved for appropriate behavior. Inappropriate behavior should go unrewarded and, as much as possible, unacknowledged.

Unresponsiveness

Some children are emotionally withdrawn in the classroom, remaining unresponsive to the teacher, to the other children, and to the equipment and activities of the program. Usually the reasons for this kind of behavior are fear and uncertainty, and most initial unresponsiveness disappears quickly as the child becomes accustomed to the school setting. However, a few children will show persistent unresponsiveness and will require individualized treatment.

Start by taking steps to make the child feel comfortable with you. Arrange your schedule to spend time individually with him, participating in games or activities that he enjoys. Try to engage him in as much conversation as possible during these contacts, to help him get used to talking with you. However, do not directly raise the problem of his general unresponsiveness. This will only make the child self-conscious and probably will undermine your efforts to put him at ease. In fact, you probably will be most successful if the child is completely unaware that you consider him a problem and are going out of your way to provide individualized treatment.

Patience is especially important with unresponsive or inhibited children; attempts to push them too far too fast are likely to backfire and cause regressions. Thus, observe the child carefully so that you can continually judge the amount of stimulation and encouragement that he can tolerate without becoming embarrassed or inhibited. Continue to impel responsiveness as long as the child is comfortable, but be ready to close the discussion and shift to a safer topic or activity if the child starts to get nervous.

If the child fails to respond to questions or responds in a mumble or whisper, teach him to speak up. Make it clear that you expect your questions to be answered, even if the answer is "I don't know." Explain this directly if necessary. Also, ask questions directly. Do not preface them with stems like "Do you think you could . . ." or "Do you want to . . ." since these phrases suggest uncertainty about whether or not the child is going to answer. Also, ask questions in an informal, conversational tone. If asked too formally, a question may sound too much like a test item and may stir up undesirable anxiety.

Look at the child expectantly after asking your question. If he answers, respond with praise or relevant feedback. If he answers too softly, praise him and then ask him to say it louder. If he appears to be about to answer but hesitates, nod your head, form the initial sound with your lips, or encourage him directly to respond ("Say it!"). If the child does not respond at all, give him the answer and then repeat the question or ask him to repeat the answer. If he mumbles or partially repeats, ask him to repeat it again and then praise him. Repeat such procedures until the child gets the idea that he is expected to answer your questions and that you will not allow him to remain silent or to mumble or whisper.

Do not allow a child to practice resistance or nonresponsiveness. If the above techniques calling for verbal responses do not succeed, make the child respond in some nonverbal way, such as by nodding his head, pointing, or performing some physical action. If he does not do so himself, guide him by taking his hand in your own and going through the physical motions with him. As he becomes accustomed to responding in these situations, build back up to verbal responses. For more details on dealing with the unresponsive child, see Blank (1973).

If unresponsiveness or inhibition of this type is a widespread problem in your class, it is likely that you are causing or contributing to it. You may be doing things like overvaluing correct answers, showing impatience or disgust when a child does not respond correctly, or being unnecessarily critical towards the children. If you cannot identify the problem yourself, ask your supervisor or some other adult to observe you and attempt to discover what you might be doing to inhibit or frighten away the children.

ANALYZING AND DIAGNOSING

There are many kinds of emotional or personality problems that you may be confronted with in addition to the more common types already discussed. Prescriptive advice cannot be given here because of the great variety of such problems and the need to take into account the individual factors in each case, but certain general guidelines for how to proceed in dealing with them can be given. The following sections outline a general process that should succeed in helping you make decisions about how to handle such special problems.

Should You Do Anything at All?

First, ask yourself whether you really should do anything about the problem. Perhaps the "problem" involves some minor habit that particularly irritates you but which would not be perceived as a problem by almost everyone else. Or, the problem might be in the family rather than in the child, and your relationship with the family and the nature of the problem might be such that it is unlikely that an attempt to do something about the problem would succeed. Thus, before attempting to solve a problem, make sure that it is important enough to merit special attention and that you can reasonably expect to be able to solve it on your own.

Find out What Behavioral Symptoms Mean

Question the child and conduct systematic observations of him in order to gain a better understanding of what his symptomatic behavior means. Why does he act the way he does? Bear in mind that the child's behavior may be just a symptom of a more important underlying problem, and that *the behavior itself is often not as important as the reasons for it.*

If the behavior appears to be simply a habit and is not part of a larger complex of problems, it can be handled straightforwardly. Insist that the child drop the irritating habit and learn more appropriate behavior instead. In addition to making explicit demands for improvement, provide an appropriate supporting rationale (appealing to classroom rules, to social convention, or to the Golden Rule). Where a habit is not fundamentally immoral but is merely a violation of classroom rules or your own personal preferences, be sure to make this distinction clear to the child. Do not make him feel guilty or feel that his habit is a sign that there is something wrong with him. Tell him straightforwardly that his behavior is not particularly wrong in itself but that you are asking him to change because it interferes with your teaching or because it irritates you.

If the problem seems to be more serious or complex than a simple habit, and if the child has not been able to explain it to you adequately, careful observation will be needed. Begin by trying to diagnose the behavior more precisely. Is it a ritual behavior that is repeated pretty much the same way over and over (masturbation, spitting, nose picking), or is it a more general tendency (aggression, suspiciousness, sadistic sense of humor) that is manifested in a variety of ways? Can you observe a recognizable pattern or learn to describe the behavior more specifically? For example, if a child is suspicious, do his suspicions center around the belief that others are talking about him behind his back, or does he think that he is being picked on or cheated? If he does think that he is being talked about, what does he think the other children are saying about him? If he laughs inappropriately, what makes him laugh? Answers to questions like these will provide clues about what the behavior means.

Also, try to observe the particular conditions under which the behavior occurs. It is unlikely that it occurs all of the time. Is it a chronic problem, or something that started suddenly in the recent past? Does it happen especially often during particular activities? Can you identify any common elements in the different situations in which you have observed this behavior? Identification of such common elements might lead to identification of the events that trigger off the behavior. Also, ask yourself what you were doing immediately before the child acted out. This might reveal that you tend to trigger off the behavior yourself by treating the child unfairly or at least treating him in a way that he thinks is unfair. By asking yourself such questions and making such observations, you can move towards a more accurate diagnosis of the problem and a more prescriptive treatment.

BRINGING IN PARENTS AND OTHER ADULTS

Think twice before involving parents or other adults in the problem. By doing so, you automatically escalate the seriousness of the problem in the minds of all concerned, singling out the child as a "problem." Thus, the benefits that you expect to derive from involving additional adults in the situation must be weighed against the possible damage that can result from such labeling.

There usually is little point in having a child tested. General intelligence or personality tests usually contribute little or nothing to the solution of a problem, and few good tests for use with young children are available in any case. Similarly, merely sending out the child to a principal or other school official for discipline is not likely to help either. If the child's behavior problem is in your classroom, you must deal with it there.

Referral for testing may be useful if you suspect a physical problem, a sensory deficit (poor vision or hearing), a motor problem, or one of the sensorimotor-coordination problems usually called *learning disabilities*. A special-education teacher or diagnostic clinic has tests designed to reveal such problems, and will be able to provide prescriptive advice (and perhaps special materials) for teaching the child.

If you are not achieving success in dealing with a child's behavioral or emotional problems, try to get help from a school psychologist or counselor, or consider referring the child to a psychological-treatment facility. Usually it is best if you work in cooperation with a counselor, ideally one who has observed you and the child in your classroom. Again, to the extent that a child's problems occur in the classroom, they will have to be handled there. However, if you have access to a counselor or other resource person who has had specialized training and who has been successful in the past helping with such problems, take advantage of this valuable resource. If such a resource person is not readily available, consider a referral to an outside counselor or clinic. Think carefully before doing so, however, because this will label the child as a special case, or problem child. Again, the potential dangers of this labeling must be weighed against the probability of getting genuine help when you make such referrals.

Contacting the parents about a child's behavior problem also can be risky. First, to the extent that a child has general emotional or behavioral problems, his parents are probably the greatest single reason for them. Merely informing the parents about the problem will do little good and may well do harm. If you give the parents the impression that you expect them to "do something," they probably will threaten or punish the child and let it go at that. Thus, if you do talk to the parents, avoid giving this kind of general impression. Instead, provide specific suggestions where possible.

Sometimes specific suggestions can be given, as when you enlist the parents' help in seeing that the child gets enough sleep or gets a sufficient breakfast in the morning. In the progress of making suggestions, you may need to tell parents about many of the things discussed in this book (particularly in the present chapter). Many parents rely too heavily on punishment, for example, and many fail to project confidence and positive expectations for their children.

In conferences with parents, make sure that you structure the meeting as a problem-solving session in which you and they will work together to help the child, and not as a gripe session, in which you complain to them about their child's behavior. Usually it is best to begin by summarizing your observations about the child and then asking the parents if they can add anything that might help you understand the child better or deal with him more effectively. Find out how much the parents know about the problem, how they explain it if they are aware of it, and what suggestions they may have for you. If a specific plan of action emerges, discuss it at length and come to a clear agreement with the parents. Also, discuss and agree upon what the parents should tell the child about the meeting.

If no specific action is agreed upon, be sure to bring the conference to some kind of closure. Thank the parents for talking with you and helping you achieve a better understanding of their child, and promise to keep in touch with them about his progress. Also, ask them to relay to you any information that might be helpful in the future. Again, be sure that you and the parents are in agreement about what the child is to be told about the conference.

Whether or not a specific plan is agreed upon, be sure to voice positive expectations about effecting change in the child and about your confidence in receiving full parental cooperation. The parents should leave with the feeling that you are deeply interested in their child and in what they have to say. They should see you as a friendly resource person who is trying to help and not as a threatening authority figure who has lectured them or rejected them because of their child's problem. Where the parents are not expected to do anything after the meeting other than inform the child about it, be sure that they are clear about this. The parents should not go away with the idea that you expect them to do something different with the child unless some particular change in their behavior has been discussed and agreed upon.

SUMMARY

The key to successful classroom management is prevention—teachers do not have to deal with misbehavior that does not occur. Many problems begin when children are crowded together, forced to wait, or idle because they have nothing to do or do not know what to do. Crowding can be minimized by planning classroom arrangement and equipment storage so that cross traffic is avoided and equipment items can be easily obtained by the children themselves. The problems that result when everyone needs to use the same item at once can be eliminated by stocking the item in several small containers rather than in a single large one. Waiting can be minimized by allowing the children to handle management tasks on their own, eliminating needless rituals and formalities, staggering the children so that different subgroups do different tasks at the same time, and establishing rules to handle special situations. Idleness and confusion can be minimized by insuring that the children know how to use the equipment available in the classroom and by teaching them to use it independently.

Teachers who enjoy working with children and who establish and maintain credibility and respect should have little difficulty in establishing classroom rules. It is helpful if rules are kept to a minimum, but the rules that are presented should be insisted upon. This must be done in a positive way, however, stressing desirable behavior and praising children who show it, rather than calling attention to undesirable behavior and making threats or punishments. Teachers should be sure to praise regularly and appropriately, and, in particular, to call attention to the specific behavior that is being praised.

Problems of inattention and distraction during group activities can be minimized if the teacher uses a standard signal or phrase to focus attention when beginning an activity, keeps the activity moving at a good pace, monitors attention carefully throughout the activity, shows variety in asking for responses, stimulates attention periodically through indirect changes in voice or gesture or through direct stimulating comments, models appropriate behavior such as listening carefully and watching what is supposed to be watched, and stops the activity before the children's attention spans have been exhausted.

Problems of minor inattention and misbehavior in the classroom should be dealt with in ways that will disrupt the class minimally and avoid calling attention to the misbehavior if possible. Such incidents can be prevented in large part if the teacher monitors the class regularly, ignores minor misbehavior that is quickly corrected by the children themselves, and generally avoids giving the children the impression that they can get attention through misbehavior. Where intervention is required because the misbehavior is repeated or grows in intensity, it should be done as nondisruptively as possible. The teacher may be able to handle the misbehavior without calling attention to it at all by using eye contact, touch or gesture, or physical closeness, or by calling on children for responses or praising desirable behavior in children seated nearby those who are misbehaving.

Where this is not possible and the behavior must be stopped through more direct intervention, the appropriate action to be taken will depend upon whether the situation is quite clear to the teacher or whether an investigation is needed before action is taken. Where the situation is clear, intervene directly by naming the child or children involved and giving a short instruction or rule reminder. Tell the misbehaving child what he should be doing; avoid nagging or dwelling on his misbehavior.

Where the situation is unclear but is serious enough to call for an investigation (i.e., it simply cannot be ignored), the investigation should be conducted in a private session that includes only the parties involved, away from the rest of the children. This will avoid the possibility of public humiliation and will minimize face-saving gestures. In conducting investigations, make it clear that you will hear out each party involved and that you are attempting to understand what happened in order to make decisions about how best to resolve the problem, not simply trying to find out who is to blame. Do not take any action until you are satisfied that you have all the facts. The action that you do take will depend upon the situation, but again, the main point is to stress desired and expected behavior and to minimize threats, punishments, or stress on undesirable behavior.

Punishment is sometimes necessary when a child repeatedly misbehaves despite continued warnings and explanations. It should be used only as a measure of last resort, since it escalates the seriousness of the problem and makes it more difficult to solve in the long run because it usually damages the teacher–child relationship. Further, it does not teach desirable behavior; it only stops the child from behaving in an undesirable fashion (and even here, it does not lessen his desire to behave this way; it only reduces the likelihood that this desire will be expressed in overt behavior).

The most effective methods of punishment are those that have some direct relationship to the child's misbehavior and that place responsibility for both the punishment itself and for self-improvement upon the child rather than the teacher. The child should understand that he has brought the punishment upon himself through his own misbehavior, but at the same time he should be told how he can redeem himself by showing improvement, so that the punishment will be lifted and he will return to normal status. Such punishments might include exclusion from an activity or from the group, removal of privileges regarding the use of particular equipment, or other restrictions on the child's privileges or freedom. Physical punishment and intense personal criticism should not be used, since they are unlikely to have positive effects and very likely to have negative ones.

Certain children with more serious and generalized personality disturbances may require some kind of specialized treatment beyond those discussed above. The specifics of such treatment will differ with the nature of the child's behavior problem and the reasons behind it. However, some general considerations include: avoiding isolating the child or labeling him as unique, stressing desired behavior and minimizing focus on undesirable behavior, stressing the child's school-related behavior rather than problems that exist outside the school, building a close personal relationship with the child and using it both to understand him better and to motivate him to want to please you, and observing and questioning the child carefully in order to analyze his misbehavior and diagnose the reasons behind it.

Think twice before involving the parents in a classroom-behavior problem, since such involvement might make the problem worse rather than better. If you do involve the parents, be sure to establish a problem-solving focus and avoid giving the parents the impression that you have called them in to blame them or to have them "do something about" their child. After explaining the problem, find out what information they can add and ask if they have any suggestions to offer. Throughout the discussion, treat them as partners who share with you an interest in the child's welfare, even where they appear to be primarily responsible for the problem. Ideally, the discussion should produce some agreement about steps to be taken by you and/or the parents. Whether or not it does, be sure to provide a definite closure to the discussion so that the parents go away with a clear understanding of what you expect them to do (or an understanding that you do not expect them to do anything in particular, where this is the case), as well as a clear understanding about what they will tell the child about the meeting.

Finally, bear in mind that patience is necessary in dealing with severe emotional or behavioral disorders. Most serious problems develop over a long period of time, and they are not going to disappear in just a few days, no matter how expertly you handle them. Thus, guard against the temptation to become angry, frustrated, or disgusted when children fail to show progress or regress to earlier forms of misbehavior. Instead, strive to communicate confidence in the child's goodwill in attempting to improve and faith in his ability to do so. Meanwhile, take every opportunity to reinforce any and all improvement attempts that you observe. Also, take advantage of any effective resource persons that are available to you and likely to be of help in situations that you are having trouble handling on your own.

QUESTIONS

1. Describe in your own words the essential attitudes a teacher must possess to be an effective classroom manager.

2. Cite specific examples to illustrate the ways in which you have observed teachers communicating their attitudes (either positive or negative) to children. Were teachers generally aware or unaware of these communications?

3. Explain how a teacher's day-to-day behavior serves as a model for children. In what specific ways can a teacher model respect for individual differences and cooperative play?

4. Devise a simple coding sheet to profile a teacher's managerial strengths and weaknesses. What variables would you include in your attempt to give teachers helpful, specific feedback (percent of time positive language is used when children are being corrected, how long transitions take, etc.)?

5. You have excluded Johnny from the group two times in the last hour. He acts up again in a moderately serious way. How would you handle the situation?

6. What factors must be considered in deciding whether to ignore misbehaviors or to intervene? Taking those into account, state a rule of thumb for this decision. Compare and discuss these rules of thumb with classmates.

7. You have a dependent, immature child who continually hangs on to you. How should you react (taking into account the child's emotional needs, your own emotional reactions, and your responsibilities to the rest of the children)?

8. Role play common management problems with classmates, taking turns playing the teacher and various kinds of "problem" children.

9. Usually you are bright and cheerful, but today you find yourself snapping at the children. What should you do? Discuss your ideas with classmates.

10. Try to become more conscious of the things you say *to* and *about* children, and the *way* you say them. Better yet, tape record yourself. Are you acting appropriately? If not, where do you need to improve?

11. Most probably you will like the majority of children you teach, but there will be a few that you dislike in spite of yourself. What should you do if you discover a personality clash of this sort? Discuss alternative ideas with classmates.

12. What should you do if an angry child "cusses you out" in front of all the children (using a combination of brash threats and "powerful" obscenities)? Discuss alternative ideas with classmates.

13. Suppose a child repeatedly leaves the room and hides, or tries to run home. What various reasons might explain such behavior in different children? How would you try to discover the child's motives and make decisions about handling the problem?

14. List, *in order,* the steps you would take in reacting to a child who loses control and defecates in his clothing before he can reach a toilet. Com-

pare and discuss your list with those of your classmates. Can you agree on the number and order of steps to take?

READINGS

Bandura, A. *Principles of behavior modification.* New York: Holt, Rinehart & Winston, 1969.

Blank, M. *Teaching learning in the preschool: a dialogue approach.* Columbus, Ohio: Merrill, 1973.

Dollar, B. *Humanizing classroom discipline: a behavioral approach.* New York: Harper & Row, 1972.

Good, T. and Brophy, J. *Looking in classrooms.* New York: Harper & Row, 1973.

Grinspoon, L. and Singer, S. "Amphetamines in the treatment of hyperkinetic children." *Harvard Educational Review, 43* (1973), 515–555.

Hamblin, R., Buckholdt, D., Ferritor, D., Kozloff, M., and Blackwell, L. *The humanization processes: a social, behavioral analysis of children's problems.* New York: Wiley-Interscience, 1971.

Kounin, J. *Discipline and group management in classrooms.* New York: Holt, Rinehart & Winston. 1970.

Krumboltz, J. and Krumboltz, H. *Changing children's behavior.* Englewood Cliffs, N.J.: Prentice-Hall, 1972.

13
PARENT PARTICIPATION

In earlier chapters we have pinpointed the critical role that parents play in enhancing or depressing the affective and cognitive growth of children. We have known for some time that parent behavior is correlated with children's intellectual development. For example, Van Alstyne (1929), after controlling for mothers' IQs, found positive correlations between their willingness to read to children and the children's vocabulary levels. Parents' involvement and interaction with their children is necessary for child development from early infancy on, and their involvement in and support for a preschool program is necessary if their children are to make significant progress.

We agree with Bronfenbrenner (1970) in stressing that good, effective parent models can be absent at all socioeconomic levels. However, the focus in this chapter will be on working with the *disadvantaged parent,* because a major emphasis of the book is on programs for the disadvantaged child. Disadvantaged parents often face special problems in serving as educational models for their children. Largely because their own parents did not provide them with appropriate models, they usually are not aware of the need for and the ways to provide their children with intellectual stimulation (reading, verbal interaction, etc.). Furthermore, their own history of school failure and/or frustration often has reduced their interest and self-confidence in approaching school officials. Thus, in addition to not knowing how to complement school activity, many are reluctant to seek information from school personnel.

However, the disadvantaged parents' concern for the progress of their children is just as strong as that of advantaged parents. The problem is not concern; it is simply that they have not had the appropriate education or exposure to know how to help their children optimally, and the demands of their working schedules often leave little time for them to interact with their children.

307

In this chapter we will quickly review the ways in which parents may facilitate the affective and cognitive growth of their children. We will see that disadvantaged families are less likely to provide an effective learning milieu than are advantaged parents, and then we will provide data to show that ineffective parent behaviors and attitudes can be changed. Furthermore, we will see that parent programs do pay off in terms of child language and IQ gains. Finally, we provide some practical tips for involving parents in the preschool program.

DESIRABLE PARENT BEHAVIORS

Most researchers and teachers involved in early education agree that more responsive parent–child relationships are needed. Many writers have divided desirable parent behaviors into sets of cognitive and affective behaviors. Gordon (1971b), for example, presents nine parental cognitive factors that laboratory and/or field research has shown to be correlated with the intellectual and behavioral development of children. The factors he cites are:

1. Amount of academic guidance provided for the child.
2. Parents' cognitive style in reacting to the environment.
3. Presence of planned cultural activities.
4. Amount of direct instructional time with the child.
5. Educational aspirations for the child.
6. Use of external resources (enrolling children in nursery school).
7. Intellectual climate in the home (availability of books).
8. Verbal facility of parents.
9. Frequency of verbal contact between parents and child.

He also identifies ten affective home factors that appear to be associated with positive development. These affective factors are:

1. Consistency of management.
2. Helping the child to differentiate and become aware of himself.
3. The nature of discipline.
4. The emotional security and self-esteem of parent.
5. Parents' impulsivity–reflectivity.
6. Parents' internality–externality.
7. Amount of babying protectiveness toward child.
8. Parents' trust of "establishment" institutions.
9. Parents' willingness to devote time to child.
10. Parents' work habits.

Hess (1969) has organized important parental influences in the following ways:

1. Maximization of verbal interaction.
2. Engagement with and attention to child.

3. Optimal, effective maternal teaching behavior.
4. Diffuse intellectual stimulation.
5. Feeling of high regard for the child himself.
6. Pressure for independence and self-reliance.
7. Clarity of disciplinary rules and use of conceptual rather than arbitrary regulations.

Various investigators have synthesized characteristics of effective parent behavior, and we have presented lists from two different sources to illustrate the point that desirable parental behaviors included on such lists are commonly agreed upon. Such information has been obtained largely from correlational rather than experimental research however, so some caution must be exercised when reacting to these conclusions.

Note that the parent behavior and home environments described above are similar to the findings that were reviewed in detail in Chapters 2 and 3. In general, the most important aspects of parent involvement are direct interaction with the child in educational (teaching) situations, and the ability to respond in expansive verbal ways to child behavior (induction techniques, etc., as described in Chapter 3).

SOCIAL CLASS DIFFERENCES IN PARENT BEHAVIOR

Some writers have argued that the desirable behaviors listed in the section above are more likely to occur in advantaged rather than disadvantaged homes. Independent of the cause, we do know that the relationship between social class and intellectual development is clearly observable by age 2. The Kagen et al. (1971) longitudinal study reported no social class differences in early infancy (4 months), but by age 2 children from more advantaged homes were superior in such skills and coping mechanisms as verbal competence, sustained attention, and reflectivity. These findings lead Kagan to suggest that if language comprehension, sustained attention, and a reflective attitude have value for school success, early education training is necessary because such skills apparently are established at an early age.

Previously we have discussed several features that distinguish the learning environments of affluent homes from those of disadvantaged homes. The information will not be repeated here, but we do want to highlight special teaching problems that many disadvantaged parents experience.

Again, most parents' inadequacies as educational models and teachers occur because of their lack of experience and opportunity for observational learning, rather than any lack of concern for their children's progress. Perhaps the chief failing of disadvantaged parent-teachers is their failure to place behavior in a context of meaning. Events take place with little verbal description or explanation, so that it is difficult for the child to structure and predict his world. Parents who regularly explain to a child where they are going to go and what will be expected of the child are doing much to help the child to prepare for the situation that he will be exposed to. Such anticipatory parent behavior is often called *proactive*. We will return to this term later.

Brophy (1970) provided evidence for the *meaningful context* hypothesis by coding the behavior of advantaged and disadvantaged mothers as they attempted to teach their own children to sort blocks. The greatest and most consistent difference in teaching behavior was the fact that advantaged mothers devoted much more time to pretask orientation and preresponse instructions than did disadvantaged parents. For example, the advantaged mothers were more likely to explain what the child was going to try to do and to suggest that it would be fun or worthwhile. Further, they were more likely to demonstrate the task to the child and to provide specific directions ("Pick up the block. See how some are tall and some are short? The one you're holding is a tall one. Find me another tall one," etc.) before allowing the child to start the task. In contrast, disadvantaged mothers were more likely to give a quick orientation (if any) for the task and then react to the responses that the child made. As would be expected, the maternal teaching styles described by Brophy were correlated with children's subsequent reading readiness and school-achievement scores and IQs (Hess, Shipman, Brophy, & Bear, 1969).

Thus, it would appear that adult comments which help the child to *see* salient aspects of his environment and to break tasks down into manageable steps are very important in that they help him respond more efficiently. The instructive parent is constantly helping the child learn by providing him with such verbal mediators for structuring his world. Independent of social class, parents who behave in this responsive fashion will probably maximize their children's cognitive development.

For example, in an earlier description of the mother's teaching behavior in this same study, Brophy, Hess, and Shipman (1966) noted that both proactive and reactive teaching styles appeared in all three social classes studied and that, in the middle- and the upper-lower-class groups, maternal style related to reading readiness. Thus, to the extent that these parents did engage in proactive teaching, they were helping their children to develop reading-readiness skills. However, maternal teaching style did not correlate with reading-readiness scores in lower-class families. Perhaps this was due to the very low frequencies of proactive teaching behavior that these mothers showed in the research tasks (and presumably in the home). More studies of parent teaching behavior, especially in naturalistic, day-to-day home activities, are needed.

The chief point to note here is that disadvantaged mothers *did not fail to respond* to their children, but they did fail to help them understand the task and make sense of it. It is this *proactive* dimension that is apt to be missing in parent–child interaction in low-income families, and it is here that parent programs can make a major contribution.

Thus, middle-class mothers are more likely than working-class mothers to engage in *meaningful* verbal exchanges while teaching their children. Tulkin and Kagan (1972) recently examined naturalistic mother–child interaction during the first year of life, and found that better-educated mothers provided their children with much more verbal interaction and cognitive stimulation than did working-class mothers. Interestingly, though, working-class mothers provided more physical stimulation than middle-class mothers.

These results are similar to those of previous reports showing minimal social-class differences in mother–child affective patterns (e.g., Bayley & Schaefer, 1960) but large differences in cognitive stimulation (e.g., Shipman & Hess, 1966). Working-class mothers clearly care about their children as much as do middle-class mothers, but may not provide them with optimal cognitive stimulation because they don't know what to do or how to do it.

Tulkin and Kagan also note that there were large intragroup differences in addition to the differences between social classes. This means that many of the working-class mothers behaved as did the majority of middle-class mothers, and vice versa. Much of the class difference could be attributed to a subgroup of middle-class mothers who were especially verbal. Thus, it is incorrect to view disadvantaged mothers categorically as poor teachers.

Educationally Disadvantaged

The fact that sharply different levels of parental teaching effectiveness can be found within same-SES-level families is similar to White's findings (reviewed in Chapter 3) concerning competence. When researchers examine differences across SES levels, notable overlap is observed, despite significant group differences. Also, too often data are not examined (or reported) for differences that exist *within* social-class categories. The common pattern is to describe *differences* and, inadvertently, to overemphasize such differences. When we speak of disadvantaged children, we mean those children who are not responded to in appropriate cognitive or affective fashions in their homes, regardless of social class. Unfortunately though, the literature mainly stresses lower-class versus middle-class differences. Here, consistently, the averages do favor middle-class homes, but overlap across groups is seldom acknowledged. Thus we do know that on the average middle-class homes are more responsive, but we must recognize that such results are *not* indicative of the behavior of all children and parents who fit a particular SES definition based on education and/or income.

Social Class Differences in Parent Attitudes

Parent attitudes are also of critical importance. Kagan et al. (1971), on the basis of parent-interview data, report that *a major difference between lower- and middle-class parents is that the latter believe that they can influence their child's mental development.* Tulkin and Kagan (1972) suggest that much of the lack of verbalization in working-class parents stems from the mothers' beliefs that they do not and cannot have much influence on the development of their children, and that it is pointless to interact with their infants. They noted that some of the working-class mothers felt it useful to speak to the infant only after he begins to speak. Again, we see *the lack of proactive behavior.* Weikart and Lambie (1969) noted a similar hesitation of working-class mothers to interact with infants because they believed that talking to a baby was foolish.

Beyond this general level of perceived effectiveness, other, more focused attitudes also appear to be important. One of the more notable issues is the belief in encouragement for the female learner. Kagan (1971) reports that the relationship between social class and intellectual drive is consistently higher for girls than boys, and further notes that well-educated mothers are three times more likely to chide their daughters for not performing well than are lower-class mothers. A similar opinion that middle-class mothers project a sense of the importance of achievement upon their daughters was expressed by Hess, Shipman, Brophy and Bear (1969). Further Herman (1970) reports that mothers' improved self-concept, positive attitude toward the preschool, and increased amount of verbal participation were notably related to gains in intellectual performance by boys on the Bayley scale. Parents may need *specific* encouragement if they are to expect and stress achievement for their daughters.

Thus, it may well be that parents' behaviors will have different effects upon male and female learners. Much more research is needed on this point. However, *it seems clear that parents' lack of confidence and feelings of powerlessness can be communicated and taught to children.* Thus, if parents' effectiveness in rearing children is to be enhanced, they may need help in seeing themselves more positively and in correcting certain self-defeating attitudes, in addition to gaining information about how to utilize their teaching skills.

WHY PARENT INVOLVEMENT IN EDUCATION ACTIVITIES?

We feel that parent support (and hopefully active participation) is necessary if a preschool program is to have lasting effects upon children. We noted in the last section that most parents do not view themselves as educators, and often do not use proactive-initiating teaching skills. Clearly, they are unlikely to improve upon their existing skills for teaching their children if they do not receive help and information. To the extent that these skills are deficient, their children will suffer. Furthermore, if parents are not aware of what takes place in school, there is no way that they can complement these activities at home. Indeed, the endless requests from children for crayons to use, books to read, and for parents to play games or sing new songs may irritate the mother or father who comes home tired and has little money to pay for the new interests that the preschool has created. Under such circumstances, the parent may react negatively to these requests, and, in time, may teach the child that school achievement is not desired at home. Alternatively, parents who realize the importance of such activities and who are aware of the program's lending library (where parents can check out books, equipment, etc.) or of inexpensive ways to make play equipment (play dough, for example) are in a position to actively encourage the emerging interests of their child. After becoming actively involved in the preschool education of their children, parents will always enhance and support school-related activities in the home. Thus, time spent working with them may not only pay current dividends but also future ones as well.

In addition to their important role in supporting educational activities in the home, parents can also play a direct and valuable role in the preschool program itself. Parents can serve as teacher aides by reading stories and helping with managerial matters, thus allowing the teacher more time to interact with children in instructional activities. Reducing the child-to-teacher ratio doubtlessly has a number of advantages in addition to freeing more of the teacher's time for instructional activity. For example Hayden, Murdoch, and Quick (1969) report that the presence of teacher aides in kindergarten and first-grade rooms improves the attention span of children—at least in an experimental testing situation. Parents can also assume small-group instructional responsibilities and can help the program by building needed equipment, and so forth.

Yet another way in which parents' involvement may improve their child's performance is participation that leads to changes in the school program itself. Parents can be valuable not only by lowering the child-to-adult ratio or by modeling concern for the children, but also by helping to change the school staff and school curriculum in appropriate ways. Clearly, parents must have some decision-making power in the program if this potential gain is to be realized.

We suggested earlier that a cognitive versus affective orientation toward preschool programs was a needless and inappropriate designation. So too, we feel, is the dichotomy between communal or school control versus family control of young children's lives. Responsibility for young children is *shared* when a child is enrolled in a preschool, and we suspect that maximum progress will come about when family and school are fused in mutual respect and cooperation.

We have reviewed some hypothetical reasons why parent involvement is desirable. Does parent education make a difference? Can parents change attitudes and learn new skills? We will now review evidence related to these questions. *Can school staff listen to and learn from parents?* Unfortunately, no direct data are available on this important question.

Parent Involvement:
Some Data

One of the effects of involving parents in preschool programs is that parents' behaviors (the way time with children is spent) and attitudes are altered. Klaus and Gray (1968) collected annual interview data from parents over a period of years, and found that experimental parents reported that they spent more time reading to their child and engaging in school-type activities than did control parents. Control parents reported more noneducational, shared experiences with their children (watching TV, house cleaning, playing games). Furthermore, experimental parents reported more interest in their child's achievement than did control parents.

However, it seems that parents are affected by particular program emphases (Bissel, 1971). Questionnaire data collected from parents suggested that they had internalized the particular program model they had been exposed to. Parents with children in regular Head Start programs reported that they were glad they had found a place for their child to stay, while parents from Planned Variation programs were more likely to stress parent–child relationships and changes in their own or their child's self-concept. Apparently, parents' attitudes are differentially affected by the kinds of programs they come into contact with. Programs that do not help parents to become more aware of and skilled in their educative role fail to develop a major part of the potential influence of preschool education upon the child. Bissel also reported that it was possible to change mother–child interaction patterns, and that program mothers learned to use more praise and to become more task oriented. The parent-training program of the Boston University Project (reviewed in Gordon, 1971b) augmented parents' self-esteem and brought about shifts in their parental roles.

Apparently it is possible to change parental attitudes and behavior. There are also data to show that parents' involvement in and support for preschool activities may have direct effects upon children's preschool performance. Bittner, Rockwell, and Matthews (1968) report that children of parents who had a high level of participation retained gains better than children of parents who did not have a high level of participation.

Furthermore, Holmes and Holmes (1969) found that children of parents who had voluntarily enrolled them in Head Start programs sustained better gains than those children who had been actively recruited for the program. Stein and Smith (1973) report that over 200 home-based programs to help parents help children are now operative. They further suggest that evidence concerning effectiveness is generally positive and encouraging. Gordon (1971b) reviews 20 or so efforts to help parents develop selected skills and, although less encouraged than Stein and Smith, he does underline the potential viability of such programs.

An Example

Karnes, Teska, Hodgins, and Badger (1970) report one of the many attempts that have been made to help parents to become more effective educators—

helping parents become major intervention agents. In this study, mothers of 12- to 24-month-old infants attended weekly meetings to learn to implement a sequential education program. Mothers were taught teaching principles, and field visitors made home visits at least monthly to help each mother establish a good working relationship with her baby and also to reinforce the teaching skills that the mother had been taught previously.

Major working principles that mothers were encouraged to follow included:

1. Establish a strong working relationship with child (an essential prerequisite step for teaching).
2. Be positive. Model correct answers and provide praise. Attempt to minimize child mistakes.
3. Break tasks into separate, small steps and move from one step to the next only when the child shows complete mastery.
4. If the child does not attend to tasks, put away toys until later. The teaching time should be natural and fun for both of you.

Toys and games were the activities utilized for intellectual and language stimulation. These activities were demonstrated in group meetings or by the field worker to the mothers, who learned key words and specific teaching techniques for each activity. These specific demonstrations enhanced the general principles that had been communicated to them. Mothers also were exposed to general information and a variety of inexpensive books and toys, and were encouraged to engage in special projects with their children. For example, mothers and children made their own books by cutting pictures from magazines, pasting them in scrapbooks, and frequently going through the books together.

Mothers attended two-hour weekly meetings, for which transportation and baby-sitting money were supplied. Further, mothers received at least monthly visits from a project staff member. On the basis of information gained from group meetings and home visits, mothers implemented a home-intervention program. After two years, there was a 28-point difference in Binet IQ scores in favor of the experimental infants over the matched controls. Indeed, there was little overlap in the range of IQ scores. The range for experimental infants was from 99 to 134, whereas the range for controls was from 71 to 102.

There were 20 mothers (including two grandmothers) when the study began. Five of the mothers eventually left the program. These mothers attended less than 60 percent of the meetings during the first seven months. Mothers who stayed with the program averaged more than 80 percent attendance. Apparently, mothers who do not become active in such programs early are likely dropouts, so that special efforts may be needed to retain them.

Despite the fact that the program included few mothers (and an even smaller number of matched subjects for the experimental comparisons), the results suggest that improving mothers' skills as educational agents can do much to prevent or reduce the cognitive and language deficiencies that are often associated with disadvantaged children.

Schaefer (1972) reviewed several home-interaction programs and concluded that: (1) parents have great influence upon the intellectual and academic achievement of their children; (2) programs that teach parents educative skills are viable supplements or alternatives for preschool education; and (3) neglecting parent education with an exclusive focus upon academic child education will not solve the problems of disadvantaged children. These conclusions are, of course, consistent with those that have been expressed throughout this chapter.

However, parent involvement per se is not a panacea solving all problems. Indeed, we have seen that parents are sensitive to the program goals they are exposed to, and under many circumstances they will internalize these program goals as their own stance or attitude. Hence, programs that communicate vague or inappropriate goals or place diffuse requests upon parents will be ineffective even if parents are involved.

One special aspect of parent-education programs deserves comment. Programs that are parent centered (as opposed to purely child centered) appear to have equal effectiveness in producing short-run gains, but are less expensive and have greater long-term effectiveness (Schaefer, 1972). We suspect that programs that deal with the parent and his problems are also more likely to involve parents in the preschool program itself as well as to receive parent cooperation in the home. Schaefer also suggests that research data on early education gains not only show the need for early and continuing involvement of the child, but also the continuing involvement of the parent as an educator. Parents who experience direct benefit are more likely to become involved in the preschool programs than parents who do not see any immediate advantages for themselves.

Involving Parents

In this section we will provide recommendations concerning how parents might assume supportive and active roles in preschool and day-care programs. We have seen that parents can play an educative role, and that time spent in contacting parents and attempting to work with them is well worth the effort. Clearly there is no such thing as *the* program for working with parents. The nature and frequency of parent activities vary with such factors as the presence of a parent coordinator or "freed" teacher time to provide leadership for a parent-activity program, the experience level of the teaching staff (experienced teachers who can effectively get the program off to a good start in their room will have more time to work with parents or volunteers than will beginning teachers), the number of new parents in the program, the educational level of parents, and so forth. Parent programs, like all other phases of the preschool program, need to be geared to local needs and restraints. At the end of this chapter, the reader will find a list of references that can be profitably consulted for information and practical ideas about working with parents. In the remainder of this chapter, we will describe some major goals of parent-involvement programs and illustrate ways in which these goals may be reached. Specific details necessarily must be planned to meet local needs.

Goals

The goals you set for a parent-involvement program will dictate when and how you contact the parents as well as the subjects of conversations and meetings you have with them. We believe that the goals of a parent-involvement program should include the following:

1. To react to parents in a human way, helping them to obtain information or direct aid in solving some of the difficult problems that confront them as parents and to become more aware of how they can help themselves.
2. To help them to become aware of their educative role and to become familiar with cognitive and affective factors that facilitate child growth.
3. To involve the parents in relevant home activities, and when possible, to enlist their direct aid in the preschool program.

If the first goal is seen as primary, we suspect that little will be done to antagonize parents. Remember, preschool parent-involvement programs are established to help parents in areas where they express a need for assistance. If parents do not view the program as helpful for them and their children, everyone's time is wasted. Communicating a direct interest in their involvement and growth is a good first step.

Demonstrating interest in the parents themselves is important when making first contacts, especially with parents who are extremely busy and/or who might feel uneasy in the presence of school officials. Indeed, it may take a series of visits and meetings before mutual liking and respect between teacher and parents is established. The initial visit is best viewed as the *first* attempt to build a bridge of cooperative interest between home and school. Continuing efforts by the teacher are often needed before the parent begins to participate in the program.

Your First Visit with a Parent

Your first meeting with parents should specifically stress goal one: to react to parents in a human way and show interest in them. Teachers who see parents as objects to manipulate, of value only to help "train" children, will not be effective. The major purpose of the initial visit is to meet with and relate to parents. Collecting and receiving information (that ultimately will be useful in achieving goals two and three) are secondary considerations.

Previously, the point was stressed that parents need to establish a strong working relationship with their child as an essential prerequisite for teaching. Similarly, if parents are to learn new behaviors and enjoy participating in parent activities, teachers must first establish a strong working relationship with them.

Specifics of the first visit are determined largely by the exercise of common sense. However, the following areas might profitably be touched upon. Call or visit the parent to set up a convenient time for a visit at the start of the year. Express interest in the parents (their work, etc.) and talk with them about the general activities that go on in the preschool program, noting that they are welcome to observe the program in action. Take a schedule of planned meetings with parents along, so that meetings, activities, dates, and the overall purpose of parent-involvement activities can be briefly discussed.

It is especially important to explain that the preschool program is (or will be) advised by a parent board and that at parent meetings there is ample opportunity to swap ideas, discuss common problems, and learn about services and resources that are available in the community. The emphasis should be on parents' sharing information and learning together with the project staff and on ways to have enjoyable contacts with children.

If you have an established program with an active parental group, it would be useful to have a participating parent visit new parents and explain in his own terms how the parents' group functions. Different persons should be called upon at different times to fulfill this role, so as not to overburden cooperating parents.

During your initial visit, give the date of the orientation meeting and ask if the parent can or will attend. If possible, it is a good idea to provide infant-care facilities for parents who cannot find baby-sitters. If the parent makes no immediate response to your question, point out that if baby-sitting services are needed they can bring their children to the center (but be sure to write down the number and ages of such children so that appropriate planning can take place) and that arrangements can be made for transportation.

If the parent can attend the orientation meeting, you might point out that in addition to providing information about the program there will be a general time for exchanging ideas. Then proceed to ask the parent if there is any problem area he would like to have discussed at the meeting. It would be useful to point out that the most commonly mentioned problems will be dealt with sometime during the year and that a major goal of the parent program is to allow parents to swap ideas and to find solutions to common problems.

Finally, time permitting, briefly suggest ways in which the parents might participate in the preschool program and describe why they are needed. But try to keep the conversation light and pleasant. If information is needed on the children, fill out forms at the end of the visit, but explain fully the reason you need such information and make every effort to minimize the amount of information collected. Limit the visit to forty-five minutes or so.

If the parent is unable to attend the orientation meeting leave simple materials describing (1) the goals and activities of the preschool program, (2) a few suggestions describing the importance of and how a parent can play a teaching role in the home, and (3) possible direct ways in which the parent can aid the preschool program (more on these later). Arrange a visit in a few weeks so you can discuss the child's progress and subsequent parent-meeting activities, and can elaborate on the written material.

In review, it is especially important to begin by building toward a relationship of mutual liking and respect in the first meeting with the parents. Although you have goals you hope to accomplish and information you want to communicate, be responsive to the parent. Building the relationship is the first step. Key steps here are listening to parents, discussing areas that have some interest to them, and being open and honest with them. The "we" approach is vitally necessary. The goal is to help parents see the value of involvement for themselves and their child. Nothing communicates this to them as directly as being responsive, being helpful in answering their questions, and so on. Keep notes and attempt to find information relevant to particular parent concerns. Stein and Smith (1973) suggest that behaviors communicating that "we're interested only in helping your child" are especially harmful and should be avoided. Show the parents that you are interested in *them* too. This theme has been communicated several times because it is fundamental to the success of the program.

Initial Orientation Meeting   Since resources for the parent-involvement program will vary from situation to situation, the role and format of the initial orientation meeting must also vary. Complete orientation goals would include:

1. Providing a general orientation to school facilities and program goals.
2. Providing information about parent activities and the creation of a parent-advisory group.
3. Conducting a needs assessment to identify parents' interests and/or problems.
4. Discussing ways in which parents can help in the home and in the school.
5. Demonstrating practical teaching ideas.
6. Providing an opportunity to visit the preschool program.
7. Finding a role in the program for the interested parent.

Clearly this is a great deal to do in one meeting and will probably have to be accomplished in three separate orientation meetings spread over a period of six to eight weeks. However, in a preschool program composed mainly of children from middle-class, advantaged homes, the time period could be condensed considerably. Indeed, with a great deal of preparation

In making home visits, the teacher stresses solidifying her relationship with the mother and child, even in situations such as this, where she is showing the mother how materials available in the home can be used for teaching.

(summarizing in written form information relevant to goals one, two, and four, so that only the highlights need be explained in the meeting) and planning, it could be accomplished in one long meeting. Here, however, we assume that the parents are motivated to read and to carry out activities in their homes and that the program will have resources for providing home demonstrations when requested by parents.

Probably the most typical program situation is the case where: (1) there is no parent-involvement director, (2) parent activity meetings are run by teachers, and (3) thus, parents receive most of their skills and information at parent meetings (as opposed to special demonstrations in the home, etc.). Under these conditions it probably makes sense to work on orientation goals one, two, and three at the first meeting. Goals four and five are developed at the second meeting, and systematic work on goals six and seven is delayed until the third meeting.

GETTING OFF TO A GOOD START

If money is available to pay the staff for a few days of work prior to the opening of the preschool, it would be helpful to have the orientation meeting *before school begins.* The goal for the orientation meeting is to provide an efficient exchange of information, but in a pleasant, enjoyable way. Obviously, the best way to prevent boredom or alienation is not to make parents sit through needless discussions or rehashings of ideas.

If there are numerous new parents, meet with them separately during the first part of the meeting (while parents already familiar with the program tour the building to see new equipment, have a social hour, or discuss parent–child techniques) so that they can receive a brief orientation to the preschool program and have a chance to ask general questions.

Within the restraints suggested above, three activities appear especially relevant for the first meeting: (1) to provide general information about the preschool program, (2) to provide general information about the parent program and to select a parent steering committee and (3) to conduct a needs assessment.

Electing a Parent Steering Group

During the orientation meeting, it would be useful to elect a self-selected (volunteer) group of parents who would be willing to serve as an advisory board for the preschool program and actively help run the program. Explanation of the duties of the board would be necessary, and although the nature and function of steering groups would vary from community to community, the major functions appear to be: (1) establishing and reviewing curriculum goals with teachers, (2) reacting to parents' criticisms of program and staff and helping to bring about responsive change when such criticism is justified, (3) hiring teachers, and (4) planning useful parent-activity programs with the help of the teaching staff. Also, information about the frequency of board meetings and an oral summary from a previous board member would do a great deal to help potential board members understand what they are being asked to do. Such boards do a great deal to help parents see that they are responsible and do play a vital role in making *their* preschool program function. We agree with Gordon (1971b), who noted that often a self-fulfilling phenomenon is at work. When parents are expected to play vital and important roles, they do.

Conducting a Needs Assessment

Parents are individuals with widely different needs and interests. Parent programs are often less effective than they might be because they have only one program agenda. Although resources are always limited and no parent-involvement program can be completely individualized, it does seem reasonable to divide the whole parent group into smaller, self-selected groups so that at each meeting parents can deal with some topic of interest and concern to themselves. Common interests (e.g., how to interact with a child) can, of course, be discussed in the total group setting. The development work for designing meetings that are of value to parents can and should be started during the teacher's first home visit and continued at the first meeting.

A needs assessment is simply a gathering of information about parent interests, concerns, and so on, and is no different from a needs assessment for teachers (see Chapter 5). The teacher's goal is to collect information that realistically describes parents' interests and to convey the idea that part of the monthly (or biweekly or whatever, depending upon local resources and restraints) parent meeting is *for them*. There is a variety of ways to collect such "interest" data:

1. Set up a general brainstorming session wherein parents call out all ideas that occur to them and eventually place themselves into one of several groups.
2. Begin by listing two or three of the activities that parents worked on the previous year ("Enjoyable, inexpensive things to do on a weekend;" "Bedtime without riot or conflict; "Home safety;" etc.) and summarize some of the practical ideas that emerged (to illustrate that groups do come up with interesting answers to real questions).
3. Break the parents down into small groups of four or so for ten minutes, allowing each small group to come up with three or four possible topics and then meet as a total group to decide upon study areas.

We could go on listing possibilities, but again we stress that there is *no one way* to gather parents' ideas. Much more important than the process to be used is to communicate that all interests are appropriate, and that even though it may be possible to study only some of the topics, efforts will be made to help parents locate information about their unique needs or interests. Staff members should use the procedures they feel most comfortable with, and not let the method get in the way of what they are trying to accomplish.

Following the needs assessment, the program staff will be able to plan, in cooperation with the parent advisory board, a series of parent meetings that might include the following:

1. General report on progress of program and current activities.
2. Demonstrations of skills and games that can be used in home-teaching situations.
3. Meeting of parent-interest groups.
4. Helping interested parents to identify active roles in the preschool.

PARENT PROGRAMS DURING THE YEAR

So far, discussion has centered on the first orientation meeting and the need to illustrate to parents that the program is interested in them and their needs as well as their children's. If parents' goodwill and respect for the program have been won, the parent program has been successful. Parents' interest in and support of the preschool program (as they communicate it to the child) create the conditions necessary for the child to participate fully and not feel ambivalent about school. Even if parents cannot participate in direct ways, their good will and acceptance is important in and of itself.

In the remainder of this chapter we will talk about teacher activities and parent programs that can be undertaken as the year progresses. Earlier we stressed the difficulty of placing these activities into specific program definitions, because resources vary so widely from program to program. However, the general order in which parent in-service topics are discussed conveys a sequence in which they might profitably unfold during the year in a particular preschool program.

Demonstration

Demonstrations of activities or teaching skills are a fundamental aspect of the parent–teacher program, once the initial orientation activities are completed. It is especially important that the first exposure to a teaching-learning episode be conducted in such a way as not to threaten new participants. At the start of the year, it might be useful to have parents who had children in the program the year before demonstrate with the child or role play with another parent some of the techniques they developed the previous year. After the demonstration (live or video), new parents should have the opportunity to discuss the skills, to practice, and to receive feedback. Depending upon the nature of the program, it may make sense to organize the parents into smaller groups (parents of 3-year-olds and parents of 5-year-olds, for instance), so that immediately applicable skills and techniques are being learned. When this occurs, the parent has direct proof that attending the meetings is useful and fun.

Hopefully, at each meeting parents will learn a new skill or item of information that enhances their personal coping skills or their ability to teach their child. It is especially important to illustrate to parents that attending group meetings or having a home visitor is a pleasant experience that helps them deal with problems.

Discussion sessions can also include some demonstration activities. Topics for demonstration might include "games for a rainy afternoon," "dealing with children who want the same toy," or problems that parents have identified as important to them. Where possible, it is useful to *see* the problem (video tape—role play) first, and then to involve parents in exchanging ideas. Successful resolutions can then be shown or acted out. The advice here seems simple and straightforward. If you want someone to enjoy a program and to become a part of it, find out the problems or interests that the person has and illustrate how the program is helpful in dealing with these interests.

Information Describing Parents' Educative Role

Written summaries of demonstrated teaching skills would be useful to give to parents. Also useful are simple, general-orientation fact sheets that help parents to remember special rules. Such description of home activities for parents is a good way to involve them at home even if they drop out of parent meetings. However, if such information is to be useful in the homes of parents who have trouble reading or who are extremely busy, teachers will have to review these sheets and demonstrate certain skills when they visit in the home. Tips on parent-education activities depend on the goals of the particular program to some extent, but we suspect the following points could profitably be made to any parent group.

1. Stress the need for parents to talk to infants even when the infant cannot respond verbally.
2. Provide information about how the child learns through games as well as descriptions of games that parents and children can play together.
3. Stress the use of language in adult–child interactions, especially games that encourage the child to sequence events ("First we pick up grandmother, then we go to the library, and then we'll have lunch") and to make inferences ("If the glass fell off the table, where would it be?").
4. Stress that nothing special needs to be done; that parents can help children by talking to them about what they do and how they do it as they carry out normal, routine household chores. The importance of enjoyable parent–child dialogue cannot be overstressed, as this is the way the child learns that things occur for predictable reasons.

5. For suggestions in teaching situations, see the guidelines suggested by Karnes et al. (1970) that were reviewed earlier in the chapter.

Countless items could be added to this list (e.g., story time, making up a story that involves something special in the child's life, how to make a walk in the neighborhood or a trip to the zoo an educational experience). What is on the list is not as important as *having a list*. Indeed, several lists could be circulated during the year. The idea initially is to suggest to parents that they can and should become educators in the home, and to provide them with a few ideas to try. Too many ideas at once may confuse the adult or make him feel that it is too complicated for him to be an educator.

Observation

As the year progresses, parents should be invited to observe in the preschool even if their child is progressing satisfactorily. Parent visitation serves several useful purposes:

1. It communicates directly that the parent is welcome.
2. Parents will doubtlessly learn some techniques that may be applicable to the home situation.
3. It assures more teacher–parent contact and the opportunity for finding the parent a *role* in the preschool program.
4. Parents who observe regularly in the program can provide useful feedback about the teacher's behavior and program implementation.

However, visits per se are not necessarily good. For example, parents may not know how to respond to children who approach them (if they talk, they may fear disrupting the activities; if they don't talk, they may fear being aloof, etc.). Thus, successful visits require preparing parents for their observational experience. In advance, parents should know: (1) when to arrive (between activities), (2) where to sit, (3) how to react to children who approach, (4) what to look for, and (5) when to talk to the teacher. Especially needed are cues telling the parent what to look for during the visit. The specific cues depend upon why the parent is visiting the program (general information, specific problem with his own child, supplying feedback for teachers, etc.) and the particular curriculum being taught during the observation period.

The point is a simple one. So much occurs in a short period of time that the parent will see very little unless he has something specific to look for. Afterwards, the "points to look for" can become the subject of a "shared" parent–teacher discussion. Again, such a list depends upon the purpose of the visit. For the sake of illustration, the following questions might be presented for a parent on a routine visit who wants to see his child in the program setting.

1. Does he seem to enjoy the various activities?
2. Does he participate fully?
3. Does he listen to the teacher?
4. Does he interact with other children?

Finding a Role

If the parent is to be an active supporter of the early education program, he must feel that his contribution is necessary. And to *feel* needed, he must *be* needed! A direct expression of need is finding a clear-cut role for each parent who wants to be involved. Initially, such role responsibilities (duties in the preschool program) should be limited. Reducing the scope of work serves two major purposes: (1) the parent is not frightened away by seemingly impossible demands; and (2) if the parent proves undependable (and this is always a risk), large gaps are not left to be filled. If the parent enjoys working in the program and it is desirable to increase his involvement, it is always possible to do so later in the year. Thus, early in the year a variety of roles can be explained to parents, and willing volunteers can be scheduled into active roles. Remember, too, that many working parents will want to play a role also, and it is good to schedule a few activities that can be performed at times other than from 8:00–5:00. Weekend field trips, a monthly curriculum night (where materials for the children are made), and other similar activities are needed to allow willing working parents to help.

Fathers, Too

Many fathers are potentially helpful contributors, but due to their lack of familiarity with preschool programs and certain role attitudes (it's unmanly to read to or play with children), they may need special encouragement initially. The easiest way is to ask fathers to do something that is "natural" for them, such as helping to build a fence around the play yard or to construct, paint, or repair play equipment. In Chapter 6 we mentioned that, with clever arrangements, even rooms with large physical problems can be turned into functional learning and play centers. Fathers and mothers with building skills can be a real asset in constructing storage racks, room dividers, and so on. Subsequently, fathers can be phased into other roles (such as reading stories to the children occasionally). The father's involvement at any level is clear, direct proof to the child of his interest in and support for school-related activities.

Filmed models may be particularly useful in getting fathers involved. Especially helpful is awareness of the fact that famous actors, sports stars, and average, working men are all playing roles in preschool programs. Such awareness is helpful in unfreezing role-bound behavior and getting the father to attempt new roles.

Parents have varying levels of interest and time for helping with the program. The trick is to find a meaningful role for a parent that meshes with his interest and available time. Possible parent roles include:

Capitalize on the special talents and interests of adult volunteers. Here, a father visits the preschool and tutors children in the use of tools.

327

1. Classroom observation and minimum supervision responsibilities (e.g., the free-play area).
2. Playground supervision.
3. Car pools for day-to-day schooling as well as for special trips.
4. Seeking information or speakers for parent-interest groups.
5. Repair, maintenance, or building of projects.
6. Classroom supervision (active help in setting up the classroom, dealing with discipline cases, or other special problems).
7. Classroom teaching assistance (reading stories, puppet acts, etc.).

PARENT INTEREST GROUPS

We have previously discussed conducting a needs assessment and the formation of special-interest groups. In review, parent-night meetings should allow some time for parents to discuss and to obtain information about their interest areas. Possible interest areas include: nutrition and menu planning, identifying and eliminating health and safety hazards around the home (paint chips, etc.), making inexpensive toys, availability of free or inexpensive community resources (legal representation, insect control, library services), and so on. Clearly the list could be much longer, but the point we want to make is that all of these activities are viable, important areas, and the only ingredient that makes one any more important than another is *parent interest*. Just as children's interests should dictate the free-play aspects of the curriculum, so, too, should parent interests dictate a part of each parent meeting. No single, set program is likely to be of service and interest to all parents. It is much better to let parents identify study groups and problem areas that are of interest to them, and at that time divide the parents into the three or so study areas that they have selected. The information and recommendations that each group provides can be shared across groups as the year progresses.

The point here is that parent-interest groups are a continuing program and will need staff time periodically throughout the year. Once formed, the groups can function in a quasi-independent fashion. However, teachers need to find resources, help summarize implications, and form new groups as needs arise.

Sharing Parents' Ideas

Another way of expressing interest in parent involvement and underlining its importance is through the collection and sharing of parent ideas. When parents discover new language games or activities for interacting with children, these ideas should be communicated during parent meetings or through newsletters. Parents will want to try out ideas and share their own activities as well. In addition to communicating parents' ideas, we think an occasional (e.g., every six weeks) newsletter from the program is useful. Such newsletters should be brief and provide a mix of information (reminding parents of important school or meeting dates) of interest to parents and enjoyable educational ideas (a recipe for play dough; how to build a toy-storage box). Ideas provided in the newsletter (by staff or parents) will stimulate other parents.

Newsletters will also reach the parent who does not observe in the preschool or who does not attend parent meetings. Although the best way to reach such parents is through home visits, it may be possible to provide them with and motivate some of them to try new ideas in the home through newsletters, especially if they are brief and highly specific.

Evaluation of the parent program should be continuous. What is a good program? It would seem that the program is healthy when parents feel that they can be and *are* participating.

Similarly, when teachers feel (and can cite specific instances) that they are learning from parents, the program is healthy. If either of these attitudes is missing, the program is less than it could be. Such assessment of teacher–parent reaction can be informal (a simple question at the end of interest-group meetings), observational (who talks at parent meetings or curricular meetings?), or formal (a questionnaire designed to obtain parent and teacher evaluation of and recommendation for the program). Form is not critical; it is critical that teachers and parents jointly plan and implement a procedure for collecting information about their success in communicating. General suggestions about collecting feedback information are presented in Chapter 15.

Follow-up Home Visits

Parents who do not attend the initial parent meeting should be visited again as soon as possible to assess their interest in the program and to see if they have special needs. Parents who express interest in learning more about ways they can become involved in parent groups and/or activities should be given such information, and parents who want to learn more about home-educational activities should receive appropriate materials and information. Sometimes interested parents will be unable to free themselves for any evening meetings (elderly, feeble grandparent living in the home, etc.), and it may be necessary to schedule a series of home visits.

If parent-involvement activities have been successful, most parents will see the demonstrations and so on at parent meetings; thus, teachers will have the time to visit and share skills with those parents who are interested but unable to attend scheduled activities. Occasionally parents will express no interest or even open hostility toward continued visits or requests upon their time. In such situations, continued visits may do nothing but place pressure on the child (for example, when he mentions an enjoyable school activity, the parent may become irritated immediately, etc.). It is best to go very slowly in these situations. "Writing off" the parents would be an unfortunate self-fulfilling prophecy, but continued short-run efforts are more likely to increase problems than to reduce them. Here, the best strategy is to stop visiting the parent and/or making requests, but to continue to send relevant preschool information and newsletters, and, after a few weeks, call the parents and ask for a brief, fifteen-minute appointment to talk about the child's progress in school.

If the parents are willing, make a *brief* visit and relate how the child has adjusted to school and what he is doing at present. Unless the parents are visibly irritated by the visit, this would be a good time to invite them to visit the program if their schedules allow. Above all, in meetings with reticent or reluctant parents, describe mainly the good behaviors of the child, but in a matter-of-fact, low-key fashion. Too much praise or enthusiasm may raise suspicions rather than please such parents.

Uninterested parents are unlikely to help with school-related behavior problems and are most likely to escalate them. However, one must distinguish between busy, overworked parents and disinterested ones. At all SES levels we will find a few parents who are too busy or who simply do not care about their children. Fortunately we find few such parents, but they do exist. Here, it is best to maintain loose periodic contact with them, but to make no demands on their time until and unless they make a positive expression of interest. Appropriate action, of course, depends upon the specific problem and personalities involved. For example, if the problem is not lack of parent interest but resentment toward the program ("Who are these people to tell me how to raise my children?"), it would be useful to have sensitive neighbors describe the program in their own terms. In any case, a home visitor who is willing to *listen* and who does not react inappropriately to parent behavior is making the beginning steps in forging a good home–school relationship.

Parent Visits: Requests for Help

In general, home–school conflict can be greatly reduced if teachers visit the homes early in the year, before major problems develop, and if they are careful to tell the parents about the good things that the child has been doing and to communicate awareness of special traits that the child possesses. It is easy to establish a relationship with most parents early in the school year before problems develop. However, after problems develop, it is exceedingly difficult to establish firm links of understanding. All too often, the parent thinks of problems as the school's fault, and vice versa. To save face, it is easy to fall into the trap of blaming someone else for the problems, and teachers and parents are often both victims of this trap. When trust and confidence have not been established between home and school, conversations are apt to be filled with "It's your fault" innuendos ("Well, he doesn't do that at home," implicitly suggesting that the teacher is causing the problem). Thus, if some problem exists and a parent that you are familiar with needs to be contacted, it is best to use a "we" exploratory approach. Express your concern for the child, your willingness to help, and your interest in discussing the problem with the parent.

A "we" exploratory approach suggests that, first, as a teacher you are willing to consider your classroom behavior as a possible cause for the child's problem, and second, that you approach the parent with a tentative description of the problem ("As I see it, but I don't or can't watch Johnny all the time") and a willingness to listen to the parent ("Does he behave this way at home? Does he dislike school?"). Beyond this, it is simply a matter of discussing with the parent what can be tried at home *and* at school, and drawing up a specific plan of action. After agreeing upon the plan, it is generally useful to meet with the child and explain to him what was discussed and what the parent and teacher expect of him in the future. Such a conversation with the child allows him to see that no private conversations go on behind his back without him being informed, demonstrates the solidarity of teacher and parent, and gives him a chance to tell his side of the story and to make suggestions. If the child makes relevant suggestions, the parent and teacher should listen and take appropriate action. Parents should receive a feedback visit or call from the teacher after a few days, and if satisfactory progress has not been made, new plans should commence.

If parents are unwilling to discuss the problem or if they deny the problem ("My boy would never act like that!"), invite them to visit and gather firsthand information. Subsequent conversation should be delayed until after the parents' visit.

However, for the most part, school problems should be dealt with at school, and no special efforts should be made to contact parents. To begin with, parents may overreact if contacted by a school official, and may become excessively worried about a relatively minor problem. Such parent concern may escalate the problem rather than reduce it. Also, some child behavior at home and school is controlled by situational factors that are not under the control of the parent or child, so that a home visit is likely to do little good. Thus, we recommend involving parents in problems only when they are major ones and are potentially solvable by parental action.

CONCLUSION

Expressed parent attitudes and parent interactions with children are very important determinants of affective and cognitive development. We have seen that appropriate attitudes and behaviors can be taught in parent-involvement activities. Programs that communicate a "can do" attitude, equip parents with new insights and interaction skills, and use parent resources are doing much to build an environment in which children develop their potential fully. Programs that do not utilize parent resources or use them ineffectively are unlikely to create programs that have lasting value for children.

1. Attend a preschool parent meeting. Evaluate the effectiveness of the program. Was it successful? Why or why not? Questions that you might want to consider in writing your evaluation include: What were the goals for this meeting? Who established them? Were "convenience" provisions made for parents (transportation, baby-sitting)? Who planned the program and who were active participants in the program? Did parents have a chance to ask questions? Learn skills? Discuss problems of interest?

2. Describe, in specific terms, how subsequent meetings might be improved.

3. Interview parent and teacher members of the parent-program committee. Do parents and teachers hold shared goals? If not, describe and explain the discrepancies. If so, describe the nature of these goals (Policy? Program? Social?).

4. *Keep a diary* (with individual parents or with a parent group) based on at least three interviews or attendance at three parent meetings.

   Summarize:

   a. What are parents getting out of the program?
   b. What is the level of parent communication with the school or individual teachers? Does communication seem to be improving?
   c. What are parents being asked to do with their children (e.g. are they serving as teachers)?
   d. What specific concerns do parents have with the program?

5. Role play an initial home visit with classmates. Try to communicate respect and interest in the parent, but also to accomplish relevant task goals. Classmates can provide feedback describing strengths and weaknesses in your approach.

6. Role play an attempt to get a father to participate in program activities. Classmates can provide feedback and suggest alternatives.

7. Role play working with a disinterested or hostile parent. Show the actions and techniques you would use.

8. Role play the demonstration of a teaching skill to a parent group (What language, examples, handouts, etc., would be necessary to teach the skill?). Be sure to give parents a chance to practice the skill and to receive corrective feedback from you or fellow participants.

9. Write up a home activity for parents who cannot attend group meetings. Communicate one idea or concept illustrating how parents can be home educators.

10. Prepare instructions for parents to use when they observe. Define the situation (e.g., a general visit), and then provide specific observation guidelines for that situation.

11. Describe what you would include in a parent newsletter (define the tar-

get parent group and discuss format, content, and language level of the newsletter).

12. Develop a list of "free" resources for parents in a local preschool program. Attempt to find all free or inexpensive opportunities that exist in the local community.

13. Several areas in which *fathers* could participate in the preschool program were outlined in the chapter. Expand this list by finding other potential roles for fathers.

14. Describe how the problems of initiating and maintaining effective parent programs would vary with the nature of the program and the characteristics of the target population.

15. Should parents have decision-making power regarding teaching practices and/or program activities? Why or why not? Discuss this issue with classmates, and determine the implications of your ideas regarding your attitudes towards parents and the kinds of programs in which you would or would not want to work.

16. If parents are to be involved in decision making, what are some practical arrangements to be made to solicit their involvement?

READINGS

Books

Brill, N. *Working with people: the helping process.* New York: Lippincott, 1973.

Casavis, J. *Principal's guidelines for action in parent conferences.* West Nyack, N.Y.: Parker, 1970.

Combs, A., Avila, D., and Purkey, W. *Helping relationships: basic concepts for the helping professions.* Boston: Allyn & Bacon, 1971.

————. *The helping relationship sourcebook.* Boston: Allyn & Bacon, 1971.

Newman, S. *Guidelines to parent-teacher cooperation in early childhood education.* New York: Book-Lab, 1971.

Pickarts, E. and Fargo, J. *Parent education: toward parental competence.* New York: Appleton, 1971.

ERIC Abstracts*

Brown, D. *Parent education: an abstract bibliography* (supplement #1). Champaign, Ill.: ERIC Clearinghouse on Early Childhood Education, 1972. (1300–34).

Coller, A. *Systems for observing parent-child interactions.* Champaign, Ill.: ERIC Clearinghouse on Early Childhood Education, 1972. (1300–28).

Howard, N. *Mother–child home learning programs: an abstract bibliography.* Champaign, Ill.: ERIC Clearinghouse on Early Childhood Education, 1972. (1300–21).

Kremer, B. *Parent education: abstract bibliography.* Champaign, Ill.: ERIC Clearinghouse on Early Childhood Education, 1971. (ED 056782).

Journal References

Baldwin, A., Kalhorn, J. and Breese, F. "The appraisal of parent behavior." *Psychological Monographs, 63* (1949), 4.

---

* These inexpensive publications are especially useful because they provide a thumbnail sketch of every report included in the bibliography and provide a comprehensive review of material available in the ERIC retrieval system.

Baumrind, D. "Child-care practices anteceding three patterns of preschool behavior." *Genetic Psychology Monographs, 75* (1967), 43–88.

Berhrmann, P. "Help from home." *Grade Teacher, 89,* 5 (1972), 16.

Bishop, D. and Chace, C. "Parental conceptual systems, home play environment and potential creativity in children." *Journal of Experimental Child Psychology, 12* (1971), 318–338.

Brezeinski, J. and Howard W. "Early reading—how, not when." *Reading Teacher, 25* (1971), 239–242.

Brophy, J. "Mothers as teachers of their own preschool children: the influence of socioeconomic status and task structure on teaching specificity." *Child Development, 41* (1970), 79–94.

Comer, J. "Child development and social change: some points of controversy." *Journal of Negro Education, 40* (1971), 266–276.

Eveloff, H. "Some cognitive and affective aspects of early language development." *Child Development, 42* (1971), 1895–1907.

Freshour, F. "Beginning reading: parents can help." *Reading Teacher, 25* (1972). 513–516.

Friedberg, M. and Millsom, C. "Communal child care: isolation or constellation." *New York University Education Quarterly, 3,* 2 (1972), 6–12.

Gordon, I. "Children under three—finding ways to stimulate development." and "Some current experiments: stimulation via parent education." *Children, 16* 2 (1969), 57–59.

———. "Reaching the young child through parent education." *Childhood Education, 46* (1970), 247–249.

———. "Self-help approach: parents as teachers." *Compact, 3,* 6 (1969), 32–35.

Gray, S. "Home visiting programs for parents of young children." *Peabody Journal of Education, 48* (1971), 106–111.

———. "Symposium on parent-centered education: 1. The child's first teacher." *Childhood Education, 48* (1971), 127–129.

Greenfield, S. "Going to bed with Captain Marvel and a flashlight is not a home reading program." *Academic Therapy Quarterly, 7* (1971–72), 117–122.

Greenglass, E. "A cross-cultural comparison of maternal communication." *Child Development, 42* (1971), 685–692.

———. "A cross-cultural study of the child's communication with his mother." *Developmental Psychology, 5* (1971), 494–499.

Gross, L. "Some thoughts on communal child rearing." *Childhood Education, 48* (1972), 201–203.

Grotberg, E. "Early childhood education: institutional responsibilities for early childhood education." *National Society for the Study of Education Yearbook, 71* (1972), 317–338.

Hamilton, M. "Evaluation of a parent and child center program." *Child Welfare, 51* (1972), 248–258.

Harmer, W. "To what extent should parents be involved in language programs for linguistically different learners?" *Elementary English, 47* (1970), 940–943.

Heilbrun, A. "Maternal child-rearing and creativity in sons." *Journal of Genetic Psychology, 110* (1971), 175–179.

Jones, E. "Involving parents in children's learning." *Childhood Education, 47* (1970), 126–130.

Karnes, M. et al. "Educational intervention at home by mothers of disadvantaged infants." *Child Development, 41* (1970), 925–935.

Katz, L. "Children and teachers in two types of Head Start classes." *Young Children, 24* (1969), 342–349.

Laing, H. "Using parents effectively in the school." *Instructor, 81,* 6 (1972), 35.

Levenstein, P. "Symposium on parent-centered education: 2. Learning through (and from) mothers." *Childhood Education, 48* (1971), 130–134.

Levine, G. "Attitudes of elementary school pupils and their parents towards mathematics and other subjects of instruction." *Journal for Research in Mathematics Education, 3,* 1 (1972), 51–58.

Little, R. "Newark's parent-powered school." *American Education, 7,* 10 (1971), 35–39.

Luterman, D. "A parent-oriented nursery program for preschool deaf children—a followup study." *Volta Review, 73* (1971), 106–112.

Lytton, H. "Observation studies of parent-child interaction: a methodological review." *Child Development, 42* (1971), 651–684.

Niedermeyer, F. "Parents teach kindergarten reading at home." *Elementary School Journal, 70* (1970), 438–445.

Ney, R. "A comprehensive approach to educational day care." *Educational Technology, 11* (1971), 65–66.

Pieper, A. "Parent and child centers—impetus, implementation, in-depth view." *Young Children, 26* (1970), 70–76.

Radin, N. "Father–child interaction and the intellectual functioning of four-year-old boys." *Developmental Psychology, 6* (1972), 353–361.

———. "Maternal warmth, achievement motivation and cognitive functioning in lower-class preschool children." *Child Development, 42* (1971), 1560–1565.

Schaefer, E. "Children under three—finding ways to stimulate development. II. Some current experiments: a home tutoring program." *Children, 16* (1969), 59–61.

———. "Parents as educators: evidence from cross-sectional, longitudinal and intervention research." *Young Children, 27* (1972), 227–239.

Seltz, J. "The teacher as mother." *Grade Teacher, 89* 8 (1972), 60–63.

Slater, B. "Parent involvement in perceptual training at the kindergarten level." *Academic Therapy Quarterly, 7* (1971–72), 149–154.

Smith, A. "Will my child succeed in school?" *Independent School Bulletin, 31,* 2 (1971), 41–44.

Smith, M. "To educate children effectively—we must involve parents." *Instructor, 80,* 1 (1970), 119–121.

Stern, D. "A microanalysis of mother–infant interaction, behavior regulating social contact between a mother and her $3\frac{1}{2}$–month-old twins." *Journal of the American Academy of Child Psychiatry, 10* (1971), 501–517.

Streissguth, A. and Bee, H. "Mother–child interactions and cognitive development in children." *Young Children, 27* (1972), 154–173.

Swift, M. et al. "Preschool books and mother–child communication." *Reading Teacher, 25* (1971), 236–238.

Tanner, D. and Tanner, L. "Parent education and cultural inheritance." *School and Society, 99* (1971), 21–24.

Tulkin, S. and Kagan, J. "Mother–child interaction in the first year of life." *Child Development, 43* (1972), 31–41.

Weikart, D. "Symposium on parent-centered education: 3. Learning through parents: lessons for teachers." *Childhood Education, 48* (1971), 135–137.

"Where learning is a family affair." *Applachian Advance, 6,* 1 (1971–72), 13–16.

Wittes, G. and Radin, N. "Two approaches to group work with parents in compensatory preschool program." *Social Work 16,* 1 (1971), 42–50.

14
DIFFERENTIATED STAFFING PATTERNS

Staffing patterns will vary greatly from one early education center to another. The number of people employed will be determined by the size of the center, the type of institution that houses the program, or the level of funding that supports it. The kind of staff employed, the relationship of one staff member to another, and the administrative structure are also very much dependent upon the particular type of setting. Early education programs can be found in public schools, churches, neighborhood centers, or operating independently as private businesses. Licensing regulations vary from state to state and from one local setting to another, creating even greater variations in staffing.

Teachers should be aware of the factors that influence the patterns of staffing likely to be found in various settings. The size of the sponsoring agency greatly affects the kinds of resources available to the classroom teacher. If the preschool program is housed in a large school district, the staff will probably include a curriculum coordinator, a principal, an assistant principal, a secretary, cooks, bus drivers, a custodian, as well as teachers and teacher aides. The staff at a small church school, on the other hand, will probably consist only of a director, teachers, teacher aides, and a custodian. Because the size of the institution affects the number of people assigned to the program, teachers should be aware of how this will affect their professional role as they function in the classroom. The teacher has to be prepared, when working for a large institution, to interact with many different kinds of people. While a number of supportive services are provided, other problems related to coordination and effective communication become fairly common. In a smaller institution, teachers do not have access to as many supportive resources, but they do have many more opportunities to exercise their own initiative and judgment in making decisions.

There are still many preschool settings where the teacher works alone in the classroom. A full-time teacher aide or assistant is not always available, and the teacher is expected to supervise a group of children without any outside help. The teachers in this situation, if they are to function effectively, must learn to make feasible program decisions based on this staffing pattern. One option to be considered is the extensive use of volunteers. Parents, community people, or students can be organized and trained to assist the teacher in the classroom. Extensive use of volunteers does require a great deal of the teacher's time. The teacher must be prepared to meet with the volunteers, brief them on their responsibilities, train them if necessary, and consider them in planning daily and weekly schedules.

In addition to extensive use of volunteers, the teacher who works in the classroom without any full-time adult assistance can train the children themselves to assume a great deal of responsibility for routine kinds of tasks. Young children can be extremely helpful to a teacher if expectations are clearly described to them. The teacher can explain from the first day of school that the children will be expected to assist in keeping the room neat and clean. The children can learn to return toys and materials to the shelves when they have finished working with them. They can also assist in serving snacks, cleaning up spills from tables and floors, and otherwise keeping their environment neat and orderly. They can help each other by monitoring their own behavior and assuming responsibility for seeing that everyone follows the classroom rules. The teacher who works alone in a classroom will need all of this assistance to be able to spend much time actually teaching and interacting with the children. While this is not the most ideal situation, it can work well with careful planning and sharing of responsibilities.

In the following sections we shall review some of the major responsibilities of administrators, teachers, and paraprofessionals in early education settings. Although the staffing patterns in many centers will include ancillary and supportive staff services, the discussion in this chapter will concern itself mainly with the responsibilities of those who work directly with children.

THE ROLE OF THE DIRECTOR

The director is a key person in an early education program. The director has major administrative responsibility for coordinating all aspects of the program. Ideally, the director also has the substantive knowledge necessary for serving as the instructional leader at a particular center. Very often, however, this is not the case, and the director's role is limited to administrative and management functions.

The director is usually responsible for identifying and hiring staff members: duties include interviewing and hiring teachers, teacher aides, and ancillary supportive staff members. The director also formulates operating policies or sees to it that they are enforced.

Coordinating the operation of any early education program involves scheduling and planning for the total program. The director makes basic decisions related to use of outdoor playground facilities, scheduling of meals, transportation to and from school, and hours of operation. Other major functions include budgeting and purchasing, working with the school board or advisory group, and implementing final decisions regarding the allocation of funds. A director who is thoroughly familiar with the goals and objectives of a particular program can be of great help in setting appropriate priorities for the allocation of often limited amounts of money.

THE ROLE OF THE SUPERVISING TEACHER

The supervising teacher is the major decision maker in the classroom, with final responsibility for the health and safety of the children, the kinds of learning experiences that will be presented to them, the quality of the interaction between adults and children, and the design of an environment that is truly responsive to the unique needs of each child. The supervising teacher's role is a key one in any preschool program. The curriculum developed for the children will be as good and effective as the teacher who supervises and implements the daily program.

Setting Up the Classroom

One of the teacher's first responsibilities is setting up the classroom so that the environment becomes truly responsive to the needs of a particular group of children. The supervising teacher must make basic decisions regarding the number and kinds of learning areas that will be available at any one time. Once the learning areas are selected, the teacher must choose the kind of equipment and toys to place in the different areas. Materials must be displayed in such a way that they are easily accessible to the children. Wall displays must be designed by the supervising teacher and, if this is done well, they will relate to and support other activities planned at that particular time. An attractive and well-organized classroom usually reflects a teacher who understands the role of manager and creator of a responsive environment.

Selecting Objectives

The supervising teacher is also responsible for selecting the content and objectives of the instructional program. The degree of freedom available to the teacher will vary from center to center. Some centers are committed to implementing a prepackaged instructional program, while others expect the supervising teacher to create the instructional program. Even if a prepackaged program is being implemented, the teachers still have the primary responsibility of selecting particular objectives for each day. They must also exercise their own judgments in modifying content where they feel it might be inappropriate for a particular group of children. There is no such thing as a teacher-proof curriculum. The teacher is the key person who can make any curriculum come alive. But this cannot happen unless the teacher carefully exercises judgment in modifying and adapting as necessary. Selecting objectives and content is one part of this process, and it is an important function for the supervising teacher.

Scheduling

Another major responsibility of the supervising teacher is the planning and scheduling necessary for a well-functioning classroom. To plan effectively, the supervising teacher must work with the assistant and communicate decisions to any volunteers who spend time in the classroom. The supervising teacher makes the major decisions related to the scheduling of events. We assume that the supervising teacher will have the academic background and skills needed to creatively plan and schedule appropriate activities for the children. As teachers plan the schedule, they also group the children for different kinds of objectives. It is the supervising teacher's responsibility to see that each child has an opportunity at some point during the day to excel in one or more learning experiences. For example, some children are more highly skilled in the area of motor coordination than in the area of oral-language expression. The teacher capitalizes on the child's special abilities by regrouping for various kinds of experiences. By carefully grouping, the teacher sees to it that each child is involved daily in an experience in which he has the opportunity to feel especially good about himself and his particular abilities. This approach to grouping demands a high level of skill and sensitivity to each child and his unique capabilities.

Presenting Activities

After teachers plan and schedule program activities, they assume responsibility for presenting specific learning experiences to the children. Usually, these are the types of activities that demand a high level of teaching expertise. The teacher would, for instance, present special problem-solving activities that require the use of questioning strategies involving simplification or expansion techniques. Knowing when to simplify and when to ask a more complex question is the kind of decision that an experienced teacher can make spontaneously and appropriately. This would be difficult for a paraprofessional or teacher aide. Other kinds of activities would include concepts related to language arts, science, and mathematics.

Demonstrating Equipment

The supervising teacher's responsibility for creating an effective learning environment does not end after the classroom is arranged. It is not at all unusual for a classroom to be physically attractive, with materials displayed and accessible to the children, while at the same time most of the children ignore this equipment. One cannot assume that children will spontaneously know what to do with a particular toy or piece of equipment. The supervising teachers should schedule equipment demonstrations throughout the school year. They can demonstrate in a dramatic and exciting fashion different uses for basic equipment. They can stimulate language development through the kinds of questions they ask the children. A creative teacher can encourage the children to discover new and innovative uses for basic toys and equipment. Knowing how to demonstrate and work with equipment in an effective, exciting manner requires special skills. It is the responsibility of the supervising teacher to be sure that equipment is being used regularly, that children are being stimulated to explore new and innovative ways of working with learning materials, and that more complex skills are being mastered through effective utilization of materials placed in the learning environment.

Individualizing Instruction

Individualized instructional materials to meet the needs of each child require careful monitoring of daily performance. The supervising teacher has major responsibility for constructing observation scales and assessment instruments that can assist both the teacher and the teacher aide in systematically collecting information related to the progress being made by the children. The supervising teacher is also responsible for making certain that the information is used to make decisions. Very often teachers find themselves spending much time collecting information and very little time *using* the information to make program decisions. The supervising teacher must know how to limit the amount of information collected through observation and checklists to those areas of child development most useful for making program decisions. A system for analyzing the information and incorporating the results into program activities must also be established. This process should be part of weekly and daily planning sessions, so that both the teacher and assistant teacher may systematically exchange information regarding the needs of the children in the classroom.

Supervising Adult Resources

The effectiveness of the adult resources available in an early childhood classroom will vary as a function of the quality of leadership provided by the supervising teacher. Teacher aides, parent and community volunteers, and student teachers can all be extremely helpful in the classroom. However, the supervising teacher must be prepared to spend the time necessary for maximizing their effectiveness. Very often a classroom teacher will ask that resource people be assigned to the classroom and then find that they provide little assistance in working with the children. To maximize their effectiveness, the supervising teacher must first plan to conduct briefing sessions on the major objectives of the program and review the function of each of the resource people. The teacher must also conduct additional training focused on specific responsibilities in the classroom. These sessions might include demonstrations on reading a story to young children, supervising outdoor play, assisting at meals, or teaching to a specific objective. This sort of training must continue throughout the school year if the teacher is to truly capitalize on the assistance that can be provided by resource people.

It is the supervising teacher's responsibility to make certain that adults assigned to the classroom understand the amount of time that must be committed to their own personal development. If it is not possible for these various adults to commit the in-service training time necessary for upgrading their skills, then the teacher should use their services only for housekeeping types of chores. Without training and time for group discussion and interaction, they will be ineffective in the classroom and will not be able to provide any real assistance to the teacher. The supervising teacher must realize that each extra pair of "helping hands" will require many hours of her time for training and staff development.

In addition to the major responsibilities described above, the supervising teacher must maintain contact and communication with the parents. Parents play the *most* critical role in supporting the optimal development of the young child. Schools, unfortunately, rarely capitalize on the strengths of the home by involving the parents actively in the child's educational experiences. This does not necessarily mean insisting that the parents come to school or spend time in the classroom. Many parents work or have younger children at home. The teacher can maintain contact with parents through home visits or newsletters sent out on a regular basis. It is the supervising teacher's responsibility to see to it that parents are informed of the skills the children are acquiring, the goals that have been established for the future, and the kinds of things the parents can do at home to complement the school program.

Major Responsibilities of the Teacher Aide

The teacher aide's responsibilities are generally shared with the supervising teacher. While aides usually do not have sole responsibility for any particular task, their role as an assistant to the supervising teacher is a critical one.

The teacher aide usually has responsibility for teaching or presenting particular kinds of learning activities to the children. Some program models are consistent in requiring that the teacher aide present specific activities, while others allow the supervising teacher to make the final decision. However, the aide should be expected in any case to function in a teaching capacity and to demonstrate mastery of basic teaching skills.

In addition to teaching responsibilities, the aide assumes a major role in managing the classroom environment. If, for instance, the teacher is working with a small group of children, the aide would be responsible for monitoring the behavior and activities of the other children. This supportive role becomes very important in assuring a classroom that operates smoothly with minimal disruptions.

The teacher and the aide work with each other in preparing the weekly and daily schedules. Communication must be maintained if the teacher and aide are to function effectively as a teaching team. Planning sessions are important events for maintenance of communication and discussion of problems that have arisen.

Setting up the classroom is another task shared by both teachers. After planning decisions have been made, changes in the classroom environment are usually indicated. Equipment must be rotated, new displays constructed, learning areas rotated, and damaged equipment repaired. Sharing this function allows both teachers extra time to plan and discuss how the program is progressing.

The teacher aide also assists the supervising teacher in maintaining contacts with parents. Very often the contacts occur informally as the children are picked up on the bus, or when the parents bring their children to school in the morning or pick them up in the afternoon. It is not at all unusual for a teacher aide to live in the same neighborhood as the parents of the children enrolled in the center. Informal contacts are thus maintained after school hours. Very often parents are less hesitant to discuss concerns about their children with the teacher aide than with the supervising teacher. The aide can be of great assistance to the supervisor by sharing some of these problems. Again, both communication and cooperation between the teachers in the classroom can help strengthen the bond between school and home.

PLANNING AND MAKING DECISIONS FOR BEST USE OF AVAILABLE RESOURCES

The kinds of resources that might be available will vary from one setting to another. Ultimately they might include a teacher aide, parents, community volunteers, college students, high school students, and any number of professional people providing ancillary, supportive services. The key question for a teacher is, what kinds of resources are needed for meeting particular goals? Supervising teachers must remember that every time an adult walks into the classroom, they must be prepared to spend whatever time necessary supervising and interacting with that person to insure maximal benefit from him as a resource. Very often, teachers do not consider all the ramifications of using adults as resources. Before teachers make a decision regarding other adults who will work in the classroom, they should ask themselves the following questions:

- What kinds of things do I want to happen that will be supportive of the program?
- Whom do I need working with me if these things are going to happen?
- Why do I need this particular kind of person?
- When do I need this particular person to work with me?
- How much of my time will be necessary in briefing and training this resource person?

As the teacher reviews these questions, it should become clear that different functions call for differing levels of participation. Regardless of the program model being implemented, the teacher, after reviewing the questions listed above, must then consider the kinds of tasks necessary to make optimal use of available adult resources.

A great deal of the planning related to effective use of resources occurs during the daily and weekly planning sessions that are part of the ongoing operation of any program. As teachers select the goals and objectives for a particular time period, they should consider carefully any external resources that might be brought into the classroom in order to assist the children in achieving the objectives. As they block in activities that are to occur at a particular time of the day, they can also schedule the adult resources that will assist them in presenting the activity. Early in the school year, they should prepare a card file of all known, available external resources. This file can be updated regularly so that the teacher constantly has an ongoing catalogue of available resources. It then becomes a simple matter to schedule particular activities during the school year as the special needs arise. For example, while planning a field trip on a certain day, the teacher should check the file of volunteers to see which people would be available to assist on the trip. Information regarding special talents or interests of each resource person could also be considered when planning certain kinds of activities. The teacher can capitalize on the resources available by carefully matching talents and interests to classroom events.

Once teachers have planned the schedule for a specified period of time, they should meet with the resource people who will be in the classroom during that time period. This would include the teacher aide, parents, volunteers, students in training, and other resource people. At this meeting they should review the objectives, goals, and learning activities that they have planned. Group discussion at this meeting would encourage the resource people to make additional suggestions regarding their own ideas for the program. Very often these suggestions can be easily incorporated into the schedule and can add immeasurably to the creation of a program that is truly unique to a specific group of children. The teacher, however, should make the final decision as to the kinds of learning experiences that will be included in the curriculum. Meetings with resource persons, if planned properly, can be held once a month. If the teachers have organized their time well, they can cover a great deal of information at this meeting and can review specific assignments with each resource person.

Since the teacher and the resource people might expect the planned schedule to change on a daily basis, the supervising teacher must be responsible for posting schedule changes. The updated schedule can be displayed in a prominent place in the classroom. It is a simple matter for every adult who works in a particular room to check the bulletin board as he arrives for any last minute changes in activities or assignments.

What kind of assistance can a teacher count on when utilizing resource people who cannot be in the classroom on a daily basis? Certainly, a teacher aide assigned regularly to a classroom can be trained over a period of time to be effective in interaction with the children. Realistically, a teacher can expect a great deal of assistance from other kinds of resource people. The basic assumption, however, is that these resource people are committed to working with young children. If the commitment is there, then they will be willing to invest the time necessary for learning new skills and will be open to critical feedback regarding their effectiveness.

Supervising teachers can expect that, if they prepare suggestions for activities and review these suggestions at a group meeting, a resource person can come into the classroom, be handed an activity card, and follow through on that particular activity. A teacher can also expect a resource person to learn to interact appropriately with young children in many of the classroom's learning centers. For example, after a demonstration and role-playing session, a resource person should be able to tell a story effectively to a small group of children. Supervising teachers must assume responsibility for this sort of training and preparation. They should not expect a nonprofessional to assume the responsibility for presenting a learning experience requiring sophisticated knowledge of child development, but they can assume that with practical training involving demonstration and role playing, a resource person can work effectively in many teaching situations.

Another area in which resource people can provide a great deal of assistance is in the preparation of materials. Most early education programs operate with a limited amount of funds. Usually, programs cannot afford to purchase all of the commercial materials they need or want. But very often these materials can be made. Preparation time is often long and tedious, however, and resource people who can contribute their time and assume the responsibility for creating the materials make an invaluable contribution.

Very often the teacher plans a special kind of learning experience that requires a particular talent. Suppose a series of activities dealing with musical instruments is planned. What could be more appropriate than to ask members of the local high school band to come to the classroom and play their instruments for the children? If a class were studying some of the cultural traditions unique to a particular community, it would be most appropriate to ask a mother of one of the children to visit the classroom and cook special food. Capitalizing on the talents available in every community does take time and planning, but it can add immeasurably to your program.

It is not unusual to find, among a group of parents or community people, one resource person who becomes tremendously interested in the early childhood program. If a teacher is fortunate, a leader will emerge from the group who will be willing to volunteer a large amount of time to the preschool. This resource person, with training, can provide invaluable assistance. The time and talents of this person can be used to organize other volunteers and train them to work more effectively in the classroom. Teachers cannot expect this to happen in every instance, but they should be aware of and ready to respond to any adult who displays this level of commitment.

ON-THE-JOB TRAINING FOR THE TEACHER AIDE

The supervising teacher has the major responsibility for training the teacher aide. The effectiveness of this person will vary in direct relation to the amount and quality of training he or she receives from the supervising teacher. Usually, a new teacher aide comes to the classroom with very little formal training. Criteria for selecting early childhood teacher aides vary from community to community. The educational background required can range from a ninth-grade education to a high school diploma. The only criterion for selection that is consistently applied is that the person demonstrate a willingness and commitment to working with young children.

How can a supervising teacher, who is already overwhelmed with the complexity of the job, find the time to train an inexperienced teacher aide? Examining this problem realistically, it becomes evident that most of the training must occur on the job. While this requires a great deal of thought and work on the parts of both teacher and aide, much of the training is actually possible in the course of ongoing classroom routines. For example, if the teacher and aide routinely conduct weekly and daily planning sessions, a great deal of in-service training information will be naturally and informally transmitted to the aide. Jointly, they will discuss events that have occurred, the progress made by different children, the problems that have been encountered, and some possible solutions. As new kinds of learning activities are scheduled, the supervising teacher will demonstrate how to present them. Very often the teacher and aide will role play a certain kind of lesson together. This can be done in a very relaxed fashion, but at the same time a great deal of learning is taking place. During the school day, the supervising teacher can always schedule time to stand back and observe the aide interacting with different children. The practice allows the teacher to observe some of the teaching techniques and interaction strategies utilized by the aide. Constructive feedback can be offered at a later time. If this feedback is presented honestly, respectfully, and in a helpful, friendly manner, the aide should be able to benefit from it. The attitude of the supervising teacher is extremely important in creating an atmosphere of mutual trust. If expectations are positive, if the teacher truly believes that a paraprofessional can make a unique contribution, the aide will be much more likely to accept feedback as constructive and helpful. On the other hand, if the supervising teacher does not believe that a paraprofessional can function effectively, then this attitude will be clearly conveyed. Paraprofessionals are generally very sensitive about their lack of formal training, and they may feel inadequate regarding their ability to interact effectively with young children. Teachers must learn to be equally sensitive to these feelings of inadequacy and should take every opportunity to positively reinforce good teaching done by the aide. Just as the teacher plans carefully for the children, taking care to match demands of the learning experience to the child's level of functioning, so must the supervising teacher match teaching demands to the aide's level of functioning. Responsibilities should be added gradually and only as the paraprofessional demonstrates mastery of each new skill.

Later in the school year, after a positive working relationship has been established, the supervising teacher and aide can begin to examine their teaching performance in the classroom in a more critical manner. A tape recorder can be used to tape a particular session between the teacher aide and a group of children. At the end of the day, both teachers might listen to the tape and critique the interaction session. If both teachers can be open to honest feedback and criticism, then great potential for professional growth might be realized. This topic will be described in greater detail in Chapter 15. If the feedback presented by the supervising teacher is to be meaningful, it must be related to the specific kinds of responsibilities assigned to the teacher aide. For example, if the teacher aide is assuming partial responsibility for classroom management, then the teacher ought to observe and comment on specific skills related to effective management techniques. Teacher aides will be much more likely to improve their teaching behavior if they are assisted in thinking about teaching in terms of specific kinds of competencies. The supervising teacher is the person best qualified to define and operationalize desired competencies.

MAXIMIZING RESOURCES Let us review, once more, a day in the life of Jane Global and Mary Withit, our two teachers from Chapter 1. As you follow the events of the day, evaluate how effectively each of the teachers used the resources available to her. How would you rate the behavior of each?

Jane Global sat at her desk and looked around the classroom. The day had been long, discouraging, and frustrating. She remembered how exciting her teacher preparation program had been, and how much she had anticipated her first teaching job. Somehow, nothing was working out as she had imagined, and she was beginning to dread each day. As she thought back over what had happened that day she remembered the steady rain that was just beginning to slacken. The bus that picked up the children had arrived twenty minutes past schedule. The weather had been so bad that all playground activities had been canceled. Within two hours it seemed as though every child in the room was either whining, throwing equipment, or moving around aimlessly. The schedule that Jane had worked out in her head late the night before was simply inappropriate for a rainy day.

While waiting for the bus to arrive that morning, Jane had decided to reschedule the day for free-play activities, and she had placed as much equipment as possible out on the shelves. There was no time to discuss the change of plans with her teacher aide, who rode the bus with the children and arrived with them. Jane remembered that Mary and Bobby, her two most disruptive pupils, had spent most of the day fighting with other children or throwing temper tantrums. Her teacher aide had been no help whatsoever. Throughout the day she had ignored the mess that was accumulating on the floors and on the tables, and she seemed totally confused regarding her duties and responsibilities. Jane was beginning to feel that if her aide couldn't show more initiative and more concern about her job, she would simply have to ask for a replacement.

To make matters worse, one of the little girls had suddenly vomited in the middle of the classroom and the janitor, who was busy in another part of the building, could not come in to clean up the mess. All Jane had on hand were some paper napkins that were totally inadequate for the job. She sponged the child's clothes off as best she could, but the odor pervaded the classroom for the rest of the day. In the midst of all this confusion, Mrs. Rogers, Bobby's mother, arrived for a classroom visit. Jane had invited her to sit in the corner of the room and observe the children, but she noticed that after fifteen minutes Mrs. Rogers quietly stood up and left the classroom. Having parents drop by unexpectedly was really a nuisance but Jane knew that parent participation was a policy of the school and there was really nothing she could do about it.

Now, as a fitting end to the day, Jane was waiting for Mrs. Brown to arrive. Mrs. Brown had been scheduled for a parent conference that afternoon and it was obvious that she didn't care enough to take the time to come by. Jane was really beginning to wonder if teaching was what she wanted to do. The working hours had sounded great and teaching was always something you could fall back on, but she was beginning to wonder if she really wanted to spend all of that time with young children.

When Mary Withit woke up that morning and heard the rain pounding the roof she hurried to get to school early. She knew that the bad weather would probably delay the bus and that the children would arrive late. She would need all of that extra time to prepare for the day. When Mary arrived at the school, she immediately went to her desk and got a copy of the rainy-day schedule that she and her teacher aide had prepared earlier in the school year. She knew that her aide, who rode the bus with the children, would check the bulletin board when she arrived at school in order to review any last minute changes. The bad weather would give them a chance to try some new musical group games with the children, Mary thought. She and her aide had listened to records a few weeks before, and had selected two or three activities that they felt the children would particularly enjoy.

Mary's eye quickly scanned the equipment and materials in the various learning centers and she decided to make a few changes. She found some books on rain and weather and placed them in the book area. Some outdoor dress-up clothes and an umbrella had been stored in the closet; she put these in the housekeeping and role-playing areas. She checked her art supplies and added two baskets of collage materials to the shelves where they would be readily accessible to the children. Finger painting also would be a good rainy-day activity, and the children were ready to try mixing two colors. She prepared paints for the whole group.

Mary reviewed the checklist that she and her teacher aide had been keeping on each child's progress. She would divide the children into small groups, and she and her aide would each demonstrate some new uses of equipment that had not been placed in the classroom previously. Finally, she pulled out her copy of *The Three Bears.* By now the children were thoroughly familiar with the story, so that today would be a good time to try some role playing and dramatization. The children arrived twenty minutes late, and, as they were putting their coats away, Mary's aide quickly checked the posted schedule. She asked Mary a few questions about the equipment she was to demonstrate, and then helped the children assemble for a large circle meeting.

Mary told the children that since it was raining, they would change their usual routine and do some new and exciting things. She briefly outlined some of the activities that had been planned, and then she asked the children if there were any other special stories, games, or activities they would like to include during the day. After the circle meeting, the children moved into independent and small-group activities. The day moved along nicely. The children, the teacher, and the teacher aide cooperated in cleanup. The children had been taught that they were responsible for replacing equipment on the shelves after they had finished using it. Mary handled some minor spills while her aide made certain that the collage materials that had fallen on the floor were picked up and replaced in the baskets.

One unexpected disaster happened when a little girl vomited suddenly in the middle of the classroom. The janitor was busy in another part of the building, but Mary had an emergency bucket and mop in the bathroom. She quickly cleaned up the floor and then helped the little girl change into some other clothes which her mother had sent to school earlier in the year.

About 10:30, Mrs. Rogers, Bobby's mother, came into the classroom for a scheduled visit. Mary was delighted to see her, and since they had already discussed at a parent's conference some of the things that Mrs. Rogers could do in the classroom, Mary simply handed her three cards which described some of the things she could do with small groups of children. Mrs. Rogers quickly scanned the posted schedule, and moved quietly to the book area. Within five minutes a small group of children had gathered, and Mrs. Rogers was reading one of the class's favorite stories.

When the children left at the end of the day, Mary reviewed the events that had occurred. Her aide would be coming back after the children had been delivered safely home, and they would have about thirty minutes to plan for the next day. Mary felt good about how smoothly the day had gone. She was delighted at the amount of satisfaction she derived from her job as a teacher. Even when she was in college she enjoyed working with young children, and the hours of volunteer work that she had done had really paid off in terms of helping her to feel comfortable and confident in her classroom. Her teacher aide was a tremendous help and seemed to anticipate where she would most be needed. Having parents come in as volunteers was enjoyable and a lot of help.

Mary had visited each one of the parents before school started, and they had already had three parents' meetings at school in the evening. Mary had prepared a number of suggested activities for the mothers and fathers and these were easily accessible on small file cards. Having an extra adult in the classroom was always helpful for both the teacher and her aide. Mary remembered that Mrs. Brown had been scheduled for a parent conference after school. She knew that Mrs. Brown, who did not have an automobile, would not be able to make it in the bad weather, so Mary decided to stop by on her way home and reschedule the visit. Mary looked forward to the rest of the school year. Working with these children was exciting and challenging, giving Mary the opportunity to apply all that she had learned as well as forcing her to constantly acquire new skills.''

The basic staffing pattern in both of these classrooms consisted of a supervising teacher, a teacher aide, and a parent observer or volunteer. It is obvious that the available adult resources were used quite differently in each classroom. The key to maximizing the effectiveness of the available staff clearly rests with the skills of the supervising teacher. A review of the events of the day, as they occurred, reveals basic differences in how each teacher perceived her roles and responsibilities.

Making Decisions

Jane Global makes decisions by default. Instead of anticipating a possible crisis, she hopes that one will not occur. Although she knew at the beginning of the school year that on some days the weather would be inclement, she never planned a schedule for bad weather. Mary Withit, on the other hand, clearly perceives herself as the major decision maker in her classroom. As a decision maker, she reviews relevant information constantly and tries to anticipate conditions that might arise in the future. She clearly accepts responsibility for the events that occur in her classroom, and takes action as necessary, to avert unexpected crises.

Planning a Schedule

Why did Jane Global's day turn into such a disaster? As noted above, she had no contingency plan for rainy weather. Her aide was assigned to ride the bus with the children, and Jane knew that a planning session could not be scheduled for early morning. Because a contingency plan had not been developed, Jane quickly had to revise a schedule that had been prepared the night before. She did not realize that it was necessary to share this new information with her teacher aide, and instead became irritated with her aide's performance in the classroom. Mary, on the other hand, was routinely planning well in advance. She had anticipated activities that could be used in rainy weather and had reviewed these activities with her teacher aide. Even though her aide was also assigned to ride the bus with the children, she and Mary both knew that any last-minute schedule changes would be posted on the bulletin board. Careful planning paid off for Mary, her aide, and the children in the classroom. The time spent anticipating what they would do when the usual schedule could not be followed yielded positive results.

Selecting Objectives and Learning Experiences

Jane obviously had no clear idea of the kinds of learning experiences that needed to be scheduled for that particular day. She placed materials on the shelves haphazardly, never really considering what kinds of things she wanted to happen. Just as her planning had been haphazard, so was the behavior of the children. Mary and her aide, on the other hand, had been carefully monitoring the progress of the children. Both of them had filled out checklists dealing with different skill areas, and Mary was able to select special activities for the rainy day that matched the children's level of functioning. Although both Mary and her aide assumed responsibility for filling out the checklists, Mary's role required that she make the decisions that converted skill-acquisition information into specific learning experiences. She knew, for instance, that the children had sufficient experience working with finger paints of one color to experiment with mixing two colors. As the supervising teacher, she obviously was concerned with working toward some clearly specified goals. Making decisions within the framework of an instructional day was much easier for Mary than for Jane because of adequate planning and preparation.

Planning Related Activities

Jane rarely planned any related activities. Her strategy for handling the inclement weather was to place as much equipment as possible on the shelves and to schedule free-play activities for the entire day. This kind of planning ignored every principle of effective teaching that Jane had been taught. Basic principles of pacing, such as alternating active and passive activity periods, teacher-directed and child-selected learning experiences, and varying the adults who interacted with the children were not capitalized upon in any sort of manner. Mary, in contrast, placed additional collage materials on the shelves where they were readily accessible to the children. She added some rainy-day dress-up clothes to the housekeeping area and placed some books dealing with the weather in the book area. Mary was not sure how the children would use these materials, but she knew that an opportunity would probably arise during the day when spontaneous interest would be shown by some of the children. Mary's intent was to be sensitive to any display of interest, so that she could capitalize upon the "teachable moment." The contrast between the two teachers becomes evident when you review how each considered the planning of related activities. There is actually no way that Jane would have recognized a teachable moment, let alone have been sensitive enough to interact appropriately with the children. Because she functions ineffectively as a supervising teacher, the same is true of her teacher aide.

Using Parent Resources Effectively

Jane Global clearly does not see the value of bringing parents into the classroom. Again, as in so many of her other functions, Jane has neglected to plan and think through the kinds of things that she wants to happen in her classroom. Since she didn't believe that parents had anything worthwhile to contribute, she clearly transmitted this expectation to them when they were present. Mary believed that parents really could help her and her aide in the classroom. Mary and her aide both took the time to visit each of the parents and to conduct group meetings at school. Ideas for activities had been prepared in advance and were available in the card file on Mary's desk. When a parent came into Mary's classroom, it was a simple matter to hand her some of these suggestions. Advance planning enabled Mary to capitalize upon the parent's visit by using her as a teaching resource.

Effective Use of Adult Resources

At the end of the day Jane Global has very negative feelings about her experiences in the classroom. By contrasting the way she plans her use of the resources available with the strategies used by Mary, some of the conditions that account for the differences in the two teachers' effectiveness become clear. Jane has very negative expectations regarding the potential effectiveness of the adults who spend time in the classroom. She did not schedule time for planning or substitute any other means for communicating. Jane did not provide these adults with any feedback regarding the adequacy of their performance. Her major problem is that she does not clearly understand her role as a decision maker. Responsibilities extend beyond interactions with the children and include planning for, supervising, and communicating with every adult who spends time in the classroom. Mary, who fully grasps the responsibilities she must assume, capitalizes fully upon the available adult resources. She understands that a great deal of preplanning must occur if she is to be able to use the services of resource people to her best advantage. The preplanning time becomes a wise investment for both Mary and the children in the classroom. Her instructional day, in contrast to Jane's, moves smoothly and purposefully.

CONCLUSIONS

Regardless of the particular staffing pattern in any center, the key to effective use of available resources lies with the classroom teacher. The complexity of this role and the demands associated with it go far beyond interactions with the children. We have described the teacher as a decision maker and facilitator of learning. Many of the decisions to be made are most effectively addressed before school begins in the morning and/or after the children are dismissed. Teachers must learn to anticipate needs that are beginning to emerge as well as to be able to respond appropriately to unexpected events. If they have planned carefully and communicated their plans and expectations to every adult who will work in their classrooms, they will be able to respond to the children sensitively and with the degree of skill required for effective teaching.

QUESTIONS

1. Explain the cooperative, flexible arrangement that should exist between supervising teachers and teacher aides.

2. Describe the relationship that exists between the supervising teacher and the aide in the room(s) you observe. How might the talents of these teachers be distributed more efficiently?

3. In general, describe the provisions for supervisory adult resources (e.g., parents). Are they effective? What use is made of other adults? Are teachers you observe more like Ms. Withit or Ms. Global?

4. In your observation room, make a list of the rules that are in effect. How many of the rules are explicit? Implicit? Are there unnecessary rules? Is there need for additional rules?

5. Appropriate use of praise, effective punishment, and exclusion techniques are all management tools. How do the three fit together in a total management program? Role play each of the three skills in specific situations. Why is it that many teachers have trouble praising children in a normal voice?

6. What should you do if it becomes clear that you and your teaching partner have important philosophical or personal differences? Take into account the welfare of the children, the other teacher, and yourself.

7. To the extent that you are successful in training an aide or other available adult, that person can take over some of your functions. Is this good? What should *you* do if someone else becomes capable of doing what you have been doing?

8. We have discussed objectives and scheduling for the *children.* What are some important objectives for improving assistant teachers? What planned activities intended to attain these objectives should be included in daily or weekly *schedules?*

9. Role play a session between a supervising teacher and a teacher aide. Do these roles inhibit openness and communication? If so, why?

READINGS

Heffernan, H. *Guiding the young child.* Boston: Heath, 1951.

Leyser, S., Dales, R., Skipper, D., and Witherspoon, R. *Good schools for young children.* New York: Macmillan, 1968.

Litman, F. Supervision and the involvement of paraprofessionals in early childhood education. In R. Anderson and H. Shane, eds. *As the twig is bent.* Boston: Houghton Mifflin, 1971.

Prescott, E., Jones, E., and Kritchevsky, S. *Group day care as a child-rearing environment.* Pasadena, Calif.: Pacific Oaks College, 1967.

15

IN-SERVICE DEVELOPMENT

This chapter is written primarily for staff employed in existing preschool programs. It provides suggestions for designing and implementing meaningful in-service programs. The chapter should have some transfer value for the teacher in training who wants to engage in self-evaluation activities, but the primary audience is the in-service teacher.

WHY IN-SERVICE PROGRAMS?

Teaching is a difficult job that demands a variety of skills. Few teachers can perform every teaching act with excellence. Most of us have strong and weak qualities, so that good teaching is a continuous process of improving upon our weaknesses. One major way that teachers can learn new skills and improve their classroom effectiveness is to become involved in meaningful in-service activities.

Successful preschool programs are team efforts. To achieve the necessary coordination between teachers and teacher aides, between instructional activities and program goals, and so on, it is necessary to build a milieu in which all staff members can share ideas and coordinate activities. Thus, in-service programs potentially can (1) help teachers to develop instructional skills, and (2) provide the camaraderie and coordination necessary for a successful program.

The suggestions we make here are mostly straightforward common sense. Principles that apply in teacher–parent situations (e.g., be open, honest, find the parent a useful role) or even in teacher–child situations (don't provide gratuitous praise, be specific) are equally applicable in teacher–teacher or teacher–supervisor situations.

Many points stressed previously in our discussion of parent involvement will be reiterated here. Strangely, principles that are learned in one situation (individualize the curriculum) do not automatically transfer to another (individualize in-service training for teachers). This ironic situation in which people don't do for themselves what they know how to do and what they repeatedly prescribe for others (cancer researchers who smoke, behavior modifiers who are obese due to compulsive eating habits, etc.) is quite common. Teachers who can successfully help *children* to learn new principles or gain confidence are often stymied when trying to help a fellow *teacher,* even though the general principles are the same. Thus, if some of the topics in this chapter seem vaguely familiar, they are!

IN THE BEGINNING

The center director starts in-service training on the first day a teacher is hired. Stress should be placed on the fact that in-service training is an important time in which *teachers* assume responsibility for evaluating curriculum progress, sharing materials and ideas, and generally helping one another as well as the program to grow. We noted earlier that when parents are expected to play important roles and are given the opportunity to do so, they usually do. Similarly, we feel that teachers and aides who are given real responsibility are much more likely to identify with program goals and to strive to make the program work than are "employees" who simply carry out someone else's program. The program director can help by weeding out teachers who are unduly hesitant about engaging in cooperative programs of staff evaluation and planning. For their part, teachers should be leery of job situations where they are not provided ample time for planning and in-service sharing.

GOALS FOR IN-SERVICE TRAINING

The goals for in-service training vary with a number of factors: target population, program goals, composition of teaching staff, and so on. *Appropriate* goals are clearly dependent upon the local situation. For example, a staff composed of veteran teachers may be able to work on special problems at the beginning of the year, while a staff with several new teachers may need to emphasize the basics.

The guiding principle is that the goals of in-service training should be related to the real interests of the teaching staff. Too often in-service programs are based upon the availability of experts in a particular area who "do their thing" at the request of the supervisor. Experts should be brought in, but they should be scheduled to deal with real, identifiable problems rather than to fill time. Arbitrary programs are needless intrusions upon teachers' time.

If teachers do not schedule in-service activities at their center and are displeased with its programs, they should meet with the supervisor and make their needs known. Too often, in-service meetings (like parent meetings) drift along without purpose or payoff for the participants. Concrete goals and opportunities for self-satisfaction must be built in for the program to have value.

Program Goals

Clearly, some program goals can be discussed profitably in large-group staff meetings. If the program is a good one, it will have model checklists or lesson formats for teaching in each curriculum area. The techniques and goals in each curriculum area (motor, math, auditory, visual, conceptual reasoning, etc.) have identifiable characteristics that can be profitably reviewed and role played by staff members working with one another.

Review of major teaching principles is a good example of a *common staff need* that yields concrete in-service results. Teachers can discuss the principles that underlie the teaching strategies in the auditory and visual lessons, for example, and then critique video tapes of themselves or other teachers teaching such lessons, or else role play these lessons and share suggestions for improvements.

The first criterion for selecting relevant content for in-service activities, then, is that they be concentrated on those skills, behaviors, and attitudes that are logically necessary for the successful implementation of the preschool program. For instance, knowledge about the rationale for the sequence of visual lessons, ultimate student-learning goals, relationships between different curriculum areas (What has to be mastered first?) and strategies for teaching lessons would all seem to be necessary for success.

What then are the logical areas that one should master to successfully implement a preschool program? The following list includes the major factors (but not all of them):

- Rationale and techniques for presenting curriculum lessons.
- General management skills (discipline, smooth transitions).
- Setting up the classroom (physical separation of areas, appropriate display and rotation of equipment).
- Testing techniques.
- Coordination of materials, media, and lessons.
- Scheduling (the day, the week, the unit).
- Planning remedial activities.
- Coordination of parent-involvement program.
- Grouping and regrouping children appropriately.

Another way to identify topics for in-service work is through program feedback. Criterion-referenced test results may show that a teacher needs special work in a particular curriculum area. Similarly, the collective results from several classrooms may reveal common problems that can be dealt with in a group setting. Thus, two major sources can be used to identify common and potentially relevant in-service topics: (1) those activities central to the curriculum and (2) deficiencies identified by test results. Another potential criterion, teacher interest, will be discussed later.

Schedule of In-service Events

The schedule of topics in an in-service program is always affected by special circumstances (e.g., new criterion-referenced forms are being used, so that testing must be dealt with early in the year) and, as we noted previously, the experience and skill of the teaching staff.

Thus, no single schedule can serve the needs of any two preschool day-care programs. For example, a program that has several new teachers must provide them with a chance to get their classrooms going and with special time for developing management and "setting-up" skills. To overinvolve these teachers in parent work or other activities is to reduce their classroom effectiveness. If the staff is balanced between new and old teachers, it may even be desirable to run dual in-service programs early in the year.

Clearly, it is impossible to sketch out *the* schedule, but it is possible to advance a few guidelines.

1. Early in the year, even veteran teachers will benefit from a review of management, room-equipment set up, and criteria for grouping children. Discussion of anticipating and dealing with first-day and first-week problems will be especially useful.
2. Teachers and aides need time to draw up concrete plans for the first units and to coordinate their activities. Typically, most time in the first few weeks needs to be devoted to these two areas.
3. Early in the year, teachers need to exert much effort in *parent involvement* activities. Clearly, there will be some contact with parents while teachers are working on their rooms and coordinating activities with fellow teachers, but much of the early work will be done by the parent-involvement staff. Once the program is underway, however, teachers can devote more time to this activity. Similarly, after the year begins, teachers can spend more time in studying appropriate *test-administration techniques* and exchanging information about using criterion-referenced test results. Teachers can begin to review the various *model activities* in the program, to develop further their teaching skills in each area, and to begin special *study groups* and *individual self-evaluation* activities.
4. Roughly one-third of the way through the year, teachers can begin to devote serious attention to analyzing criterion-referenced test results and noting their implications for *remedial teaching* and for *regrouping* children. Of course, these activities must necessarily begin early and continue throughout the year, but at some point (after the completion of a few units), a systematic effort should be made to improve understanding and utilization of test results. Again, we emphasize the arbitrary nature of this list. For example, if the program had many new teachers, it probably

would be useful to conduct extended work in interpretation and use of test results prior to initiating systematic study of the model lessons.

5. Toward midyear, it would be useful to explore additional ways in which parent resources might be utilized in the preschool program. By this point, much more time can be devoted to study-improvement group activities.

6. After midyear (and especially following a long vacation period such as Christmas), it is useful to *review management and transition principles,* as midyear "regressions" are apt to occur even in good centers. This is also a good time to review opportunities for adding *variety* in the classroom and for using ideas initiated by the children. Such "pre-spring-cleaning" activities can do much to boost child and staff morale.

7. After dealing with post-midyear problems, it is useful to assess staff interest for the remainder of the year. If things are moving effectively, then staff interest should be the biggest factor in designing work programs.

8. Two-thirds of the way through the year is another good time to look at testing and to consider regrouping the children. This will help teachers avoid forming rigid stereotypes of children and also will help strengthen the notion that children should be regrouped as their abilities change. Study groups working on other topics can, of course, continue.

9. Late in the year an evaluation-planning session should be conducted wherein teachers receive group-program results (70 percent of the 4-year-olds successfully completed all auditory units) and where program problems are dealt with and goals are set for the subsequent year. Evaluation of the in-service program itself is also appropriate.

The above tentative suggestions need to be blended into local needs. Only a creative, responsive staff that is working together can intelligently decide when such topics need to be discussed together as a staff, in small groups, or between individuals. There is no single, best format; the best format for a particular program can only be discovered through the *formal and informal exchange of ideas.* Conditions that allow for this kind of interaction among staff members must be established early and maintained throughout the year.

INDIVIDUALIZATION: IDENTIFYING INTERESTS

Just as there are *program* topics and needs, there are also *teacher* needs and interests. Some teachers may be especially interested in making or obtaining more physical equipment, other teachers may be interested in finding appropriate ways to use puppets in instructional activities, and so forth. The only thing that makes one goal more important than another is interest. If in-service time is to be satisfying, time for individual interests must be found.

Finding a Role

If teachers are to be involved in directing and becoming responsible for their own self-development, they must be given a real role and must be needed. Teachers regularly should be put in charge of particular programs, such as leading discussions or preparing demonstrations. They must be active and responsible participants. For example, teachers may become "local experts" in searching for and presenting information on classroom equipment or some other special topic. All teachers should be co-participants with the director in designing how in-service time will be spent.

Meetings need structure if in-service activity is to be a good experience. Simple things such as scheduling the meeting at the same time each week so that teachers habitually plan for it are important. Meetings should start and end on time. Meetings that fail to begin promptly irritate people who take care to arrive on time. And, once off to a bad start, regularly occurring meetings have a tendency to start later and later each week as people learn that there is no reason to be on time (and indeed that it is unpleasant to be on time and have to wait). Meetings that go beyond the scheduled time may be even more destructive to group morale than meetings that start late. The problem here is that people have commitments (need to pick up their children, for example), and that time beyond the scheduled dismissal is likely to be "psychologically absent" time. People begin to think about their needs and do not follow the substantive discussion ("If this goes ten more minutes, I'm going to leave"; "I'll try to catch Wanda's eye and see if she is going to leave"). Further, at the next meeting, personal thoughts and irritations begin to build up much earlier ("Could this meeting last as long as the last one?"), so that even more time is lost.

Conducting In-service Meetings

In addition to the simple, structural meeting properties described above (have a regular time and place, start and end on schedule), people need psychological structure. What will happen at the meeting? What is scheduled? What type of advance preparation is necessary? Just as these proactive skills are important in teaching, they are also important in conducting in-service meetings. Teachers who plan their own in-service programs are simultaneously developing their own psychological structures.

Previously, we have called for proactive skills that identify program needs and teacher needs and blend these into an appropriate sequence. Beyond this, for a specific meeting we would suggest that concrete goals be established. For example, a teacher or the in-service director should announce the specific purpose of the next meeting (e.g., review motor lessons) at the end of the scheduled activity.

The format of the meeting (e.g., discussion/demonstration) and the preparation necessary for the next meeting should be specified (e.g., read pages 21–35 in the curriculum manual, watch tape number 2, and identify better ways to conclude the lesson; be prepared to illustrate your ending).

Without specific orientations and concrete demands, it is difficult to come to a meeting in the appropriate frame of mind. However, if the goals are clear and you have already attempted to construct an answer to the problem, it is much easier to enjoy the meeting and to share and learn with others.

Leading the discussion or demonstration is simple if the appropriate spade work has been done. With veteran teachers, the in-service leader can immediately call on a teacher and get started. However, if a number of new teachers are present, it may be desirable to make a few comments about the importance of providing honest and open feedback (more on this later) and then model this by obtaining corrective feedback from the staff. If a discussion is scheduled, the staff leader might provide an answer to the first assigned discussion and then call on a veteran teacher ("Mary, what important points did I miss?"). The idea is for the discussion/demonstration leader to *model* interest in learning and/or sharing. Such behavior at the first meeting is important in determining whether the staff learns to share or to avoid each other's problems and attitudes about the program. Behavior, not words, makes the difference.

In addition to the prediscussion structure and an open and honest chance to share ideas, a definite closure to the meeting is necessary if people are to continue working. If new policies are agreed upon, specific implementation plans need to be worked out. Closure can be communicated directly to the staff by memo ("As we decided at the last meeting . . .") or at the next in-service meeting ("Today the format is changed because of the decision we made last week"). *Implementation* of discussion "products" is the most important proof for the participant that his time and involvement were worthwhile.

Observational Feedback

A special type of in-service training comes in the opportunity to observe, to be observed, and to share developmental information. In-service coordinators can do much to improve the quality of teaching in the program by regular visits to classrooms and detailed feedback to teachers. The idea is to create a learning attitude, where teachers are interested in developing more effective techniques and in helping others grow. Too often, teachers view visits from the coordinator or fellow teachers as a test, and tend to see only the possible negative consequences of such participation by "outsiders" in their classrooms.

The job of the staff in-service director is to create a climate that maximizes the positive effects of feedback and minimizes negative consequences. Teachers need to accept the fact that they do make mistakes, but that the only real mistake is to leave error undetected and uncorrected. Systematic feedback can improve performance. But just as teachers are sometimes hesitant to label children's errors as mistakes, so too are some teachers hesitant to point out to fellow teachers their errors and ways to improve.

The program director can do much to increase teacher willingness to benefit from in-service feedback. Teachers benefit from feedback when (1) their strengths are acknowledged, and (2) specific criticisms are made with accompanying suggestions for change. Supervisors who provide this type of information to teachers will play a valuable role in helping teachers to *listen* and develop new skills.

Some common sense rules should be observed in providing feedback:

1. Be positive but honest. Try to emphasize good teacher behavior as well as average or problem behavior.
2. Provide only specific *developmental* criticism. (Developmental criticism is feedback that describes what the teacher did and that advances *alternative ways* in which the teacher might have behaved. Detrimental feedback focuses upon *evaluation* rather than description and alternatives.)
3. The major condition present in developmental feedback is that it contain suggestions for improvement ("Read pages 16–37," "Watch the tape of Mrs. Wilson teaching," "I'll come in tomorrow and model this lesson," etc.). If simple information is to be conveyed, teachers can be *told* directly ("You'd reduce some of your management problems by sitting so that you can see most of the children in the room while you work with a small group," "Get more individual responses to questions and fewer group-chorus responses"). More complex teaching skills are probably better *modeled.*
4. Allow teachers to become increasingly self-sufficient and responsible for their own improvement. Teachers should be involved in charting their own in-service remedial activities. For example, "We talked about your problem with transitions, and you can read the principles in the staff manual, but you would also benefit from seeing these principles being implemented. Would you prefer to watch video demonstrations, visit another teacher, or have me demonstrate them with your class? . . . I'll be interested in seeing your improvement. Contact me when you want me to visit next week."
5. Don't overwhelm the teacher with several criticisms, especially if the criticisms involve several different aspects of teaching. Too much criticism lowers morale and immobilizes people: They simply do not know where to begin. It is better to focus improvement discussions on the one or two most important weaknesses that teachers exhibit, and then help them develop a specific remediation plan. Guided criticism helps teachers mobilize their efforts and improve. Too much criticism is debilitating.
6. Whenever developmental criticism and a program of action have been developed for the teacher, it is imperative that the supervisor return (hopefully in response to a teacher-initiated request) and provide subsequent feedback. The rules here are still the same: Look for areas of improvement, be positive but honest, provide specific criticisms and specific recommendations. Teachers need and want to know the degree of progress

they have achieved. When an observer notices progress on dimensions that were discussed previously (even if they are not the subject of the present conference), such progress deserves comment. We all want to know when we have overcome deficiencies or obstacles, and regular "progress" feedback will help supervisors to create the role of being a helpful advisor rather than a carping critic.

7. Opportunity for teacher self-evaluation should be built into the program. Progressively, teachers should be requested to evaluate their own teaching ("What was your general evaluation of the lesson? How might it be improved?"). Also, the supervisor should attempt to progressively become more of a facilitator rather than an initiator of the teachers' in-service requests.

8. For example, teachers can be encouraged to study and to code the teaching behaviors of model video lessons (more and more centers are purchasing video equipment and hence have the opportunity to purchase or make model lessons as well as to tape live teacher behavior in the center). Teachers should have the opportunity to visit one another's classrooms periodically for the dual purposes of providing feedback and learning new techniques. Teachers might meet regularly in self-selected study groups to observe one another's tapes and to provide feedback. The desirable sequence and format of these activities will naturally vary from site to site. However, a good in-service program will provide opportunities for watching video lessons, observing fellow teachers, and self-study.

Self- and Group Study

Most of the above points were written in the context of a teacher or director providing feedback to another teacher on a one-to-one basis. However, the same general points operate whether one is engaging in self-study or group study. Individuals engaging in self-study should: focus attention on a small manageable area, such as handling transitions (you can't change everything at once, and an attempt to do so is self-defeating); make an assessment of their skills in the area (if okay, move to another area); develop specific plans for correcting the problem; and develop a system for obtaining developmental feedback (save the present tape and replay it with a new tape in two weeks, etc.).

Group self-study teams should serve the interests of the *individual participants* and endeavor to provide them with the feedback that *they* want. The teacher whose tape is being viewed should provide the focus for the group by describing the type of feedback that is especially relevant. Some teachers may be concerned about questioning or pacing skills, whereas other teachers are concerned about how they begin and end lessons. Group resources can be directed toward meeting individual goals. That individuals obtain satisfaction is especially important early in the year when teachers in the group are still entertaining such thoughts as "Do I really want to expose myself to a group?" Progressively, teachers may encourage the group to criticize or comment upon anything that occurs in the teaching segment. However, when group meetings are "getting off the ground," it is best to limit the focus of feedback to assure that criticism will not be overwhelming.

Another good operating rule is to let the "taped" teacher react to the tape first, providing a personal evaluation and explaining any special circumstances that were operating that day. Group members then should attempt to find the good things that occurred as well as the things that could be changed, and should make specific recommendations for bringing about suggested changes. Role playing alternative techniques is desirable, when it is appropriate and when time allows. Clearly, the group should provide information to the teacher about how well she did in particular areas of concern, but more importantly, the group should operate as a mechanism for suggesting desirable teaching and program changes.

Study groups are useful, then, in that they can help teachers become more aware of what they do and how they affect children. Furthermore, study groups help provide the emotional support for looking objectively at one's own behavior and attempting to change. Thus, self-study groups are viable in-service alternatives for relatively mature teachers who want to learn with others. Certain teachers may benefit initially from extended self-study and one-to-one work with the director or a respected veteran teacher. However, most teachers who remain in a program for consecutive years should be able to move into at least a small study group.

Once functioning, study groups do not demand the regular attendance of the in-service director. This savings in time can be used to work with teachers who have special problems or who prefer not to work in study groups. Study groups, like any part of the in-service program, need to be regularly evaluated.

**TEACHER-DIRECTED
IN-SERVICE WORK**

To this point, we have written with the assumption that the program has a director or coordinator who has formal responsibility for establishing a climate and procedures for facilitating staff development. The time a director can devote to in-service work varies widely from program to program. Often a director has so many responsibilities (or does not realize the importance of in-service work) that little time is spent in creating and maintaining in-service programs.

Indeed, many programs have no provision for supervisory in-service training whatsoever. This is unfortunate, because we feel that efforts to aid the professional development of all staff (teachers, aides, cooks, etc.) will contribute ultimately to better programs for young children. Unless program monies are unduly restricted for legitimate reasons, it seems reasonable to expect programs to invest at least a small portion of the budget in further developing human resources.

Ideally, every program would free some time for a teacher or director so that a staff member would have time to provide leadership for the in-service program. However, at some centers we realize it will be impossible to provide money for in-service training. Even then, it is possible to build meaningful and systematic in-service programs.

As noted earlier, the principal task of in-service coordination is to establish a climate for sharing and learning together and to allow teachers to assume control of their own professional development. Teachers who are willing to cooperatively develop their own training program can proceed, independent of any outside help, along the lines suggested earlier in the chapter.

Indeed, there has been nothing mentioned in this chapter that couldn't be accomplished by an enthusiastic group of teachers. Wherever the word director appeared in the text, we could have substituted *lead teacher.* Teachers rotating the role of lead teacher or *in-service planner* guarantee that no teacher would be overburdened continually with in-service details. Teachers who elect to initiate, plan, and conduct their own in-service programs will reap the same benefits as they would under the director-led program.

Getting Started

Teachers interested in creating an in-service program should discuss their idea with the local director in order to invoke the director's participation and to explain why they want to hold regular in-service meetings. Such a meeting might even get the director involved! If not, at least teachers would gain permission to hold periodic group meetings, invite community resource persons to meetings, leave their own room to observe other teachers, and, perhaps, to obtain some monies for the purchase or rental of video or audio recorders.

If approached by teachers in a straightforward fashion, most directors would make every effort to support teachers' efforts. After obtaining the director's permission, the teachers initiating the action could then circulate a brief letter explaining interest in creating an ongoing in-service program and acknowledging the director's support. The purpose of the first meeting would be to assess interest and to forge a framework out of which the in-service program would eventually evolve. Relevant framework "areas" to explore might include: (1) How often do we want to meet? (2) Initially, do we want to observe live situations or teach only simulated lessons? (3) What types of lessons do we want to see demonstrated? (4) Who will organize the first meetings?

These questions are not meant to be *the* agenda but are merely the kinds of questions that interested teachers might ask themselves. Prior to such a meeting, it would be useful to make copies of the first part of this chapter or some other materials on in-service training so that teachers could begin to "try out" in-service ideas and see if they really want to make a commitment to group-help activities.

The ultimate in-service plan would depend upon the needs and interests of the teachers at a particular center. The goal is to build a program that helps teachers to grow in skill areas where they want to improve. Again, it is worth noting that disinterested teachers should be able to decline in-service involvement without undue or critical comment. A cooperative in-service program that is vital and useful can only be built around a core of teachers who want to improve and who want to help others grow. To the extent that in-service programs are dull and unproductive, it is typically because they involve people who are disinterested or because the program content is irrelevant to the participants.

Obviously, it should be easy for teachers to join an in-service group when they are ready to do so. If teachers are enjoying and learning in in-service sessions, the word will spread and other teachers will want to be part of a good thing. Eventually, in-service participants can invite (in a low-key fashion) other teachers to join group activities. Initially, though, it is best to allow people who have strong reservations to stay away and concentrate on building a satisfying program with willing participants.

We have stressed the need for in-service training and "shared" teacher activities because of our belief that a group structure can evolve into a system that supports an individual's effort to explore new ideas, attempts to try different teaching strategies, and so on. An isolated teacher who tries to become a more effective teacher does not benefit from the stream of ideas and encouragement that groups can provide. Group support (e.g., Weight Watchers) can be a powerful aid in helping an individual to change his behavior. At the risk of distorting the memory of Will Rogers, we can summarize by sincerely saying that we have never met a teacher we could not learn from nor a teacher who could not learn from us. Potentially we can learn from fellow teachers if they and we are motivated to exchange ideas.

Other Ways of Getting Help

However, this is not to reify the concept of group in-service training. As noted previously, groups formed by uncommitted teachers will operate in stultifying ways. Thus, if it is impossible to attract several teachers at a center, or if the group fails to help you, there is no reason to remain in it. The only reason to stay in a teacher-directed group or program is that it facilitates learning. Still, the teacher who wants to develop his talents would do well to find one or two other teachers who have similar interests and at least periodically observe one another. Such "paired" observation is the only real alternative for a teacher at a small center, unless such teachers are willing to seek out teachers in other centers (and this is often impossible due to scheduling or transportation problems).

The chief advantage of being observed is to become more aware of our classroom behavior and its effects on children. There is evidence to show that when teachers are busily engaged in the teaching role of responding and running the class, they are unaware of much that occurs in the class-room . . . even their *own* behavior (Good & Brophy, 1973).

The teacher and teacher aide can provide each other with some useful feedback. This is especially true if the classroom is structured so that the teacher (or aide) occasionally has no responsibility for a half hour or so and can function as an observer rather than as an actor. Such free time from responding to program demands could also be used to have *sustained* dialogue (five to ten minutes) with one or two children. Such procedures help the teacher to break the class down into smaller units and observe more intensely than is usually possible. For example, sustained contact may help teachers to see individual children more fully and react to them and their unique developmental levels rather than to some stereotype or group norm.

Although attempts to see the classroom from the viewpoint of an observer will help to some extent, teachers and aides will be blind to many events because they have built up expectations about children and ideas about how particular lessons should be taught. Stress has been placed upon bringing other teachers into the room because they may not hold the same assumptions, commitments, beliefs about particular children, and so on, and hence many see things that would go unnoticed by the participant teacher and aide. Obviously, visiting teachers also gain by expanding their repertoire of teaching skills.

Child Test Performance

The chief source of feedback to the teacher not participating in "shared" teacher activities is child performance on criterion-referenced tests (see Chapter 10). Low performance, particularly consistently low performance, is a signal that something is wrong. Unfortunately, the test score itself does not always *specifically* suggest what the teacher should do. Low scores only note that the child has not learned the material.

Again, the potential value of group in-service work is that a rich pool of information is available to the teacher (e.g., several strategies for teaching a particular concept). However, teachers working alone can use test performance to cue attention more closely to particular aspects of their behavior. Generally low scores in a particular curriculum area would suggest the need to tape-record lessons in that area and analyze them—identify weaknesses, seek new techniques, review general goals for that area, and so forth. Low scores from the same two or three children would signal the need to have sustained contacts with them and to generally be sensitive to the ways that you interact with those children.

EVALUATION

In-service meetings, like any other aspect of the curriculum, need to be evaluated. The evaluation can take many forms. For example, with new teachers it is desirable to periodically collect anonymous feedback. Written responses can be collected from teachers in a variety of ways. For example, teachers may be asked to respond anonymously and in their own fashion to such questions as: Has time spent in in-service activity been useful to you? What topics have been most helpful? What suggestions do you have for improving the format? Are there topics or special problems you would like to discuss?

Responses to such questions are useful in providing a general global reaction to the quality of the program and for sounding out topics or issues that would not have occurred to the person who prepared the inventory. For example, some of the teachers (after Christmas vacation) may express the need for reviewing management skills and ideas for regaining the pre-vacation smooth-flowing classroom. Thus, in addition to getting a general reaction to the program, "free" teacher responses may yield ideas not contained in the questionnaire.

The disadvantage of open-ended questions is that they usually fail to yield specific, clear-cut recommendations in and of themselves. Therefore, if decision-making information is to be collected, it is best to phrase specific questions:

How helpful was the demonstration that was held last week on the visual lesson?
____very valuable __ some value ____undecided
____little value ____waste of time

How helpful was the discussion that followed?
____very valuable ____some value ____undecided
____little value ____waste of time

How valuable was the feedback you received in the small-group session following your presentation of the model lesson?
____very valuable ____some value ____undecided
____little value ____waste of time

What three changes would you suggest in order to make in-service model-lesson programs more meaningful to you?

1.

2.

3.

Should we continue with more model-lesson demonstrations? (specify why not below.)

_____yes _____only if the following changes are made _____no

1.

2.

3.

Specific and open-ended questions can be combined in collecting relevant information. Consider the following example: "Examine the list below that contains the topic and format for the next six in-service meetings. For each topic, mark the anticipated value of the meeting for yourself. After rating each topic, respond to the following questions: Should any of these topics be deleted? Should the order be rearranged? Are there other topics that should be discussed?"

The type of question asked depends to some extent upon the cohesiveness of the staff. For a new program or a program that has experienced a number of staff turnovers, it may be best to ask broad questions in order to survey general interests and attitudes first, saving specific follow-up questions until later (e.g., if role playing rather than tape demonstrations is reported to be a more valuable learning experience, then questions can be raised that pinpoint the reasons for the global preferences and dislikes).

Relatively cohesive staffs typically would be assessed best by specific questions, since the in-service coordinator has a good understanding of general staff feelings and attitudes. Here the need is for decision-making information (Would you prefer to firm up parent-involvement activities before we start working out difficulties with auditory lessons?). The need for frequent formal (written) evaluation of in-service training should dissipate as a group of teachers work together for a longer period of time. Just as teachers openly provide suggestions for improving observed teacher behavior, so too should they be able to provide director feedback about in-service activities.

Feedback is the key if teachers are to continue to provide honest, detailed reactions. Feedback from the director is especially critical when teachers provide their evaluations in written form. Participant (live and direct) evaluation provides its own form of feedback, but it is easy for teachers to underestimate the value of their feedback, especially when they do not see program changes despite their suggestions and criticisms. Supervisors should regularly provide group statistics describing the results of teacher evaluations of in-service programs (67 percent voiced strong approval for more live demonstration, 33 percent voiced strong approval for less live demonstration). Such information allows teachers to see that their opinions are taken seriously and in some instances shows that opinion is balanced and, hence, does not lead to major program changes. However, this information may be used at some point in the future to make in-service activities more meaningful. If teachers are opting for more taped lessons for positive reasons (they can see several examples in a brief period of time, they want to discuss the rationale, etc.) rather than for negative reasons (afraid to perform, have skill deficiencies, etc.), they can be placed into different format groups. But teacher needs and interests change just as do the needs of children. In-service groups should not become permanent and should be rotated as the teachers' needs change or as program needs dictate (to prevent cliques, to assure wider teacher–teacher contacts, etc.).

EVALUATION: GENERAL COMMENTS

The comments suggested above apply to all areas of the preschool program. Whether we are evaluating the arrangement of the playground equipment, parent involvement, or curriculum materials, the first step is to state in specific terms what we want to happen (e.g., at least 70 percent of the parents involved in some type of program activity; 50 percent of the parents will voluntarily serve in a direct instructional role, etc.), and then to design a procedure for collecting information that specifically measures progress toward the goals we have established. Let's take an example and see how the process works.

How can the outdoor curriculum be evaluated? Again, the first task is to *identify goals* (large-muscle development, development of social skills such as equipment and yard arrangement that calls for group play and imagination, etc.), and to then develop a procedure to collect evaluative information. Established goals indicate the type of process information that should be collected. The goals (or at least the emphasis) of outdoor curricula will vary from center to center. Here our purpose is not to dictate goals, but to suggest that useful evaluation depends upon clear goal statements.

Collection of specific observational data could provide information necessary for describing how present playground activities mesh with program goals. Simple records collected for a week or so can provide rich decision-making information. Simple frequency measures might include: How often is each playground area and each piece of equipment used? What type (sex, age) of child uses the various pieces of equipment? What percent of the time are specific children engaged in solitary, group, aimless, or "conflict" activity?

For illustrative purposes, let's describe a few results that might emerge and briefly explore the implications of these findings for the outdoor curriculum. If we find that many children are engaged in aimless or conflict activity for an unacceptably high percentage of time, then *general* changes in playground equipment and/or arrangement would seem appropriate. Perhaps too much equipment in too little space? Not enough or the right kind of equipment (equipment areas going unused)? Too many children on the playground at one time? Too little planning and/or adult coordination?

In this example, the data tell us that one program goal is not being met. Some of the questions raised above probably could be answered by the collected data. However, it should be stressed that, normally, evaluation data do not tell us what to do—only that something needs to be done (if the results are negative). After changing the program, it is *necessary* to collect information to determine if a more desirable form of outdoor involvement *has been achieved.*

Equipment that is seldom used should be carefully evaluated. Should you demonstrate some of the various ways in which it could be used? Should it be rotated? Careful records should be kept to see if usage improves when such changes are made. If nothing seems to help, perhaps the equipment is inappropriate and should be discarded. Equipment that is very popular might call for the purchase of identical or similar items if such usage appears appropriate.

Areas that are congested also call for scrutiny. If the pattern of activity is fun and children are *involved* (exercising, etc.), then high-density areas may be okay. However, if areas that attract large numbers of children are associated with high-aimless and/or conflict scores, then such patterns must be investigated and changed (e.g., are popular areas dominated by 5-year-old participants surrounded by several 3-year-old observers?).

The balance of group- to solitary-play usage may yield useful information. Assume that such a balance is three to one. Clearly, the desirability of this ratio varies with program type, time of the year, and so forth. However, if the balance is supposed to be five to one or two to one, then such results would call for adjustment in the curriculum and subsequent data collection. Of interest, too, would be information about where solitary and group play are most likely to occur. If more solitary-play area is needed, then some of the areas showing the least profitable group play could be abandoned to provide more area for individual-skill development. Such manipulations are of course more easily accommodated if schools buy versatile equipment that can be used for individual or group activity than if most equipment has a "fixed" purpose (e.g., swings).

If but a few children fail to use the outdoor area successfully, selective changes (rather than general changes) are suggested. Children who are disengaged and aimless on the playground will merit careful observation and appropriate treatment. Children who engage exclusively in individual-outdoor play may or may not benefit from new opportunities. If such children voluntarily play with other children indoors, there may be no problem; however, when children's individual indoor style is matched by unproductive solitary-outdoor play, staff efforts to encourage group play are in order. Although the possible unproductive aspects of solitary play were discussed in their research, Moore, Evertson, & Brophy (1974) reported that a preference for solitary play is not necessarily maladaptive.

Above we have illustrated the two keys to evaluation: (1) define your goals, and (2) collect data relevant to these goals. The same two principles apply in every area of program evaluation. For example, we have pointed out repeatedly in this chapter the advantages of observing other teachers and being observed by fellow teachers. Such observation provides a basis for learning about what we actually do (Where are we?), and such knowledge is a prerequisite for sensible change. However, without goals or points to look for, it is very difficult to observe profitably.

To observe profitably, it will be necessary for teachers in a program to develop checklists of teacher and child behaviors that are central to their particular goals and/or teaching philosophies. Records of specific behaviors will describe regular classroom behavior and provide *clues* about what to change if criterion-testing results are poor for the class or individual students. Process-evaluation data do not provide simple prescriptive information, but they do tell what present practice is and afford a profile from which reasonable hypotheses may be formed.

Stress is placed upon the fact that checklists need to be developed for the *local* program. There is an understandable but unreasonable tendency for preschool programs to look at *outside* experts to tell them how they should teach. This is impractical for several reasons:

1. "Good" teaching varies with the characteristics of individual children.
2. Different goals demand different milieus.
3. The same effect (on students) can probably be achieved by several different types of teacher behaviors, so that successful teaching is in part a function of the teacher's own style.
4. It is impossible to specify process teacher behaviors that invariably relate to child gains.
5. Scales developed by others are often too general to be of use in a particular program.

Teachers need to *define* their teaching goals and then develop scales to measure their behaviors. Teachers who construct scales are better able to understand that information collected by such scales is valuable, not in and of itself, but only in combination with product information describing child progress. Teachers who use the observation scales developed by "experts" sometimes develop the implicit but erroneous assumption that if they perform behaviors on the scale they are doing good teaching.

This assumption is invalid. Good teaching occurs when children make satisfactory progress on important program goals. Process information is useful to describe how present practice matches with general teaching intent and to make planned changes in classroom behavior.

A variety of coding schedules are available for use to collect data to describe teacher–child classroom interaction. Several sources of observational examples are provided in the suggested reading list that appears at the end of the chapter. Some of these describe data collection results and/or systems for preschool children; other articles focus on older children but provide valuable tips to observe when collecting interaction data. However, *all* of the materials that are listed would most likely have to be *modified* before they could be used to best advantage in a particular program. The purpose of these materials is to provide the reader with a variety of examples to illustrate *how* to code various behaviors; *what* to code should be dictated by local program goals and local conditions.

Each area of evaluation within a preschool program will have its unique problems, but the principles are the same in each area. *Define* what you want to accomplish and design *specific* measures to provide *information* about those goals. If these principles are adhered to, useful information will be collected. Clearly, a very important part of in-service training is for the staff to gain a firm but mutual understanding of program goals. If this understanding does not exist, in-service work is likely to be fragmented and pointless.

SUMMARY

We have suggested that a successful in-service program has to be built with local needs in mind. Different programs have different in-service needs. In particular, in-service programs must be matched with specific program demands (logical needs and weaknesses identified by testing) and the individual needs and interests of teachers and teacher aides. Staffs that are mature enough to discuss problems openly and to provide helpful feedback to one another are establishing the conditions necessary for high staff morale and a productive learning center. Above all, teachers must insist that an in-service program be responsive to their (and the children's) real needs. Regular feedback and evaluation of in-service activities will do much to guarantee that in-service activities are responsive to teachers' needs.

QUESTIONS

1. Explain why self-evaluation is a critical dimension in changing teacher behavior. Given our stress on teachers' lack of awareness, why do we encourage self-exploration?

2. Watch films of teaching behavior and identify specific weaknesses and strengths. How would you give feedback to a fellow teacher? If you were the director? Should there be any differences? What are the principles for providing helpful feedback?

3. Review the various tasks and teaching skills that have been mentioned in the previous fourteen chapters (preventing managerial problems, dealing with overly active children, diagnosing error sets, daily planning, etc.), and draw up a list containing the twenty most important skills that were mentioned. Compare your lists with those prepared by classmates. Discuss the differences. List the three general areas and three specific skills within these areas that you most have interest in knowing more about. Compare your priorities with those of other students. To what extent could the collective interests of the entire class be served by one in-service course or theme?

4. From the list, select *your* three weakest areas. How do you know that these are your weaknesses? Write out a specific plan for improving your skills. How will you assess your progress?

5. Right now you are probably very self-conscious regarding your teaching behavior. However, five years from now you may have formed a large repertoire of teaching habits (including some bad ones) without awareness. What steps can you take to avoid this by remaining alert and aware of your own behavior? What steps could you take to check to see if you are doing things unconsciously?

READINGS

Coller, A. *Systems for the observation of classroom behavior in early childhood education.* Champaign, Ill.: ERIC Clearinghouse on Early Childhood Education, 1972 (1300–28).

Flanders, N. *Analyzing teacher behavior.* Reading, Mass.: Addison-Wesley, 1970.

Gage, N., ed. *Handbook of research on teaching.* Chicago: Rand McNally, 1963.

Goldhammer, R. *Clincal supervision.* New York: Holt, Rinehart & Winston, 1969.

Good, T. ed. *Trends in classroom observation.* New York: APS Publications, 1975.

Good, T. and Brophy, J. *Looking in classrooms.* New York: Harper & Row, 1973.

Jackson, P. *Life in classrooms.* New York: Holt Rinehart & Winston, 1968.

Ober, R., Bentley, E., and Miller, E. *Systematic observation of teaching: an instructional approach.* Englewood Cliffs, N.J.: Prentice-Hall, 1973.

Simon, A. and Boyer, E., eds. *Mirrors for behavior: an anthology of observation instruments continued, 1970 supplement,* Vols. A and B. Philadelphia: Research for Better Schools, 1970.

Travers, R., ed. *Second handbook of research on teaching.* Chicago: Rand McNally, 1973.

BIBLIOGRAPHY

Aiken, L. "Attitudes toward mathematics." *Review of Educational Research, 40* (1970), 551–596.

Ainsworth, M. "Object relations, dependency, and attachment: a theoretical review of the infant–mother relationship." *Child Development, 40* (1969), 969–1025.

Ainsworth, M. and Salter, D. "The development of infant–mother interaction among the Ganda." In B. Foss, ed. *Determinants of infant behavior,* vol. 2. New York: Wiley, 1963.

Anglin, J. ed. *Beyond the information given.* New York: Norton, 1973.

Bandura, A. *Principles of behavior modification.* New York: Holt, Rinehart & Winston, 1969.

————. "Social-learning theory of identificatory processes." In D. Goslin, ed. *Handbook of socialization theory and research.* Chicago: Rand McNally, 1969.

Bandura, A. and Mischel, W. "Modification of self-imposed delay of reward through exposure to live and symbolic models." *Journal of Personality and Social Psychology, 2* (1965), 698–705.

Bandura, A. and Walters, R. *Social learning and personality development.* New York: Holt, Rinehart & Winston, 1963.

Baumrind, D. "Child-care practices anteceding three patterns of preschool behavior," *Genetic Psychology Monographs, 75* (1967), 43–88.

————. "Current patterns of parental authority." *Developmental Psychology Monographs, 4,* 1 (1971), Part 2.

Bayley, N. "Development of mental abilities." In P. Mussen, ed. *Carmichael's Manual of Child Psychology,* 3rd ed. vol. 1. New York: Wiley, 1970.

Bayley, N. and Schaefer, E. "Relationships between socioeconomic variables and the behavior of mothers toward young children." *Journal of Genetic Psychology, 96* (1960), 61–77.

Beilin, H. "The status and future of preschool compensatory education." In J. Stanley, ed. *Preschool programs for the disadvantaged: five experimental approaches to early childhood education.* Baltimore: Johns Hopkins Press, 1972.

Belgau, F. *A motor perceptual developmental handbook of activities for schools, parents, and preschool programs.* La Porte, Texas: Perception Development Research Associates, 1967.

Beller, E. "Impact of early education on disadvantaged children." In S. Ryan, ed. *A report on longitudinal evaluation of preschool programs.* Washington, D.C.: Department of Health, Education and Welfare, Office of Child Development, 1972.

————. "Research on organized programs of early education." In R. Travers, ed. *Second handbook of research on teaching.* Chicago: Rand McNally, 1973.

————. "The evaluation of effects of early educational intervention in intellectual and social development of lower-class disadvantaged children." In E. Grotberg, ed. *Critical issues in research related to disadvantaged children.* Princeton, N.J.: Educational Testing Service, 1969.

Beller, E., Zimmie, J., and Aiken, L. "Levels of play in different nursery settings." Paper presented at the annual meeting of the International Congress for Applied Psychology, 1971.

Bereiter, C. and Engelmann, S. *Teaching disadvantaged children in the preschool.* Englewood Cliffs, N.J.: Prentice-Hall, 1966.

Bernstein, B. "Social structure, language, and learning." *Educational Research, 3* (1961), 163–194.

————. "Some sociological determinants of perception." *British Journal of Sociology, 9* (1958), 159–174.

Bessell, H. and Palomares, U. *Methods in human development.* San Diego: Human Development Training Institute, 1967.

Bilingual early childhood program. Austin, Texas: National Educational Laboratory Publishers, 1974.

Bilingual kindergarten program. Austin, Texas: National Educational Laboratory Publishers, 1973.

Birch, H. and Gussow, J. *Disadvantaged children: health, nutrition, and school failure.* New York: Harcourt Brace Jovanovich, 1970.

Bissell, J. *Implementation of planned variation in Head Start.* Washington, D.C.: Department of Health, Education and Welfare, Office of Child Development, 1971.

————. *The cognitive effects of preschool programs for disadvantaged children.* Washington, D.C.: National Institute of Child Health and Development, 1970.

Bittner, M., Rockwell, R., and Matthews, C. *An evaluation of the preschool readiness centers program in East St. Louis, Illinois, July 1, 1967—June 30, 1968. Final Report.* East St. Louis, Ill.: Southern Illinois University, 1968.

Blank, M. *Teaching learning in the preschool: a dialogue approach.* Columbus, Ohio: Merrill, 1973.

Blank, M. and Solomon, F. "A tutorial language program to develop abstract thinking in socially disadvantaged preschool children." *Child Development, 39* (1968), 379–389.

————. "How shall the disadvantaged child be taught?" *Child Development, 40* (1969), 47–61.

Block, J. "Conceptions of sex role: some crosscultural and longitudinal perspectives." *American Psychologist, 28* (1973), 512–526.

Bloom, B. "How learning begins." *American Child,* 1966, *48,* (Spring), 14–18.

————. *Stability and change in human characteristics.* New York: Wiley, 1964.

Bloom, B., Davis, A., and Hess, R. *Compensatory education for cultural deprivation.* New York: Holt, Rinehart & Winston, 1965.

Bowlby, J. *Maternal care and mental health,* 2nd ed. Geneva: World Health Organization, Monograph Series No. 2, 1951.

Bronfenbrenner, U. *Two worlds of childhood: U.S. and U.S.S.R.* New York: Russell Sage, 1970.

Brophy, J. "Mothers as teachers of their own preschool children: the influence of socioeconomic status and task structure on teaching specificity." *Child Development, 41* (1970), 79–94.

Brophy, J. and Evertson, C. "Appendix to first year data of Texas Teacher Effectiveness

Project: complex relationships between teacher process variables and student outcome measures." *Catalog of Selected Documents in Psychology, 3* (1973), 137.

Brophy, J. and Good, T. "Feminization of American elementary schools: female chauvinism or cultural socialization?" *Phi Delta Kappan, 54* (1973), 564–566.

———. *Teacher-student relationships: causes and consequences.* New York: Holt, Rinehart and Winston, 1974.

Brophy, J., Hess, R., and Shipman, V. "Teaching behavior of mothers in structured interaction with their four-year-old childen: a study in frustration." Paper presented at the annual meeting of the Midwestern Psychological Association, 1966.

Bruner, J. "Poverty and childhood." In R. Parker, ed. *The preschool in action.* Boston: Allyn & Bacon, 1972.

———. *Toward a theory of instruction.* Cambridge, Mass.: Harvard University Press, 1966.

Caldwell, B. "Can young children have a quality life in day care?" *Young Children, 28* (1973), 197–208.

Caldwell, B. "On designing supplementary environments for early child development." In R. Anderson and H. Shane, eds. *As the twig is bent.* Boston: Houghton Mifflin, 1971.

Caldwell, B. "What is the optimal learning environment for the young child?" *American Journal of Orthopsychiatry, 37* (1967), 8–21.

Caldwell, B. and Richmond, J. Programmed day care for the very young child—a preliminary report. *Journal of Marriage and the Family, 26* (1964), 481–488.

Caldwell, B., Wright, C., Honig, A., and Tannenbaum, J. Infant day care and attachment. *American Journal of Orthopsychiatry, 40* (1970), 397–412.

Cazden, C. "Environmental assistance to the child's acquisition of grammar." Unpublished doctoral dissertation. Cambridge, Mass.: Harvard University, 1965.

Coopersmith, S. *The antecedents of self-esteem.* San Francisco: Freeman, 1967.

Corsini, D., Pick, A., and Flavell, J. "Production deficiency of nonverbal mediators in young children." *Child Development, 39* (1968), 53–58.

De Hirsch, K., Jansky, J., and Langford, W. *Predicting reading failure.* New York: Harper & Row, 1966.

Deutsch, M., Levinson, A., Brown, B., and Peisach, E. "Communication of information in the elementary school classroom." In M. Deutsch ed. *The disadvantaged child.* New York: Basic Books, 1967.

Diggory, S. *Cognitive process in education: a psychological preparation for teaching and curriculum development.* New York: Harper & Row, 1972.

Dinkmeyer, D. "Top priority: understanding self and others." *Elementary School Journal, 72* (1971), 62–71.

Eichenwald, H. and Fry, P. "Nutrition and learning." *Science 163* (1969), 644–648.

Epstein, S. "The self-concept revisited: or a theory of a theory." *American Psychologist, 28* (1973), 404–416.

Epstein, S. "Toward a unified theory of anxiety." In B. Maher, ed. *Progress in experimental personality research,* Vol. 4. New York: Academic, 1967.

Erikson, E. *Childhood and society,* 2nd ed. New York: Norton, 1963.

Fantz, R. "The crucial early influence: mother love or environmental stimulation?" *American Journal of Orthopsychiatry, 36* (1966), 330–331 (abstract).

———. "Identity and the life cycle." *Psychological Issues Monograph, 1, 1* (1959).

Flavell, J., Beach, D., and Chinsky, J. "Spontaneous verbal rehearsal in a memory task as a function of age." *Child Development, 37* (1966), 283–299.

Forrester, B., Harge, B., Outlaw, D., Brooks, G., and Boismeier, J. *The intervention study with mothers and infants.* Nashville, Tenn.: Peabody Demonstration and Research Center in Early Education, 1971.

Fraser, C., Bellugi, U., and Brown, R. "Control of grammar in imitation, comprehension, and production." *Journal of Verbal Learning and Verbal Behavior, 2* (1963), 121–135.

Frostig, M. and Horne, D. *The Frostig program for the development of visual perception.* Chicago: Follett, 1964.

Fuller, F. "Concerns of teachers: a developmental conceptualization." *American Educational Research Journal, 6* (1969), 207–226.

Gates, A. *The improvement of reading: a program of diagnostic and remedial methods.* New York: Macmillan, 1947.

Good, T., Biddle, B., and Brophy, J. *Teachers make a difference.* New York: Holt, Rinehart & Winston, 1975.

Good, T. and Brophy, J. *Looking in classrooms.* New York: Harper & Row, 1973.
———. "The influence of teacher attitudes and expectations upon classroom behavior." In R. Coop and K. White, eds. *Psychological Concepts in the Classroom.* New York: Harper & Row, 1974.

Gordon, I. *On early learning: the modifiability of human potential.* Washington, D.C.: NEA, Association for Supervision and Curriculum Development, 1971a.
———. *Parent involvement in compensatory education.* Urbana, Ill.: University of Illinois Press, 1971b.

Gordon, I. and Jester, R. "Techniques of observing teaching in early childhood and outcomes of particular procedures." In R. Travers, ed. *Second Handbook of research on teaching.* Chicago: Rand McNally, 1973.

Hayden, R., Murdoch, R., and Quick, C. "Teacher aides improve attention span." *Elementary School Journal, 70* (1969), 43–47.

Herman, S. "The relationship between maternal variable scores and infant performance in a Negro experimental stimulation training population." Unpublished doctoral dissertation. Gainesville: University of Florida, 1970.

Hess, R. "Social class and ethnic influences upon socialization." In P. Mussen, ed. *Carmichael's manual of child psychology,* 3rd ed., vol. 2. New York: Wiley, 1970.
———. "Parental behavior and children's school achievement: implications for Head Start." In E. Grotbert, ed. *Critical issues in research related to disadvantaged children.* Princeton, N.J.: Educational Testing Service, 1969.

Hess, R. and Shipman, V. "Early experience and the socialization of cognitive modes in children." *Child Development, 36* (1965), 869–886.

Hess, R., Shipman, V., Brophy, J., and Bear, R. (In collaboration with A. Adelberger). "The cognitive environments of urban preschool children: follow-up phase." Report to the Children's Bureau, Social Security Administration, HEW, 1969.

Hodges, W. "Behavior-oriented prescriptive teaching approach skill objectives for children." Working paper: SEDL-SCA, Austin-Conway, 1969.

Hodges, W., McCandless, B., and Spicker, H. *The development and evaluation of a diagnostically based curriculum for preschool psycho-socially deprived children: Final Report.* Grant No. OEG-32-24-0210-1011. U.S. Office of Education. Bloomington, Indiana: Indiana University Press, 1967.

Hoffman, M. "Moral development." In P. Mussen, ed. *Carmichael's manual of child psychology,* 3rd ed., vol. 2. New York: Wiley, 1970.

Holmes, M. and Holmes, D. "Evaluation of two associated YM-YWHA Head Start programs." In E. Grotberg, ed. *Review of Research 1965 to 1969.* Washington, D.C.: Project Head Start (OEO), 1969.

Honig, A. and Brill, S. "A comparative analysis of the Piagetian development of twelve-month-old disadvantaged infants in an enrichment center with others not in such a center." Paper presented at the annual meeting of the American Psychological Association, 1970.

Hunt, J. "How children develop intellectually." *Children, 11,* 3 (1964), 83–91.

Hunt, J. *Intelligence and experience.* New York: Ronald, 1961.

Hyman, I. and Kliman, D. "First grade readiness of children who have had summer Head Start programs." *The Training School Bulletin, 63* (1967), 163–167.

Itard, J. "*The wild boy of Aveyron.*" New York: Appleton, 1962. (Originally published in 1799).

Jencks, C., Smith, M., Acland, H., Bane, M., Cohen, D., Gintis, H., Heyns, B., and Michelson, S. *Inequality: a reassessment of the effect of family and schooling in America.* New York: Basic Books, 1972.

Jensen, A. "How much can we boost IQ and scholastic achievement?" *Harvard Educational Review, 39* (1969), 1–123.

Johnson, S. "Relationships among cognitive and affective outcomes of instruction." Unpublished doctoral dissertation, Los Angeles: University of California. Ann Arbor, Mich.: University Microfilms, 1967, No. 67–6179.

Kagan, J. et al. *Change and continuity in infancy.* New York: Wiley, 1971.

Kagan, J. and Moss, H. *Birth to maturity.* New York: Wiley, 1962.

Kagan, J., Pearson, L., and Welch, L. "Conceptual impulsivity and inductive reasoning." *Child Development, 37* (1966), 583–594.

Kahn, S. and Weiss, J. "The teaching of affective responses." In R. Travers, ed. *Second handbook of research on teaching.* Chicago: Rand McNally, 1973.

Karnes, M. *Investigations of classroom and at-home interventions: Research and development program on preschool disadvantaged children: Final Report.* Bureau No. 5-1181, Bureau of Research, Office of Education, U.S. Department of Health, Education, and Welfare, 1969.

————. "The evaluation and implications of research with young handicapped and low-income children." In J. Stanley, ed. *Compensatory education for children ages two to eight.* Baltimore: Johns Hopkins Press, 1973.

Karnes, M., Teska, J., Hodgins, A., and Badger, E. "Educational intervention at home by mothers of disadvantaged infants." *Child Development, 41* (1970), 925–935.

Karnes, M., Zehrbach, R., and Teska, J. "A five-year longitudinal comparison of a traditional versus structured preschool program on cognitive, social, and affective variables." Paper presented at the annual meeting of the American Educational Research Association, 1972a.

————. "An ameliorative approach in the development of curriculum." In R. Parker, ed. *The preschool in action.* Boston: Allyn & Bacon, 1972b.

Katz, L. "Four questions on early childhood education." *Child Study Journal, 1* (1970), 43–51.

Keeney, T., Cannizzo, S., and Flavell, J. "Spontaneous and induced verbal rehearsal in a recall task." *Child Development, 38* (1967), 953–966.

Keyserling, M. *Windows on day care.* New York: National Council of Jewish Women, 1972.

Klatskin, E., Jackson, E., and Wilkin, L. "The influence of degree of flexibility in maternal child-care practices on early child behavior." *American Journal of Orthopsychiatry, 26* (1956), 79–93.

Klaus, R. and Gray, S. "The early training project for disadvantaged children: a report after five years." *Monographs of the Society for Research in Child Development, 33,* 4 (1968).

Kohlberg, L. "Development of moral character and moral ideology." In M. Hoffman and L. Hoffman, eds. *Review of child development research,* vol. 1. New York: Russell Sage, 1964.

———. "Early education: a cognitive-developmental view." *Child Development, 39* (1968), 1013–1062.

Kohlberg, L., Yaeger, J., and Hjertholm, E. "Private speech: four studies and a review of theories." *Child Development, 39* (1968), 691–736.

Korner, A. "Some hypotheses regarding the significance of individual differences at birth for later development." *The Psychoanalytic Study of the Child,* vol. 19. New York: International Universities, 1964, 58–72.

Korner, A. and Grobstein, R. "Visual alertness as related to soothing in neonates: implications for maternal stimulation and early deprivation." *Child Development, 37* (1966), 867–876.

Kounin, J. *Discipline and group management in classrooms.* New York: Holt, Rinehart & Winston, 1970.

Krech, D. "The chemistry of learning." *Saturday Review, 51* (1968), 48–50, 68.

Lazroe, J. "An investigation of the effects of motor training on the reading readiness of kindergarten children." *Dissertation Abstracts, 29,* 8 (1969), 2609a.

Lenneberg, E. "On explaining language." *Science, 164* (1969), 635–643.

Levenstein, P. "Cognitive growth in preschoolers through verbal interaction with mothers." *American Journal of Orthopsychiatry, 40* (1970), 426–432.

Levenstein, P. "Mothers as early cognitive trainers." Paper presented at the biennial meeting of the Society for Research in Child Development, 1971.

Levenstein, P. and Levenstein, S. "Fostering learning potential in preschoolers." *Social Casework, 52* (1971), 74–78.

Levenstein, P. and Sunley, R. "Stimulation of verbal interaction between disadvantaged mothers and children." *American Journal of Orthopsychiatry, 38* (1968), 116–121.

Lichtenberg, P. and Norton, D. "Cognitive and mental development in the first five years of life." DHEW Publication No. (HSM) 72-9102, Washington, D.C., 1970.

Lorenz, K. "The enmity between generations and its probable ethological causes." In M. Piers, ed. *Play and development.* New York: Norton, 1972.

Maccoby, E. "Sex differences in intellectual functioning." In E. Maccoby, ed. *The development of sex differences.* Stanford, Calif.: Stanford University Press, 1966.

Maccoby, E. and Masters, J. "Attachment and dependency." In P. Mussen, ed. *Carmichael's manual of child psychology,* 3rd ed., vol. 2. New York: Wiley, 1970.

Maccoby, E. and Zellner, M. *Experiments in primary education: aspects of Project Follow-Through.* New York: Harcourt Brace Jovanovich, 1970.

Mager, R. *Preparing instructional objectives.* Palo Alto, Calif.: Fearon, 1962.

McNeill, D. *The acquisition of language: a study of developmental psycholinguistics.* New York: Harper & Row, 1970.

———. "Developmental psycholinguistics." In F. Smith and G. Miller, eds. *The genesis of language.* Cambridge, Mass.: M.I.T. Press, 1966.

Medinnus, G. and Curtis, F. "The relation between maternal self-acceptance and child acceptance." *Journal of Consulting Psychology, 27* (1963), 542–544.

Meeker, M. "Intelligence in the classroom: individualized curriculum based on intelligence patterns." In R. Coop and K. White, eds. *Psychological concepts in the classroom.* New York: Harper & Row, 1974.

Meichenbaum, D. and Goodman, J. "Training impulsive children to talk to themselves: a means of developing self-control." *Journal of Abnormal Psychology, 77* (1971), 115–126.

Meier, J., Nimnicht, G., and McAfee, O. "An autotelic responsive environment nursery school for deprived children." In J. Hellmuth, ed. *Disadvantaged child: Head Start and early intervention,* vol. 2. New York: Brunner/Mazel, 1968.

Miller, L. et al. *Experimental variation of Head Start curricula: a comparison of current approaches: Progress Report No. 5.* Research Grant #CG 8199, Office of Economic Opportunity. Louisville, Ky.: University of Louisville Press, 1969–70a.

————. *Experimental variation of Head Start curricula: a comparison of current approaches: Progress Report No. 7.* Research Grant #CG 8199, Office of Economic Opportunity. Louisville, Ky.: University of Louisville Press, 1970b.

————. *Experimental variation of Head Start curricula: a comparison of current approaches: Progress Report No. 9.* Research Grant #CG 8199, Office of Economic Opportunity. Louisville, Ky.: University of Louisville Press, 1971.

Miller, L. and Dyer, J. *Two kinds of kindergarten after four types of Head Start.* Louisville, Ky.: University of Louisville Press, 1970.

Mischel, W. "Sex-typing and socialization." In P. Mussen, ed. *Carmichael's manual of child psychology,* 3rd ed., vol. 2. New York: Wiley, 1970.

Moore, N., Evertson, C., and Brophy, J. "Solitary play: some functional reconsiderations. *Developmental Psychology, 10* (1974), 830–834.

Murphy, L. "Infants' play and cognitive development." In M. Piers, ed. *Play and development.* New York: Norton, 1972.

Myklebust, H. *Auditory disorders in children: a manual for differential diagnosis.* New York: Grune & Stratton, 1954.

Neidt, C. and Hedlund, D. "Longitudinal relationships between cognitive and affective learning outcomes." *Journal of Experimental Education, 37,* 3 (1969), 56–60.

Nimnicht, G. "A model program for young children that responds to the child." In R. Parker, ed. *The preschool in action.* Boston: Allyn & Bacon, 1972.

Painter, G. "The effect of a structured tutorial program on the cognitive and language development of culturally disadvantaged infants." *Merrill-Palmer Quarterly, 15* (1969), 279–294.

Palmer, F. "Children under three—finding ways to stimulate development: II. Some current experiments: learning at two." *Children, 16* (1969), 55–57.

————. "Concept training curriculum for children aged two and three years old and eight months." New York: The City University of New York, Institute for Child Development and Experimental Education, 1968.

————. "Minimal interaction at age two and three and subsequent intellective changes. In R. Parker, ed. *The preschool in action.* Boston: Allyn & Bacon, 1972.

Piaget, J. *The origins of intelligence in children.* New York: International Universities, 1952.

Piaget, J. and Inhelder, B. *The psychology of the child.* New York: Basic Books, 1969.

Prescott, E., Jones, E., and Kritchevsky, S. *Group day care as a child-rearing environment: an observational study of day-care programs.* Pasadena, Calif.: Pacific Oaks College, 1967.

Rist, R. "Student social class and teacher expectations: the self-fulfilling prophecy in ghetto education." *Harvard Educational Review, 40* (1970), 411–451.

Robinson, H. and Robinson, N. "Longitudinal development of very young children in a comprehensive day-care program: the first two years." *Child Development, 42* (1971), 1673–1683.

Rohwer, W. "Images and pictures in children's learning: research results and educational implications." *Psychological Bulletin, 73* (1970a), 393–403.

————. "Implications of cognitive development for education." In P. Mussen, ed. *Carmichael's manual of child development,* 3rd ed., vol. 1. New York: Wiley, 1970b.

Rosner, J. *The development and validation of an individualized perceptual skills cur-*

riculum. Pittsburgh: University of Pittsburgh, Learning Research and Development Center, 1972.

Rubenstein, J. "Maternal attentiveness and subsequent exploratory behavior in the infant." *Child Development, 38* (1967), 1089–1100.

Ryan, S., Hegion, A., and Flavell, J. "Nonverbal mnemonic mediation in preschool children." Mimeographed report. Minneapolis: University of Minnesota, 1969.

Schaefer, E. "Home tutoring, maternal behavior, and infant intellectual development." Paper presented at the annual meeting of the American Psychological Association, 1969.

————. "Parents as educators: evidence from cross-sectional, longitudinal and intervention research." In U. Bronfenbrenner, ed. *Influences on human development.* Hinsdale, Ill.: Dryden, 1972.

Schaefer, E. and Aaronson, M. "Infant education research project: implementation and implications of a home tutoring program." In R. Parker, ed. *The preschool in action.* Boston: Allyn & Bacon, 1972.

Schaffer, H. and Emerson, P. "The development of social attachments in infancy." *Monographs of the Society for Research in Child Development, 29,* No. 3(a), (1964).

Schroder, H., Driver, M., and Streufert, S. *Human information processing.* New York: Holt, Rinehart & Winston, 1967.

Schuckert, R. and Touchton, R. "An experimental method of relating variations in teacher participation to measures of child fatigue in preschool training programs." *Journal of Educational Research, 62* (1968), 123–125.

Seguin, E. *Idiocy and its treatment by the physiological method.* New York: Columbia University Press, 1907. (Originally published in 1866).

Shane, H. "The renaissance of early childhood education." In R. Anderson and H. Shane, eds. *As the twig is bent.* Boston: Houghton Mifflin, 1971.

Shipman, V., and Hess, R. "Early experience in the socialization of cognitive modes in children: a study of urban Negro families." Paper presented at the Conference on Family and Society, Merrill-Palmer Institute, 1966.

Skeels, H. "Adult status of children with contrasting early life experiences: a follow-up study." *Monographs of the Society for Research in Child Development, 31,* 3 (1966).

Skeels, H. and Harms, I. "Children with inferior social histories: their mental development in adoptive homes." *Journal of Genetic Psychology, 72* (1948), 283–294.

Skeels, H., Updegraff, R., Wellman, B., and Williams, H. "A study of environmental stimulation: an orphanage preschool project." *University of Iowa Studies in Child Welfare, 15,* 4 (1938).

Smilansky, S. *The effects of sociodramatic play on disadvantaged preschool children.* New York: Wiley, 1968.

Soar, R. *Follow-through model implementation.* Interim report on Project No. OEG-0-8-522471-4618(100), U.S. Office of Education. Gainesville, Fla: University of Florida, Institute for Development of Human Resources, College of Education, 1970.

Spitz, R. "Hospitalism: an inquiry into the genesis of psychiatric conditions in early childhood." In U. Bronfenbrenner, ed. *Influences on human development.* Hinsdale, Ill.: Dryden, 1972.

Stein, S. and Smith, C. "Return of mom." *Saturday Review of Education, 1* (April 1973), 37–40.

Stevenson H. "Learning in children." In P. Mussen, ed. *Carmichael's manual of child psychology,* 3rd ed., vol. 1. New York: Wiley, 1970.

Swift, J. "Effects of early group experience: the nursery school and day nursery." In M. Hoffman and L. Hoffman, eds. *Review of child development research.* vol. 1. New York: Russell Sage, 1964.

Tanner, J. "Human growth and constitution." In G. Harrison, J. Weiner, J. Tanner, and N. Barnicot, eds. *Human biology: an introduction to human evolution, variation, and growth.* New York: Oxford University Press, 1964.

————. "Physical growth." In P. Mussen, ed. *Carmichael's manual of child psychology,* 3rd ed., vol. 1. New York: Wiley, 1970.

Thomas, J. "Tutoring strategies and effectiveness: a comparison of elementary age tutors and college tutors." Unpublished doctoral dissertation. Austin: University of Texas, 1970.

Thomas, S. "Nutrition and learning in preschool children." Champaign, Ill: ERIC Clearinghouse on Early Childhood Education, 1972. (1300–32).

Thompson, W. and Grusec, J. "Studies of early experience." In P. Mussen, ed. *Carmichael's manual of child psychology,* 3rd ed., vol. 1. New York: Wiley, 1970.

Torshen, K. "The relationship of evaluations of students' cognitive performance to their self-concept assessments and mental health status." Paper presented at the annual meeting of the American Educational Research Association, 1973.

Trowbridge, N. "Self-concept and socioeconomic status in elementary school children." *American Educational Research Journal, 9* (1972), 525–537.

Tulkin, S. and Kagan, J. "Mother-child interaction in the first year of life." *Child development, 43* (1972), 31–41.

Van Alstyne, D. "The environment of three-year-old children: factors related to intelligence and vocabulary tests." In *Columbia University Teachers College Contributions to Education.* New York: 1929, No. 366.

Vygotsky, L. *Thought and language.* Cambridge, Mass.: M.I.T. Press, 1962.

Weikart, D. "A comparative study of three preschool curricula." Paper presented at the biennial meeting of the Society for Research in Child Development, 1969.

————. "Relationship of curriculum, teaching, and learning in preschool education." Paper presented at the Hyman Blumberg Memorial Symposium on Research in Early Childhood Education, 1971.

————. Results of preschool intervention programs. In D. Weikart, ed. *Preschool intervention: a preliminary report of the Perry Preschool Project.* Ann Arbor, Mich.: Campus Publishers, 1967.

Weikart, D., Deloria, D., Lawser, S., and Wiegerink, R. *Longitudinal results of the Ypsilanti Perry Preschool Project.* Ypsilanti, Mich.: High/Scope Educational Research Foundation, 1970.

Weikart, D. and Lambie, D. "Early enrichment in infants." Paper presented at the annual meeting of the American Association for the Advancement of Science, 1969.

White, B. "Fundamental early environmental influences on the development of competence." In M. Meyer, ed. *Third symposium on learning: cognitive learning.* Bellingham, Wash.: Western Washington State College, 1972.

Wolff, P. "Operational thought and social adaptation." In M. Piers, ed. *Play and development.* New York: Norton, 1972.

Zigler, E. Paper presented at the Education Commission of the States Meeting, Denver, Colorado, December 7, 1972.

NAME INDEX

SUBJECT INDEX

75 76 77 9 8 7 6 5 4 3 2 1